CAMBRIDGE CLASSICAL STUDIES

General editors: M.I.Finley, E.J.Kenney, G.E.L.Owen

IMPERIALISM IN THE ANCIENT WORLD

Imperialism in the Ancient World

THE CAMBRIDGE UNIVERSITY RESEARCH SEMINAR
IN ANCIENT HISTORY

Edited by

P.D.A. GARNSEY
Fellow of Jesus College and Lecturer in Ancient
History in the University of Cambridge

and

C.R. WHITTAKER
Fellow of Churchill College and Lecturer in
Ancient History in the University of Cambridge

CAMBRIDGE UNIVERSITY PRESS
Cambridge
London : New York : Melbourne

Published by the Syndics of the Cambridge University Press

The Pitt Building, Trumpington Street, Cambridge CB2 1RP

Bentley House, 200 Euston Road, London NW1 2DB

32 East 57th Street, New York, NY 10022, USA

296 Beaconsfield Parade, Middle Park, Melbourne 3206, Australia

© Faculty of Classics, University of Cambridge 1978

First published 1978

Printed in Great Britain by
Redwood Burn Limited
Trowbridge & Esher

Library of Congress Cataloguing in Publication Data

Main entry under title:

Imperialism in the ancient world.

   (Cambridge classical studies)
   Bibliography: p.
   Includes index.

   1. History, Ancient--Addresses, essays, lectures.
2. Imperialism--Addresses, essays, lectures.
I. Garnsey, Peter. II. Whittaker, C.R. III. Series.
D60.I56   320.9'3   77-85699

ISBN 0 521 21882 9

CONTENTS

FIGURES

PREFACE

This is the second volume arising from the Cambridge Seminar in Ancient History directed by Professor Moses Finley. We take this opportunity to express our appreciation for the active assistance and encouragement he has given us as editors and scholars.

This volume reflects the aim of the architect of the Seminar to approach the subject of imperialism on a broad front. Unlike its predecessor, *Studies in Roman Property* (1976), it ranges over a wide expanse of history and covers a number of different societies, from New Kingdom Egypt to Rome under the Principate. Despite the inevitable gaps and unevenness of coverage, all important aspects of imperialism are given detailed and systematic attention in one or more studies. There is sufficient overlap of subject matter and interests to invite comparative assessment. Uniformity of viewpoint has not been sought after, nor has it been attained. In this, the volume reflects the present state of the debate on imperialism in the ancient world.

We wish to thank R. Van Dam for his valuable help in editorial matters.

July 1977

C.R.W.
P.G.

1: INTRODUCTION

P.D.A.Garnsey and C.R.Whittaker

The first and major problem in discussing imperialism is one of definition.[1] 'Imperialism' has become a term of abuse, implying unjust
or oppressive rule or control of one people by another. These pejor-
ative connotations are central to the meaning of the word as it has
been interpreted by numerous historians of antiquity, with the result
that it has been all but eliminated from their accounts of inter-
state relations. In the case of the Delian League, where it was not
at all obvious that the dominant state ruled benignly or in the
interests of its subjects, scholars have fallen back on the assertion
that Athenian-allied relations were 'hegemonial' in character rather
than 'imperialistic' in the first decades of the existence of the
League (if not through the entire inter-war period); meanwhile Thucydides' characterization of the Athenian empire as a tyranny has been
attributed by some to the historian's political prejudices, which
led him to overlook the popularity of Athens among the lower classes
of the empire.

   The requirement that an imperialist power must have imperialist
aims and motives has further narrowed the concept of imperialism and
limited its applicability. In this case discussion has centred on
the growth of Roman power; the debate has its origin, not in the
strictures of a critic, a Roman Thucydides, but in the viewpoint of
an enthusiastic admirer, Polybius. Polybius asserted, indeed took
it for granted, that Rome aimed at empire.[2] Modern scholars influenced by anti-imperialist currents of thought were bound to challenge
this assumption. In 1920, Maurice Holleaux demolished an extreme
version of the Polybian theory, according to which Rome was an aggressive and Machiavellian power advancing systematically and deliberately towards the goal of world dominion. His thesis, put simply,
is that the Romans did not want an empire and did not look for one.
War and empire were imposed on them from outside, by chance factors
beyond their control. Thus, for example, Holleaux concluded his
discussion of the outbreak of the Second Macedonian War in this way:

'In 200, as thirty years earlier, it was simply an accident that drew the Romans out of Italy and set events in motion. It was by accident and through an error of judgement that the senators committed themselves to this course.'[3]

The concept of accident has found its way into English historical writing. Cary wrote of the First Punic War: 'Both parties may be acquitted of using the affair of Messana as a pretext for a predetermined war. The collision which brought on the First Punic war was wholly accidental.' Badian in discussing Rome's Illyrian policy came to this conclusion: 'It was the accident (if we may call it such) of the failure of Rome's attempt to live at peace with other great powers, that led to the need to subdue them and thus to the establishment of the Roman Empire as we know it.' A recently published book by Errington begins with the startling sentence: 'Rome's rise to power was one of the most important accidents in European history.'[4]

The doctrine of 'accidental imperialism' rests on an improper use of the word 'accident', as a reading of Aristotle's discussion of chance in *Physics* ch. 4ff. makes clear.[5] In the first place, it would be difficult to concede that a state which made a whole series of territorial conquests or political gains was acting without having foreseen possible consequences. If the Romans consistently failed to coexist with their rivals, the proper inference seems to be that their wars were inevitable not accidental. The broader the perspective we adopt on Roman foreign policy, the less appropriate the language of accident becomes - Polybius, it will be recalled, began with the Gallic invasion of the early fourth century and the steady conquest of Italy that followed. Secondly, if the Romans, as we are told, were forced to expand their area of control, then the proper notion to introduce, following Aristotle's discussions in both the *Physics* and the *Ethics*, is that of a reluctant not an accidental action or set of actions.

An amended version of the thesis might run as follows: Rome's chief aim in expanding its frontiers was self-defence; the empire grew only under the stimulus of threats and provocation from outside; Rome was not involved in empire-building for its own sake. Here it is tacitly admitted that expansion was in some sense an end, and its accomplishment therefore neither accidental nor unforeseen. But the initiative for warlike action lay with other powers, and the

Romans are therefore freed from the opprobrium which is attached to aggressors. We have thus slid into the thesis of 'defensive imperialism'. This popular thesis, which draws its strength from the apparent inconsistency of Roman foreign policy, the slowness with which their rulers acted (or reacted), and their reluctance to annex, has yet to be subjected to systematic and searching criticism.

The most recent proponent of the view that imperialism is to be associated with a palpable intent is Veyne.[6] In an article asking whether there was such a thing as Roman imperialism Veyne argues that what is important is not so much dependence and superiority as 'a sense of dependence', 'a sense of superiority'. Imperialism, as distinct from an empire, does not exist unless one acquires a taste for unsought conquest. Desiring only the freedom to behave as she wished, Rome was the victim of circumstances, being forced into a series of pragmatic decisions, the consequences of which she never considered. In this jungle, where dog eats dog and every neighbour is either subordinate or a threatening enemy, war was a normal part of life in which the aristocracy took part for the public good without asking why. To be sure, there were ambitious individuals anxious for their measure of glory, but their personal behaviour must (by this argument) be separated from the collective intention of the state and the oligarchy.

The studies in this volume illustrate the problems of conceptualization that are discussed above. On the one hand are those papers which employ a restricted definition of imperialism and empire. Griffith describes the Second Athenian Confederacy as 'no *arche*, but a genuine and respectable hegemony', and argues that the 'mentality of *arche*' can be detected with certainty only in Athens' relations with allies who were not members of the Confederacy. Briscoe declares it 'wrong to see Macedon as an imperial power consciously seeking to extend its control in Greece', and draws a parallel between Macedonian and Roman behaviour, which was 'purely defensive'. In arguing for the lack of rational choices open to the Hellenistic rulers, he comes close to a modern view of imperialism as being a natural consequence of international power relations, which are necessarily unstable. Andrewes' question-mark over Spartan imperialism hinges on the difficulty he finds in distinguishing between the ambitions of individuals and the policy of the state.

On the other hand are those papers which seek to define imperialism purely in terms of the exercise of power. However difficult the abstraction, commonsense tells us that we are dealing with a reality, the relationship of ruler to subject, which can be evaluated with reference to some set of criteria. Finley suggests six ways in which power might be exercised by one state or community over another - restriction of freedom, political interference, compulsory service, tribute, confiscation of land or emigration, and other forms of economic exploitation or subordination. Whittaker and Kemp have followed this suggested typology with minor variations when discussing Carthaginian and Egyptian imperialism.

The reader must make his or her own choice as to how this debate is to be conducted or resolved. Motives, real or assumed, are of interest. The problem is, how are they to be ascertained? It may be significant that Kemp, who is dealing with the heavily stylized and formulaic sources of the Egyptian New Kingdom, and Whittaker, who has to rely on the largely hostile Greek sources for Carthaginian history, are the most ready to adopt Finley's view that motives are irrelevant to definitions of imperialism. Neither in the events of Egyptian nor of Carthaginian imperialism can they confidently detect the immediately pragmatic rationale of action.

Conquerors can hardly be expected to explain their motives as a deliberate attempt to increase their *Machtbereich*. The British in India did not admit to a doctrine of imperialism. Louis Faidherbe, architect of French imperial expansion in West Africa, declared: 'Our motives are pure and noble, our cause just.' Kaiser Wilhelm II of Germany was supposedly 'profoundly penetrated by the ideal of peace'. So although we may feel in retrospect that actions ought to relate to a declared philosophy of conduct, in practice the information available usually consists of either the pragmatic rationale of the frontiersmen, the men on the spot, for whom the action itself is sufficient without a clear policy, or ritual justifications and pretexts: claims of honour at stake, security at risk, necessary war measures and the '*mission civilisatrice*'.[7] Athenian tribute was necessary to protect the allies from Persia; freedom and autonomy were the gifts which every imperial power wished to confer on willing or unwilling subjects. Brunt's study of Roman concepts of empire in the age of Cicero shows how important it is to differentiate between explanations

of the genesis of empire ('the true driving forces' behind imperialism), the ideology which keeps it going, and the reality.

As for the conquered, their point of view (or more correctly,
points of view) is usually inaccessible to us, or at least until such
time as the empire itself has produced its own beneficial ideology
among those subjects who have cooperated.

Motives can be understood only with reference to a background of
the structure and institutions of society. This is the lesson of
Andrewes' study, which shows that the Spartans were not so much imperialists who arrived too late (as Veyne suggests), as half-imperi-
alist; their actions abroad laid bare the basic contradictions of a
society which produced a militarist ethos with no military mission to
complement it. New methods of warfare abroad were necessarily evolved in the Peloponnesian War, but new political relations never developed internally. A structuralist approach is prominent in Finley's
unromantic assessment of the economic benefits and burdens of Athenian
imperialism, which he finds was designed to serve the interests of the
Athenian democratic state. By contrast, the rational interests of the
commercially-minded Carthaginian oligarchy lay in avoiding confrontation but increasing control. This volume lacks a structuralist
study of the Roman republic along the lines proposed by W.V.Harris in
a recent article.[8] Such a study might stress the ever-increasing need
for warfare in the acquisition of personal riches, glory and clients
among a competitive political elite, which was bound to produce an
empire. Brunt refers briefly to the militarism of the traditions of
old Rome, such as the ancient prayer of the censors for the aggrandizement of Rome, or the soothsayers' habit of predicting that a war that
was imminent would advance the boundaries of the empire. Such practices in his view undermine the argument for defensive imperialism.
When all such justifications have been swept away, it is *laus imperii*,
the doctrine of power, which remains. And this is simply the ancient
belief, expressed by Thucydides and implicit in the works of Polybius,
that it is natural for the stronger to dominate the weaker.

Roman writers under the Principate produced no new thoughts on
the subject of imperial rule. Such 'advances' as were made in the
philosophy of empire were the work of the Greek intelligentsia. This
class, which in the fluid and dangerous period of the late republic,
according to Crawford, exploited the Greek intellectual pretensions

of leading Romans in order to win protection and other concessions
for the Greek communities, two centuries later, as Nutton shows, produced the ideology of participation and turned *imperium populi Romani*
into *imperium orbis terrarum*. Aelius Aristides, Plutarch, and the
other Greek intellectuals who became vocal supporters of the empire
were representative of the class of provincials which benefited most
from Roman rule, the local aristocracy. On the one hand, the new
phase of imperialism ushered in by the Principate of Augustus was
characterized by a more rational exploitation of the subjects of
Rome; on the other, the Roman imperial system that Augustus and his
successors created brought real material benefits for subjects as
well as rulers. There is no paradox here, for the benefits and burdens of empire were unevenly distributed. In order to reap the
fruits of power the Romans were forced to utilize their provincial
clients and thus to share power with them. As Garnsey shows, the
real effect of empire was to increase social differentiation.

Resistance within the empire was not to be expected, and did
not come, from the *évolué*, who despite his provincialism was committed to the values of the empire, and was prepared, even anxious, to
participate in the exercise of power and the economic exploitation
of the mass of provincials. There were Rabbinic protests − although
Jewish attitudes were not uniformly hostile, according to de Lange −
and some dissentient Christian voices. But the spirit of rebellion
was by and large the preserve of the poor and the fringe members of
Roman provincial society. Their resistance was the least likely to
be effective.

2: IMPERIALISM AND EMPIRE IN NEW KINGDOM EGYPT (c. 1575-1087B.C.)

B.J.Kemp (Faculty of Oriental Studies, Cambridge)

The treatment of a period of ancient Egyptian history under a heading
which belongs very much to the modern world requires something of a
defensive introduction. The charge is easily made that simply by
using the words 'imperialism' and 'empire' a host of complex and de-
batable issues are prejudged and cast into a misleading and inappropriate mould. Certainly the ancient Egyptians themselves seem to
have known of no words which can be translated as 'imperialism' or
'empire', but neither, for that matter, did they have words for
'government', 'administration' and 'history', nor even, despite its
pervasiveness in Egyptian civilization, was there a word 'religion'.
This is something that can be encountered across the whole range of
subjects on which the Egyptians wrote. Thus, they possessed a technical vocabulary for solving mathematical problems, but no word which
can be translated 'mathematics'. They acted without seeing the need
to abstract and refer separately to the activity as an independent
phenomenon. The verbal and mental sequence in Egypt was not from the
particular to the abstract, it was to metaphor and religious symbol-
ism. Yet, conversely, whilst we may judge the Egyptian vocabulary to
have been weak in just those areas that we rate most highly, it is
also true that our own vocabulary and range of concepts is inadequate
for coping with the heart of the Egyptian intellect for which we can
offer only the sadly degraded term 'religion'. It is not just a matter of difficulties in translation; there is a major intellectual
disjunction between us and the ancient Egyptians. Yet, with a large
bureaucratically-run country and having important interests in neighbouring lands, they also faced some of the same practical problems
that more recent societies have faced. Their solutions, though justified in religious terms, seem firmly rooted in political reality. It
is in our assessment of politically real behaviour that the answer is
to be found as to whether they acted in a manner analogous to states
of later periods who have conceived of 'empire' with a greater degree
of abstraction and clarity.

From the New Kingdom, a considerable body of inscriptions and
scenes has survived related to the theme of conquest and subjection
of the outside world to the rule of the king of Egypt. Some of them,
in alluding to specific instances of triumph, are termed 'historical'
by modern scholars, but from their language, and very often from
their context within a temple, one can judge them to be more truly
theological documents and sources for our understanding of divine
kingship. Within them the divine king is depicted fulfilling a
specific role with historical actuality entirely subordinated to a
predetermined format. Presented as a form of cultic drama the conquest theme is one element in the broader and fundamental role of
divine kingship: that of reducing chaos to order.[1] Sometimes one
finds scenes of the king's subjection of foreign humanity paired
with hunting scenes where a chaotic animal world is subdued, and
certainly in later periods the symbolic connection between the two
was explicitly formulated in scenes of the king snaring birds in a
clapnet which illustrated the text, or 'book', called 'The subduing
of the nobility', which was evidently intended to assist the king's
supremacy over his enemies.[2]

It is a mistake, too, to explain the endless repetition of victory as just propaganda. Little of it would have been visible to
the people as a whole, being often well within the body of the temple, or at least screened off by the great temple-enclosure walls.
It represents rather a constant restatement of theological formulae,
particularized for each king. It is also likely that the great
scenes of victory and the listing of conquered places which frequently occur on temple walls, particularly on the towers of pylon
entrances, were regarded as magically efficacious in protecting
Egypt from foreign hostility. This interpretation can be supported
by reference to a ritual of humiliation in which the names of the
king's 'enemies' were written upon little statuettes of bound captives which were then burnt or buried, or on pottery vessels subsequently smashed. This ritual is known from as late as the Graeco-
Roman period, and many actual statuettes bearing long lists of
foreign places and princes have survived from the earlier period of
the Middle Kingdom (when they are referred to as 'Execration Texts').[3]
The lists on the temple walls of the New Kingdom, and around the
statue bases of kings, were probably intended, by their attitudes of

permanent subjugation, to achieve the same end, having shared in the
'Opening of the Mouth' ritual which animated temple walls and statues
alike.[4]

These formal scenes and texts contain elements of a fairly consistent and coherent view of Egypt's position in the world, or more
correctly, of the king's position, for at times the Egyptian people,
including the army itself, are presented as being on a level little
different from that of the foreign nations. These statements can be
abstracted and put together to make up a single account. It is important, however, to realize that Egyptian religious texts in general
are not constructed as logical treatises intended to explain or to
persuade, but consist instead of series of concise statements whose
logical connections may not be made explicit. Hence, any modern
account which seeks a logical presentation is bound to be quite alien
to the spirit of the texts themselves.

In the theology of the New Kingdom the single most important
element was still the sun (Ra), whose manifestations were many, but
most importantly the Theban god Amen, whose almost total absorption
into solar theology was marked by the common divine designation Amen-
Ra. Akhenaten's religious reform was evidently an attempt to separate the sun cult from extraneous elements, particularly that of Amen,
and to emphasize its true nature by constant reference to the sun's
disk (Aten). The theme that the sun god was the creator and sustainer
of all life, both animal and human, throughout the universe was made
the subject of hymns, some of great poetic beauty.[5] Some passages
briefly include the foreign lands and peoples within the scope of the
sun god's power,[6] but more generally Egyptian theologians seem to
have displayed little interest in the details of the creation of the
physical world. Nevertheless, a simple, unelaborated claim that the
sun-god of Egypt, and occasionally other gods as well, was the creator and sustainer of the whole universe was not infrequently stated
or implied in contexts involving the king in his role of foreign
conqueror. Of more particular interest to the gods were those lands
which yielded products for themselves and for their temples. These
places were sometimes referred to as 'god's land'. The Lebanon
where grew the cedar trees for the great temple flagstaffs and barges
was one; Sinai of the turquoise mines was another; so also was the
greywacke quarries of the inhospitable Wadi Hammamat (*KRI* VI 11.4,

VI 13.11). But most important was Punt, a term for some coastal area
somewhere between Eritrea and northern Somaliland which the Egyptians
regularly visited by voyages from ports on the Red Sea coast.[7] Here,
through trade probably at a coastal entrepot, incense was obtained.

Considerable prominence was given in the New Kingdom to detailed
expositions in temples by texts and pictures of the king's conception
and birth from a union between his mother and Amen-Ra, who had assumed
the form of the reigning king.[8] Being made in the divine image the
land was described as becoming at his accession as perfect and har-
monious as it had been 'in the time of Ra', on the 'First Moment' immediately after creation had taken place (e.g. Urk IV 2119-20), and
as the son of the gods he inherits all that they have made, 'that
which the sun's disk encircles',[9] in order to administer it on their
behalf (e.g. Urk IV 368.13-14, 1327.1-3). This could include a claim
to universal rule abroad. Thus Amenhetep III says of Amen: 'He has
handed over to me the princes of the southlands, the southerners and
the northerners as well, every one made equal to the other, and their
silver, their gold, their cattle, all the precious stones of their
lands in millions, hundreds of thousands, tens of thousands, and thousands. I shall act for him who begat me with a steadfast purpose,
just as he appointed me to be "Ra of the Nine Bows".'[10] The 'Nine
Bows' is a common collective expression for the nations of mankind,
including the Egyptian people, and here the king's equivalence to the
sun god is expressed by simply calling him 'Ra'.

Sometimes this transfer is represented as a contract in which
the king provides for the gods, building temples and ensuring a plen-
tiful supply of offerings, and the gods in their turn are then obliged
to grant universal power, as well as health and good fortune (e.g. Urk
IV 563.4-5, 817.2-5, 864.5, 1754.4-7, 2043.6-9). But the transfer
should not be understood as something which took place at one point in
real time. It belongs to a mythopoetic dimension outside time, and
describes rather an ever-active relationship. And whilst the king is
most commonly the heir to certain gods of outstanding power and importance, principally Amen-Ra, the inheritance myth could also be invoked to describe his relationship to lesser divinities as well, an
aspect of the interchangeability of Egyptian deities. In the little
temple at Semna in Nubia, for example, the king's inheritance stems
from Dedwen, a probably Nubian god long before brought into the

Egyptian pantheon, to whom this temple happens to be partially dedicated (*Urk* IV 199.13-15). At the great temple of Amen at Karnak both
Dedwen and Sebek, a crocodile god, hand over to the king the rule of
foreign lands (*Urk* IV 774.13-15, 574.8-9).

Although the theme of the king replacing chaos with order was
very occasionally given an Egyptian setting,[11] normally Egypt was depicted as accepting a new rule with joy. The foreign lands, however,
were regarded as much closer to the primeval chaos and possessed of a
naturally rebellious disposition, so that force was necessary before
the king's claims might be accepted, though eventually they too would
come to rejoice in his rule. Military campaigns thus appear as part
of the duties which the gods pass on to the king. Scenes which illustrate Rameses III's defeat of Libyans, for example, commence with Amen
symbolically handing him a sword, whilst Thoth, god of writing, says:
'Thy father Amen sends thee forth to destroy the Nine Bows' (*KRI* V
10.9-10 = *HRR* 4). Elsewhere kings receive the sword which commissioned
conquest from Ra-Horus of the Horizon, Ptah, Atum and Seth.[12] One
text, of the reign of Tuthmosis IV, suggests, too, that the king may
have consulted an oracle of Amen before setting out on a Nubian campaign (*Urk* IV 1545.14-1546.3). The final act was the king's presentation of his conquests to the gods, most often to Amen.

Implicit in this relationship between king and gods was a simple
theory of causation: piety brought blessings, and victory was one of
them. The converse - impiety bringing failure and defeat - is found
in a formal context only once in the New Kingdom. Akhenaten's attempts
to destroy the existence of Amen in favour of the wholly non-anthropo-
morphic solar cult of the Aten were afterwards thought to have had
this effect: 'The land was in distress. The gods, they had turned
their backs on this land. If expeditions were sent to Palestine to
enlarge the boundaries of Egypt, they met with no success' (*Urk* IV
2027.11-14).

In view of the divine assent to campaigns, texts describing them
tend to be very sparing in providing strictly historical explanations.
One common introductory cliché which provides a setting rather than a
cause describes a report brought to the king in his palace outlining
the mustering of specific enemies, and their hostile intentions and
initial actions. Immediately the king prepares for battle and the
campaign commences. In other cases the purpose is said to be simply

'to enlarge the boundaries of Egypt', a ritual phrase which was applied to actions well within the regular sphere of Egyptian activity,
or just for the king to 'give vent to his desires throughout the
foreign lands' (Urk IV 9.8-9). It is interesting to note that the
machinations of the enemy are normally a purely human affair, spring-
ing from perversity and wickedness. In one instance defeated Libyan
invaders claim to have been deliberately made the playthings of 'the
gods', but these can only have been Egyptian (KRI V 64.2-3 = HRR 82).
In another text, unfortunately fragmentary, the king charges his officials with the responsibility of guarding the boundaries of foreign
countries, 'according to the design of the fathers of your fathers',
a collective term apparently for the principal Egyptian gods, who are
thus seen as the source of order abroad.[13] There is never a recognition of an alien superhuman power. The Egyptians were, of course,
aware that other gods were worshipped in foreign lands, at least in
western Asia. But when encountered during the New Kingdom they were
increasingly regarded as peripheral members of the Egyptian pantheon.
Sometimes in the Nineteenth and Twentieth Dynasties they were seen
as forms of the Egyptian god Seth who represented, amongst other
things, all that was strange and disturbing in foreign lands,[14] and
who was given great prominence at this time, though partly for local
historical reasons. Thus the Egyptian version of the treaty between
Rameses II and the Hittite king Hattusilis concludes with the names
of divine witnesses, and the Hittite gods appear in such guises as
'Seth of Hatti', and 'Seth of the town of Zippalanda', substituting
for forms of the Hittite storm-god Teshub.[15] It is also Seth who in
one text appears as the fickle god of the Libyans: 'The Libyans have
been burnt up in a single year. Seth has turned his back on their
chief. Their settlements have been destroyed at his utterance' (KRI
IV 15.9-11 = ANET 377). Seth is one of the gods who hands the sword
of conquest to the king, and in the later New Kingdom the king's
might is often compared both to Seth and to the Palestinian god Baal.
This recognition of foreign, or at least western Asiatic, gods would
seem to have been the ultimate logic of claims to universal sovereignty made for Egyptian gods, and presumably deprived Egypt's foes
of sources of divine assistance, at least in Egyptian eyes.

    This theology of conquest which not only justified, but, because
of the magic latent within words and pictures, also helped to bring

about the king's universal rule, was illustrated with a characteristically vivid and powerful iconography.[16] Some themes – the king
smiting bound captives with a mace, or in the form of a sphinx trampling on contorted figures – were of great antiquity. But the tech-
nological innovation of the chariot in the New Kingdom added a further important artistic element. Although most familiar to us from
temple walls, the themes of conquest and dominance over enemies were
employed in the decoration of palaces,[17] on state barges,[18] and in
the designs on pieces of jewellery and small trinkets such as
scarabs.[19] This would have accorded well with the growing fashion
for militarism in the New Kingdom.

Alongside the theme of conquest, it is not uncommon to find inscriptions which represent universal Egyptian rule as an already
accomplished fact: 'Heaven and all the foreign lands whom god has
created serve her [Queen Hatshepsut] in totality' (*Urk* IV 341.15).
The hyperbole is extravagant to the point of including lands beyond
the likely reach of Egyptian power: 'Commands are sent to an unknown
land, and they do everything that she commanded';[20] 'Giving praise
to the good god, doing obeisance before the son of Amen, by the
princes of all foreign lands who are so distant as to know not Egypt'
(*Urk* IV 1866.16-18). This figure of speech is found stretched to
cover even countries with which the Egyptians were actually familiar.
So Queen Hatshepsut's expedition to Punt, a place regularly visited
by Egyptians, becomes a marvellous discovery, with the astonished
princes of Punt expressing incredulity at the Egyptian discovery,
yet admitting that they live by the breath which the king of Egypt
provides.[21] The detailed lists of subject places which regularly
accompany scenes of the victorious king likewise were influenced by
this attitude.[22] Although some of the earliest of the preserved
lists from the New Kingdom, of the reign of Tuthmosis III, seem to
reflect fairly faithfully the state of Egyptian power abroad, the
universalist ideal begins to make itself felt from the reigns of
Tuthmosis IV and Amenhetep III, so that into these lists there enter
the names of places and of great kingdoms from the limits of the
Egyptians' geographical knowledge: Babylon, Assyria, Mitanni, Hatti,
and, from the reign of Horemheb, Arzawa on the west coast of Anatolia.
Crete was included as well, and one of the more recently discovered
lists from the reign of Amenhetep III contains what appears to be a

list of towns in Crete and the Aegean, including Knossos, Amnisos,
Mycenae and its port of Nauplia, and just possibly Troy as well.[23]

In this type of context the only relationship which could be
appropriate between Egypt and other countries was that of overlord
and vassal. Diplomatic gifts from foreign rulers beyond Egypt's empire, material received in trade, as well as levies exacted from
places that were actually subject, all is depicted and referred to
in the same way, as if tribute. The word that is frequently translated 'tribute' more strictly means 'produce' or 'revenues', but the
individual contexts frequently are such that 'tribute' conveys better
what was intended.[24] In the reign of Amenhetep II the diplomatic
preliminaries between Egypt and her principal enemy at the time, the
kingdom of Mitanni, which were eventually to lead to a marriage alliance were recorded in one formal text: 'The princes of Mitanni
came to him, their *tribute* on their backs, to beg peace from His
Majesty, seeking his sweet breath of life. A famous occasion, quite
unheard of in all the days of men and gods – this country which Egypt
knew not making supplication to the good god' (*Urk* IV 1326.1–12).
Very similar terms were employed to record the marriage between
Rameses II and a Hittite princess which took place thirteen years
after the signing of a peace treaty in which, being a real diplomatic
document, both kings appear as equals, and 'brothers'. In the Marriage Stele the king of Hatti is given the words: 'Our land is deso-
lated, our lord Seth is angry with us, and the skies do not give us
water... Let us despoil ourselves of all our possessions, with my
eldest daughter at the head of them, and let us carry gifts of fealty
to the good god, so that he may give us peace and we may live' (*KRI*
II 246.7–247.3 = *BAR* III §§415–24).

Texts of this type, and the scenes they sometimes accompany,
belong to an idealized, or ritualized, counterpart of the real world,
a dimension similar to that in which other aspects of Egyptian religion were presumed to operate. The king as a mortal man fought and
negotiated in a real political world, but the true significance of
his actions at the level of 'intellectual' interpretation emerged
only after translation into this cosmic dimension. In this process
the record of actual events was edited to bring out just how the im-
mutable forces and roles had been present on a particular occasion.
The two most revealing cases of editing of this nature are the Battle

of Megiddo text of Tuthmosis III,[25] and the texts and scenes recoun-
ing Rameses II's battle with the Hittites at Kadesh.[26] The former
was composed by creating a narrative framework from the concise and
factual entries in the daily scribal journals, and grafting on to
this lengthier passages in a more varied literary style which depict
the roles of the main participants, and in particular the king's sole
responsibility for successful strategy and ultimate victory. The
role of the Egyptian army is essentially to act as a foil to the
king's superiority, and to receive the blame for not having followed
up the king's instant routing of the enemy. In the Battle of Kadesh
record there is a curious and presumably unintended contrast between
the pictorial record, an extraordinarily imaginative composition
which hints at the strategic weakness of the Egyptian tactics, and
the literary record which was written in a uniform heroic style,
where victory is the responsibility solely of the king, assisted by
Amen who is reminded in a speech of his contractual obligations to
Rameses as a pious king. Even more than in the Megiddo text the
Egyptian army has a wholly inglorious role, and in the end is depicted as being scarcely more worthy than the enemy. These texts
are about divine kingship, not about national greatness.

This material poses large and difficult questions. The historian may well be left with the feeling that if it were possible to
discover the full history of international relations at this period
in some other way, the surviving sources would turn out to be of interest only in illustrating the tenuous relationship which they had
to historical reality. Then one is entitled to ask: did the king
and his advisers ever really speak in this way? To what extent was
belief in this mythohistorical world spread through government
circles? Obviously it provided a good source of metaphors, and the
satisfaction of the justified cause.[27] But there is enough documentation to show that in the Near East the Egyptians were participating
in a form of international relations which was conducted very much at
a truly political level. Apart from a great deal of background material from western Asia, not involving Egypt but going back to
earlier periods,[28] there are two groups of sources for Egypt's direct
involvement. The later group concerns the single most important aspect of international relations in the ancient Near East: the treaty.[29]
Many were between a dominant state and less powerful ones who thereby

became vassals under various obligations, but in this case the treaty,
between Rameses II of Egypt and the Hittite king Hattusilis after a
long period of hostilities (including the Battle of Kadesh), was between two great powers.[30] In the text, known from both Egyptian and
Hittite versions, both kings appear as equals and 'brothers'. It was
said to be binding on successors, it declared a pact of mutual non-
aggression and aid in the event of one party being attacked from without or within, arranged for extradition of refugees, and assistance
in the case of a disputed succession. Nothing was said about boundaries and spheres of influence, presumably because these things were
evident from treaties which each side had with individual Syrian
princes. An impressive list of deities were invoked as witnesses,
many from the Hittite contribution being translated into forms of
Seth, but also adding Amen and Ra at the end. The contradiction inherent in having a peace treaty guaranteed by gods who at the same
time supported the king's conquering role appears also in the striking fact that the Egyptian version has survived only because it was
inscribed in at least two temples, an interesting break in the logic
of temple texts, although, as noted above, the subsequent Marriage
Stele is in the old stereotyped formula. The new cordiality between
the two countries was affirmed at a more personal level by letters
of friendly, though restrained, greetings sent to the Hittite king
and to his wife, Padu-Hepa, by Rameses II, his wife Nefertari, his
mother, Queen Tuya, the then crown prince, Seth(Amen)-her-khepshef,
and by the vizier Paser.[31] These letters were accompanied by presents of gold and cloth.

        The earlier source group is the cache of tablets from Akhena-
ten's capital, el-Amarna, written in cuneiform script employing a
dialect form of Akkadian.[32] Amongst the texts are a few intended
to help Egyptians learn Akkadian, and vice versa. The bulk of the
tablets are letters from western Asiatic courts, and copies of letters sent in return. In political terms the letters fall into two
main groups which immediately delimit the real sphere of Egyptian
power abroad. One is correspondence between Egypt and other states
of great power status where the mutual mode of address is 'brother'.
These are the states of Babylonia, Assyria, Mitanni, Hatti, and
Alashiya (Cyprus).[33] The content is mainly personal, but might include a political element, as with the King of Alashiya's advice

not to align with the kings of Hatti and Babylon (EA 35). With the
letters went exchanges of presents, a practice taken very seriously
and about which kings were most sensitive in balancing what they
gave against what they received. The second group concerns the city-
states of Palestine and Syria: their princes and their resident Egyptian officials. They address Pharaoh as 'my lord'. Those closer to
Egypt had little prospect of an improved alternative, but the Syrian
princes were in a position to make choices of major importance for
themselves. Their aims have been summarized as: preservation of
their own local autonomy, extension of their own rule over neighbours, maintenance towards the Egyptians of a show of loyalty to secure men and money, and either opposition or submission to the Hittite king according to circumstances.[34] Their letters tend to have
the form of a long introductory protestation of absolute loyalty
couched in obsequious language: 'This is the message of a slave to
his master after he had heard what the kind messenger of the king
[said] to his servant upon arriving here, and [felt] the sweet fra-
grance that came out of the mouth of Your Majesty towards his servant'; thus Abi-milki of Tyre (EA 147). In such cases the direct
political message tends to be reserved for a brief final sentence or
two, although some writers, notably Rib-addi of Byblos, could sustain
loquacious pleas for support for much of their letters. A constant
element is denunciation of a neighbouring prince on grounds of dis-
loyalty to the king of Egypt. Since the accusations at times extended to the murder of one prince by another (e.g. EA 89, also 73,
75, 81, 140), these were not necessarily to be dismissed as inven-
tions.

The obvious conclusion to be drawn from this material is that,
although no trace has survived of anything like an objective comment
on an international situation, Egypt's foreign relations were politically based, required careful interpretation and judgement, and involved discussion of situations in terms of human motives. For this
one may assume that the Egyptians were well equipped. In the first
place they tended to write letters to their superiors in a not dissimilar exaggerated style.[35] Secondly, the giving of legal judgements in Egypt (something which was not confined to a class of professional judges but was probably a basic attribute of holding a
significant office), although it might well involve reference back

to documentary archives, was essentially a matter of resolving conflicting testimonies and assessing human behaviour. The inspecting
committees of the Abbott Papyrus set up to make on-the-spot checks
on accusations of tomb-robbery in the Theban necropolis are a clear
example of rational independent assessment.[36]

Against the view that decisions were rationally based one might
cite the ample evidence that oracles played a significant role in
New Kingdom society.[37] The evidence ranges from minor decisions in
the lives of common people to the ratification of state decisions by
the oracle of Amen at Karnak. One is entitled to ask if this practice had a part in foreign policy and military decisions, although
apart from a single case, mentioned above, where a king implies that
he sought divine advice before starting a campaign, there is no real
evidence. But in any case, the nature of Egyptian oracles seems to
have been normally very simple, involving an affirmative/negative
reaction to a question. The formulation of questions would presumably have entailed rational prior discussion, and a negative reaction
would have involved either a retiming or a reformulation. One might
wonder if perhaps oracular guidance was sought when a major decision
proved difficult, the response by the god reflecting a decision which
had 'emerged' from a subtle interplay of inspiration and consultation
on the part of the priests involved. Nevertheless, the records of
major court enquiries – the tomb-robbery trials of the later Ramesside
period and the harim conspiracy of the reign of Rameses III[38] – give
no indication that oracles were involved in reaching decisions; nor
in the formal records of the battles of Megiddo and Kadesh do the
kings involved seem to have sought divine guidance when faced with
major tactical decisions. Indeed, the Kadesh sources imply that the
king made a wrong decision through accepting false information from
captured enemy agents.

Through their massive repetition one can perhaps too readily
come to accept the formal texts and scenes of the king as universal
conqueror as an early form of a theory or doctrine of imperialism.
But if one considers carefully the likely reasons why the Egyptians
embarked on conquest at the beginning of the New Kingdom, and the
fact that by having done so, further activity in western Asia, at
least, became circumscribed by a political situation which required
rational treatment, it is hard to see in what way the formal texts

could have guided decisions, which is presumably one important criterion for a theory of imperialism. Nor does Egyptian behaviour in
western Asia bear any distinctive stamp which marks it out from that
of other major states. In Nubia the results of conquest were in fact
more distinctive, mainly through the massive temple building programme. But even here, whilst a definite positive policy must be
presumed, it is not something which can be read from the formal texts.
Thus, in searching for a form of imperialism in New Kingdom Egypt it
is necessary to look beyond the formal texts on kingship, and to consider both the patterns of Egyptian activity abroad, and certain features of Egyptian society itself.

For the present, two very basic interests in conquest and control can be pointed out. One was the economic return. From the
south this involved not only trade goods encountered closer to their
sources and therefore diminished less by customs dues levied by a
succession of native kingdoms, but also gold and copper and possibly
other things as well from direct exploitation of the land,[39] although
gold was presumably the most important. In western Asia the return
was more in the nature of booty: the capture of spoil during campaigns, and the levying of taxes in those areas where a degree of
control could be exercised. Some of the Amarna letters refer to caravans, some originating from beyond the areas of Egyptian control and
evidently vulnerable to robbery (EA 7, 29, 52, 226, 255, 264, 295,
316), but how important overland trade was (and some of these caravans
may have been carrying tribute or diplomatic gifts) compared to maritime trade with places such as Byblos and Ugarit is impossible to
know, as is, therefore, its influence in determining policy. Booty
and tribute and its presentation to the temples was a constant theme
of the formal texts, and one which, in the detailed enumerations,
brought out the bureaucratic side of the Egyptian character. But
this is not to say that it was a prime consideration in making decisions rather than just a desirable by-product of policies formulated from rather different considerations. Economic exploitation
as a prime motive in imperialism has been doubted in the history of
more recent colonial empires,[40] and one might well conclude from a
review of all the evidence that in New Kingdom Egypt other considerations had equal and probably greater value.

Later manifestations of imperialism also prompt one to ask the

question: was there an aristocratic pursuit of 'glory' in the New
Kingdom? Although no personal commentaries on the politics of the
age have survived - almost certainly none was made - there is sufficient circumstantial evidence to suggest the existence in New Kingdom society of a group or class of high social standing for whom
militarism and the military arts were things to be pursued for their
own sake. The prestige of militarism was enhanced by its ready association with kingship, in which in ways far more diverse than in
previous periods the king as conqueror and mighty man was celebrated.[41] Its symbol was the chariot, a striking innovation for
Egypt in the New Kingdom. This group must have been a creation of
the policies of conquest, but increasingly must have come to play a
major part in perpetuating it. There is ample documentation for the
increasing political role of men with military backgrounds, culminating in the eventual transfer of the throne to an army general,
Horemheb, and his succession by a military family who founded the
Nineteenth Dynasty.[42]

If glory and booty had been the main stimuli for the Egyptian
effort abroad, then the search for rational explanations would be
curtailed. The Nubian evidence in particular suggests otherwise,
but it is also worth noting that militarism was evidently not
characteristic of educated Egyptian society as a whole. The army
and the empire in the end depended on the civil administration,
from whose ranks also came politically powerful individuals. At
school, through the texts which served as models for copying, young
scribes were taught a disdain for all professions other than their
own. This extended to military careers, and scorn was poured on
the soldier and on the chariot officer and on service abroad.[43]
These texts evince no positive side other than selfishness - being
a scribe 'saves you from toil, it protects you from all manner of
work'[44] - but simply in preferring power through orderly administration to glory through action and adventure people who had accepted this ethos must have been a source of counter-arguments to
those of the military. At a very general level it might be said
that Nubia was an administrative creation, whilst western Asia
provided the main scope for military shows, though even here, as
the Amarna letters imply, identifying the enemy was itself a task
for home-based officials.

THE EGYPTIAN EMPIRE IN NUBIA[45]

Nubia is the southward continuation of the Nile valley, beyond the
ancient frontier at the First Cataract. Below the Third Cataract the
agricultural potential of the valley must have been relatively small
compared to most of Egypt, and there must be a degree of doubt as to
whether the fertile Dongola Reach to the south, above the Third Cataract, was much exploited by a settled crop growing population.[46]
During the earlier Middle Kingdom the Egyptians had held Lower Nubia
by a series of great fortified towns and a group of frontier fortresses all of which seem to have been culturally isolated from the
surrounding population who continued with a material culture which
still bore marked resemblances to that of late prehistoric Egypt.
Upper Nubia had remained independent, but, perhaps from the wealth
that trade with Egypt brought, a coalition of kingdoms with a striking material culture of their own, now named after the most important one at Kerma, grew up.[47] During the two centuries or so of
internal governmental weakness which resulted in a withdrawal of
rule from Nubia and a partitioning of Egypt between an Upper Egyptian
state ruled from Thebes (the Seventeenth Dynasty) and a northern
kingdom under the rule of Palestinian kings (the Hyksos), a Kingdom
of Kush, based on Kerma, emerged as a significant state whose power
extended into Lower Nubia. Towards the end of its existence it is
known to have been in diplomatic contact with the Hyksos kingdom,
and was recognized by the Thebans as a threatening presence beyond
Elephantine.

The New Kingdom was initially the result of an expansion of the
Theban kingdom of the Seventeenth Dynasty, northwards against the
Hyksos, a move which eventually reunified the country, and southwards
against the king of Kush. An important group of inscriptions provides an account of the beginning of the most important phase, and
does so in terms of an aggressive initiative of the king for reasons
of political honour.[48] From a point of terminology, for which other
examples can be found,[49] it would appear that it was felt that Nubia,
or at least the more northerly part, was a sort of quasi-extension of
Egypt at more than a purely geographical level, and it would doubtless have been well known that at an earlier period Lower Nubia had
been held by the Egyptians through their forts and fortified towns.
There is no mention of a long-term economic gain - trade-goods and

gold - from Nubia, although the booty theme appears in the sections
on the attack on the Hyksos which is the major interest of the preserved parts of these texts. The power of the king of Kush, with his
fortified court at Kerma, may well have been known to the Thebans,
not least from Egyptians who are known to have spent periods in his
service, and since power readily provokes notions of great and plun-
derable wealth, there may be no need to look further than the motives
provided by the immediate political setting and the promise of glory
and booty.

The conquest of Nubia was effected relatively rapidly. By year
3 of Kamose (c. 1555 B.C.), last king of the Seventeenth Dynasty,
most of Lower Nubia was already in Egyptian hands,[50] and within fifty
years, in the reign of Tuthmosis I, the kingdom of Kush in Upper Nubia
had been destroyed, and an Egyptian expedition had penetrated as far
as Kurgus, above the Fourth Cataract.[51] In Lower Nubia, the old
Middle Kingdom towns and forts, suitably refurbished, formed the basis
of the new Egyptian occupation, and it is possible that new fortresses
were built, the evidence being as yet confined to a hill fort in Lower
Nubia, Gebel Sahaba, and to a rock-cut ditch beneath the later temple
town of Sesebi in Upper Nubia,[52] and a statement in a formal inscription which refers to 'fortresses' built by Tuthmosis I 'to repress the
rebellious lands of the Nubian people' (Urk IV 138.16-139.1). Formal
records of campaigns in Nubia continue into the reign of Merenptah,[53]
and where specific places and events are referred to some historical
basis can be accepted, but even then the scale or significance may
have been magnified. Certainly the archaeological record does not
suggest serious opposition to Egyptian rule. Such disturbances as
there were probably arose either as attacks by eastern desert nomads
on Egyptian mining expeditions and perhaps on caravans, or in Upper
Nubia as attacks on officials by Nubians not resident in the temple
towns.[54] In contrast to the scenes of warfare in western Asia where
the object of attack in the battle reliefs of the later New Kingdom
is frequently a fortified town on a hill, the only Nubian scene where
there is any indication of a setting depicts Nubians fleeing to a
village set amidst trees.[55]

The conquest of Nubia began in a particular political context.
By a century later, say the reign of Tuthmosis III, Egypt had become
a major power in the Near East; Nubia could no longer have appeared

as a serious threat, and trade and mineral exploitation were things
which were dependent upon security in relatively remote desert areas
where a permanent Egyptian presence was hardly feasible. Thus the
pursuit in the period between the reigns of Tuthmosis III and Rameses
II (about two centuries) of an essentially civil policy requiring
considerable effort and expenditure should be seen as a development
within a relatively stable and established situation and not as a
direct consequence of whatever might have been in the minds of Kamose
and his immediate successors. The most enduring sign of the new direction in Egyptian policy was the large number of stone temples
which appeared not only in the old fortified towns inherited from the
Middle Kingdom, but also on many sites, new as far as the Egyptians
were concerned, in both Upper and Lower Nubia. Some of them were of
considerable size, the most splendid having almost certainly been the
great temple of Amenhetep III at Soleb.

With a few exceptions in remote desert localities,[56] Egyptian
temples were not isolated structures. Although our knowledge of
towns in ancient Egypt is still disappointingly slight, enough is
known to suggest that normally a temple was the focal point, at physical, symbolic, and spiritual levels, of an urban community. In Nubia,
evidence from a number of sites offers a fairly consistent setting
for the stone temples. It took the form of a rectangular area en-
closed by a mud-brick girdle wall with external towers along the wall
faces and at the corners, but normally without a ditch. Despite the
application to such places of the term 'fortress',[57] the lack of a
ditch and of extra protection at the gates suggests that serious
attacks were not expected, and it is as well to remember that in
Egypt temple enclosure walls were in some cases given a fortified aspect largely for symbolic reasons.[58] Within the Nubian enclosures,
however, were not only the temples and their ancillary buildings, but
also areas of houses, including a residence for the civil governor.
Extra-mural settlement is also known to have existed, but its extent
has never been fully investigated at any one site. An important
point to note is the size of the storeroom block in the most completely revealed example at Sesebi (fig.1). Because these towns were
for the most part constructed of mud-brick their survival has often
not matched that of their temples. But in view of what has been
learned from a selection of sites, together with what we know of the

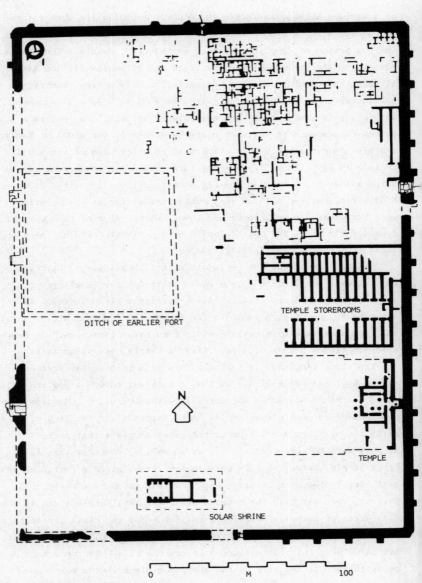

FIG. 1 THE TEMPLE TOWN OF SESEBI

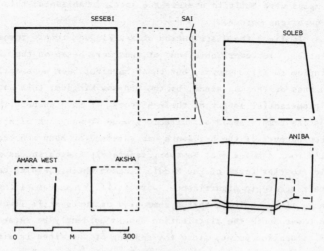

FIG. 2.   OUTLINES OF SIX NUBIAN TEMPLE TOWNS

role of temples generally in New Kingdom society, it seems reasonable
to assume that wherever a stone temple stood on flattish ground not
far from the river it was built to be the centre of a brick town.
During the long reign of Rameses II temple building and embellishment
reached obsessive proportions in Egypt, and this extended to Nubia as
well, particularly in the creation of a group of rock-cut temples in
Lower Nubia, of which Abu Simbel is the most famous. Although the
normal programme of temple town building continued as well (e.g.
Aksha and Amara West), these rock temples, being out of all proportion to the size of the local communities, are a gross extension of
an aspect common to all temples: that whatever their local role might
be, they were also manifestations of royal power. Here, this aspect
was treated independently of the local context. This is evident at
Wadi es-Sebua (fig.4), where the mud-brick enclosure around the front
can have accommodated only the priestly group, the local community
having apparently lived in a small unwalled village down by the river
bank (see p.42 below). It is not enough to say that these rock

temples were built to overawe the local inhabitants; this had happened
generations before.

In fig.3 the distribution of New Kingdom temple towns has been
plotted. In Lower Nubia some of them were based on the old Middle
Kingdom fortified towns, but these have not been separately distinguished on the map since, by the mid-New Kingdom, this had become a
circumstantial aspect of their history. I have assumed that wherever
a stone temple stood on suitable ground it was part of a town, even
when no part of the brickwork has survived or been reported. Rameses
II's rock temples are, however, separately indicated, as are those
old frontier forts of the Middle Kingdom which, despite having lost
their strategic significance, were still given a small temple and
where finds indicate that a community of sorts still lived there.
In Lower Nubia the distribution should evidently be regarded as close
to saturation point, since the spacing of the sites is similar to
that obtaining in the more southerly part of Upper Egypt, whose agricultural potential may not have been much more. A map of likely
temple town sites in this area is included as an inset. Upstream
from Lower Nubia there lies a rocky and inhospitable region known as
the Batn el-Hager, 'Belly of the Rock', which detailed archaeological
survey has shown to have lacked a significant settled population in
ancient times, except for a gold-working site or two.[59] But beyond
roughly the Dal Cataract, the valley begins to open up a little more
and significant areas of flat ground and river bank appear. The sequence of temple towns follows this resumption of limited fertility
closely, until it is again broken by the Third Cataract zone. By
contrast, between Kerma and the Fourth Cataract the Nile flows across
a vast flat plain of sandstone, and the Dongola Reach, as this
stretch is called, has broad and continuous alluvial banks watered by
the Nile floods, as well as some shallow basins (the largest being at
Kerma, Argo and Letti), although unless their drainage and irrigation
is improved with canals and banks their yield is said to be poor, and
in a year of low Nile negligible. Thus their value in ancient times
is uncertain, but even so, this 300 kilometre stretch is the most fertile region south, probably, of Gebel Silsila in Egypt. Consequently
the absence of evidence for temple towns in this area south of Kawa
is a matter that calls for some comment.[60]

There are three points to be made here. In the first place, the

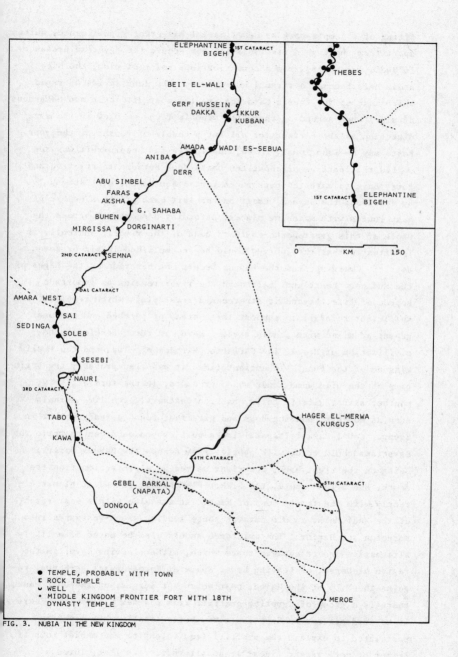

FIG. 3. NUBIA IN THE NEW KINGDOM

siting of a temple town at Gebel Barkal has great significance, quite
apart from showing in its isolation how secure the Egyptian presence
in Nubia was. For, from a communications point of view, the Nile
above here becomes a virtual cul-de-sac. The long series of rapids
which make up the Fourth Cataract are the most difficult and hazardous
of all. When ascending them, the wind is found to blow in the same
direction as the current for all but a couple of months of the year.
Boats may be laboriously towed, and in the last century it was reported that parties of about ten boats took between thirty-five and
forty days to make the passage as far as Abu Hamed, near Kurgus.[61]
By contrast, the Bayuda Desert on the left bank offers a number of
easy routes with watering places, affording a short-cut across the
whole of this great north-eastward bend of the river. Anciently it
is attested that the journey could be accomplished in six or seven
days.[62] Emerging from the Bayuda Desert one has reached the edges of
the Sudanese heartland. Although the river remains an important
source of life, beyond it stretches a great plain which receives just
sufficient rainfall to support large areas of parched and seasonal
grassland mixed with acacia trees. Here, in turn, developed the
civilization of Meroe, the Christian kingdom of Alwa, and the Muslim
kingdom of the Fung. In ancient times it was also probably the beginning of the wild game lands whose products, in the form of ivory,
panther skins, giraffe tails, ostrich feathers, even live animals
such as monkeys, hunting-dogs and giraffes, found a ready market in
Egypt. Gebel Barkal (Napata) looks well chosen as a centre where the
Egyptians could trade with peoples from across the Bayuda Desert.
Being on the right bank, the river served as a protection from the
south, and a land route, the Sikket el-Meheila, linked it almost directly with the temple town of Kawa. It was also within easy reach
of the Wadi Melh, an old caravan route leading south-westwards into
Kordofan and Darfur. The existence should also be noted of a likely
alternative desert caravan route which, either leaving Egypt in the
region of Daraw, or leaving Lower Nubia at Korosko/Wadi es-Sebua, re-
gains the Nile at Abu Hamed, near which, at Kurgus, on the east bank,
there is a group of Egyptian graffiti from the New Kingdom.[63] There
is no evidence for an Egyptian town, but a local market might be
postulated to explain the graffiti (equivalent to the market town of
Berber of more recent times[64]); an alternative is that, lured by

reports of wealth or by the possibility of a direct land route to
Punt, these graffiti mark the passage of Egyptian armies.

The second point on the distribution of temple towns is that
they may be following the existing pattern of political power. Although our knowledge of the archaeological record of the Dongola
Reach is still disappointingly slight, the principal area of the
Kerma culture would seem to be just this stretch of river between
Kawa and Amara.[65] This would readily be explained if the wealth and
eventual power of this area, in the form of the kingdom of Kush, was
derived from the use of the same overland trade route in those
earlier times when the Egyptian frontier was further north at the
Second Cataract. This leads to the third point. When, after a cultural hiatus of some three centuries following the end of the Egyptian New Kingdom control of Nubia, the kingdom of Meroe suddenly
emerges from obscurity and for a while, as the Twenty-fifth Dynasty,
ruled Egypt as well as Nubia and an area of uncertain extent to the
south, four sites were given particular prominence in Nubia as
centres for the cult of Amen and for the rites of coronation: Gebel
Barkal (Napata), Sanam, Kawa and Argo.[66] Although Sanam appears to
have been a new foundation (opposite Napata), the other three sites
belong to the same distribution pattern as the temple towns of the
New Kingdom. Furthermore, the two earliest of the Meroitic royal
cemeteries were in the vicinity of Gebel Barkal: Nuri and el-Kurru.
At the latter site an earlier phase extends back into the period
between the end of the New Kingdom and the beginning of the Twenty-
fifth Dynasty, and probably contained the burial of ancestral native
rulers of this area. Important Meroitic cemeteries have also been
found at Soleb and Sedinga. This continuity of importance in these
two separated areas - the Amara-Kawa stretch, and the Napata region -
carries with it the implication that one should seek to locate here
the most important of the Nubian kingdoms or regions which occur in
Egyptian lists of captured or defeated enemies. Amongst these,
Kary can in fact be localized in the Napata region,[67] and Irem (and
the possibly adjacent Gwerses and Tiurek) in the Kawa-Amara area.[68]

With the temple towns went a full administration on Egyptian
lines.[69] As in Egypt, most officials were either representatives of
the king and departments of the central government, particularly
those concerned with various forms of wealth, with a viceroy of Kush

at the head corresponding to the vizier in Egypt; or they were officers of the local temple, not merely in a hierarchy of priests, but
including 'scribes' and 'stewards' and suchlike, and more minor figures, such as a 'cultivator for the divine offerings (i.e. temple
income)',[70] or a 'herdsman of the cattle of Horus, Lord of Miam',[71]
who also exemplify the fact that temples were normally owners of
agricultural resources, although a title like 'official in charge of
the cattle of all the gods of Wawat (Lower Nubia)' also implies that
ultimately temples came under some central accounting system.[72] Two
other groups of officials should also be noted: military officers,
and 'mayors' of the temple towns.[73] This last office, although it
possessed little by way of its own officialdom, was the basic local
government office in Egypt, and one of its responsibilities was the
delivery of local taxes, paid in kind as well as in gold, to the
vizier, presumably those levied on private land.[74]

The agricultural land of Nubia seems to have been apportioned
according to the fragmented pattern of landholding characteristic of
Egypt. The evidence is not very abundant, but is nevertheless
fairly specific. In the reign of Rameses VI a deputy to the viceroy
called Pennut made a pious donation of land for the benefit of a
cult of a statue of the king in the temple of Aniba (Miam).[75] The
donation consisted of five plots of land varying between about $1\frac{1}{3}$ and
$5\frac{1}{3}$ acres, in no case adjoining one another, and mostly narrow strips
running back from the Nile to the desert. They were bordered by
fields belonging to Pharaoh, to the office held by Pennut and in one
case apparently rented to the crown, to a herdsman called Bahu, and
to other existing statue cults: one of a former deputy, one of the
king administered by the chief priest at Aniba, and another to a
cult of the dead queen Nefertari, wife of Rameses II. A remarkable,
and possibly exceptional, case of a major temple in Egypt having
wide-ranging possessions in Nubia is provided by the Nauri Decree of
Seti I, intended to protect the temple possessions and the transfer
of revenues back to Egypt from the interference or misappropriation
of officials.[76] The siting at Nauri implies that in part the possessions were in the more southerly region. One clause concerned
with the protection of the 'staff' of the temple in Kush, the name
of the more southerly part of Nubia (Upper Nubia), gives a vivid
idea of the diversity of temple holdings and involvement in local

activities, for listed are: 'guardians of fields, inspectors, bee-
keepers, cultivators, vintners, gardeners, crews of transport boats,
hunters (?), stoneworkers (?), foreign traders, transport troops for
the gold miners, carpenters', and another clause adds fishers and
fowlers. An alternative method of endowing temples and their communities, by tax rather than ownership, appears in a decree of
Tuthmosis III which re-establishes the 'offerings', or income, of
the little temple at Semna, perhaps too remote to be able to look
after its own lands. Most of it was in the form of corn from Lower
Nubia, to be provided by an annual tax collected by the 'mayors and
district officials of the Elephantine part of the "Head of the
South"' (another term for Nubia),[77] the same officials who were, in
Egypt, responsible for delivering taxes to the vizier. Finally,
there is a record of a grant of land to a chief priest at Buhen in
the reign of Tuthmosis IV (*Urk* IV 1637.11-14).

There are two important implications of this. One is that the
Egyptians were attempting to introduce agriculture in a far more
systematic way than is likely to have existed before, probably not
an easy task in view of the height of the river banks which requires
the lifting of water, unless the area happens to be an abandoned
river channel and therefore lower. Agriculture and a complex system
of land tenure must have transformed Nubian society at the lower end,
since the need was now for peasant agriculturalists. Secondly,
doubts must be raised as to the reality of a significant Nubian
'tribute', as depicted in formal scenes and texts. The products of
trade and of the mines may well have flowed straight to Egypt. But
the logic of the temple town/mayor system is that they passed on to
the central government (represented by the viceroy of Kush) only
something equivalent to the taxes which similar places in Egypt re-
mitted to the vizier. The Egyptian economy contained a large redistributive element based on the king, but at least by the later New
Kingdom (and probably a lot earlier) both the evidence from texts
and the simple fact of the size of their storage facilities strongly
suggest that temples carried out at a local level a large share of
the total redistributive operation in the country, perhaps leaving
the army and the various palaces as the principal responsibility of
the king. For the mid-Eighteenth Dynasty some figures are available
for cattle, an apparently highly-priced commodity in Egypt.[78] The

Rekhmira tax list indicates that taxes rendered to the vizier's office on a mainly town basis in the southernmost, i.e. poorest part
of Egypt, between Elephantine and Thebes, amounted to a figure almost certainly well short of 100 head of cattle.[79] The annals of
Tuthmosis III give as the revenues (bkt) of Lower Nubia the figures
92, 104, 94, 89, and 114 head of cattle for five almost consecutive
years,[80] figures that compare closely with the Upper Egyptian taxes.
For Upper Nubia the figures, at 343, 419, 275, and 296, are much
larger, and perhaps imply that the fertile areas of the Dongola
Reach were given over more to herding than to settled agriculture.

     The evidence from Egypt shows that temple involvement in land
holding was an extremely complex business. Over long periods of
time the temples built up holdings as a result of royal donations,
usually, it would seem, in the form of numerous widely-scattered
plots. A practice, going back to the pyramid age and still apparently followed, allowed for part of the income from a particular
temple holding to be diverted to become the income of another temple. A good part of the lands seems to have been farmed on a rented or sharecropping basis. A significant feature of the New Kingdom was the number of statues of kings whose cult was supported by
an income, partly or largely derived from land owned by them. This
land was donated either by kings (a very ancient practice), or by
private individuals, Pennut, quoted above, being an example in
Nubia.[81] In either case the responsibility for administration
could be granted to private individuals, the donors themselves where
the land had been a private bequest, who then became the statues'
priests and thereby received a regular income. These arrangements
could be hereditary, the attraction for private donors being perhaps
a reduction in taxes and greater security against seizure. There
are grounds for thinking that this was one way in which veteran
soldiers, including foreigners, were rewarded. This practice was a
partial replacement of an older one where the statue supported by
such a pious foundation was of the donor himself, and formed part of
his tomb. The complex and sometimes interlocking patterns of temple and statue cult income, not all on the same basis, made an overall accounting system necessary, of which one classic example, the
Wilbour Papyrus, has survived from the reign of Rameses V.[82] Since
temples were, at a symbolic as well as at a practical level, a part

of the 'state', the king being the other part, temple revenues from Nubia could perhaps also be regarded as 'tribute', although we do not have sufficient information to know if this was ever actually done.

The above discussion should go a long way towards defining the character of New Kingdom imperialism in Nubia. One can say that the system provided a ready means of exploiting Nubia to the full, but exploiting should evidently not be taken to mean a massive transfer of wealth and produce to Egypt. The logic of the system was that much of the revenue was consumed in this locally controlled manner of redistribution through the temple. Even the building of the temples themselves represented a loss to the Egyptian state of administratively and technically skilled persons and the means of payment to large building crews, all of which could have been used in Egypt. The benefit to the Egyptians must have been of a much more intangible character, namely the extension of the very area of the state, though whether piety can be distinguished from power as a motive is hard to know. Nevertheless, the idea - even the word 'vision' may not be inappropriate - was a persistent one, to judge from the period of time over which new temple towns were founded or rebuilt, and, if one is prepared to allow for the existence in ancient Egyptian society of different views as to the nature of preferred activity abroad, a product of the 'scribal' mentality rather than the military one.

This is also an appropriate moment to consider the applicability of the term 'colonization'. Since the basic form of Egyptian society differed significantly from Roman society, a point by point comparison between the temple towns and the *coloniae* is not particularly helpful. However, if the comparison is made at the level of the relationship to the parent society, then a parallel can be seen to emerge. The *coloniae*, remarked Aulus Gellius,[83] 'have the appearance of miniatures, and are reproductions of Rome herself'. Of the temple towns in Nubia, with regard to their basic physical shape and their administration, one could phrase a similar statement, although no individual Egyptian city seems to have possessed quite the symbolic role which Rome had. But reproductions of the New Kingdom city idea they certainly were. They were also the centres of a policy on land, and land is, in Finley's words, 'the element round which to construct a typology of colonies'.[84] The Egyptian policy in riverine Nubia

involved not merely annexation, but evidently a more intensive exploitation of its agricultural potential through the introduction of personal responsibility for farming strictly defined and legally based
plots of land. Insofar as one can construct a useful definition of
the word 'colony', the New Kingdom temple towns would seem to fit.

The one element of uncertainty is the extent to which the population of Nubia was increased by immigration from Egypt. The uncertainty arises from the rapid and, around the temple towns, wholesale
adoption of Egyptian culture by the local population, to the extent
that the composition of the population seems at present unascertain-
able. Imperial policies have occasionally embraced significant trans-
fers of population, and this has been raised in connection with New
Kingdom Egypt, though also strongly criticized. However, letters found
in 1969 at Kamid el-Loz in Syria do hint at some definite policy towards population. Addressed to two local rulers under Egyptian overlordship, they are concerned with the transfer of a class of captives
(*prw*) to Nubian towns whose inhabitants the king had removed.[85] As
is so often the case, wide implications from isolated sources are
incapable of being verified further. The question remains, therefore, somewhat academic. We have no evidence for a legally defined
'citizenship' in ancient Egypt. The implication of this is that
just by adopting Egyptian culture and making himself presentable
enough to enter Egyptian officialdom, a Nubian acquired a place in
Egyptian society equivalent to possession of citizenship, and with
opportunities for property-owning and promotion within the system.
Thus the effect of Egyptian policies in Nubia was to increase, perhaps quite considerably, the numbers of people who, by culture and
opportunity, were, in effect and in those respects which mattered
most at the time, Egyptian. Whether this was ever consciously intended is hard to say. During the Second Intermediate Period, when
Nubia was independent, a taste for Egyptian culture and the means
to satisfy it are evident in some Lower Nubian cemeteries, and in
any case, by the time that the temple town programme got under way
the process of Egyptianization was largely complete.[86] Egyptian
culture must have had a considerable glamour in the eyes of Nubians,
and, through the land reorganization process, few riverine communities can have escaped regular contact with Egyptian society. It is
not hard to understand how, in an age innocent of the esoteric

delights of 'folk culture', many of the local products, such as the
decorated hand-made pottery and mother-of-pearl trinkets, did not
survive the flood of cheap mass-produced Egyptian wares: the plain
but practical pottery made to fit in with Egyptian practices and
habits, and the rather gaudy jewellery of glazed frit (Egyptian
faience) which seems to have held a place in ancient Egypt equivalent to plastic in our own culture. Furthermore, once conquest was
complete, Nubians may have become anxious to display how they now
belonged to the ruling power.

The evidence which makes Egyptianization into an important issue
is not simply the ubiquitous replacement of one culture by another.
From an upper stratum of society there is striking evidence pertaining to two groups of Nubian princes. One group were princes of Teh-
khet, a region apparently between Buhen and Faras.[87] Within it, at
Debeira East, was a rock-cut family tomb of entirely Egyptian type,
decorated with wall paintings in Egyptian style, though with some
details depicting local agriculture. It belonged principally to a
'prince of Teh-khet' namely Djehuty-hetep, a common Egyptian name.
Across the river was the tomb of another of these princes with the
Egyptian name of Amenemhat, who was apparently Djehuty-hetep's
younger brother. This tomb had a small brick pyramid built above
the rock-cut chambers, a fashionable touch only just at this time
becoming popular at Thebes itself. The pottery and other grave
goods were also Egyptian. Both men seem to have lived in the first
part of the Eighteenth Dynasty. A number of typically Egyptian
statues and stelae can also be ascribed to this family. It is only
the genealogy of these princes where non-Egyptian names occur, the
fact that Djehuty-hetep himself occasionally used a second and non-
Egyptian name, and their use of the title *wr*, 'prince', which the
Egyptians normally applied to foreign dignitaries, which tell us
that we are here dealing with a prominent Nubian family who had
adopted Egyptian culture. One member of the family must have mi-
grated to the frontier town of Elephantine, where his tomb has been
discovered. The office of prince of Teh-khet is known to have
lasted at least to the reign of Rameses II.

Interestingly, Djehuty-hetep's father, Ruiu, had two namesakes
at Aniba who both illustrate the same process.[88] One, whose title
is not fully preserved, was married to a woman with a probably

Nubian name, Iret-nebia, but their son's name, although not fully
preserved, was clearly Egyptian: '...nefer'. The other Ruiu, conceivably the same man, held the office of 'deputy to the viceroy',
the highest office for Lower Nubia. He was buried in a family tomb
at Aniba with an elaborate mud-brick chapel of Egyptian type, his
name inscribed on the stone door jambs. The burials had been rich
and wholly Egyptian, and included two statues and ushabti-figures
bearing his name. A further case at Aniba of a man with a probably
Nubian name holding high office is the mayor of Miam (Aniba), Pahul,
buried in a tomb with a fine Egyptian-type heart scarab and some
imported pottery, a Syrian red lustrous spindle-bottle and an imitation Late Minoan alabastron.

The second group of princes also used the term Miam to refer
to their territory, but evidently it could apply to a stretch of
the Nile valley at least as far as Toshka, as well as to the Egyptian
town of Aniba. For a long time a prince of Miam called Heka-nefer
was known from a wall painting in the Theban tomb of the Viceroy of
Kush, Huy, who held office in the reign of Tutankhamen. In a scene
where princes of Lower Nubia, painted alternately black and brown,
are presented to the king by Huy, one of them is labelled 'Prince of
Miam, Heka-nefer', and is dressed in a richly exotic native costume.
But in this there may be more than a touch of the artistic conven-
tions for southerners. In 1961 his tomb was identified as one of
three rock tombs at Toshka East, some twenty-five kilometres away
from Aniba.[89] In its plan it closely resembles contemporary tombs
at Thebes, particularly that of the Viceroy Huy himself. Around the
entrance were carved prayers to Egyptian gods and representations of
Heka-nefer in Egyptian costume. Inside were traces of wall painting
in Egyptian style. The objects which remained in the badly plundered
burial chamber indicated interments of Egyptian type, with ushabti-
figures, and a fragment of a stone pectoral inscribed on the back
with Chapter 30 of the Book of the Dead. The contrast with the de-
piction of Heka-nefer in Huy's tomb could scarcely be more complete.
Inscriptions from the site also preserve more of his titles, including one which suggests that he had served whilst a youth as a page
at the Egyptian court, exemplifying a common Egyptian policy of
giving an Egyptian court education to the children of foreign
princes.[90]

No inscriptions have survived to identify the owners of the other two closely similar tombs adjoining Heka-nefer's, but in the vicinity was found a graffito commemorating another prince of Miam with the Egyptian name of Ra-hetep. It would seem very plausible to regard Toshka East as the site of a cemetery of native princes allowed to retain their elite status, but who, to the extent of siting their tombs at least, kept themselves separate from the Egyptian temple town at Aniba. Similarly in the case of Teh-khet, Debeira lay between the Egyptian towns of Buhen and Faras.

A further area where the extent of Egyptian penetration into Nubian society can be seen is religion. In the temples built by the Egyptians in Nubia the gods who were present in statues and to whom offerings were made were entirely the product of Egyptian theology. This suggests that, in contrast to the Egyptian reaction in Palestine, Egyptian theologians were unable to identify any well-defined local deities whom they could recognize as fringe members of the Egyptian pantheon. Nor have the indigenous inhabitants of the pre-New Kingdom phases left any traces of shrines, unless some of the groups of rock carvings of cattle and other subjects served as foci for devotion. The Egyptian gods in Nubia can be divided into three groups:

(i) traditional Egyptian deities. These appear quite unaltered, or with some specific Nubian epithet, such as 'Amen-Ra, pre-eminent in Nubia', 'Amen-Ra residing in the "island" of Miam (Aniba)', 'Maat-Ra, lord of Nubia', 'Ra, lord of the eastern bank', 'Isis the great, lady of Nubia', or 'Amen-Ra, lord of the thrones of the two lands (a term for Karnak, Thebes), residing in the holy mountain of Napata, the great god, lord of heaven'.[91] Of understandably common occurrence was the father-wife-daughter triad of Khnum, Anukis, and Satis of Elephantine and the First Cataract;

(ii) 'the Horus gods of Nubia'.[92] For reasons largely lost in obscurity both Horus and the goddess Hathor were, from early times, regarded by the Egyptians as the typical manifestations of accessible and beneficent divinity in foreign lands. Sometimes they reflect an Egyptian view of a local deity, such as Hathor, Lady of Byblos, who masks the local goddess Baalath Gebal. But in most cases, and probably exclusively in Nubia, they are likely to have been Egyptian creations, in which particular localities were assigned to their

patronage. Such immanence is very clear from the case of Hathor,
Lady of Nekhent, who, in the Middle Kingdom, was the patron goddess
of the normally uninhabited diorite quarries in the desert west of
Toshka.[93] Most important were the Horus gods: 'Lord of Baki', 'Lord
of Miam', and 'Lord of Buhen', representing the three principal areas
of Lower Nubia with their centres at Kubban, Aniba, and Buhen. Of
lesser importance were 'Horus, Lord of Meha', 'Hathor, Lady of
Ibshek', and 'Hathor, Lady of Iken'.[94] Curiously, these localities
are all in Lower Nubia, which might suggest that this particular form
of theological 'research' was primarily a Middle Kingdom phenomenon,
when the Egyptians lived in fortified enclaves and Lower Nubia must
have seemed still an alien land; and that the import of more purely
Egyptian deities was found in the New Kingdom to be more appropriate
to the changed Egyptian position;

    (iii) Egyptian kings. This again was an extension of a very
Egyptian practice, going back at least as far as the later Old Kingdom in Egypt, but possibly given more prominence now in Nubia. The
cults of statues of Tuthmosis III 'residing in Teh-khet',[95] and at
el-Lessiya temple,[96] of Amenhetep III 'Lord of Nubia' at Soleb, of
Tutankhamen at Faras, and of Rameses II at various temples, including
all of his rock-cut ones,[97] all seem to have commenced during the
particular king's lifetime. Cults of Rameses VI and probably of
Queen Nefertari are attested at Aniba by the donation text of Pennut
mentioned above. Amenhetep I as 'Amenhetep of Kary',[98] apparently
the area of Napata, was presumably a posthumous cult, and in a number
of localities a cult of Senusret III, the great conqueror of the
Twelfth Dynasty, was celebrated.

    A particularly eloquent witness to the depth of penetration by
Egyptian religion into Nubian society is provided by a shrine, a mere
ledge in a rock face at Gebel Agg, not far from Heka-nefer's tomb at
Toshka East.[99] A narrow bench had been cut at the back, presumably
for offerings, and above it was carved a scene on the overhanging
rock face. It portrayed a group of people, almost certainly a Nubian
family, two of them herdsmen, who bring offerings to three gods:
Horus, Lord of Miam, the long-dead conqueror of their country from a
previous age, Senusret III, and Reshep, 'great god, lord of heaven',
a Palestinian deity given a niche in the Egyptian pantheon, although
his exotic origin was doubtless unknown to this particular group of

worshippers. Below the scene is carved a short prayer for a number
of Egyptian officials who had 'visited Nubia', one of them a stone-
cutter and perhaps the man who had carved the scene above, although
the responsibility for this, perhaps more of a financial kind, was
claimed by one of the sons of the family. Some of the pottery found
in front was apparently in the traditions of the pre-New Kingdom culture, suggesting that this was a well-established place of offerings.
One might also wonder if at other localities this type of rock shrine
characterized the sites chosen by the Egyptians for rock temples.
Outside the walls of Sesebi in Upper Nubia a small single-chambered
shrine had been erected, around which skeletons of snakes had been
buried in pottery vessels. Unfortunately no inscriptions survived
to show whether the cult was a local one, or of the Egyptian cobra
goddess of the harvest, Renenutet, honoured in at least three Nubian
localities.[100]

The Egyptian system established in Nubia had, perhaps not surprisingly, a powerful demographic impact. During the Eighteenth
Dynasty, the number of sites, mostly cemeteries, declined dramatically in Lower Nubia until, by the beginning of the Nineteenth Dynasty, it becomes virtually impossible to isolate significant groups
of graves outside the cemeteries attached to the temple towns. This
has been taken to show an equivalent absolute decline in population:
'During the fifteenth century B.C. there occurred a general exodus
of what remained of the indigenous population, until in the later
Eighteenth Dynasty the only Nubians who remained in the region were
those who had been absorbed into the Egyptian colonies. These colonies themselves rapidly declined in size and importance, and prac-
tically ceased to function after the Eighteenth Dynasty. Small
numbers of Egyptians remained on frontier duty for another two centuries, building monuments to proclaim the glory and sovereignty of
their pharaoh over a deserted land.'[101] Explanations have been
sought in natural ecological reverse,[102] and in the effects of too
energetic an exploitation. One might note that the names of the
last three kings of the New Kingdom, Rameses IX, X, and XI have been
found at widely separated temple towns in Nubia, and more significantly the Pennut donation text referred to above provides indisputable evidence that in one part of Lower Nubia the Egyptian agricultural system was still operating in the reign of Rameses VI, implying

the existence of peasants, even if they did not leave much in the way
of archaeological traces behind them. But for a better understanding
of the archaeological evidence two general points must be made. The
first is that, probably by about the beginning of the first millennium, thus subsequent to the New Kingdom, the practice of burying
quantities of household goods in tombs in Egypt had largely ceased,
and had been replaced, though probably not so universally, by the
inclusion of amulets and other purely religious objects. The first
part of this process - decline in the burial of household goods -
had almost certainly begun in the late New Kingdom, producing in
Egypt an effect which bears some resemblance to that visible in Lower
Nubia. It can be demonstrated in the relatively well-surveyed Qau
area of Middle Egypt,[103] and at the important palace site at Medinet
el-Ghurab, whose cemetery seems to display the same decline in the
numbers of burials that can be ascribed to the later New Kingdom.[104]
The second point is that in the larger New Kingdom cemeteries in
Nubia, the Egyptian type of family vault was adopted, served by a
single chapel, sometimes quite elaborate.[105] These have been ter-
ribly robbed being very vulnerable, but in addition to containing
several burial chambers, it is clear that each chamber might contain
several bodies,[106] so that the numbers of tombs in one of these
cemeteries give one no idea at all of the numbers of burials involved, nor how they might have been distributed in time. Since the
comparison that is being made is with the older indigenous cemeteries where burials were made singly and marked clearly with a
stone tumulus, there is a real danger of being misled by a simple
tomb count.

      To illustrate this demographic aspect I have chosen one fairly
well surveyed area of Lower Nubia, fig.4. The stretch of Nile valley upstream and downstream of Wadi es-Sebua seems anciently to have
been one of the less prosperous parts of Lower Nubia, although
Burckhardt in 1813 reported that he found it 'the best cultivated
part of the country which I met with, between Assouan and Derr',[107]
as well as the home of merchants who used a long overland desert
route to trade with the Sudan, at Berber. The principal area of
cultivable alluvium was at es-Sebua itself, on the left bank, and
extended to a maximum width of about one hundred metres, which has
probably been reduced since ancient times by heavy sand drifting.

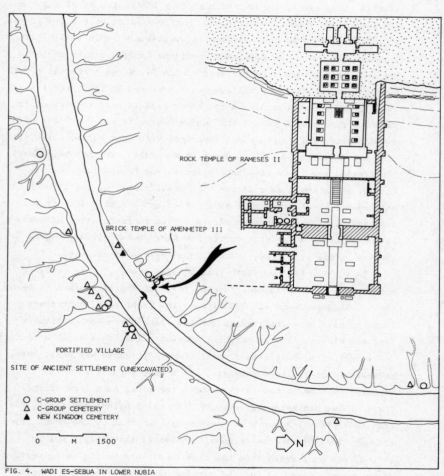

ROCK TEMPLE OF RAMESES II

BRICK TEMPLE OF AMENHETEP III

FORTIFIED VILLAGE

SITE OF ANCIENT SETTLEMENT (UNEXCAVATED)

○ C-GROUP SETTLEMENT
△ C-GROUP CEMETERY
▲ NEW KINGDOM CEMETERY

0   M   1500

N

FIG. 4.   WADI ES-SEBUA IN LOWER NUBIA

During the Middle Kingdom a population bearing C-group culture was
distributed as a scatter of small communities on both sides of the
river, and with an obvious concentration in the vicinity of es-Sebua
itself. They can be recognized both from little groups of stone huts
and from stone tumulus cemeteries. Many contained only a few graves,
and although part of the evidence is available only in preliminary
reports, altogether no more than about one hundred graves may be
present. Almost opposite the site of the New Kingdom temples a much
more substantial C-group village was discovered in 1965, comprising
about forty stone houses. On the river side it used the low cliff
edge for protection, but on the landward side it was fortified with
a thick stone wall containing loopholes, with spur walls to protect
the main gate, though all on a miniature scale. In the preliminary
publication the finds have been dated to the Second Intermediate
Period, which would make it one of a small number of fortified
settlements which grew up at this period.[108] If this date is substantiated, it would suggest strongly that the nucleation of population which is so evident in the New Kingdom had already begun
shortly before this time, and for local defensive reasons.

In the New Kingdom, both this village and any other outlying
settlements were abandoned. Except for some sherds claimed to be of
the New Kingdom found in isolation on the right bank, settlement
seems to have been confined to the left bank where the cultivable
land was widest. In the reign of Amenhetep III, thus about a century
and a half after conquest, a small mud-brick temple was built here,
dedicated principally to Amen-ra, but a more popular form was
honoured on some private stelae under the name 'Amen lord of the
roads'. One had been dedicated by 'the chief priest and mayor, Pia',
from the reign of Rameses II, presumably the head of the community
at this time.[109] In the reign of Rameses II this temple was restored, and on a fresh site the rock temple was built, using western
desert nomads captured for the purpose as labour.[110] Both temples
stood back from the river at the beginning of the slope up to the
desert. No trace was found here of a New Kingdom town or village,
but in the report of a 1906-7 survey it was remarked that the 'mounds
which mark the site of the ancient town are to be seen at the river's
edge in front of the temple, the surface pottery being mainly late'.[111]
No attempt was made to excavate it, and it subsequently fell victim

to the raised level of water in the reservoir created by the successive damming of the Nile at Aswan. Consequently, a New Kingdom horizon must remain a matter of conjecture, but this situation also illu-
strates the particular vulnerability of one class of settlement,
that lying on the river bank. The cemetery record, likewise fragmentary, also suggests that the community was divided into two: a handful
of people living around the temple, the officials, who were apparently
buried in a small cemetery with rock tombs near the temple; and the
inhabitants of a small village down by the river who continued to use
an old C-group cemetery about a kilometre upstream, which was used
again in Meroitic and modern times, a fact which suggests, despite
gaps in the archaeological record, a degree of continuity in the local
population. It had been plundered, and deeply buried beneath drift
sand so that full excavation was not possible. In one campaign of
excavation forty-one graves were ascribed to the New Kingdom, all
shallow oblong pits for one burial and all extremely poor, even when
unplundered. Indeed, half of them contained no objects at all, and
most of the remainder only a single pot. It is thus not really
possible to see how these burials were distributed in time.

The conclusions to be drawn from Wadi es-Sebua are that the
size of the New Kingdom temples, especially the rock temples, is no
guide to the size of the population, even at the outset of the New
Kingdom; and that with such a modest population the archaeological
record becomes highly vulnerable and makes quantitative assessment
difficult. Wadi es-Sebua may not be typical of all 'country' areas,
away from the main towns, and it should be noted that no assessment
is yet possible at all for Upper Nubia. But when other evidence,
such as the Pennut donation text which concerns an area not all that
distant from Wadi es-Sebua, is considered as well it should be concluded that whilst the later New Kingdom was not a period of particular prosperity for Lower Nubia, and may have seen an agricultural
population with very little material wealth at all existing beside
small groups of officials, it is not justified to invoke almost total
depopulation.

THE EGYPTIAN EMPIRE IN WESTERN ASIA[112]

From the point of view of the history of imperialism, the western
Asiatic side of the Egyptian empire is of less interest than Nubia,

in that it was merely a variation on the common theme of vassalage
and tribute. As in Nubia, the initial conquests were rapid, in
succession to the expulsion of the Palestinian Hyksos dynasty,
reaching the Euphrates in the reign of Tuthmosis I (c. 1500 B.C.).
Some fifty years later, this same limit marked the peak of Tuthmosis
III's successes. At this distance the Egyptians were close to the
frontiers of major states – Mitanni across the Euphrates, and by the
late Eighteenth Dynasty the Hittites in Anatolia – and evidently did
not possess the overwhelming military strength to defeat rival great
powers and occupy their territories, as the Assyrians and later the
Persians were able to. Since the same was true, *vis-à-vis* Egypt,
for these other two powers, the history of this period is essentially
one of military struggle for the domination of Syria, not only for
whatever economic gain might accrue (this being something that the
texts say little about), but more for the power or sense of power
brought by military success and diplomatic coercion in a region which
was, by the standards of the age, an advanced one. The limits of
effective Egyptian control seem normally to have stretched no further
north than, say, a line between Ugarit (or a point to the south) and
Kadesh, although this should not be understood as a frontier, but a
zone beyond which Egyptian power to dictate the course of events and
collect tribute was greater or lesser, according to circumstances.
Only with the treaty between Rameses II and the Hittites (c. 1270
B.C.) does a degree of relative stability seem to have appeared, and
was effective probably because it represented a mutual recognition
of the limitations of power, and although it contains no geographical
definitions, it must have been based on this dividing zone which had
gradually emerged and which left most of Syria within the Hittite
empire. Behind this treaty lay some three centuries of Egyptian
military effort since the beginning of the Eighteenth Dynasty, of
garrisoning punctuated by major campaigns. The basic lack of territorial advance over this period may have mattered less compared to
the satisfaction of the New Kingdom military urge, since the well-
equipped armies of western Asia must have seemed a more fitting
challenge than Nubian raiders or rebels. The increase in power
brought by success was marked by diplomatic courtesies from far
afield, from the courts of great kings. Nubia could offer nothing
like this.

Syria and Palestine had been the scene of a relatively sophisticated urban society for as far back as the initial emergence of the
Egyptian state at the end of the fourth millennium, and indeed beyond.
This has been emphasized recently by the discovery at Tell Mardikh
(the ancient Ebla) of about 15,000 tablets dating to the twenty-
fourth or twenty-third century, part of the contents of which are
said to deal with international diplomatic exchange.[113] It says
something about the character of the early Egyptian state that,
apart from forays and perhaps some attempt at control in that part
of Palestine closest to Egypt, it was not until the New Kingdom that
a serious attempt was made to establish hegemony in Palestine and
Syria. Little is actually known in Palestine of political organization for the earlier periods, but the archaeological record shows
every sign of an inherent city-state pattern. This reached a peak
of wealth and development during the latter part of the Middle
Bronze II period, and probably produced the Hyksos dynasty in Egypt.
The material culture of Middle Bronze II Palestine was for a while
transported to the eastern Nile delta.[114] Although there is no
really unambiguous written evidence, the general historical situation
raises the serious likelihood that the overlordship of the Hyksos
kings extended over at least the southern part of Palestine as well,
whither they retired in the face of the successful Theban revolt
which led to the establishment of the Eighteenth Dynasty. The importance of considering this is that, if true, the early Eighteenth-
Dynasty kings may have found themselves heirs to an existing vassal
system which required only a limited display of military determination to take over.

Egyptian hieroglyphic sources say remarkably little about imperial organization. But considerable incidental detail emerges
from the Amarna letters, augmented to a small extent by finds of
similar tablets on other western Asiatic sites (e.g. Ta'anach, Gezer,
Tell el-Hesi, and Kamid el-Loz).[115] The careful sifting of allusions
in letters written by and to people well acquainted with the background, to which certain Egyptian hieroglyphic references can be
added, has produced the following rather hazy picture.[116] The city-
states continued to retain their kings or princes (more than one term
was used to differentiate status) once they had sworn an oath of
allegiance to Pharaoh, a formal ceremony to which the Egyptians gave

FIG. 5   TENTATIVE POLITICAL MAP OF PALESTINE AND SYRIA IN THE 14TH CENTURY B.C.

great symbolic importance. Some of their children might be sent to
the Egyptian court to be brought up in Egyptian ways, and from them
the successor might have to be chosen. Loyalty and a flow of tribute
was maintained by Egyptian-appointed commissioners who frequently,
though not always, possessed Egyptian names. The powers of these
commissioners were evidently wide, and extended to protecting the
local prince from his own people and quelling disturbances in the
cities, and to settling local disputes between city-states by a court
of arbitration consisting of a group of them. Where Egyptian supremacy was an established fact, the commissioner was a figure who
could help support a ruling house in the local political intrigues
which could reach serious proportions, and his character was of obvious concern to the individual prince. One Amarna letter (EA 106)
from Rib-adda of Byblos, in requesting a new commissioner for Simyra,
asks for a particular Egyptian fan-bearer by name, for 'I have heard
from others that he is a wise man and everyone loves him'. It is
possible to interpret the evidence of the Amarna letters to point to
the existence of a division of the whole area under Egyptian hegemony
into three provinces (though there appears to be no ancient term for
such): Amurru (taking its name from the dominant city-state), a northerly coastal province; Upe, stretching inland over Syria; and Canaan,
comprising much of Palestine. Each contained a city in which the
senior Egyptian representative had a more permanent residence, respectively Simyra, Kumidi and Gaza. Garrisons, which could be quite
small, were stationed at some places. At Jerusalem, the local prince
Abdu-heba faced a revolt of a garrison of Nubian mercenaries, poorly
supplied, who broke into his house and, so he claimed, tried to kill
him (EA 287). It is interesting to note that, in contrast to the
conditions of Hittite vassalage, the city-states were evidently not
required to assist the Egyptians militarily.[117] The Egyptian government was kept in touch by envoys, chariotry personnel carrying clay-
tablet letters to and from Pharaoh and his chief ministers on the
one hand, and the various princes and Egyptian commissioners on the
other.

Naturally, an important feature was the assessment of tribute,
paid in kind and probably on an annual basis (cf. *Urk* IV 1442.3-7),
carried out by Egyptian officials. The possibility that this implies
at least a limited Egyptian bureaucratic presence in addition to the

commissioner is increased by the discovery at two sites (Tell el-Duweir[118] and Tell esh-Sharia[119]) of a small number of Ramesside hieratic texts, probably preliminary book-keeping jottings. The former group is concerned with 'wheat' and 'harvest tax'; of the latter group one is concerned with taxes coming to the 'house', though whether this refers to the local sanctuary or to the local Egyptian residence is not yet apparent. If the Egyptians were running a full tax assessment system, a much greater degree of organization and staffing is implied than is visible from other sources.

Basic to the character of this empire was the Egyptian acceptance of a well-established way of life. Politically, it was a classic city-state situation with some, particularly in Syria, the centres of confederacies with their own vassals. Typically, the urban centre stood on a mound of accumulated strata from earlier periods, surrounded at the top by a massive towered perimeter wall with strongly fortified gateways, and possessing some form of keep or strong point. In size the cities varied considerably, sometimes reaching proportions which, for the ancient world, were fairly large. Within they presented a tightly-packed congested appearance, crossed by only narrow crooked streets. House units are often not easy to isolate, and there has been little serious analysis of the articulation of town plans. At some sites palaces have been found, likewise varying greatly in size: 400 square metres at Ta'anach; some two and a half acres at Ugarit, a city of very considerable wealth. Public buildings separate from the palace are difficult to isolate. Particularly important for the contrast with Egypt are their temples, relatively modest constructions without their own precincts.[120] For Syria, some further written evidence exists for social and economic structure.[121] It was not an ethnically homogeneous society. As a result of southward migrations in the preceding period, a significant new element was now to be found in the ancient Near East. Their language was Hurrian, their ultimate homeland may have been Armenia, and amongst them was an aristocratic class called *maryannu*, bearing Indo-Aryan names, who formed a ruling element in Syria and parts of Palestine, though not exclusively so. They were particularly associated with chariotry, and indeed must have provided the model for the military aristocrats of New Kingdom Egypt, as well as an enemy whose defeat or

capture was prestigious. The term *maryannu*, however, was not only
hereditary, but could also be conferred on a man as a mark of honour.
The kingdom of Mitanni was itself a Hurrian confederate state across
the Euphrates.

These city-states were ruled by hereditary kings who in some
cases still attempted to maintain an aura of divinity, and who fulfilled a wide range of administrative and judicial functions, although their power was to a degree circumscribed by a council of
'city lords'. Census records provide a good sign of a bureaucratic
control of society, in which people were classed, taxed and rendered
liable to service. This last demand, in particular, is probably a
sign that the existing system was in essence no less onerous for the
majority of the people than anything the Egyptians might have introduced, although the extent or frequency of the burdens might have
been increased by Egyptian demands for revenue. Members of the aristocracy could be granted lands and villages in perpetuity in return
for payment of certain taxes and the rendering of certain obligations
to the king. Slavery existed, but not apparently on a particularly
large scale. Farming, trade and industry (e.g. purple dye from murex
shellfish) were pursued, and made some places, such as Ugarit, very
rich. Quite apart from the great practical problems, the Egyptians'
general weakness in abstract thinking must have rendered very unlikely any attempt at reorganizing the law, government, or society
of this region following some great master plan or set of elegant
concepts. Since this was a society which the Egyptians could not
alter but only hope to keep favourably disposed towards them, it is
possible that, outside the special conditions created by rebellions
and campaigns, they acted with some regard for established exchange
procedures. Thus Pharaoh might seek to acquire weaving slave-girls
'in whom there is no blemish' not by peremptory demand, but by sending an official to one of the local princes (in this case Milkili of
Gezer) with a consignment of precious things to exchange for them
(*ANET* 487). This debit side to the imperial balance sheet is, as in
Nubia, impossible to quantify.

Nor does the question of colonization or town-building arise in
this area. Some towns or districts are known to have been made into
Egyptian royal domains (e.g. Gaza and Kumidi), others of the temple
of Amen at Thebes,[122] but there is no indication that this went

further than placing an existing town or area somewhat more firmly
within the Egyptian grasp, no indication that anywhere a significant
building programme was undertaken. Even in the important copper
mining desert region around Timna in the Wadi Arabah the local cult
set up by the Egyptians, a form of Hathor, was served by only a rudi-
mentary rough stone sanctuary, in contrast to the great temples of
Lower Nubia which must likewise, in some cases, have served insig-
nificant communities.[123]

In assessing the impact of Egyptian imperialism in western Asia
in cultural terms, allowance must be made for the fact that this was
an age of great international exchange in technology, religious
ideas and artistic motifs in which Egypt was only one party, although
the distinctiveness of Egyptian art makes its influence more readily
apparent. Furthermore, these exchanges of ideas, material objects
and persons went beyond the bounds of empires. As examples revealed
by texts but of a type not normally documented by archaeology one
might cite the Mitanni loan to Amenhetep III of a statue of the heal-
ing goddess Ishtar of Nineveh (EA 23), and the requests by the prince
of Ugarit for an Egyptian doctor to be sent (EA 49), and by the
Hittite king to Rameses II for medical assistance for his ageing sister.[124] The artistic eclecticism of the age is well exemplified by
the Megiddo ivories,[125] and survived into the very different political world of the early first millennium in the carved ivories of
Phoenicia and North Syria, where it is possible to discern still
Egyptian, Hurrian, Hittite and Mycenaean motifs.[126] Small objects
of value from Egypt - faience, stone and glass vessels, scarabs and
bronze objects - are found in relatively limited quantities on Syro-
Palestinian sites, although the general record does include 'pockets'
of Egyptian or Egyptianizing material, the background to which is
not always easy to understand. The Fosse Temple at Tell el-Duweir,
for example,[127] which was evidently not the main city shrine since
it lay outside the city limits at that time, included a strong
Egyptian element among the large quantity of votive objects, despite
the lack of Egyptian inscriptions referring to the deity there (unlike the temple at Beth-Shan, see below). The question as to
whether the devotees numbered Egyptians amongst them, or whether objects of value suitable for pious temple gifts would inevitably often
have been Egyptian imports or imitations, is as yet unanswerable.

Identifiable Egyptian pottery, the most distinctive being the blue-painted vessels developed during the later Eighteenth Dynasty, is generally rare. This is in marked contrast to the quantities of pottery imported from elsewhere or imitated locally which could, in tomb groups, reach fifty per cent.[128] This included Mycenaean pottery, but even more so Cypriote, which became a dominant feature of the Palestinian pottery repertoire. Its range is noticeably wider than that found in Egypt, where Cypriote pottery imports seem the result of a more specialized trade, and presumably is a sign that local trading patterns in Syro-Palestine continued under Egyptian overlordship. It is a common comment that trade in Egypt, particularly with the outside world, was a royal monopoly, in contrast to other parts of the ancient Near East, but the evidence on which this is based is not very satisfactory. One reference, in a scribal school exercise in which the writer is made to describe the luxurious and successful life of his teacher, contains the intriguing statement: 'Your ship has returned from Syria laden with all manner of good things.'[129] Although one can scarcely base a case for private merchant ventures in Egypt on a single isolated reference, it should at least serve as a warning against making too sweeping a generalization on this topic.

During the Second Intermediate Period, as noted above, Palestinian material culture was to be found in the eastern Nile delta, but with the coming of the New Kingdom this influence seems largely to have died away. Apart from a line of forts or way stations along the north Sinai coastal road leading to Palestine (one recently located at Bir el-Abd),[130] the cultural division between Palestine and Egypt was a sharp one in the New Kingdom, as can readily be seen by comparing the excavation reports of east delta sites such as Tell el-Yahudiya[131] with that of Tell el-Ajjul,[132] one of the closest large Palestinian Late Bronze Age sites to Egypt, and possibly the city of Sharuhen whither the Hyksos king retired when expelled from Egypt.[133] On many sites in Palestine (even Tell el-Ajjul) the purely archaeological record would not of itself incline one to the view that an Egyptian empire existed at all.

However, one particular facet of culture does deserve to be singled out for further consideration. The temples on Late Bronze Age sites display little in the way of architectural grandeur. Their

basic forms, of one or more modest chambers, were still rooted in a
long tradition reaching back to the Early Bronze Age, and were also
widespread beyond Palestine and Syria. The contrast with Egypt was
not just in forms and monumentality, but also in the absence of important identifiable ancillary structures, particularly a temple
precinct and capacious warehouses. There are some indications, however, that they were given a significant role in the Egyptian imperial
presence. It might indeed be thought that in this area at least the
Egyptians were better placed for introducing changes, but even here
they seem to have accepted basic cult practices and divine ident-
ities, some Syro-Palestinian deities acquiring a limited recognition
in Egypt (Reshep at the Gebel Agg shrine in far-distant Nubia was
referred to above).[134] The most revealing site in this respect is
Beth-Shan (Tell el-Hosn), a town set on a mound lying to the west of
the Jordan valley.[135] During the period equivalent to the New Kingdom the edge of the mound was fortified with a towered wall, and behind it, at one period (level VII of the thirteenth century) a small
fortified keep was built, of the sort that appears in Egyptian artistic representations of western Asiatic towns, and at another (level
VI, about the reign of Rameses II) a house was constructed for the
Egyptian army commander employing inscribed stone doorframes of the
type found in houses in Egypt. The site of the temple was close by,
and over a period between the mid-thirteenth and the tenth centuries
it had been successively rebuilt. For much of this time it was a
relatively modest building of mud-brick, of locally inspired layout
but employing certain Egyptian design elements, such as stone papyrus
capitals. The inscribed stones belong to two groups, representing
two very different levels of patronage. One consists of stelae dedicated to local deities: Anat, possibly Astarte, and 'Mekal of Beth-
Shan', this last god depicted in Egyptian style though with Asiatic
headdress and features, and dedicated by a builder named Amenemope
and his son Paraemheb. There is no obvious trace at this personal
level of Egyptian deities. The other group, which very surprisingly
had been re-erected in front of a yet later temple belonging to the
period following the end of the New Kingdom, when it is generally
assumed that the Egyptian empire had ceased to exist, consisted of
formal, 'official' stelae of kings Seti I and Rameses II, depicting
only Egyptian gods, and containing either military epithets or

accounts of local campaigns, just as if they had belonged to a purely
Egyptian temple.

Along with the reused stelae was found a life-size statue of
Rameses III. This may not have been the only royal statue on a
Palestinian site, for another from an unknown provenance in Palestine
is in the British Museum,[136] and a battle text of Rameses II may refer to a statue of his in Tunip.[137] Royal statues, particularly in
the Ramesside period, imply statue cults with supporting foundations,
and may suggest, for the later New Kingdom at least, an attempt at
creating a psychological focus for Egyptian rule, in the shape of a
ruler cult. Evidence for other Egyptian cults is slight.[138] The
most specific is a reference to a 'mansion' built by Rameses III at
Gaza to contain a statue of Amen to whom the people of Palestine
would bring tribute (P Harris I 9.1-3). The term 'mansion' may well
have referred to something fairly modest,[139] and Gaza itself was too
closely linked to Egypt for this statement to signify a policy more
widely adopted. The unusually close relationship between Egypt and
Byblos during the Middle Kingdom had left a legacy in the form of a
local Hathor cult, and this continued to receive Egyptian patronage
during the New Kingdom.[140] Another Hathor cult, at Timna, see above,
belongs to an extension of Egyptian desert mining activities. From
the major role played by temples in the society of New Kingdom Egypt
and Nubia one might have expected a greater effort at establishing
Egyptian cults, especially of Amen and of the king, or perhaps of
Seth even, in the western Asiatic provinces. One should not over-
estimate the size of Late Bronze Age archaeological exposures on
Palestinian town sites, and it should be pointed out that statues or
other cult objects of Canaanite deities are equally lacking. The
Beth-Shan temples themselves contained nothing in their architectural remains to suggest that a large royal Egyptian statue had been
present, nor does P Harris I (a summary of Rameses III's achievements) refer to it. One should perhaps not, therefore, be too ready
to deny that this basic aspect of the Egyptians' ordering of society
was scarcely represented in this part of their empire.

As with Nubia, it has been claimed that under Egyptian hegemony
there was a general decline in prosperity in Palestine (though not
in Syria) during the later New Kingdom, corresponding to the later
phases of the Late Bronze Age and the beginnings of the Iron Age. It

has been further claimed that this was the direct result of maladministration and rapacious taxation.[141] A literal acceptance of the
Amarna letters, with their desperate pleas and grievances might indeed create the impression of a system degenerating in disorder. But
at the same time, the self-interest of those who wrote is hard to
discount, as hard as the seriousness of their complaints is always to
accept at face value. Although in tone they are a valuable correc-
tive to the bombast of official texts, they are likely to be, in
their way, almost as tendentious.[142] The archaeological record is
far more complex than in Nubia, and still a lot more fragmentary.
As excavation proceeds – it has now reached the stage of second expeditions to some of the original key sites and to inevitable re-
interpretations of basic findings – a bewildering variety of local
histories is emerging, punctuated by destruction levels for which
attempts at correlation with known Egyptian campaigns sometimes seem
forced and somewhat arbitrary. In general, the period equivalent to
the establishment of the New Kingdom empire seems to have witnessed
the decline, even abandonment, of some places in Palestine (such as
Bethel, Jericho, Tell el-Duweir, Shechem, Tell Beir Mirsim and Tell
el-Fara'ah), and at others a period of destruction followed shortly
afterwards by rebuilding (e.g. Beth-Shemesh and Tell el-Ajjul).
Destruction temporarily overtook Megiddo and Ta'anach somewhat later.
But by the later Eighteenth Dynasty it would seem that almost every
town for which there is evidence in the Middle Bronze Age was once
more occupied, and some, such as Tell Abu Hawam, had been newly
founded. Significant new buildings might be constructed (e.g. the
Late Bronze II palace at Tell Aphek[143]). But for the later New Kingdom, any growth that was in Palestinian society seems to have stopped. Individual places (Beth-Shan is a striking case, and one might
cite places in the plain of Accho[144]) survived to the end of the New
Kingdom without apparently suffering a serious destruction, but a
great many more were wrecked in about the reign of Rameses III.

It is thus evident that the Egyptian empire did not usher in a
golden age of peace and prosperity in western Asia. The fate of
city-states evidently depended a great deal on local circumstances
so that generalization is now extremely difficult. Some clearly
went through periods when survival itself was uncertain. Whether or
not the added taxation for Egypt depressed local economies, the

really serious weakness of the empire in this part of the world was
almost certainly that the Egyptians were just not strong enough militarily themselves to impose their rule absolutely. They evidently
had no real supremacy over the armies of Mitanni or of the Hittites,
and could only with difficulty prevent local rebellion or inter-
city warfare.

The texts of the period also expose a further threat to order
which one imagines the armies of the day were even less able to cope
with: a disruptive element outside the recognized power structure of
the region. The better-documented group were referred to by the
terms SA.GAZ or *hapiru*, and occur in cuneiform documents both from
the preceding period and from a wide area of the Near East, as well
as in the Amarna letters.[145] They may not be ethnic terms, and in
the Amarna letters could be used as pejoratives in referring to one's
enemies generally. The people they describe appear as donkey ,
drivers, smugglers, migratory farmers and slaves. Occasionally they
turn up as independent raiders, but more frequently as mercenaries
employed by one city-state against another. Their origin remains
obscure, though one might guess at a mixture of people drawn in from
the deserts, refugees from wars, and simply criminals. Some were
captured on Egyptian campaigns, and appear in Egyptian texts as *'prw*,
working on winepresses and in quarries. A further group whose niche
in society may for a time have been similar were called by the
Egyptians the Shasu, although with them a homeland in Transjordan and
a more specific origin amongst organized pastoral nomadic tribes
seems substantiated.[146] They too were encountered by the Egyptians
on campaigns in Palestine, were captured alongside the *'prw*, and, by
the late New Kingdom, were serving as mercenaries in the Egyptian
armies. In the battle reliefs of Seti I, the Shasu are defeated
just over the borders of Egypt in north Sinai. It is impossible to
measure how seriously this undercurrent in society affected the prosperity and well-being of urbanized life in Palestine, and difficult
as yet to discover at what point this element took on the character
of the more direct assault which was to lead to the establishment of
the kingdom of Israel, although it is noteworthy that from the reigns
of Rameses II and Merenptah, alongside general terms for unruly elements, more specific names appear: Israel, Moab and Edom.[147]
In the thirteenth century these disruptive elements were

augmented by migrants or refugees from western Anatolia and perhaps
the Aegean, termed the Sea Peoples by the Egyptians. By the end of
this century they had destroyed both Hatti and Ugarit, and some went
on to settle on the coastal plain of Palestine, as the Philistines.[148]
The peace treaty between Egypt and Hatti in the reign of Rameses II
may not therefore have had much effect in improving security within
the areas of Egyptian control. The Egyptians took through taxation
or tribute, but could not provide the peace and security needed to
maintain or enlarge the economic base.

The first part of this paper made the point that, as a contribution
to the history of imperialism, New Kingdom Egypt should not really
be studied primarily on the basis of the formal texts of conquest,
which reflect a philosophy of glorified pillage. It is necessary
from other, often less explicit sources - both written and archaeological - to seek the rationale behind Egyptian foreign activity of
this time. Furthermore, an imperial balance sheet would almost certainly show a significant debit side.[149] Whatever specific motives
may be discerned, however, empires are ultimately about power and
the sense of power, and belong to a stage of internal political development. In Nubia, the exercise of power was in extending the
Egyptian way of life and administration, and the form it took involved investment in the creation of a particular type of colony,
whose form points to certain emphases in the character of Egyptian
society at that time. In the long term it was not successful in
that, when eventually the administrative impetus was withdrawn at
the end of the New Kingdom, the life of the temple towns seems to
have faded away. But some recognition, at least, should be given
to the positive side of this early attempt to extend what, to the
Egyptians themselves, was a civilized way of life.

In western Asia there was no scope for anything like this. A
strong indigenous culture and a relatively sophisticated society
would doubtless have swamped any Egyptian colonies had they been
set up, and this must presumably have been appreciated at the time.
The contrast with Nubia can in a rough way be compared to the contrast in numbers of colonies in the eastern and western parts of
the Roman empire. But here the sense of power for the Egyptians
came partly from trying to match the well-equipped and presumably

well-trained armies of western Asia, and perhaps even more so, from participating as a major power in the well-established prestige forum of international relations. Satisfaction came from the exchanges of presents, compliments and envoys with other great powers whose respect had been won, and from the oaths of loyalty of vassals, and the many other ways in which vassals expressed their inferior status.

From its establishment to the end of the reign of Rameses II, the empire was a going concern for something like two and a half centuries. The lack of prosperity in Nubia in the subsequent century, the failure in Palestine to maintain order and security, and the similar lack of growth: these are things which cannot be entirely explained by saying that the Egyptians exacted too much, or were too punitive in their treatment of subject territories. Rameses II was the last major New Kingdom builder in Egypt outside Thebes, and the period following his reign was also evidently one of stagnation and of many changes in the character of society which are as yet barely understood. Decline embraced Nubia, Palestine and Egypt.

3: CARTHAGINIAN IMPERIALISM IN THE FIFTH AND FOURTH CENTURIES

C.R.Whittaker (Churchill College, Cambridge)

INTRODUCTION[1]

Phoenician colonization of the western Mediterranean from the eighth
century B.C. was never a coordinated movement under the direction of
a single mother country or state. If therefore Tyre, who was most
prominent of the Phoenician colonizers, exercised no direct control
over the Phoenician diaspora, neither did Carthage, the new Tyre in
the West, inherit any hegemonial role. Carthage began as merely
one of a number of colonies, founded almost certainly after Gades
and Utica but, like other western Phoenicians, in response to pressures at home and in quest of land on which to settle in the West.
Tradition, which is probably correct, gave to Carthage only one distinctive feature from the rest - a restricted territory. From the
start Carthage was bound by a compact with her Libyan neighbours to
remain confined to a narrow neck of land, the Megara, and checked
from expanding into her natural hinterland of Cape Bon (e.g. Justin
18.5.14; Livy 34.62.12).

For a long period this was the condition which pertained. As
the colony grew in size she was compelled to seek beyond her confines for food and for land for her surplus population. Already in
the mid-seventh century B.C. archaeology has revealed that she established a trading presence on the corn-rich Syrtic coast of
Africa. And according to Diodorus (5.16), she sent out her own
first colony to Ibiza in 654 B.C.

In the next century, even though Carthage broke out of her
narrow territory into the *peraia* of Cape Bon, native Libyans still
resented and resisted Carthaginian expansion inland. Meanwhile
social and political norms had become established over a period of
two hundred years. The result was that Carthage, more than her
sister colonies, looked towards the sea for her livelihood. The
Carthaginian aristocracy discovered profit and prestige from long
distance trade - principally in corn and precious metal - as well
as from the land they held in Carthage itself. Shipping and

overseas interests, long familiar to Phoenician grandees, because
they too had suffered restricted access to their Lebanese homeland,
became an inherited tradition and a way of life among the nobility
of Carthage. In the Mediterranean Carthage was a force to be
reckoned with by the Greeks and Etruscans.

The aim of this paper is to examine how far Carthage's overseas
interests and the actions she took to maintain them can be categor-
ized as 'imperial' from the late sixth century, when she first took
a hand in Sicily, until the fourth century when Agathocles invaded
Africa. By the latter date Carthage had expanded into a territory
beyond Cape Bon and, although there were never the same social barriers as in Greece or Rome against participation in trade, the aristocracy had begun to return to the land. As landowners their
values changed, so that in the third century a new attitude to empire and territorial expansion developed just as Rome appeared in
Southern Italy.

What I shall argue is that up to the third century imperialism
by most criteria cannot, as is generally believed, be proved by the
evidence or argued on a *priori* grounds. Only in one or possibly
two respects can imperial control be detected: one is emigration
under what might be considered privileged conditions to states who
owed obligations to Carthage, although it is difficult to prove
that these colonial settlements maintained formal political bonds
with Carthage; the other is in the control of ports of trade. But
that control must be carefully understood. It was not through
colonization nor through territorial annexation but - as far as one
can judge - through grants of privileged treaty status in foreign
ports, not unlike what later came to be called 'Capitulations'.
The third century, however, was a different story of land empires
and annexation and one that will not be told here. The concern in
this paper is the period when Carthage, like Venice before the
fifteenth century, still remained 'bride of the sea'.

THE TRADITION AND LANGUAGE OF IMPERIALISM
The 'imperialism' of Carthage is more or less taken for granted by
both ancient and modern writers.[2] As early as the sixth century,
according to Justin (19.1.1, 18.7.19), the great dynast Mago, following the campaigns of the mysterious 'Malchus', laid the

foundations of the *imperium Poenorum*; and this process was supposedly
carried on by the Magonid house in the fifth century, particularly in
Sardinia and Sicily. Diodorus Siculus, too, writing of the archaic
period of Sicily, speaks of Carthaginian 'hegemony of the Phoenicians'
(4.23.3, 10.18.6, 12.26.3) and the whole ideological presentation of
the Battle of Himera, as first reported by Herodotus, was based on
the presumption that Carthage in the fifth century intended the enslavement of the Sicilian Greeks - just as Persia had intended to enslave the mainland Greeks (e.g. Hdt. 7.158 and 166).

There is therefore a powerful and early historiographic tradition of Carthaginian imperialism which derives its strength from
the supposed ambition of Punic barbarians to dominate the civilized
Greeks. A Platonic epistle of the mid-fourth century specifically
warned of the dangers of Sicily being transformed into a Phoenician
or Opician 'empire' (*dynasteia kai kratos*, *Ep.* 8.353e). Even if the
hostility and chauvinism stemmed more from Greek aggressiveness and
their fierce inter-city rivalries in Sicily than from any clearly
revealed Carthaginian design,[3] in the end there were no pro-
Carthaginian historians whose work survives, nothing to redress the
balance. And these distortions continued. Under the Romans there
is a spate of horror stories illustrating the supposed Punic lust
for power which justified the initiative of her enemies. One thinks
of Roman claims of attacks by Carthaginians upon their shipping to
justify their annexation of Sardinia, which even Rome's best propagandist, Polybius, found impossible to defend (3.28.1-2). Strabo's
story of how Carthaginians used to drown all strangers attempting to
sail to Sardinia or Gibraltar is another tale from the same book
(17.1.19).

The problem then resolves itself into two strands. First, how
much of the historiographic tradition of a Carthaginian empire, including the semantics of imperialism, must be saved? And secondly,
assuming there is something to preserve, how can ancient views of
Carthaginian imperialism be conceptualized?

It is plainly impossible to reject a Carthaginian 'empire' out
of hand. The weight of Thucydides, Plato, Aristotle, Diodorus and
Polybius is more than we can resist. If Thucydides, through the
mouth of Alcibiades, could speak of a Carthaginian *arche* (6.90.2)
and through Hermocrates could declare Carthage 'more powerful than

any other people of her day' (6.34.2), contemporary readers must
surely have imagined some resemblance, however remote, to the
Athenian empire of the time. The question is, What?

The same question attaches itself to that other favourite word
of ancient authors, *epikrateia*. The term was first employed in relation to Carthaginian power in Sicily by Plato (*Ep*. 7.349c) and
subsequently adopted by Aristotle to describe Carthaginian control
over some miraculous source of oil (*de mirac. ausc*. 841a; cf. 837a).
It then became the word regularly used by secondary sources, such
as Diodorus and Plutarch, as the technical term for Carthaginian
presence in Sicily in the fourth century B.C. Since it is unclear
what these varied authors meant by the term - whether vaguely 'influence' (as in Xen. *Hiero* 6.13) or more generally 'power' (as
Polyb. 2.39.7) - it cannot be simply assumed they intended the
sense of an imperial province of the later, Roman sort, for which
the normal Greek word was *eparchia*.

On the other hand, Diodorus at least would appear to convey
something rather more formal by *epikrateia* than the word *hegemonia*
by which he regularly and deliberately characterized the much less
coherent Carthaginian relations in Sicily in the sixth and fifth
centuries B.C. (e.g. 10.18.6, 12.26.3). Diodorus, or his source,
had presumably come to the conclusion that Carthage by the fourth
century had become in some sense a counterweight and similar to
the expansionist power of Syracuse under Dionysius I and his successors, who are said to have 'used fear of Carthage to be masters
of the other cities without risk' (Diod. 13.112.1-2; cf. 13.91.1).
But Diodorus is far from unambiguous about his terms. In Sardinia
he says that Carthage had from a very early date 'possessed'
(*krateo* is his word) the island (5.15.3-5; cf. Strabo 5.2.7), yet
in a subsequent passage, in which he probably derived his information from the historian Timaeus, he calls this Carthaginian control in the fourth century no more than *hegemonia* (15.24.2).

Finally we come to Polybius, whose major concern was the anat-
omy of Roman imperialism in the second century B.C. Polybius had
no hesitation in employing terms like *eparchia* of Carthaginian
territorial relations in Sicily (e.g. 1.15.10, 1.17.5) and
eparchousi to translate an archaic Latin verb that described Carthage's control of Sicily under the terms of the treaty of 509 B.C.

(3.22.10, 3.24.12). In Roman parlance the terms ought to correspond
to *provincia* and some such word as *imperare*, meaning 'to rule over'
or 'control'. So on the face of it this appears to mean a good deal
more than simply alliances or hegemony. But the oddity is that the
terms are conspicuously not employed in the treaty to define Carthage's relations with either Sardinia or Libya which were, if any,
'ruled over' by Carthage. To say that the whole of Sicily was some
sort of direct Carthaginian province as early as 509 B.C. was in
any case preposterous, as Polybius himself realized when he explained that the clause must refer only 'to as much of Sicily as
falls under Carthaginian control' (3.23.5). But that was not what
the treaty itself said, and we must either accept that Carthage
really ruled over all Sicily or the terms do not mean rule at all.
Since the treaty which Polybius saw was in archaic Latin, we can
only speculate about what Latin words Polybius saw which led him to
his Greek translation. But this and the treaty of 348 B.C., which
Polybius also recorded, were drawn up long before Rome herself did
control *provinciae* in a territorial sense. Could it be therefore
that the term *provincia* did actually appear in the treaty but only
in the original latin sense of 'sphere of influence',[4] which Polybius wrongly assumed to mean what it did in his own day? Perhaps
all the treaties were really saying was that Rome would recognize
certain regions over which Carthage had influence.

If the language of the ancient writers is ambiguous or unclear, we
must now ask how far the evidence of historical events will support
the reality of a Carthaginian empire - the reality, that is, in
terms of domination, control or manipulation of one previously
autonomous agency by another by whatever mechanism, whether political, moral or economic. Since this control need not be to the disadvantage of the weaker party, all question of the willingness of
the subject and the popularity of the imperial power, even if it
could be measured, is an irrelevancy. For this judgement I shall
examine Carthaginian power under the following headings, any one
of which, if present, must be regarded as a mark of imperialism:
direct territorial conquest and annexation, a system of provincial
administration, the levying of tribute, a method of exploiting
land, unequal alliances and, lastly, trade monopolies and controls.

CONQUEST AND ANNEXATION

Most explicit of all the ancient evidence is the contrast and implied
parallel between Carthage and the imperial ambitions of the Sicilian
tyrants culminating in the open rivalry between Dionysius I of Syracuse and Carthaginian interests in the fourth century B.C. There is
no doubting Carthaginian intervention in Sicily over a long period
from at least the later sixth century B.C. and it was in this context
that Thucydides described Carthage as a force to be reckoned with.
Whether or not Malchus in the sixth century was the name of a historical person, or a title, or even a corruption of the name Mago
(since his name appears in one manuscript as 'Mazeus'), and whatever
his intentions in Sicily,[5] in the end it is impossible to show that
Carthage was either the only resistance or even the main Phoenician
resistance to the early encroachment and attacks mounted by Greek
cities and adventurers. Presumably all Phoenician colonies in
Sicily had an interest in the supply of silver and in the ports of
trade in Sicily; certainly all had armies of their own, even if
Carthage was among the more powerful. Their call to Carthage for
aid probably derived from a straightforward need for manpower, since
the Phoenician colonies in Sicily were not only smaller than their
Greek counterparts at the time of their foundation but did not increase significantly in size from the continuous flow of immigrants
that was characteristic of cities like Syracuse. But why should the
effort to resist be thought primarily Carthaginian? In both the
Pentathlus episode at the beginning of the sixth century and in the
Dorieus episode at the end the evidence is less than unanimous as
to whether Carthage even participated, and there is perhaps a natural
tendency among Greek authors to think of all Phoenicians as Carthaginians.[6]

There were of course Carthaginians resident in Sicily by the
beginning of the fifth century B.C. and their close ties with some
of the Phoenician and Greek colonies are discussed later. But this
does not make an empire. It is not too difficult to see how the
rise of the turbulent Deinomenids in the early fifth century and the
arrival of Greek refugees in eastern Sicily might upset some of the
trade agreements and in particular the safety and accessibility of
ports such as Syracuse or those on the Straits of Messina (e.g. Hdt.
6.17; see below, p.84). So it is not surprising that *emporia*

figure as one important issue in this period (Hdt. 7.158). The
Magonids, whose political power in Carthage was dominant, were also
enmeshed into Sicilian and Syracusan politics (Hdt. 7.166-7) and were
naturally interested parties in these developments.

But having said all that, we must recognize once again that
Carthaginian merchants were not likely to have been the only or even
necessarily the main defenders of port of trade rights and reciprocity
agreements in Sicily. At Himera in 480 B.C. Herodotus pointedly
speaks of other allied forces, with Phoenicians as well as Libyans
ranged against Syracuse, even though their leader was Hamilcar, the
Magonid king (7.165). Carthage, that is, played a role of one among
many of the Phoenician colonists and seems to have been present at
Himera largely through the mediation of the Greek tyrants Terillus of
Himera and Anaxilas of Rhegium, who must surely have supplied some of
the funds. It is typical of the historiographic tradition that the
huge quantity of silver and gold taken after Himera should be said to
have been taken from the defeated Carthaginians in spite of the known
wealth and probable access to silver of Selinus, Motya and others of
the allies.[7]

After this it is the supposed cataclysmic size of the disaster
of Himera which has frequently been adduced as the event which reduced Carthage to economic impotence and isolation for the rest of
the fifth century, thereby checking the imperial designs of the
Magonids. But, as it turns out, the propositions upon which the hypothesis was based have been eroded. Politically the Magonids were
not immediately discredited and economically it is unbelievable that
Carthage suffered economic isolation while other Phoenician cities
such as Motya or even Kerkouane on Cape Bon flourished.[8] Yet it is
worth reminding ourselves that the existence of the theory of re-
cession was in order to explain the objective fact of the lack of
aggressive action or opportunism by Carthage in Sicily during the
rest of the fifth century - including her failure to take advantage
of the Athenian invasion of Sicily in 415 B.C. If now by contrast
we regard Magonid policy in Sicily as one not of territorial imperialism but of alliance and the preservation of independence for those
cities who offered them rights of access and protection for their
trade, then Himera, for all its losses, was not an unmitigated disaster. For it was in fact a warning to Acragas and Syracuse and it

preserved Carthaginian trade and alliances in Sicily. In spite of
the barrage of Greek propaganda, it now becomes intelligible why
Hamilcar, the dead general, was honoured in every Phoenician city
(Hdt. 7.167); the proof of his success was nearly seventy years of
uninterrupted freedom, peace and prosperity in Sicily. The fame of
Carthage's supply of gold and silver by 415 B.C. is matched by the
wealth of Motya in 397 (Thuc. 6.34.2; Diod. 14.53.3). But neither
Carthage nor the Phoenician cities needed territorial empires to
achieve this. What they needed was peace.

The real puzzle is why Carthage should have abandoned this
beneficial quiescence in Sicily at the end of the fifth century for
a more active policy which served her rational interests less well.
The theory of Magonid revenge for Himera (Diod. 13.43.6) loses its
force if what was said earlier was correct. The theory in any case
finds little support in the narrative of 410-409 B.C. Renewed
Carthaginian intervention, for instance, came at the request of
Segesta and it was an Elymian general who commanded the first battle
(Diod. 13.43.4, 13.44.4). Every effort was made to avoid rousing
Syracuse (Diod. 13.43.6, 13.54.5) and in 406 Carthage made an offer
of an alliance and neutrality to Acragas in spite of earlier Greek
hostility (Diod. 13.85.2). On the Greek side, the attacks upon
Panormus and Motya in 408 by Hermocrates were not supported by Syra-
cuse in spite of Hermocrates' efforts to legitimize his position.
Thus far there was little to show a radical departure from earlier
Carthaginian policy and nothing to explain the massive display of
force in 406 - certainly nothing to justify Diodorus' words that
Carthaginians were 'eager to be overlords of the island' (13.80.1).
No doubt there was a degree of war hysteria in Carthage and an impetus produced by the events themselves into which Carthage was
sucked, where it is easy to understand Magonid interests in revenge,
among other things, pressing for intervention. And no doubt there
was the inducement of the massive booty which Carthage did in fact
gain by the virtual annihilation of Himera, Acragas and other Greek
settlements. But it is difficult to avoid the conclusion that the
real reason behind Carthage's greater involvement in Sicily in this
century was more directly a response to the truly dominating position of Syracuse, which began with Hermocrates and Dionysius I,
than the result of some radical reappraisal of Carthaginian interests.

It may be therefore that Diodorus and his sources were right
to select a different word, *epikrateia*, to describe this new Carthaginian presence in Sicily. It was a more formal acknowledgement of Carthage's role as protector of Phoenician interests. Several agreements and treaties, beginning with that of 405 B.C., recognized a territorial region, eventually marked off by the River
Halycus, of Carthaginian paramountcy (Diod. 13.144, 14.96.4, etc.),
and this corresponds to the Carthaginian 'sphere' of Sicily within
which Romans were offered the same facilities as Carthaginians by
the treaty of 348 B.C. (Polyb. 3.24.12). This is important because
it shows that Carthage could now in some respects speak for the
communities of western Sicily. But does it go further than the
system of alliances in the fifth century? Although Diodorus talks
of cities 'drawn up under Carthage' (15.15.1), the actual relationship was in fact still determined by bilateral agreements. Hali-
cyae, Solus, Segesta, Panormus, Entella and others, including native Sicani, were all called 'allied cities' (*symmachousai poleis*)
in 397 (14.48.4) and this term continued to be applied to the cities in the *epikrateia* (e.g. 13.62.5, 14.55.7, 14.85.4). The description in itself need not, of course, mean any more real independence for Phoenician and Elymian cities than Athenian 'allies'
possessed in the Delian League. To some extent that impression is
borne out when we read that Segesta 'put herself into the hands'
of Carthage in 410 in return for her aid (Diod. 13.43.3-4). But
the parallel with Athens ceases when we read that Carthage in
345/4 had to 'court' her allied cities in Sicily for their support
(Diod. 16.67.1).[9]

It is furthermore quite wrong to regard the military resistance
to Syracuse as conducted solely by Carthaginian armies. No doubt
again Carthage's repeated expeditions created a confusion between
'Phoenician' and 'Carthaginian' which could be exploited. In 396
B.C., for instance, the fleet is described by Diodorus in alternative sentences as Carthaginian or Phoenician (16.60). But in fact
the massive fleet on that occasion could not conceivably have been
all Carthaginian, if the figures provided by Ephorus and Timaeus
are anywhere near correct (Diod. 14.54.5 and 59.7 - one thousand
ships, or perhaps half that number). In 409 B.C. Hermocrates' attack on the western Phoenician cities encountered local armies who

were manifestly not Carthaginian (Diod. 13.63.4), and it was presumably these forces which turned up alongside the Carthaginians at
Cremisus in 338 (Diod. 16.79.6-80.1). As before, money would certainly have been provided for military pay by all the Phoenician
cities, who struck silver coin.

The strangest of all features of Carthaginian behaviour in
Sicily in the fourth century is explained by this ambivalent relationship. In spite of the undoubtedly increased military activity
of expedition and counter expedition from Carthage and Syracuse,
Carthaginian aggression time and again faltered just at the critical
moment of success. In 405 B.C. Dionysius I was even politically em-
barrassed by Hamilcar's failure to pursue him and his offer of alliance at the very gates of Syracuse (Diod. 13.112.2 and 114.1-3).
In 397 the Carthaginian force was totally unprepared to assist Motya
and ended by simply running away (Diod. 14.48.1 and 50.4). Diodorus
himself is astonished at Himilco's withdrawal from Syracuse in 396
and his explanation is a devastating plague (14.70.4). In 383 (or
perhaps 374), after defeating Dionysius I at Cronion, Carthage
tamely agreed to more or less the *status quo ante* (Diod. 15.17.5).
In 344, after failing to dissuade Timoleon's force from entering
Sicily, the Carthaginians 'unaccountably' withdrew from Syracuse
(Diod. 16.69.5). To those Greeks who proclaimed the chronic, imperial machinations of Carthage the explanation had to lie in barbarian cowardice (e.g. Diod. 16.79.2) or plagues and Pyrrhic victories. The chain of mishaps is decidedly suspicious.

Sardinia too was a region colonized by early Phoenicians where
also Carthage intervened. There is no difficulty in finding an historical context for Carthage's proprietary interest. The Phoceans,
with more than a penchant for piracy, colonized Alalia and possibly
Olbia too in about 565 B.C., thereby provoking the retaliation of
Carthage and Etruscan Caere about 535 (Hdt. 1.166-7). It makes
sense to connect this event with the presence of 'Malchus' whom
tradition brings to Sardinia after his Sicilian escapades (Justin
18.7).[10] And after him there was Magonid activity on the island
in the early fifth century (Justin 19.1.6).

Archaeologists have been quick to detect confirmations of
these episodes from the signs of destruction at inland Phoenician
forts and their subsequent restoration.[11] But the precise dates

of the various phases offer by no means conclusive support, since the archaic period is deemed to end in the sixth century B.C. but the so-called 'Punic' phase does not start till the fourth century.[12] That is one difficulty. The other is whether this Punic evidence really does amount to what Moscati says was 'without doubt' a permanent Carthaginian occupation from the fifth century onwards.[13] All it really proves is that there was a close similarity between Carthaginian culture and that of many Phoenicians in Sardinia. But that would not be surprising if close trade and exchanges, including colonization, existed and need not imply a loss of autonomy by the Phoenician cities. As we have already seen, Diodorus, where he deals with better documented periods than the archaic, uses a term, *hegemonia*, which in the Sicilian context seems to mean no more than assistance and alliances with other Phoenicians. The considerable and early independent development of archaic Phoenician foundations like S. Antiocco, Tharros and Cagliari, whose exploitation of the agriculture and minerals of the hinterland have been demonstrated by the excavations at Monte Sirai, make one wonder about the extent to which Carthage could have actually controlled them or closed their ports.[14]

Then again in the early fourth century Dionysius I probably provoked the Carthaginians into sending some sort of help to protect Sardinian Phoenicians by his activity in the Tuscan Sea, an attack on Pyrgi in Etruria in 384 B.C. and an attempt to set up a base in Corsica (Strabo 5.2.8). The details are obscure but it may have been these events which were connected with a rebellion of Sardinian natives that forced Carthage to 'win back' the island (Diod. 15.24.2).[15] The circumstances explain the proprietary interest of Carthage, particularly if she relied on Sardinian corn. But it should perhaps be seen on a political level too, akin to the Carthaginian action to restore Hipponium on the Bruttian coast after it had been wiped out by Dionysius (Diod. 15.24.1); that is, measures specifically provoked by Dionysius and an attempt to neutralize his aggressiveness. It need not however (as we can be sure of in the case of Hipponium) mean Carthaginian occupation.[16]

In Spain the Carthaginian flag was never as prominent as in Sardinia. Once one accepts that Gades and other Phoenician colonies from the start had an independent life of their own and were not

simply part of a great web of Tyrian commerce that fell into
Carthage's lap when Tyre declined, the scrappy literary and archaeological evidence for the classical period does not amount to very
much.[17] There were pressures on Gades and the far-western Phoenicians from the sixth century onwards, which were to some extent
linked with the maritime activities of the Phoceans. Obscure records have survived of Phocean or Massiliote clashes with both
Gaditain and Carthaginian ships (Justin 43.5.2; Paus. 10.8.6, 10.
18.7; Thuc. 1.13.6; cf. Strabo 4.1.5), as well as the mysterious
disappearance of Greek Meinake (Strabo 3.4.2) and an otherwise unknown battle of Artemisium.[18]

But Carthaginian activity and interest in the West at the same
time as her other ventures in Sardinia and Sicily are not at issue.
The point is, does this amount to an imperial take-over of the
Phoenician colonies? The closest we come to that notion is in an
undatable passage from Justin, which reads that Gades, being under
pressure from her neighbours, was assisted by her kinsmen, the
Carthaginians, who then added a part of this 'province' to their
'empire' - *partem provinciae imperio suo adiecerunt* (44.5.3; cf.
Macrob. *Sat.* 1.20.12).[19] Certainly there is reason to suppose that
the sixth century was not an easy period for Phoenicians in Spain.
The last dated evidence from the sites of Toscanos and Trayamar on
the Malaga coast, for instance, fall in this century and thereafter they were abandoned. There are also distinct breaks on the
west African coast between the archaic Phoenician pottery, generally
thought to emanate from Gades, and the later 'Punic' pottery, which
may not date before the later fifth century. All that suggests the
ending of Gades as an independent trading city.[20]

On the other hand, it is extraordinarily difficult to authen-
ticate actual Carthaginian occupation. The long-distance ships in
the mid-fourth century which made the west African run were based
on Gades not Carthage, according to Ps. Scylax (*GGM* I. p.94 (112)),
and they are named as Phoenician not Carthaginian. That may mean
nothing. But Gades did preserve its quasi-independent status
right down to the last days of the Barca Spanish empire (*socius et
amicus* - Livy 28.37.1). If the evidence from west Africa is anything to go by, the conclusion of the most recent and thorough
study of the region is that 'Morocco knew the Carthaginians but it

never belonged to them'.[21] Polybius' vague statement about the submission of much of Spain to Carthage by 265 B.C. (1.10.5) is completely contradicted by the fairly precise information given by
Diodorus concerning the new conquests of Hamilcar Barca 'as far as
the pillars of Hercules, Gadeira (Gades) and the ocean' just before
the Second Punic War (25.10.1-4). That means either Spain was lost
and won back in thirty years without a single comment from any source
or that the nature of the relations with Spain and the western territories before the Barcas was of a much looser kind than is commonly
admitted. Let it be conceded however that the information is so
meagre that it could be interpreted in many different ways. But in
general the evidence of actual conquest and annexation throughout
the western Phoenician orbit is at best ambiguous and in many regions
unlikely in the earlier classical period, at least, even if there was
perhaps some change in the fourth century. That will be examined
later.

PROVINCIAL ADMINISTRATION
In spite of the historiographic tradition which saw in Carthage a
Persia of the West, the sources have produced no satrapy system, no
governors of satellite territories like those of the Persian empire
- or none, at least, before the third century B.C., which will be
discussed later, when for very specific reasons a change took place
in Carthage's political economy. Throughout the archaic and classical periods to the fourth century B.C. there is not a single reference to any known Carthaginian structure of imperial administration.
About the closest we can get to an imperial bureaucracy in the literary sources are the various kings and generals fighting short-term
wars abroad - like Mago, who was 'spending time' in Sicily in 393
B.C. (Diod. 14.90.2). It is significant that in the entire chapter
assigned by Gsell to 'Administration de l'Empire de Carthage' he
could find only one reference which looks anything like an imperial
official before the third century B.C. This is an inscription from
Tharros in Sardinia (*CIS* I 154) which records a scribe, whom Gsell
believed to be similar to the *grammateis* or market officials who
appear in the first Carthaginian treaty with Rome (Polyb. 3.22.8).
Similar they may have been but there is absolutely nothing to prove
this man was either Carthaginian or in Carthaginian employ and the

chances against him being so seem quite high.[22] Even in the third
century, outside Africa and the Barca empire in Spain, the only
Carthaginian official that can be found is a military officer, a
boetharch, in Sardinia; but that was after the First Punic War
(Polyb. 1.79.2).

TRIBUTE

The nearest we get to imperial tribute and the first of such references, as far as I know, is after the sack and total destruction of
Selinus in 409 B.C. (Diod. 13.59.3). Those Selinuntians who had
not taken part in the siege were permitted to work the land on payment of *phoros* to Carthage. The second reference is in the treaty
between Carthage and Syracuse in 405 B.C. which stipulated that Gela
and Camarina must pay for their defeat a *phoros* which was in explicit
contrast to the status of the Phoenician colonies, the Elymians and
the Sicani (Diod. 13.114.1). The position of Selinus, Acragas and
Himera, who also figure in the terms, is ambiguous as the wording
stands and they might also be thought to be listed as tribute payers,
although it seems easier to regard them as being recognized in this
agreement as Carthaginian allies, which was reaffirmed later. The
third and final reference comes in an imaginary speech by a Syracusan
called Theodorus, who claims in 396 B.C. that, if victorious over
Dionysius I, Carthage would impose upon them a 'fixed tribute' (*phoros
horismenos*) (Diod. 14.65.2). In all the references the *phoros* seems
to apply only to defeated enemies, not to allies and, unless it can
be shown to be a permanent imposition, looks more like a war indemnity than regular tribute. That is very much the implication of
Theodorus' speech. Perhaps the tribute was permanent for Selinus,
Acragas and Himera, but, if so, this is not stated when they were
redefined by treaty in 314 B.C. as somehow 'drawn up under Carthage'
(Diod. 19.71.7). The subordination of Camarina and Gela cannot be
documented beyond 397 and had ended by 383 B.C. (Diod. 14.47.5,
15.17.5). Further speculation about the existence of a full scale,
imperial tribute, a pre-Roman tithe system and so on, is simply unsupported by the evidence.[23]

    As far as Sardinia and Spain are concerned, the evidence of
tribute is even less. It may be that Sardinian corn came to Carthage under some sort of tributary system. But we only hear about

this source of supply when Carthage was faced with revolts by the Libyans of the interior.[24] So the record is irregular and, for all we know, the corn could have been paid for. In Spain, however much interest the Phoenicians and Carthaginians may have taken in mining the silver, we know nothing of any tribute paid in this medium to Carthage.

Tribute requires some sort of organization for collection and coercion; it may also produce a tendency towards a single coinage system, as in the Athenian empire. Yet, as we have already seen, there is no hint of an imperial civil service, inspectors and the like. Garrisons however are often thought to have existed. The standard example quoted is that of Heraclea Minoa, on the borders of the territory defined as the Carthaginian *epikrateia* in the fourth century. It was a city which Diodorus says 'was subject to' (*hypekouen*) Carthage in 357/6 (14.9.4). That looks clear enough. But in spite of mention of a 'prefect' or magistrate (*epistates* or *archon*) in the sources, there is nothing about a garrison of troops; and in the one case where we know of the officer he was not a Carthaginian but a Greek (Diod. 16.9.4; Plut. *Dion* 25). Certainly Heraclea was, like some other towns, used in the fourth and third centuries as a centre for mustering Carthaginian armies (as when Pyrrhus attacked, for instance, Diod. 22.10.2).[25]

Can we conclude from this a permanent network of imperial garrisons? In 409 B.C. Carthage retired from Sicily leaving behind some troops, but specifically for the needs of her 'allies', not to control her subjects (Diod. 13.62.6). In 404 B.C. too Campanian troops (in origin, presumably, mercenaries) were left at some unnamed place 'as a guard' (Diod. 14.8.5). But they promptly joined Dionysius I and, to judge by other Campanians settled at Entella, they were neither satellites nor a garrison but allies (Diod. 14.61.5, 14.67.3). A Carthaginian garrison in 278/6 at Enna - if the textual emendation is correct - was there explicitly at the wish of the inhabitants to protect themselves against the tyrant Phintias and they remained there until such time as the people voluntarily turned to Pyrrhus (Diod. 22.10.1). Thus the evidence of coercive control comes down to a garrison town without troops and troops who are not in garrison towns. Vague allusions to troops in Sicily cannot, in view of the contingents supplied by

the Phoenician colonies, simply be assumed to mean garrisons of Carthaginian contingents (e.g. Diod. 15.17.2 - Lilybaeum in 368; 19.106.5
- in 311; both of which are quoted by Gsell[26]).

There did develop in the fourth century, or more precisely after
410 B.C., several coinage series in Sicily with the Phoenician legend
s.y.s. whose provenance from cities such as Motya, Solus, Panormus
and even Segesta suggests a cultural and perhaps some political unity.
The question is whether this political and geographical solidarity
among Phoenician cities adds up to an imperial province controlled by
Carthage.[27] The so-called 'Carthage' types and the *s.y.s.* types were
presumably struck for the military campaigns of this decade when
there was indeed a united front in western Sicily against Dionysius.
That does not prove a Carthaginian dictat existed. Indeed there is
good reason to believe that the *s.y.s.* coins belonged only to Panormus, while die links are common among Greek cities with no more than
friendly relations. The several sources of the coins and the link-
ing of the dies between various Phoenician cities might indicate
exactly the opposite - that Carthage was only one among many allies.
The coins were certainly never an instrument and probably not even
a symptom of imperialism.

Under this heading therefore there are some signs of Carthage's
growing concern in Sicily and perhaps even a willingness to contem-
plate the formal subjection of perennially troublesome enemies within
what they regarded as their sphere of influence. But it is hazardous to go beyond that to postulate a regular system of garrisons,
tribute and officials, who exacted money, men and obedience from
friends and enemies alike.

LAND EXPLOITATION

It follows that, if there was no actual territorial conquest, land
could be acquired by Carthaginians only by private purchase under
some arrangement like *enktesis* or through colonization of some sort.
But unless the colony can be shown to have preserved real ties with
Carthage which the mother city could exploit to her own advantage
then the foundation of colonies in itself is no more imperialistic
than the movements from Greece had been in the archaic period.

Evidence of Carthaginian colonization is not hard to come by,
directed to all the territories where Carthage was active. In

Sicily, for instance, Diodorus describes Motya in the early fourth
century as an *apoikos* of Carthage, and, although he is strictly
wrong, he may be referring to reinforcements of colonists sent from
Carthage (Diod. 47.4; Paus. 5.25.5).[28] After the destruction of
Himera colonists were sent from Carthage to found the new city of
Thermae in 407 B.C. (Diod. 13.79.8), although many Greeks from old
Himera and elsewhere, including Agathocles' father, were included
in the venture (Cic. II *Verr.* 2.35.86; Diod. 19.1.2). In Sardinia
too we have a number of references to Carthaginian colonists, although some are quite certainly incorrect and confuse early western
Phoenicians with Carthaginians (e.g. Paus. 10.17.9, attributing the
foundation of Caralis and Sulcis to Carthage). We need not take
Cicero at his word that all Sardi were in origin disgraced Punico-
Libyan half-breeds (*pro Scauro* 42) to believe there is something
behind the notion that here too some Carthaginians came to settle
and reinforce the old Phoenician foundations.[29] In Spain it is
significant that, apart from the references to innumerable Carthaginian *emporia*,[30] there is only one case of a colony - *apoikia* -
cited in any author before the Roman period, when the distinction
between Phoenician and Carthaginian seems to have been lost. The
single colony is one mentioned by the fourth-century historian
Ephorus of 'Libyphoenicians from Carthage, forming a colony' (Ps.
Scymnus, *GGM* I, p.203; cf. Avienus, *Or.marit.* 421).

The term 'Libyphoenician' does however go right to the heart
of the problem. It does not matter here what the ethnic mixture
of these people was, since we are only concerned with their relations to Carthage. And for that we have Diodorus' statement that
'they share rights of intermarriage (*epigamia*) with Carthaginians'
(20.55.4). If that were true of Libyphoenicians and if Libyphoenicians could be shown to have been scattered all over the Mediterranean littoral, it would go a long way to establishing the case for
colonies formally tied to Carthage - much as the Latins were tied
to Rome, said Mommsen[31] - and would support Weber's contention
that all western Phoenician colonies assisted Carthage in 'the
forceful monopolization of trade'.[32] There is a fair number of
references to Libyphoenicians or the analogous Blastophoenices
(Spain) and Sardolibes (Sardinia), of which the earliest is probably that describing the foundations on the west African coast in

the periplous of Hanno (*GGM* I, p.1). But there are two points to
observe: one, that by far the majority of references are late and
seem to have had a geographic limitation to those who lived east of
Cape Bougaroun in Algeria; the other is that Diodorus expressly
limits his remarks about *epigamia* to 'the four categories who have
divided Libya' - and by 'Libya' he almost certainly meant the eastern Maghreb. So the remarkable 'interwoven kinship' that he mentioned could have been something which grew up in the third century
and the product of the African empire of Carthage, about which there
is more to say later. But there is slender support in these Libyphoenician examples for a tight network of satellite 'Latin'-type
cities scattered over the western Mediterranean.

If we now come back to the examples of *apoikiai*, is there any
reason why we should believe they had more than sentimental links
with Carthage? These might in some cases lead to bilateral alliances and even dependency, but not *qua* colony and not more than,
say, in the case of the old Phoenician colonies or Elymian Segesta.

There are two curious passages in Aristotle's *Politics* which
deal with Carthaginian colonization (1273b19, 1320b5). The first
concerns the use of colonization as a social manipulator to prevent
discontent against the oligarchy and the second deals with the provision of working capital to colonists 'whom they constantly send
out to the surrounding territory'. This last phrase strongly suggests that Aristotle had in mind the African hinterland, although
there is nothing to preclude overseas territories. It requires
some stretch of the imagination, however, to perceive in this passage a system of rotating native commissioners, as Gsell believed
(following Mommsen).[33] If it does refer to the overseas colonies
noted earlier and if it means the Phoenician cities of Sicily,
Sardinia and Spain were prepared 'constantly' to accept Carthaginian peasants and poor in return for the aid Carthage offered
them against their neighbours, then here indeed is an instrument
of imperialism which Carthage exploited to the advantage of her
own political economy.

ALLIANCES

What has just been said raises the question of the *quid pro quo* of
Carthaginian alliances. There is no denying the presence of

Carthaginian forces nor their concern to keep the ports open - nor
even their leadership from time to time in Sicily, Sardinia and
Spain. The ancient evidence is unassailable on this point. To
Greeks who viewed all Phoenicians in one light the question of
whether Carthage herself was always involved perhaps seemed academic. But in the early stages and before the fourth century, at
any rate, there is not enough to talk of an empire nor even, as
Merante does, of 'domination'.[34] Diodorus deliberately spoke of
hegemonia up to that date and there is nothing which happened which
could not be explained in terms of a loose system of alliances and
reciprocal treaties.

One aspect of the early alliances is a feature familiar enough
in the study of Greek history, the exchanges of hospitality (*xenia*)
and formal ties of friendship and marriage contracted between aristocratic families of different great houses across state barriers.[35]
The Carthaginian dynast Mago, who was active in Sicily around the
turn of the sixth century B.C., had married a Syracusan wife and
his sons were heavily involved with other powerful families in
Himera and Rhegium, who were themselves similarly bound by marriage
ties (Hdt. 7.165). These were the men who emerged as tyrants in
their cities and who stimulated Carthaginian intervention at Himera
in 480 B.C.

These quasi-kinship relations continued throughout Carthage's
involvement in Sicily. They are the sort of thing which is portrayed in the exchanges of *tesserae* recorded in Plautus' *Poenulus*
(e.g. 955-60) and they lasted long after the growth of central
state agreements. They characterize and underline the fact that
Carthaginian foreign policy was conducted not so much in the abstract political atmosphere of state government but through the
very personal interests and ambitions of its leading figures.
There were numbers of wealthy Carthaginian merchants resident in
the various ports of trade in Sicily (and we must presume elsewhere) and it is not surprising to find them on familiar terms
with the tyrants' courts. In a dialogue of Heraclides of Pontus,
for instance, there is a reference to 'a certain Magos' who
claimed to have circumnavigated Libya and who is portrayed in
discussion with Gelo, tyrant of Syracuse (Strabo 2.3.4). It
would be pleasant if this Mago (as I take his name to be) were

a member of the great house, but he represents a typical enough
example.[36] Carthaginian interests in alliances for security and
the benefits that accrued do not have to be explained in imperialist terms of crude annexation and booty. For the elite were often
personally and directly involved in the success of the trade (see
below p.87). As we saw earlier, the rational interest of these
men was generally conditions of peace.

The Carthaginian dilemma was on the one hand to maintain the
peace that produced economically profitable relations with many
towns such as Acragas and Syracuse, which housed resident Carthaginian and Phoenician merchants (Diod. 13.81.5, 13.84.3, 14.46.1-2),
and on the other to keep alive the alliances and treaty ports in
Sicily upon which her merchants ultimately depended. A series of
ambitious Greek adventurers, Hermocrates, Dionysius, Timoleon,
Agathocles, Pyrrhus and finally Hiero, continually threatened to
destroy the delicate balance of Carthaginian foreign policy and to
lay bare its contradictions. In particular the total destruction
of Motya and the expulsion of all Phoenician merchants from Syracuse and her allied cities in 389 B.C. by Dionysius I (Diod. 14.53
and 46.1-2) - the latter an action which, as far as I can tell, is
unique in Sicilian history - hammered home the lesson that, if
Carthage wished to maintain her interests in Sicily, a more active
foreign policy of intrigue and interventionism was necessary in the
fourth century.

It is this dilemma which accounts for the increase in political
rivalries in home politics at Carthage during this century: the fall
of the Magonid general, Himilco and his suicide in 396 (Diod. 14.76.
3-4); the rise of Hanno the Great and the disappearance of the last
known Magonid in the early 370s, at about the same time as a terrible Libyan invasion and internecine fighting in the city (Diod.
15.24.2-3); the treachery of Hanno's rival Suniatus (Eshmunyaton?)
in warning Dionysius I of an impending expedition (Justin 20.5.4;
cf. Diod. 15.73 - 368 B.C.). All these were manifestations of a
struggle for a fundamentally unattainable goal. Even the fall of
Hanno the Great at some unspecified date after an attempted *coup
d'état* (Justin 21.4; cf. Arist. *Pol.* 1272b and 1307a) is probably
linked to Sicily, since we hear of a certain Hanno in 345 who was
replaced for his failure as a general (Diod. 16.67.2; Plut. *Timol.*

19). But in 338, after the fearful defeat at the Cremisus, it was
Hanno's son, Gisco, who was recalled from exile (Diod. 16.81.3,
Plut. *Timol*. 30.3).

This does not mean there were clear-cut imperialist and non-
imperialist parties in these rivalries, nor even a clash between
African and Sicilian interests, although both these causes have
sometimes been suggested.[37] The political struggles now, as always,
were as much the product of personal rivalries and family intrigues
as of fundamentally opposed policies. Gisco's return to favour
after Cremisus was due to both the failure of his predecessors and
the personal advocacy of his Sicilian friends, Mamercus of Catania
and Hiketas of Leontini (Plut. *Timol*. 30.2); the latter was certainly a friend of Hanno, though Hanno was also known for his
African achievements (Diod. 16.67.1-2). In all the intrigues for
power there is never reported a hint of either withdrawal from
Sicily or of total conquest (in spite of vague Greek propaganda);
only of 'keeping a hand in Sicilian affairs' (Diod. 14.95.1). The
problem of how to balance the twin themes of this policy was irre-
ducible and led to constant fluctuation in one or other direction.

The truth is that the territorial ambitions of Carthage in
the fourth century seem to be not much greater than before in
Sicily. But there was a greater sense of insecurity in face of
the now dominant power of Syracuse. The development of central,
state institutions in both Syracuse and Carthage led to a shift in
balance in interstate relations from the personal bonds of friendship between the great houses to the more impersonal, collective
interests of the ruling elite, although never the elimination of
the former. Both tendencies created a greater need for formal
definitions of alliances and intercity relations, of spheres of
influence and boundaries. That would explain why men looked at
Carthage's 'province' in a different way, and why Carthage's allies became more dependent upon her aid and leadership, but it
did not in itself change the structure of the Carthaginian alliances into a centrally organized empire of provinces and officials. To some extent this is quibbling with words, since the
greater dependence of the allies made it less and less likely or
possible that they should withdraw. And that was a form of imperialism.

TRADE MONOPOLIES AND CONTROLS

Recent studies of the western Phoenicians in the archaic period,
based upon the distribution of trade goods, now stress the poly-
centric character of archaic trading in the Mediterranean and the
absence of any centralized and exclusive trade empire directed by
Tyre or Carthage. [38] We are nevertheless confronted by the awkward
fact that there are innumerable references in the sources to Carthaginian *emporia* or trading ports, particularly in Libya and Spain,
of which the most prolific are perhaps those of the fourth-century
Greek geographer whose *periplous* was attributed to Scylax. [39] We
have the literary and archaeological evidence of trade down the
kolpos emporikos (Strabo 17.3.2) as far as Mogador, if not further,
which is reinforced by the celebrated voyages of Hanno and Himilco
making their way past the Straits of Gibraltar. [40] And above all we
have the treaties between Carthage and Rome: according to the first
treaty of 509 B.C. the Carthaginians seem to be claiming control of
ports of trade in both eastern Libya and Sardinia, which in the
second treaty of 348 becomes a prohibition on all trading and settlement in those regions (Polyb. 3.22.9, 3.24.11). These provisions
Polybius interpreted to mean that Carthage in some way regarded
Sardinia and eastern Libya as their own or 'private'. The second
treaty added a provision about Spain by defining a point, Mastia
Tarseion, beyond which trade should not be conducted by Rome (3.24.4).

It has become accepted almost without question from all this
that during the course of the fifth and fourth centuries Carthage
increasingly exercised a trade blockade in the western Mediterranean.
Stories of drowning of strangers or voluntary scuttling of ships to
prevent the discovery of trade routes add to the impression (Strabo
3.5.11, 17.1.19). And yet questions arise. At the end of the fifth
century, for instance, a Spartan fleet of merchantmen *en route* from
Cyrene to Tunisia encountered no Carthaginian blockade and even put
in at the Carthaginian *emporion* at Neapolis on the southern side of
Cape Bon in supposedly forbidden territory (Thuc. 7.50). The
condottiero, Ophelas, who marched from Cyrene to Carthage in the
late fourth century, is probably the man who wrote a *periplous* of
Libya (Strabo 17.3.1), which could have had more than academic
interest for him. Herodotus seems to have received information
about natives in the Libyan *emporia* district and about the gold

trade of the far west (4.191 and 196). If all this information came
from Carthaginian sources, which is by no means certain, it at least
shows that it was not censored. So much so, that Gsell, unlike some
of his successors, was forced to argue that Polybius' wording about
the embargo on Libya in the 509 treaty must have meant Libya *west* of
Carthage, even though Carthaginian special interest in the Algerian
coast is inexplicable and unsupported in this or later centuries.[41]

In Spain, in spite of the treaty, there was no uniform trade
embargo on foreigners either. Apart from Euthymenes of Massilia who
sailed down the Atlantic coast of Africa at some unspecified date
(*FHG* IV 408), the Massiliote explorer Pytheas claimed to have travelled to Britain some time in the late fourth or third century and
he was not molested at Gades (Strabo 2.4.1-2). The Alexandrian ad-
miral Timosthenes in the 280s had good information about the western Mediterranean, including the site of Gibraltar/Algeciras, for
which significantly he gave a Greek name (Strabo 3.4.7).[42] And in
Sardinia, where the approaches were supposedly completely banned,
presumably for fear of native revolts, Eratosthenes actually says
it was only 'strangers' (*xenoi*) who were so treated (Strabo 11.1.19)
and he made his comment in the context of the ports of trade in
Egypt, where we know access was certainly carefully controlled but
never totally excluded (Hdt. 2.179). The presence of Massiliotes
in Tharros at a date which could fall within the period under discussion (*IG* XIV 609-10) rather suggests that the same was true in
Sardinia.

There is no need here to underline Carthage's continuous and
predominant role in long-distance trade. In this respect Carthage,
because of her restricted access to a rural territorium (Justin
18.5.14), differed from many of the other western Phoenician colonies in her early history, and this was doubtless the reason why
she developed into the leading Phoenician naval state during the
archaic period. It also explains why Carthage from an early date
found it necessary to dispose of her surplus population by sub-
colonization and to seek food supplies outside her territory from
districts such as eastern Libya and Sardinia. In Spain of course
the attraction was silver and in west Africa gold. But nowhere in
the archaic period or later is there anything to indicate this
trade was conducted in a commercially open and competitive market

responsive to price wars, supply and demand or diminishing marginal
utility.[43] No one, said Xenophon, has got so much silver that he
does not wish for more (*Poroi* 4.7). It follows that the Phoenician
Spanish trade in silver was not undercut or dislocated by grants of
port or trade facilities to Phoceans or other Greeks by the local
rulers (e.g. Hdt. 1.163, 4.152). What did upset Carthage was piracy
(Hdt. 1.166, 6.17; Arist. *Rhet*. 1.12.18), and this in turn provoked
general hostility to the foundation of alien colonies within the
limited range of raiding penteconters.[44] That had been the reaction
of the men of Chios when Phoceans tried to settle on the adjacent
Oenussae islands (Hdt. 1.165), and it was the same principle which
provoked Carthaginian opposition to Dorieus' attempt to colonize
the African *emporia* coast or the Phocean colonization of Alalia in
Sardinia.

In other words, none of these were examples of simple market
competition. Trade under these conditions is basically a political
activity between communities, like war, and conducted at the same
level of management.[45] Guarantees of peace and friendship are more
important than haggling for prices, which undermines security.
Complete strangers are automatically suspect, since their purpose
must be aggressive and their influence on peaceful natives disruptive. Even friendly traders are stereotyped as potential cheats,
spies and pirates (e.g. Hdt. 1.1, 1.153), whose access to markets
must be strictly supervised. Elaborate care was therefore taken to
defuse potential conflicts, either by silent trade - for which we
have the celebrated Carthaginian example in Herodotus (4.196) - or
by agreed rights to ports of the sort granted by king Arganthonius
to some Greeks at Tartessus (Hdt. 1.163).

It is the ports of trade, the *emporia*, which Polanyi first
suggested should be regarded as the principal instrument of the
Carthaginian political economy and (we may add *ex hypothesi*) of
whatever degree of imperial control they may have exercised. The
notion has been taken up by others, but with two important quali-
fications:[46] first, that the distinction between *emporia* and other
urban centres is blurred, particularly in Sicily; and secondly,
that the neutrality of ports of trade as a means of separating incompatible systems, which Polanyi emphasized, should not exclude
the possibility of a more discriminatory, political use of ports

in favour of friends and allies.

Carthaginian *emporia* must be regarded as falling into two categories. One type was in those regions where Carthaginian traders
themselves operated under the licence of foreign powers, even though
they often settled more or less permanently in the port. This was
clearly true, for instance, of those many Carthaginian and Phoenician
traders in Syracuse (Diod. 14.46.1), or in Acragas with its hundreds
of 'resident aliens' in the fifth century (Diod. 13.81.4-5, 13.84.3
- the figures are surely exaggerated). The same was presumably the
case with the Punic ghettos of *portum Punicum* and Pyrgi in the Etruscan ports of Caere and Tarquinia. It must also account for some of
the many so-called 'Carthaginian' *emporia* listed by Greek geographers
in Spain and Africa. They were not necessarily any more Carthaginian
than the port where Homer's Phoenician merchants lived for a year (*Od*.
15.416ff.); nor, to judge by what we know of Arganthonius, were they
limited to Carthaginian merchants. The independent Phoenician colonies of Spain, Sardinia and Sicily would not in principle have behaved any differently from Greeks or Iberians in their relations with
Carthaginian merchants, although in practice a common culture and
language must have created favourable conditions for trade agreements.

The second category of *emporia* consists of those under Carthaginian control, the most important of which was obviously Carthage
itself. This was state administered trade, conducted in the presence
of state officials (*kerykes* and *grammateis*), of the kind we have recorded in the Rome treaty of 509 B.C. in Libya and Sardinia (Polyb.
3.22.3). The presence of a Greek community in Carthage is attested
on many occasions (e.g. Diod. 14.77.4-5 in 396 B.C.) and it was
assuredly paralleled by an Etruscan settlement.[47] Nor was Carthage
the only site known in Libya. Neapolis (Thuc. 7.50) and later
Kerkina (Livy 33.48.3) were all very much Carthaginian.

It was presumably in Carthage's interest to determine the rights
of access to ports of trade herself rather than to rely on the possession of such rights as were granted by other powers. Direct administration of the *emporion* was not only profitable for *vectigalia
maritima* which went into the pockets of the *principes* of Carthage
(Livy 33.46.8-47.1) but, as Xenophon's Simonides advised Hiero of
Syracuse, it brought political prestige to the ruler (Xen. *Hiero* 4.7,
9.9). This means that user-rights in ports of trade were regarded as

instruments of diplomacy and power as much as special economic advantages. According to an emotional speech given by Herodotus to Gelo of Syracuse in the early fifth century, Gelo had once asked the mainland Greeks for help against Carthage, 'To free the *emporia* from which you had great advantage and profit ... But for all you did they would still be in barbarian hands' (Hdt. 7.158). Whatever the historicity of the speech, the notion was feasible in Herodotus' day.[48]

But what control? And how was it operated? In the second category of *emporia* it was exercised by the presence of Carthaginian officials, payment of tolls to Carthage and perhaps territorial occupation by Carthage - the sort of thing that seems to have pertained in Leptis Magna in the second century B.C. But that kind of evidence is lacking for anywhere else among the dozens of *emporia* outside Africa, with the possible exception of Sardinia. The silence is here surely significant. The only other possibility is Carthaginian control by treaty and indirect pressure; perhaps also Carthaginian control of the semi-autonomous enclaves established in the ports. This would be rather like the right to appoint the wardens of the port granted by Egypt to select states at Naucratis (Hdt. 2.178), or the control of the segregated *karum* by Assyrian traders in the middle of a foreign Anatolian kingdom in the second millennium B.C.[49] In the Middle Ages and later such concessions were called 'Capitulations' and are recorded from at least the ninth century, when Harun-al-Rashid granted special commercial facilities to the Frankish subjects of Charlemagne.[50] They were in effect treaties which granted to a state extra-territorial jurisdiction over its nationals within the boundaries of a foreign port, and were based on the principle that the sovereignty of a state could extend to its overseas subjects but not to the port territory. It was thereby a convenience to both parties - to the home state by providing a measure of law and order among wealthy and often powerful merchants in the port, and to the foreigners in that they were protected in their transactions and usually given some reduction of port duties. The result was the formation of virtually a foreign enclave in the midst of an alien land, sometimes, although not necessarily, to the restriction of the host's sovereignty.

How far the Assyrian *karum* or the Capitulations were precisely paralleled in Carthage's extra-territorial relations is almost impossible to say with the limited information available. But the examples prove that territorial sovereignty was not a precondition of control of port operations. Nor were these conditions necessarily exploitative of the host country - what today we might call neo-colonialist - since in this kind of trade prices were fixed by non-commercial mechanisms. But politically such user-control was of immense value in the conduct of foreign affairs. In return for Carthaginian aid against mounting Greek or native pressures, the various Phoenician cities must have agreed to permit Carthage to dictate the terms under which the ports of trade extended its rights to users, but they did not necessarily forfeit their independence.

This political instrument of determining the approaches to the ports of trade (*epibathrai* is Polybius' word, 3.24.14) is always assumed to mean a policy of *mare clausum*, trade monopolies and closed markets, based on theories of formal economics. But in conditions of administered trade the logic is perverse. The Carthaginians were concerned not to limit the number of traders who came to their ports but to increase them. Strangers, unidentifiable penteconters of warlike appearance were potential enemies, raiders and kidnappers. It is significant that Polybius automatically interpreted the treaty of 509 to refer to Roman war ships (3.23.2).[51] They caused local shipping to suffer and the population was abducted as slaves (e.g. Plaut. *Poen*. 66). Adjacent ports of trade or colonial foundations were likewise threatening, apart from drawing off potential allies. The success of treaty trade depended upon the ability to offer protection and guaranteed prices. The aim was to direct shipping to suitable sites, to assist the trader with facilities for storage and judicial authorities to enforce contracts, to keep the foreigner under surveillance rather than encourage him to smuggle at unauthorized sites.[52] The 'running in' of ships (*katagein* is the Greek word) seems to have been a fairly common practice for compulsory sales both in this period and later.[53] The essential prerequisite for the port of trade was peace (Xen. *Poroi* 5.2), and this was what motivated Carthage in Spain, Sardinia and Sicily.

TOWARDS A MODEL FOR CARTHAGINIAN IMPERIALISM

In Carthage, as in all pre-industrial and relatively undifferen-
tiated societies of a precapitalist era, the economy was 'submerged
in social relationships' and this characteristic predominated over
such principles of formal economics as the theory of indifference,
diminishing returns and economic maximization.[54] That means to
say that, even if they had had the skill to calculate the strictly
financial value of marginal production and exchange, the Carthaginians would not have had the will to create this as the over-
riding principle, to the exclusion of social and political gains.
Perhaps that is true enough of any society, but in Carthage as in
all face-to-face communities, economic rationality was modified by
social prescription to a far greater extent than in modern indus-
trial societies where social and economic spheres are largely
segregated.

Price in other words was less important than goodwill or
prestige, and external trade was merely a tool towards this end.
Commerce, insofar as it is an appropriate term at all, was directed towards the socially necessary objectives of Carthaginian
society, which had as much to do with moral obligations and status
as with private money-making. This does not mean that economic
rationality disappeared and played no part in determining Carthaginian behaviour overseas. Economic maximization is merely a taut-
ology for saying that each man does the best he can in the circumstances. But it is the circumstances that matter. We are not
dealing with prelogical mentalities but with priorities.[55]

In consideration of Carthaginian imperialism this means that,
while we must not rule out the possibility of economically exploitative domination through territorial conquest or tied trade,
socially oriented actions also provided opportunities for manipulation and self advantage that do not fit into a term like 'commercial empire'.

If the Carthaginian economy was thus embedded in the social
and political fabric of the state, there was no clear dichotomy
between the public and private sector. Personal bonds of *xenia*
and *philia* predominated in such actions of foreign policy as
Magonid support for Himera against Syracuse or in response to the
kinship call for help from Gades.[56] Phoenician merchants of

antiquity were princes and their traffickers 'the honourable of the
earth' (Isaiah 23.8) – unlike those of Greece and Rome. Whatever
the precise relationship between kings and the ruling 'order' at
various periods, Aristotle and Polybius make it clear that wealth,
largesse and conspicuous spending rather than birth were essential
for control of political power (Arist. *Pol.* 1272b–1273a; Polyb.
6.56.4).[57] Since agrarian wealth and land were in short supply until at least the fourth century B.C., it follows that Carthaginian
grandees derived their status and riches both from land and from
trade and foreign adventures. King Hanno's voyage to the west
African coast in search of gold (as we believe) was just such an
example of state-cum-private enterprise and perhaps one more
example of the interchangeable political and trading role by the
ubiquitous Magonid family.

    According to Cicero's biased view, commercial greed destroyed
Carthage's will to fight (*de rep.* 2.4.7), which more or less corresponded to Aristotle's judgement that riches in Carthage were
more honoured than merit (*Pol.* 1273a). In other words, prestige
action lay more in trade than conquest and this, not surprisingly,
baffled Cicero's agrarian sense of values. This does not mean
that military prowess was wholly despised. If we can believe
Justin, Mago, the founder of the dynasty, won great renown for
bellica gloria (18.7.19) and the crack troops of the 'Sacred Band'
in 339 B.C. were a political elite 'distinguished for bravery and
reputation as well as property' (Diod. 16.80.4). But war in general, as we saw in Sicily, endangered the very basis of the economic and political welfare of the oligarchy, which was achieved
through the careful nurture of administered trade in foreign ports
and the extension of such facilities to their allies by private
and state agreements.

    And this brings us once again to the Rome-Carthage treaties,
which are in many ways the best documents for understanding Carthaginian imperialism. The treaties, as many have seen, must be set
in the context of the *symbola* and state agreements concluded by
Carthage with several Etruscan cities (Arist. *Pol.* 1280a36). They
were therefore agreements arising out of friendship not truces
dictated from hostility. In matters of exchange and business the
parties became 'like citizens of one city', says Aristotle.

Strangers were in this fashion made like kinsmen so that they could
be incorporated as trading partners through a political and social
act outside the realm of pure market economics, and not restricted
to commerce.[58] The important point is that *symbola*, which were
similar to other types of exchange of rights, rights of sanctuary
or alien residence which can be documented in Phoenician or Leven-
tine trading history far back into the archaic period, were designed to assist traders and strangers, not to keep them out.[59]
Such state agreements were closely related to and developed out of
exchanges of *xenia*.

What this paper has sought to suggest is that such agreements
of reciprocity, which began as deals between equal partners, could
move into conditions of unequal domination for political as much
as commercial reasons. The tone of the Pyrgi gold inscriptions,
dating from near the time of the first Roman treaty, is deferen-
tial to Carthage.[60] The treaties with Rome defined political
spheres of influence where Carthage could, as it were, speak for
others. And that redounded to Carthage's prestige. But Rome in
509, while speaking for the Latin cities, could hardly claim to
control them at that date. No more could Carthage claim that Tyre
was Carthaginian territory in 348, although she was included in
the agreement (Polyb. 3.24).[61] So why should Utica or Mastia
Tarseion in Spain have been any different in the same treaty?
What had happened was that these cities under pressure of events
were prepared to permit Carthage to define their foreign relations
by jointly underwriting the protection of allied shipping in selec-
ted ports of trade. That was the attraction of the alliance and
the nature of the Carthaginian empire.

A CHANGE IN CARTHAGINIAN IMPERIALISM

Carthaginian attitudes towards trade and overseas commitments were
changing in the fourth century. This may have underlain their un-
willingness to allow Romans to approach Libya and Sardinia, although they did not necessarily demand the same conditions from
all their allies. It coincided with a change in the political
economy of Carthage and the expansion of Carthage beyond the *chora*
of Cape Bon. By the time of Agathocles' invasion in 310 B.C.
Carthage controlled a territory some forty miles deep that extended

westwards as far as Hippo Acra (Bizerta) and eastwards to Hadrumetum
and Thapsus. This implies a growth of landed property ownership,
control of labour and new relations of production, which were bound
to alter the social and economic priorities as well as affecting the
ideology of the ruling estate. It is at this time in the fourth
century, for instance, that we hear of Hanno and his support from
20,000 'slaves', who must be labourers on the land (Justin 21.4.6).
We have evidence of rich estates owned by the nobility (Diod. 20.8.4),
which probably included the exploitation of the corn lands to the
south-west and olive culture to the south-east.[62] The introduction
of the *Ceres* cult into Africa (Diod. 14.77.5) and the export of corn
in 306 B.C. (Diod. 20.79.5) are signals of the new economy. However
scathing Cicero may have been about the relative absence of a purely
land-owning class in Carthage, the large olive estates owned by the
Barca family near Thapsus (Livy 33.48.1; Pliny *NH* 17.93) demonstrate
the change.

The logic of this change, however small in the fourth century,
was growing inequality among the population of the territory as the
minority gained control of the means of production. That produced
greater unrest among those who were increasingly exploited and
therefore greater danger that foreign invasions might spark off
native rebellion - just as Agathocles and Regulus calculated. The
benefits of reciprocity agreements and foreign exchanges were out-
weighed by the disturbances caused by foreign contacts. The vulnerability of Africa led to a greater dependence on Sardinia for
emergency imports and therefore the need to limit approaches even
by allies. Sicily became less a field for enterprise than a security risk from her contiguity. Agathocles, it was said, at the time
of his death in 289 B.C. was planning to control Carthaginian routes
by holding strategic points in Africa with a large war fleet (Diod.
21.16.1).

By the end of the fourth century the stage was set for the new
Carthaginian imperialism of the third century, which is not studied
here. Basically it aimed to neutralize Sicily and produce equilibrium through chaos. It was only the Romans who claimed to perceive
in this an aggressive intent, in order to excuse their own actions.[63]
The complete loss of Spain and its silver supply made Carthage more
than ever reliant upon Sardinia and Libya. So it was that in the

third century the first extensive penetration deep into Africa took
place followed by the full panoply of a provincial system, including governors, taxes and district organization of the territory.[64]
This was the work of Hanno and Hamilcar Barca, further stimulated
by the crippling blow to Carthaginian trade by the loss of Sicily
and Sardinia in the First Punic War. Hamilcar then carried the
empire westwards along the Metagonian coast and into Spain. The
empire was described in the Macedonian treaty of 215 B.C. as 'those
who are subjects of Carthage, who live under the same laws' (Polyb.
7.9.5). Polybius used the word *hyparchoi* for subjects, not the
eparchia he had described before. The verbal shift is small but
the real change great.

A.Andrewes (New College, Oxford)

The query in my title indicates a doubt about the reality of Spartan imperialism, as distinct from the ambitions of individual Spartans and their followers. Lysander tried to create something that we can fairly call an empire; twenty years earlier we have the foundation of Herakleia Trachinia, and we must at least consider whether the thinking behind that grandiose project could be called imperialistic; earlier still the regent Pausanias after the Persian War harboured ambitions which might have tended the same way. Both these men ended badly, and the colony too failed. The question is both about the nature of the ambitions and about the opposition to them: to some extent it was personal, but I conclude that there were general factors in the Spartan system which inhibited imperialism.

I *PAUSANIAS AND THE HEGEMONY*

It would be possible to extend the enquiry backwards and include King Kleomenes I, an active king, and a good case can be made for regarding him as an expansionist eager to increase Sparta's power and his own. I doubt if this would be profitable: the evidence is in effect all from Herodotus, mainly hostile to him, and the narrative is fragmented in such a way that it is hard to be sure how his various activities hang together, and harder still to be sure about his own and his opponents' motives.[1]

The position is different with his nephew Pausanias, regent for many years for his cousin King Pleistarchos, son of Leonidas. As the youthful victor of Plataia in 479,[2] and the leader of the fleet which went to Cyprus and Byzantium in 478, he had an assured prestige and opportunities for action beyond those available to Kleomenes. We see him through the eyes of two good witnesses, who took different views of the last phase of his life but use similar phrases about his alleged aims: Herodotus (5.32) knew, but doubted, the story that he was betrothed to a Persian princess, ἔρωτα σχὼν τῆς Ἑλλάδος τύραννος γενέσθαι; Thucydides cites a letter in which

he proposed to marry Xerxes' daughter, and does not doubt his motive
(1.128.3), ἐφιέμενος τῆς Ἑλληνικῆς ἀρχῆς. Before we can go further
this has to be sorted out.

At 5.32 Herodotus had occasion to mention Darius' cousin Mega-
bates, and noted that it was to this man's daughter that Pausanias,
'if indeed the story be true, at a later time was betrothed, longing
to become tyrant of Greece'. The doubt relates directly to the be-
trothal, but as the sentence runs it must also cover the tyrannical
ambition, and it is significant that Herodotus thought it right
both to mention the story and to express his doubt. At 8.3.2 the
Athenians, in the interests of unity, nobly abandon their claim to
command at sea; but only for the moment, 'as they showed, for when
they had repulsed the Persian and the fight was about his own land,
they used the excuse of Pausanias' hybris to take the hegemony from
the Spartans'. Herodotus does not deny the hybris, but he thought
that it was not in itself grave enough to cause the allies' switch
from Sparta to Athens.[3] When Pausanias makes his substantive entry
into the narrative, Herodotus praises his victory at Plataia, 'the
fairest of all that we know' (9.64.1), and follows this with a
string of favourable anecdotes about his conduct after the battle
(9.76, 78-9, 82); at most there is a hint of corruptibility in
Pausanias' reaction to Persian luxury (82.2), and his arbitrary
execution of the Theban Medisers (88) is disquieting, but no real
shadow is allowed to mar the glory.[4]

Thucydides had no occasion to dilate on Plataia and starts
with the expedition of 478. Pausanias' violence is mere fact, not
anyone's pretext, and it is the reason why the allies turned to
Athens (1.95.1); when he was recalled and tried, it is a surprise
that he was acquitted of Medism (1.95.5). Thereafter, in the
excursus 1.128-34, his Medism and his ambition to rule Greece
under the king is assumed throughout. We are given the text of
his letter to Xerxes (ὡς ὕστερον ἀνηυρέθη, which has naturally
excited suspicion) and of Xerxes' reply (128.6-7, 129.3): the only
problem at that time, as Thucydides sees it, was to obtain certain
proof of his guilt.

Thucydides' version has encountered severe criticism, some of
it justified and some less so.[5] There is no need to rehearse the
whole controversy here. The critics have enough of a case, and

the letters are not very palatable; it is hard to feel much enthusiasm for the novelette about Pausanias' eventual detection. The different situations of the two witnesses are important. Long before
he began his famous enquiries, Herodotus heard enough discussion
among his elders about the transfer of the hegemony and about Pausanias' role; above all he heard these things outside Athens, which
makes it more difficult to disregard his judgement of the limited
extent to which he could endorse the developed story. Thucydides,
a full generation younger, was an Athenian who grew up when the
empire was fully developed; and when Athens and Sparta took joint
action against Themistokles, before Thucydides was born, Pausanias'
Medism and Themistokles' involvement had been accepted officially
as fact at Athens. We may regret that nothing stirred his powerful
and critical mind to question these agreed fables, but only his
more extreme worshippers need feel offended.

One factual detail shows that Pausanias did indeed have some
dealings with the Persians: his agent Gongylos the Eretrian received
from the king some Aiolic cities which his sons held in the 390s
(Xen. *Hell.* 3.1.6; cf. *Anab.* 7.8.8), presumably for service actually
rendered.[6] The extent of Pausanias' commitment has been variously
estimated,[7] but Herodotus' doubts incline me to minimize it: we need
imagine no more than some form of reinsurance, such as Themistokles
was alleged to have practised (Hdt. 8.109.5), or the English who
after 1688 maintained contact with the exiled Stuart court, just in
case.

His reaction to the loss of the hegemony is more important for
our purposes. Driven out of Byzantium by the Athenians, he seems
to have been left undisturbed at Kolonai for some time.[8] Thucydides' certainty about his Medism does not tell us exactly what he
was doing at Kolonai, or why the Spartans sent for him when they
did. The terms of the summons (131.1) and his imprisonment by the
ephors (131.2) suggest that his enemies at home were at this time
dominant and confident of a conviction; but then he was released,
and when he 'offered himself for trial' no one took up the challenge. Thucydides did not infer, as we might, that the evidence
proved inadequate or that Pausanias was found to have more political support in the city than had been expected; instead he remarks
on the difficulty of attacking a Spartan in the regent's position

(132.1, 5) and turns to other grounds Pausanias had given for suspicion, the inscription on the dedication at Delphi[9] and the rest.
It was the Spartan way, he comments, not to hurry into irreversible
steps against a Spartiate without sure proof.

The Spartans could indeed be cautious, but this did not stop
them putting their kings on trial;[10] and according to Thucydides
himself Pausanias offered to undergo one. If public feeling had
been strongly hostile to him, accusers would have come forward and
evidence would have been found, so the implication of Thucydides'
account is that Pausanias had enough support to make it risky for
his enemies to proceed. But if so, what did his friends support?
Not, presumably, a plan to make him tyrant or satrap under the
Persians: the likely issue is the one indicated by Diodoros, who
at 11.50 reports a debate between the young and the majority who
wished to recover the hegemony from Athens by force, and a prudent
elder who dissuaded them. Diodorus has this under 475/4, but his
introductory phrase joins easily on to the end of his account of
the transfer of the hegemony at 11.47.3, and the moment for decision was when the allies rejected Dorkis, sent out to succeed
Pausanias: Sparta must either take action at once or acquiesce in
Athens' initiative, as Thucydides says she did at 1.95.7, not
contradicting Diodoros but putting the matter in a very different
light. That was a victory for the opposition, and Pausanias'
second voyage to Byzantium was a rebellious refusal to accept
this. There is an uncertain hint in Thucydides that he said he
was going out to take action against a Greek enemy;[11] the Athenians
showed what they thought by expelling him forcibly from Byzantium,
in my belief after no long interval.[12] The proceedings in Sparta
after his second recall were an inquest on all this. It was no
longer feasible to contest the transfer of hegemony, but there was
an opportunity to strike down Pausanias and his supporters. We
might understand better if we knew the exact date and how this
fits in with other events in Sparta and the Peloponnese. The opposition won again, but it was not a complete or happy victory
(Thuc. 1.134.4), and time must have been needed to establish the
version which Thucydides accepted without question.

A design to retain or recover the leadership of the Greek war
against Persia is not in itself, or not simply, imperialistic. It

is not indeed very clear what Pausanias and the Greek leaders were
trying to create in 478, more particularly what they expected to become of Cyprus after their campaign there; [13] if Sparta had kept the
leadership she would have had to impose some measure of organization
generally. Lotze (1970) argues forcibly against assuming that the
contemporary question was about the political domination of Greece;
whatever the personal ambitions of Pausanias, the general Spartan
reaction should be seen in terms of the prestige of leadership.
This is in the main convincing, though it leaves Sparta's acquiesc-
ence in the Athenian takeover not quite transparent, and the ano-
dyne mildness of Thucydides' Spartans at 1.95.7 can hardly be the
whole story. Diodoros does not help with the motive: his Hetoi-
maridas (11.50.6) argues that naval hegemony would not be good for
Sparta (μὴ συμφέρειν), which has an Isokratean ring, reminiscent
of feelings expressed at Athens in the 350s but not suitable here.
But it is not hard to imagine, with Lotze, that the landowners of
Sparta preferred their established mode of life and were reluctant
to undertake the effort that would be needed if Pausanias' lead
were to be followed; and after the event it might seem palatable
enough to sacrifice a degree of prestige and to leave the labori-
ous job to Athens. Things were different at the end of the century, when Sparta had experience of war overseas and had developed
new mechanisms for conducting it.

II *HERAKLEIA TRACHINIA*

Thucydides distinguishes the two alliances at the outbreak of war
by saying (1.19) that the Spartans did not subject their allies to
tribute, only took care (θεραπεύοντες) that they should be ruled
by oligarchies sympathetic to herself. 'Care' might run to armed
intervention, as at Sikyon in 418 (5.81.2; cf. 82.1 for Achaia),
at a time of Spartan recovery after a period of depression; and no
doubt at all times less obtrusive pressures might be exercised.
Nevertheless, power by land required armed forces larger than
Sparta could supply from her own citizen body, so that her allies
retained their arms and got a measure of independence from that.
The Peloponnesian League held real conferences at which Sparta
might be outvoted, and the boast that the cities she led were
autonomous had some substance. [14] At the start of the war Sparta

proclaimed the liberation of Gre-ce, and if some Spartans entertained
larger ambitions, the declaration hampered open imperialism. When
war was resumed in 413 Thucydides allows the expression of thoughts
about hegemony (6.92.5, 8.2.4), but not about empire, and the theme
of liberation still shows its effects (8.46.3, 43.3).

The Archidamian War did however see the establishment of the
Spartan colony at Herakleia Trachinia (Thuc. 3.92-3; Diod. 12.59.3-5)
in 426, a venture which shows that policies which had nothing to do
with liberation might be adopted by the Spartan state. I have argued
elsewhere (Andrewes (1971), 217-26) that expansion by land to the
north was a continuing strand in Spartan policy, that Thucydides perhaps overstresses the freelance position of Brasidas in his expedition
to the north, and that the Olynthian War was not an isolated aberration. Of all this the foundation of Herakleia is the most striking
symptom, worth further discussion.

The mere size of the colony is portentous. Diodoros' ten thousand is a naturally suspect number, and his breakdown into 4,000
Peloponnesians and over 6,000 others does not much improve its credi-
bility; but Thucydides guarantees a large scale when he speaks of
πάνυ πολλούς at the start, due to confidence in the stability of a
Spartan foundation. There is no classical parallel for a colony of
these dimensions on Greek soil, supposed to be friendly: the 4,000
Athenian cleruchs of Hdt. 5.77.2 on the land of the Hippobotai were
not sent to Chalkis out of piety or friendship. We must not of
course write off the element of piety for Herakleia, the connexion
of Herakles with Trachis and the simultaneous appeal from Doris, but
protection from the Oitaioi in this style was likely to prove more
of a burden than a boon to the recipients, and there is evidence
that it was resented;[15] and the Spartans finished by expelling the
remaining Trachinians.[16]

For a second motive Thucydides gives its use in the war against
Athens: a fleet could be prepared against Euboia, with a short crossing. We are then told that they began to build νεώρια,[17] and that
the Athenians were at first greatly alarmed by this aspect of the
foundation. It remains a little mysterious. They cannot have hoped
to evade Athenian control of the sea and bring in a fleet of any
size, but it may have been intended to build ships locally, and hope
to find enough adequate seamen among the colonists, or import them

specially. In any case it would seem more economical to assemble
the force required somewhere along this coast and ferry it across
in some more surreptitious way; the Athenians, even if in general
alerted, could not keep continuous watch on the whole coastline.
Even if Spartan caution rejected that kind of risk, the naval preparations still seem somewhat overblown. Third, and most briefly
stated, the place would be useful for the passage to the north,[18]
and in 424 Brasidas stopped here to organize his transit of Thessaly (Thuc. 4.78.1); but again, a large-scale colony forty stades
west of Thermopylai was not the most economic way of securing the
defile.

Two further matters call for consideration. The first is
Agis' expedition north from Dekeleia in winter 413/12 (Thuc. 8.3.1).
His action against the Oitaioi is explained in terms of 'old enmity',
i.e. the oppression of Trachis and Doris which in 426 had excused
Sparta's intervention; it was another matter when he turned to 'the
Achaioi Phthiotai and the other subjects of the Thessalians in these
parts', over Thessalian protest, exacting money and hostages, de-
positing the latter in Corinth, and attempting to bring these tribes
into the Spartan alliance. This is markedly more aggressive than
anything that was done or threatened in 426, and the suggestion of
imperialism is much stronger. Later, after the reorganization of
Herakleia in 399 or 400 (see n.16), we find a Spartan garrison in
Pharsalos (Diod. 14.82.6), presumably drawn in the first instance
from their nearest base; and in 395 the army which followed Lysander
to Haliartos included contingents from the tribes of the Malian Gulf
(Xen. *Hell.* 3.5.6).

Secondly, the action of Eurylochos in autumn 426, very soon
after the foundation of Herakleia, when he gathered an army at
Delphi to attack Naupaktos, and it included 500 hoplites from the
new colony (Thuc. 3.100.2-101.1). It is not clear how many of them
can have got home (3.109.2-3, 111), and the blow to Herakleia was
probably severe; but the employment of these men may be one indication of the purposes which the colony was intended to serve. Lysander's army in 395 (above) also included Herakleots.

These items add up to a serious indication that some Spartans
entertained plans to subject certain areas of central and northern
Greece to a control tighter than that which they exercised over

their Peloponnesian allies. In terms of manpower this was imperialism on the cheap, calling only for governors and some staff from
Sparta; and recruitment to Sparta's later long-distance expeditions
shows that the Peloponnese could spare the colonists. These plans
cannot have been wholly secret, but the key measure, the despatch of
the colony to Herakleia, could be wrapped up as a response to the
appeal of Trachis and Doris, so we need not suppose that the average
Spartan at the start willed such action as Agis took in 413/12. I
would stress again (cf. Andrewes (1971), 225) that our knowledge of
Spartan involvement in the north depends on curious chances, and it
is certain that there is much that we do not know; but the important
fact remains that the colony failed, and failed repeatedly. In winter 420/19 it suffered a defeat at the hands of the local tribes and
some Thessalians, and in the spring the Boiotians took it over
(Thuc. 5.51–52.1). By the time of Agis' action in 413/12 Spartan
control must have been restored, though Thucydides says nothing of
Herakleia here (8.3.1); but in winter 409/8, if the chronology of
this scrappy entry in Xen. *Hell.* 1.2.18 can be trusted, Herakleia
was again defeated with heavy losses, this time by the Oitaioi and
by the treachery of the Achaioi (presumably the Phthiotai whom Agis
had recently tried to incorporate into the Spartan system). In 399
or 400 (see n.16) Herippidas intervened in a stasis, expelled the
Trachinians and reorganized the colony, but after the battle at
Haliartos in 395 the Boiotians and Argives took the place over,
sent the Peloponnesian colonists away, and restored the Trachinians
(Diod. 14.82.6–7). The later history of the city does not concern us.

Thucydides blamed the failure on the hostility of the colony's
neighbours, and on the arrogance and incompetence of its governors
(3.93.2, 5.51.2–52.1); and both charges are credible. The establishment of this outsize Spartan outpost was an affront only to be en-
dured by those whom it affected if it was forcibly and efficiently
maintained. The failure of the governors echoes a theme familiar in
criticism of Sparta (e.g. Thuc. 1.77.6), and it is probably also a
sign of uncertainty in Sparta's commitment to the enterprise. If,
as I think, there was a continuing group of Spartans who favoured
expansion by land to the north, the whole record shows that they
were not continuously in control, and so could not ensure the appointment of governors in full sympathy with the project; and

governors of a different way of thinking were unlikely to make it
work.   The project needed more whole-hearted backing than it got.

III *LYSANDER AND AFTER*

In the course of the Archidamian War Sparta evolved methods for
dealing with war in distant theatres for which the regular levy was
not suited.   Eurylochos in 426 foreshadows, and Brasidas and his
subordinate officers in 424-422 fully exemplify, the practice of
sending detached officers on special missions, and then or later
the term *harmost* was applied to them.[19]   Among his troops Brasidas
had 700 helots (Thuc. 4.80.5), liberated on their return (5.34.1);
and it must be soon after 424 that Sparta instituted the standing
force of *neodamodeis*, helots liberated in advance for hoplite service.[20]   The rest of Brasidas' force was made up of Peloponnesians
who volunteered for pay.   The record of Sparta's campaigns in the
390s shows that there was an ample supply of both types of soldier.
This again was a system which made no large demand on citizen manpower, calling only for an adequate number of zealous and efficient
commanders.   Before the end of the Ionian War it had been expanded
and developed, and it was ready to Lysander's hand for his attempt
to set up an extensive Spartan empire.

It is not in doubt that Lysander proposed to retain for Sparta
all of Athens' Aegean empire, and the mechanisms are too well known
to need long exposition here.   It is irritating that we cannot
document a dekarchy in any state but Samos (Xen. *Hell*. 2.3.7), but
general statements about them occur in contexts (e.g. *Hell*. 3.4.2,
7) such that we cannot write them off as exaggerations of a few
instances; if a harmost was installed in Byzantium (*Hell*. 2.2.2)
as well as Samos, that shows the range of Lysander's plan.   The
finance of the operation is referred to explicitly only by Diodorus
(14.10.2), to the tune of more than a thousand talents exacted from
the defeated;[21] a clause in the Athenian settlement of 403 (*Ath.Pol*.
39.2) shows that payment was actually demanded, and for some time
after the abolition of Lysander's dekarchies a fleet and an army
overseas had to be paid for.   The concentration of our sources on
Athens prevents us from discovering much more about the way in
which Lysander's dispensation affected other states.

It is hardly surprising that the attempt was made: the question

is rather why Lysander failed. His policy for Athens was wrecked by
the intervention of King Pausanias in summer 403, and his defeat was
sealed by the acquittal of Pausanias at his subsequent trial, though
the voting is said to have been close (Paus. 3.5.2); and roughly at
this time the dekarchies were abolished and the cities were given
their 'ancestral constitutions' (Xen. *Hell*. 3.4.2).[22] The alliance
still hung together for some years, and Xenophon (*Hell*. 3.1.5) comments on the continuing readiness of East Greek cities to comply
with Spartan orders; but it was no longer in the same sense an empire, and when Lysander in 396 tried to recover his commanding influence among the East Greek cities (Xen. *Hell*. 3.4.2 credits him
with an intention to re-establish the dekarchies), he was foiled
by Agesilaos.

     This was certainly in large part a matter of the internal
politics of Sparta, which we should understand more fully if we
disposed of minor sources for Sparta comparable with those we have
for the political life of Athens. But Xenophon and Plutarch make
it clear enough that Lysander was not only ambitious for Sparta,
but also energetic and ruthless in building up his personal power:
the narrative leaves no doubt that he was effectively in charge,
even when he was no longer in formal command of the fleet. That
was bound to cause trouble, and we need not doubt Xenophon when he
gives jealousy as the motive of Pausanias when he persuaded three
of the ephors to send him with a force to Athens (*Hell*. 2.4.29), to
interfere with an operation which Lysander seems to have been carrying out with complete efficiency. The question is how widespread
this feeling was, and the mere fact that Pausanias was brought to
trial on his return shows that Lysander's position inside Sparta
was still strong, whether or not we have been given the voting figures correctly. One would like to know more of the arguments by
which Pausanias persuaded a majority of the ephors.[23]

     But there is also the moral question, or if that is thought an
unsuitable formulation, the question how much the policies and
methods of Lysander offended ordinary men brought up under the
strict Spartan code. Critics of Sparta have castigated the immorality and hypocrisy of her public policy, at least from the time of
Thucydides' Athenian speakers at Melos (5.105.4), but even for them
the Spartans show conspicuous virtue in their private dealings with

one another; it would be very peculiar if the average patriotic
Spartan did not genuinely believe in the pre-eminent virtue of his
city, and the opponents of Lysander surely made use of moral argument against his treachery and cruelty. One can only take the instances as they happen to be presented. Kallikratidas, done down
by Lysander and his partisans (Xen. *Hell*. 1.6.4, 10), makes a noble
if slightly confused impression as Xenophon pictures him. The
touching scene described in Lys. 18.10-12 is a little spurious, for
Pausanias had surely made up his mind about Lysander's Athenian
policy before he left Sparta, but there is no difficulty in believing that he used the situation of Nikeratos' and Eukrates' children
as an example to show his troops how wrong it was to support the
Thirty. The ephors who ordered the suppression of the dekarchies
no doubt congratulated themselves on the righting of a manifest
wrong. The basic fact is that the able and forceful Lysander, for
whatever reason, could not persuade his countrymen to follow him
for long.

What follows is pale in comparison. Agesilaos, relying less
on force and fraud and more on his diplomatic ability and on the
charm which enslaved Xenophon, built up his own position and made
the most he could of Sparta's continuing predominance, imposing
his will most effectively in the execution of the King's Peace.
But it was noted that his prevailing passion was the advancement
of his own friends in the cities (Isoc. 5.87), a source of weakness
as well as of strength, which led him into actions which even Xenophon could not quite excuse (*Hell*. 5.3.16; cf. *Ages*. 2.21): this
was something less than a system of empire. The defeat at Leuktra,
provoked in a sense by Agesilaos' intractable enmity to Thebes,
put an end to it all.

IV *CONCLUSION*

In all three instances we detect a lack of the whole-hearted will
to empire. Comparison with Athens shows how this is rooted in the
social and political system of Sparta. At Athens the empire brought
tangible benefit to all classes: we hear most of the material gains
of the poor and of their greed for pay, but that imbalance is due
to the fact that they did not write the literature which has come
down to us, and there is no doubt that the upper classes too

exploited the empire for material advantage. A recent study[24] examines the acquisition of land in the territory of allied cities by
individual Athenians of this class; and they gained too because the
tribute of empire saved them over a long period from contributions
which they must otherwise have made from their own pockets to the
expenses of the state. There is no good evidence of anti-imperialist
feeling in the Athenian upper class,[25] least of all any sign that
they resisted the exaction of tribute or its increase.

The benefits of a Spartan empire would be spread less widely,
and might be less widely attractive to the governing class. Expansion meant for a substantial minority of helots the chance of being
freed for military service, and there were no doubt increased opportunities for individual *perioikoi* (e.g. Thuc. 8.6.4, 22.1): but
they did not determine Spartan policy. Notoriously, a section of
the aristocracy proved eager for foreign service, not only for the
hope of wealth but because they relished their standing in the
cities and the 'flattery' of the inhabitants, a total change from
the traditional discipline of Spartan life: see Xenophon's out-
burst, *Lac.Pol.* 14, most of which seems more applicable to the
beginning of the century than to the time of the pamphlet's composition. These were the men of energy and initiative, like Derkyl-
lidas whose fondness for service abroad is noted by Xenophon (*Hell.*
4.3.2): Ephoros (*FGH* 70 F 71) thought him devious and not a typical Spartan. They provoked some outcry against the corrupting
influence of the wealth that now poured in to Sparta and, however ineffective in the long run, this may be taken as genuine
protest in defence of a way of life that had satisfied many previous generations. Their estates, their hunting, a modicum of
conventional warfare with their neighbours, and the high standing
that their military reputation gave them, were enough for a good
life; to reach out further meant a sustained effort in an unfamiliar field, and it seems that there were not enough who were
ready to break out of the traditional pattern. That is the justification for setting a question-mark against Spartan imperialism.

M.I.Finley (Darwin College, Cambridge)

    I

'Every doctrine of imperialism devised by men is a consequence of
their second thoughts. But empires are not built by men troubled
by second thoughts.'[2]

    I start with that aphoristic formulation, the truth of which
has been demonstrated in the study of modern imperialisms, as an
antidote to the familiar practice of *beginning* a discussion of
the Athenian empire with aims and motives and quickly sliding over
to attitudes and even theory, thereby implying that the men who
created and extended the empire also began with a defined imperialist programme and theories of imperialism. An outstanding current
example of the procedure I have in mind is the attempt to date a
number of Athenian laws and decrees (or to support a proposed date)
by what may be called their imperialist tone. If they are 'harsh',
it is argued, they smack of Cleon and should be dated in the 420s
B.C., and not in the time of the more 'moderate' Periclean leadership, the 440s or 430s.[3] Insofar as the argument is not circular,
it implies the existence of an identifiable programme of imperialism, or rather of both successive and conflicting programmes, and
that requires demonstration, not assumption.

    A second source of confusion is the unavoidable ambiguity of
the word 'empire'. Stemming from the Latin *imperium*, 'empire' becomes entangled with the word 'emperor', and much of the extensive
discussion throughout the Middle Ages and on into modern times
ends in a tautological cul-de-sac: an empire is the territory
ruled by an emperor.[4] Everyone knows that there are, and have
been in the past, important empires not ruled by an emperor, and
I see no purpose in playing word-games in order to get round that
harmless linguistic anomaly. To suggest, for example, that we
should abandon 'empire' as a category in Greek history and speak
only of 'hegemony' does not seem to me helpful or useful.[5] It
would have been small consolation to the Melians, as the Athenian

soldiers and sailors fell upon them, to be informed that they
were about to become the victims of a hegemonial, not an imperial,
measure.

That is not to question the legitimacy of efforts to differentiate among empires. All broad classificatory terms - 'state'
is the obvious analogy - embrace a wide spectrum of individual
instances. The Persian, Athenian and Roman empires differed among
themselves in important ways, as do modern empires. It then becomes necessary, as with all classifications, to establish the
canons for inclusion or exclusion. Those who play with 'hegemony'
seem to me to give excessive weight to purely formal considerations, which, if adopted rigorously, would fragment the category
'empire' so much as to render it empty and useless. Common sense
is right in this instance: there have been throughout history
structures that belong within a single class on substantive grounds,
namely, the exercise of authority (or power or control) by one state
over one or more other states (or communities or peoples) for an
extended period of time. That is admittedly imprecise, but large-
scale human institutions can never be classified by other than
imprecise canons: again I cite 'state' as an analogy.

A notable example of the formalistic approach is the concern
of some historians to define and date the point at which a voluntary association of states was converted into an Athenian empire.
The year 454 is a favourite date, because, it is generally believed, the 'league treasury' was then transferred from Delos to
Athens.[6] At most, such an action was a symbol, a brutal statement
of the reality, but not the reality itself. The word 'voluntary'
is not even a good symbol, leading historians into remarkable verbal contortions. 'It seems possible to go farther and to state
that though coercion of members apparently was regarded as legitimate - and probably even compulsion against states that did
not wish to join - the reduction even of revolting members to the
status of subjects was contrary to the constitution.'[7] Matters
are not improved by a sprinkling of 'Weberian' terminology: 'in-
direkte Herrschaftsmittel bestehen darin, dass sie auf ein In-
teresse des Beherrschten am Beherrschtwerden bauen bzw. dieses
hervorrufen'.[8]

Thucydides, with his incomparable eye for reality, did not

confuse it with the symbols and the slogans. 'First', he writes in opening his narrative of the Pentakontaetia (1.98.1), 'they (the Athenians) besieged Eion on the Strymon River', still in Persian hands, and then the island of Skyros in the north Aegean. Their populations were enslaved *and their territories were colonized by Athenian settlers*. Next Athens compelled Carystus on Euboea to join the league; clearly the 'voluntary' principle had had a very short run. Soon Naxos tried to withdraw from the league (the precise date is uncertain), only to be besieged and crushed by Athens. Naxos 'was the first allied city to be enslaved against established usage', comments Thucydides (1.98.4), employing his favourite metaphor for Athenian interference with the autonomy of the subject-cities in the empire.

Of course the Athenian empire underwent significant changes in the more than half a century of its existence. So has every other empire of similar (or longer) duration in history. To establish and explain the changes is a valid historical concern, but I find it a misconceived enterprise to seek one point along a continuous line which permits us to say that there was no empire before and that there was an empire thereafter. Carystus refused to join the alliance and was forced in; Naxos sought to leave and was forcibly prevented. And they were only the first of many city-states in that position, subject to the authority of another state which acted to advance its own interests, political and material.

I do not dispute that the 'Delian league' (a modern name for which there is no ancient authority) was welcome when it was created in 478 B.C., both because of the popularity of the vengeance appeal and, fundamentally, because of the need to clear the Aegean Sea of Persian naval forces. The Persians had twice invaded Greece unsuccessfully, and no one in 478 could have had the slightest confidence that the Great King would accept the defeats passively and would not return in a third attempt. Control of the Aegean was the most obvious protective measure, and Athens successfully won the leadership of such an undertaking. An Athenian, Aristides, was given the task of fixing the amount of money or the number of ships equipped and manned which each member-state would provide for the combined league fleet. The Athenians supplied the league treasurers (*Hellenotamiai*) and the military-naval command. Within a dozen

years (the exact number depends on the date of the battle of Eurymedon, which no scholar dates later than 466 B.C.), the league's
formal objective was achieved. The Persian fleet of 200 triremes,
most of them Phoenician, was captured and destroyed in a great
land-and-sea battle at the mouth of the Eurymedon River in southern
Asia Minor. Yet the 'league' remained in existence without a moment's faltering and its membership grew, willingly or by compulsion as the case may have been in each instance, exactly as before
Eurymedon.

    The chief executant of Athenian policy in those years and the
commander-in-chief at Eurymedon was Cimon. He had been personally
in charge at Eion, and again in 465 B.C., shortly after Eurymedon,
when Thasos, the largest and wealthiest island in the north Aegean,
tried to withdraw from the alliance. After a siege lasting more
than two years, Thasos capitulated and was condemned to surrender
her fleet (henceforth paying tribute in money), to dismantle her
walls, to pay Athens a large indemnity, and to surrender the ports
and the mines she possessed on the mainland. And Cimon, of course,
far from being a 'radical democrat' or 'demagogue' like Pericles,
let alone Cleon, represented the traditional, oligarchically inclined, landowning aristocracy of Athens. Had he lived longer, he
no doubt would have opposed many of the policies adopted by both
Pericles and Cleon with respect to the empire. However, his opposition would not have been on moral grounds. There is no difference in 'harshness' between the treatment of the people of Eion
and Skyros in Cimon's day and Cleon's proposal nearly half a century later to massacre the people of Mytilene. Our sources, in
fact, do not reveal a single Athenian who opposed the empire as
such, not even Thucydides son of Melesias or his kinsman and name-
sake, the historian.[9]

    Certainly neither Athens nor her allies anticipated *all* the
consequences of the first step of association in 478, in particular what would happen if a member-state chose to 'secede'. Nor
can anyone today know what decision-making individuals in Athens
hoped or desired. What, for instance, were the long-range aspirations of Themistocles and Aristides for Athens and Athenian power?
The Delian league was the first of a number of major instances in
classical Greek history of the deployment of Panhellenism, with or

without the name, 'to justify the hegemony and mastery of one *polis*
over other states by proposing a common aim, war against the barbarians'.[10] Hope and aspirations do not imply a defined programme,
but their presence in Athens in 478 is demonstrated by the rapidity
with which Athens not only acquired the decision-making power for
the league but also was prepared, in manpower, ships and psychology,
to exert force in the strictest sense, to impose her decisions and
to punish recalcitrants.

This is not to underestimate the Panhellenic appeal, any more
than the real fear of further Persian invasions. The pull of ideology is never to be underestimated, nor is it easy to untangle ideology and reality. In a conflict, how does one measure the respective
importance of the two elements in determining the decision of a
weaker state? A prudent state could 'voluntarily' save itself from
the frightful consequences of resistance and 'involuntary' subjection, but some did not. An early British juridical distinction between ceded and conquered territories was soon abandoned precisely
because the two overlapped much of the time.[11] Lacking, as we do,
the data from the Athenian empire with which to attempt such refined
distinctions, we may still examine that empire operationally, that
is, analyse as best we can, and as concretely, the observed behaviour patterns, and assess the gains and the losses of both the imperial state and the subject states.[12]

For that purpose, a crude typology of the various ways in which
one state *may* exercise its power over others for its own benefit
will suffice:

(1) restriction on freedom of action in inter-state relations;

(2) political, administrative and/or judicial interference in
local affairs;

(3) compulsory military and/or naval service;

(4) the payment of 'tribute' in some form, whether in the
narrow sense of a regular lump sum or as a land tax or in some
other way;

(5) confiscation of land, with or without subsequent emigration of settlers from the imperial state;

(6) other forms of economic subordination or exploitation,
ranging from control of the seas and Navigation Acts to compulsory
delivery of goods at prices below the prevailing market price and

the like.

The present essay will focus on the economics of imperial power.
I do not imply by that concentration that the politics of the Athenian empire do not merit analysis or that economics and politics were
separable, autonomous aspects of the story. However, I have nothing
new to contribute on the foreign-policy aspect, except perhaps to
ask: Why was Athens concerned to convert other Greek *poleis* into dependent agents in inter-state relations, and, in particular, what
material benefits did Athens obtain (whether deliberately envisaged
or not) from her success in the endeavour? Interference in internal
affairs is less well understood, largely because of the inadequacy
of the evidence, and again I shall restrict myself to those measures
which either had or may possibly have had an immediate economic impact.

Because of the paucity and one-sidedness of the sources, no
narrative is possible, and that means no adequate consideration of
development and change. If what follows therefore has a static
appearance, that is not because I hold the improbable view that the
relations between Athens and her subjects were fundamentally un-
changed from 478 to 404 but because I know of no way to document
significant change, and no other way to avoid falling into the
harshness-of-Cleon trap I have already discussed. We have the impression, for example, that over the years Athens interfered with
increasing frequency and toughness in the internal affairs of some
or all of the subjects: certain criminal cases had to be tried in
Athens before Athenian juries, the right to coin money was taken
away for a period, and there were other measures. What little we
know about these actions rests almost entirely on epigraphical
finds, and although it is usually possible to offer a plausible
reason for the introduction of a particular measure at the time of
a particular inscription, there has been too much unhappy experience with the crumbling of such logic upon the discovery of a new
inscription. Besides, the dates of some of the most critical
measures, such as the coinage decree, remain the subject of open
controversy.

We know, too, that the Athenians developed a considerable administrative machinery for the empire, 700 officials, says Aristotle
(*Const. of Ath.* 24.3), about as many as the number for internal

affairs. Apart from suspicion about the duplication of the figure
700, there is no valid reason to question his accuracy. 'We do not
know enough to say that 700 is an impossible figure'[13] is needlessly
sceptical. And again the sources let us down: the evidence for the
administration is almost entirely epigraphical; it does not take us
back earlier than the Erythrae decree (*IG* I[2] 10), probably of the
mid-450s; it allows barely a glimpse into the division of functions.[14]
Nothing can be deduced from silence here: there are virtually no
Athenian inscriptions (other than dedications) before the mid-fifth
century, and even the tribute drops from sight between the original
assessment by Aristides and 454. We may safely assume, I believe,
that administrative officials (both military and civilian, in so
far as that distinction has any meaning in this context) other than
the *Hellenotamiai* began to appear at least as soon as there was
resistance to membership, that their numbers increased and so did
their duties and powers as the years went on. No long-range or
systematic Athenian planning is implied in that assumption. What
is indisputable is the existence and scale of this administration
in the end, not only very large by Greek standards but also, as has
apparently not been noticed, relatively larger than the formal administration in the provinces of the Roman empire.

II

In any study of the Athenian empire, two of the categories in my
typology - military-naval service and tribute - must be considered
together, because they were manipulated together by Athens for most
of the history of the empire. When the league was founded, the
member-states were divided into those which contributed cash and
those which contributed ships together with their crews. As time
went on, the latter group was whittled down until only two members
remained, Chios and Lesbos, although others are recorded as having
contributed a few ships to a campaign on a few later occasions, as
did Corcyra, an ally outside the league. We have no list of the
original muster of ship-contributing states nor any statement of
the principles on which the states were assigned to one category or
the other.[15] In a general way it is obvious that ships would have
been required of the larger maritime states with proper harbour
facilities, not of inland states or of very small ones. Honour

would have also played its part. In 478, at any rate, Chios or
Lesbos would not lightly have surrendered their warships and everything that their possession implied; a few decades later, they pathetically clung to their continued ship-contribution as a symbol
of 'autonomy' in contrast to the tribute-paying mass of subject
states.[16]

However, if the surviving ancient texts fail us on the situation at the foundation of the league, Thucydides is explicit
enough about the reason for the change in the pattern: 'reluctance
to go on campaign led most of them, in order to avoid serving
abroad, to have assessments made in money corresponding to the expense of producing ships' (1.99.3). 'To avoid serving abroad' cannot be taken at face value: these states had not in the past built,
equipped and manned warships merely in order to repel attackers,
and there are enough instances of their willingness to 'serve
abroad'. Now, however, they were serving an alien, imperial state
on its terms and at its command. Hence the reluctance, which first
showed itself in a refusal to meet the required contributions
(Thuc. 1.99.1), and after the high price of refusal had several
times been revealed, turned into the most abject surrender, the
conversion of the 'league' fleet into an Athenian fleet in the nar-
rowest sense, part of it consisting of ships confiscated from the
subjects (Thuc. 1.19) and another part paid for out of their annual
tribute. Thucydides openly condemns the subjects for thus reducing
themselves to impotence. But I suggest that the difference in
naval power between 478 and, say, 440 was basically only a quantitative one. Athenian control of the combined fleet was near enough
complete at the beginning to justify H.D.Meyer's judgement that the
league was 'from the moment of its creation an Athenian instrument
of compulsion (*Zwangsinstrument*)'.[17]

Some of the purposes for which the instrument was employed
will be considered later. Here I want to examine the financial
implications, without resorting to the arithmetical guessing-games
that litter the scholarly literature. The few figures in the surviving sources are too skimpy, too unreliable, and often too contradictory to underpin the mathematics, and the epigraphical data
add to the confusion rather than help to clear it. I shall therefore restrict myself to a few considerations *exempli gratia*, none

of which is undermined by a large margin of error.

First, however, it is necessary to get rid of two fetishes. One is a single numeral: 'The original tribute assessment totalled 460 talents' (Thuc. 1.96.2). It requires a powerful will to believe to accept that figure as credible, and a mystical faith to bring contributions in ships within the total.[18] The expenditure of ingenuity in the attempt to reconcile 460 with other amounts scattered among the sources could be indulged as a harmless pastime were it not that they divert attention from the realities of the situation. The objective was a fleet, not coin, yet scholars debate whether Aristides began his survey with a target of 460 talents or merely ended his work with a bit of meaningless addition, producing the meaningless total of 460. Can it be seriously suggested that in the early fifth century B.C. anyone would have begun the difficult task of assembling a coalition fleet by setting a target in cash, not in ships? And what is the point to a tribute total without a ship total, of which there is not a trace in the sources?

A major difficulty in the attempts at reconciliation is created by the totals of payments, normally under 400 talents, that appear (or are conjectured) on the 'Athenian tribute lists', a group of inscriptions which collectively are my second fetish.[19] Their discovery and study have of course been the greatest modern boon to our knowledge of the Athenian empire, but it has become necessary to insist that the 'tribute lists' are not a synonym for the empire, and that they do not represent the whole of the monetary inflow into Athens from the empire. I believe that the only figure of money income from the empire which can be defended, both substantively and contextually, is the one Thucydides (2.13.3) attributes to Pericles at the beginning of the Peloponnesian War - 600 talents. The tribute was the largest component, but from the viewpoint of Athens it was fiscally irrelevant whether the cash arrived as tribute, as indemnities or as income from confiscated mines.[20] But even if my faith in 600 talents should prove to be ill-founded, my analysis of the financial implications of the empire would not suffer in the least.

The figure of 600 talents certainly did not include the 'cash value' of ship-contributions, by then restricted to Lesbos and

Chios. For the earlier period of the empire, however, it is essential to obtain some notion of the relative burden of the two types
of contribution.[21] Unfortunately, the cost of building and equip-
ping a warship is unknown; the widely quoted figure of between one
and two talents in the mid-fifth century is a guess, but it will
serve our purposes. The normal life of a trireme was twenty-plus
years, against which must be offset damage or loss in storms, ship-
wreck and battles, all varying greatly from year to year and in-
calculable. Then there was much the largest cost item, the pay
for the crews, 200 in round numbers on each trireme, 170 of them
rowers. That ranged from one third or one half a drachma early in
the fifth century to one drachma a day at the beginning of the
Peloponnesian War, or one talent per ship per month at the higher
rate. Again there are too many uncontrollable variables - the
number of ships on regular patrol duty, on guard duty or on
tribute-collecting assignment, the number and duration of campaigns
year by year and the number of participating warships, the number
of days devoted annually to training, essential for the rowers in
triremes,[22] the share of 'allied' ships in the total activity of
the league in all these respects.

We must therefore attempt a comparative assessment without
precise figures, and one fairly late instance will serve as a point
of departure. In the spring of 428 B.C. ten triremes from the
Lesbian *polis* of Mytilene arrived in the Piraeus 'according to the
alliance' (Thuc. 3.3.4). The ten triremes, Blackman writes, were
'a small squadron for routine service; more could of course be
called for if necessary for a particular campaign'.[23] Yet this
small squadron cost Mytilene five talents a month in pay, at the
half-drachma rate, in addition to the costs of construction, maintenance, repair and equipment. The fragmentary 'tribute lists'
for the years 431-428 show such annual tribute payments, in round
numbers, as 10-15 talents from Abdera, 10 from Lampsacus, 15 or
16 from Byzantium, 9 from Cyzicus - all in the higher range of
recorded contributions, not exceeded by more than half a dozen or
so states. The comparison with the cost of ships' crews therefore suggests that, once the Persian fleet was shattered at Eurymedon, the move by the subject-states to shift from ships to tribute was motivated not only by patriotism and love of freedom but

also by public finance. For the maritime states, tribute often
meant a reduced financial burden, in some years a substantial reduction. One comparative figure may help assess the burden: the average annual outlay on the Parthenon, a very expensive temple, was
30-2 talents,[24] equal to the highest recorded tribute, a sum which
the crews of twelve triremes would have earned in pay (at the lower
rate) in one five-month sailing season (and there were times when
warships remained at sea outside the 'normal' season).

Two offsetting considerations are commonly introduced into the
calculation, as in the following statement by Blackman: '... but
the pay was mainly if not entirely going to their own citizens. A
long season probably meant active campaigning rather than routine
patrols, and this gave greater hope of booty to offset expenditure.' They 'may well have expected to cover their costs as a result; this was probably the case in the early years, at least until after Eurymedon and perhaps until the early 450's.'[25] The
'social welfare' consideration may be dismissed out of hand: it is
not a fifth-century conception, especially not among the oligarchies which still controlled some of the larger maritime states:
besides, many of 'their own citizens' quickly found employment as
rowers in the Athenian navy. As for booty, which everyone no doubt
hoped for, so long as they had to campaign and fight, there is
little evidence in the ancient sources about any campaign during
the relevant period except for Eurymedon. The silence of the
sources is not a compelling argument on one side, but it seems to
me impermissible on the other side to fill out that silence with
'may well have expected to cover their costs'. As for Eurymedon,
it is a flight of the wildest imagination to think that the Delian
league gambled its combined fleet, with their men, and the independence of Greece on a major naval battle chiefly, or even significantly, for the booty they would collect if they won.[26]

Large-scale naval (and military) engagements were both expensive and unpredictable, to the participants if not to later
historians, even those with heavy advantages on one side. It required something like a full year, from about April 440 to about
April 439, for Athens to subdue Samos.[27] The island was then
still a ship-contributor and was able to muster 70 warships, 50
of them in fighting condition, and posed the further threat, real

or imaginary, of support from a 'Persian' fleet. Athens sent several large flotillas, perhaps totalling more than 150 (a portion
of which was diverted against the 'Persian' threat) and a military
force with siege equipment; she also summoned Chios and Lesbos to
make their contributions, 25 triremes together in the first year,
30 in the second. There were victories on both sides, and then an
eight-month siege forced Samos to surrender. There was considerable loss of life and material (including triremes). The financial
cost to Athens may have been 1,200 talents (though that figure is
reached by too many textual emendations for comfort). The victor's
terms included a heavy indemnity, paid to Athens, and the surrender
of the Samian fleet, marking her permanent disappearance from the
roster of ship-contributors. We have no details of the Lesbian-
Chian involvement, but each month would have cost them 12-15 talents in pay alone, and they received not a penny for their pains,
either in indemnity or in booty.

Triremes were purpose-built warships fit for no other use.
There was no interchangeability with merchant ships or fishing vessels, nor was there any other professional employment for tens of
thousands of rowers.[28] Hence, as states lost genuine freedom to
make war, there was little point, and great expense, in construct-
ing, maintaining and manning a squadron. So they sought relief by
inviting Athens to transfer them to the tribute-paying category, a
request that could not have been *imposed* on an *unwilling* Athens.
That Athens did agree indicates that she could afford the fiscal
loss as the price for a fully Athenian navy, with all that it
meant in power and self-satisfaction. She could afford it because
the state's finances were in a healthy condition, thanks to the
imperial revenues, direct and indirect. We are unable to do the
sums, just as we cannot properly calculate how Athens managed to
put aside so much of her public revenues as a reserve fund, reaching 9,700 talents at one moment (Thuc. 2.13.3). That is a pity,
but it does not alter the reality.

III

Tribute, in its narrow sense, is of course only one way that an
imperial state drains funds from subject states for its treasury.
It is probably neither the most common nor the most important, as

compared, in particular, with a tithe or a monetary tax on the land
of the subjects. Of the latter there is no trace in the Athenian
empire, and indeed there is only one recorded instance of state exploitation of confiscated property, that of the gold and silver
mines on the mainland taken from Thasos after her unsuccessful revolt.[29] These mines continued to be worked by individuals, as
they had been before - most famously by Thucydides (4.105.1), presumably as an inheritance from his Thracian ancestors - but the
Athenian state took its share of the profits, as from the mines of
Laurium at home.

It was in the area of private enrichment, not public, that
land played a major role in the Athenian empire. The number of
Athenian citizens, usually from the poorer strata, who were given
either allotments of confiscated land or, at least in Lesbos after
the unsuccessful revolt there in 428, a substantial, uniform (and
therefore arbitrary) 'rent', roughly equivalent to a hoplite's pay
for a full year, on holdings retained and worked by the islanders,
may have totalled 10,000 in the course of the imperial period.[30]
The most naked kind of imperial exploitation therefore directly
benefited perhaps eight to ten per cent of the Athenian citizen
body.[31] Some confiscations were in places from which the defeated
population had been totally expelled, but many were in areas in
which the local people remained as a recognized community, and
there the settler pattern that has dominated so much of the history of later imperialism was evident,[32] though rather in embryo
because the settlements were short-lived.

Colonies and cleruchies are not the whole story, though most
accounts of the empire rest with them, 'too preoccupied in studying the misdeeds of Athenian imperialism through official institutions and collective decisions' to give due weight to 'the action of individuals who played their part in the general con-
cert'.[33] Individual Athenians, most of them from the upper end
of the social and economic spectrum, acquired landed property in
subject territories where there were neither colonies nor cleruchies. The evidence is scarce, but one piece is remarkable enough
for a closer look. In the surviving fragments of the very detailed record, inscribed on stone, of the sale by public auction
of the property confiscated from men convicted of participation

in the double sacrilege of 415 B.C., the profanation of the mysteries and the mutilation of the herms, there are included a few landed
estates outside Attica, in Oropus on the Boeotian border, on Euboea
and Thasos, and at Abydos on the Hellespont and Ophryneion in the
Troad.[34] One group of holdings, dispersed in at least three regions
of Euboea, belonged to one man, Oionias. It went for $81\frac{1}{2}$ talents,[35]
a sum to be compared with the largest (composite) landed holding recorded for Attica itself, that of the banker Pasion at his death in
370/69 B.C., which, we are told, was worth twenty talents (Ps.Dem.
46.13).[36]

It must be emphasized that men like Oionias were not from the
classes who were assigned land in colonies and cleruchies, and that
the properties sold up following their conviction (or flight) were
not within 'cleruchic' blocks.[37] They had acquired their holdings
by 'private enterprise', though we have no idea how that was
achieved. Throughout the Greek world in this period, land ownership
was restricted to citizens, unless a *polis* by a sovereign act
granted special permission to a non-citizen, which it appears to
have done rarely and then only for notable services to the state.
It is wildly improbable that Alcibiades and his friends had each
individually been granted this privilege by Oropus, Euboea, Thasos,
Abydos and Ophryneion in gratitude for their benefactions. It is
equally improbable that only men caught up in the escapades of 415
were in this privileged group. Were it not for the chance find of
a batch of fragmentary inscriptions, we should have known nothing
about the whole operation beyond four or five off-hand general remarks in the literary sources, yet Oionias, otherwise unknown,
turns out to be one of the richest Athenians of any period in its
history. Nor, finally, have we any idea of the number of properties abroad held by the men sold up: only some twenty of the known
fifty victims have been identified in the surviving epigraphical
fragments, and by no means all of their possessions are listed in
the texts we have.

As I have already said, we do not know how these acquisitions
were brought about. Were they obtained 'legally' or 'illegally'?
Only the Athenian answer is clear: the Athenian state accepted the
legitimacy of the title and sold the estates as the property of
the condemned men. That the Athenian empire was the operative

element seems certain to me: I need not repeat what I have already said about the ambiguity of the concept of 'voluntary action', and we are here concerned with men who had influence and power inside Athens, men to be courted by subjects. It is even more certain that there was great resentment in the empire over this breach of the principle of citizen monopoly of the land, hence the Athenian concession in the decree founding the so-called second Athenian league in 378/7 B.C., that neither the Athenian state nor any of its citizens will be permitted 'to acquire either a house or land in the territories of the allies, whether by purchase or by foreclosure or by any other means whatsoever' (*IG* II^2 43.35-41). No one would have requested and been granted the inclusion of such a blunt prohibition unless there were strong feelings on the subject, which are reflected in the excessive formulation and which can have resulted only from the bitter experience of the 'first Athenian league'.[38]

IV

The moment we turn to the sixth category of my typology, 'other forms of economic exploitation or subordination', we are immediately plunged into the contentious field of Greek 'trade and politics'. On that I have stated and argued my views at length elsewhere.[39] My chief concern at present is with the consequences of Athenian imperial power in assisting individual Athenians to derive direct economic advantage other than through employment in the navy and related industries or through the acquisition of land in subject territories. Indirect gains were inevitable: power always attracts profits, as in the much vaunted plenitude and variety of commodities available in Athens, from which shippers, artisans and peddlers made gains. Many of the latter were not Athenians, however, and Hellenistic Rhodians were in the same advantageous position without the same political power behind them. Nevertheless, that such gains were a by-product of the Athenian empire is indisputable, though the magnitude of the gain cannot be measured and its place, if any, in Athenian policy cannot be deduced simply from its existence. *Handelspolitik* is not a synonym for *Machtpolitik*, no matter how often historians make the slide.

The problem can be stated in this way. Control of the Aegean
was for Athens an instrument of power. How was that instrument employed to achieve ends beyond collection of tribute, land settlement, interference in internal political arrangements, suppression
of petty wars and the more or less complete elimination of piracy?
More precisely, was it in fact employed for any ends other than
those I have just listed, and, in particular, for commercial ends?

Given the nature of the ancient economy, two of the most important and most profitable forms of modern colonial exploitation
were ruled out, namely, cheap labour and cheap raw materials; in
more technical language, the employment, by compulsion if necessary,
of colonial labour at wages well below the market wage at home, and
the acquisition, again by compulsion if necessary, of basic raw
materials at prices substantially below the market prices at home.
A third form of exploitation, which was available and which loomed
so large in republican Rome, seems to have been absent in the
Athenian empire. I refer to the lending of money to subject cities
and states at high rates of interest, usually in order to provide
the latter with the cash required by them for their tax (or tribute) payments to the imperial state. The possibilities of
Handelspolitik are therefore narrowed to competitive commercial
advantages sought by non-economic means, that is to say, by the
exercise of power without manipulating prices and wages.

The evidence is notoriously slight, almost to the point of
non-existence. In the second chapter of the *Constitution of the
Athenians*, Pseudo-Xenophon hammers the point, repeated in blunt
words in the next century by Isocrates (8.36), that imperial Athens
'did not permit others to sail the sea unless they were willing
to pay the tribute'. These two writers are so notoriously tendentious that any of their generalizations is suspect, but not *ipso
facto* false. Not so easily dismissed is the provision in the
Athenian decree of 426 B.C. allowing Methone on the Thermaic Gulf
to import a fixed amount (lost) of grain annually from Byzantium,
upon registering with Athenian officials there called *Hellespontophylakes* (Hellespont Commissioners). Similar permission was given
in the same period to Aphytis (near Potidaea). Only two texts, but
they go some way towards documenting Pseudo-Xenophon and Isocrates.
The inscriptions do not say that Methone and Aphytis could not

sail the sea without paying tribute; they say both less and more: both cities were guaranteed the right to 'sail freely' but neither could purchase Black Sea grain without Athenian permission.[40]

The presence of the *Hellespontophylakes* implies that all other cities were, or could be, similarly controlled. Whether or not the *Hellespontophylakes* represented 'a system of strict organisation'[41] cannot be determined but they deserve more attention than they customarily receive. Potentially, with the backing of the Athenian navy, they could deny any and every Greek city access to the Black Sea, and therefore access to the main seaborne route not only for grain, but also for slaves, hides and other important products. When were they installed? The temptation to label them a 'wartime measure' must be resisted. Not only does it introduce the argument from silence, about which I have already said enough, but it ignores the fact that very few years since 478 were not 'wartime' years.[42]

I do not suggest that the *Hellespontophylakes* were introduced early in the history of the empire. They were, after all, only the capstone of the structure, an organization designed to bring about a closed sea. What I do suggest is that such an aim was the automatic consequence of naval power, within the Greek *polis* system, and that steps in that direction would have been taken by the Athenians when and as they were able, and found it advantageous, to do so.[43] Short of going to war, there was no more useful instrument for punishing enemies, rewarding friends, and persuading 'neutrals' to become 'friends'.[44] And if employment of the instrument meant going to war, *tant pis*. The revolt of Thasos, Thucydides writes (1.100.2), arose from a quarrel 'about the *emporia* on the Thracian coast and about the mines the Thasians exploited'. That was as early as 465 B.C., and, though we do not know the issue dividing Athens and Thasos over the *emporia*, it can scarcely be unrelated to the 'closed sea' ambitions of the imperial state, which then simply took over the *emporia* after Thasos was defeated. Of course Athens did not yet have the ability to close the sea which she was to have later, but it is surely wrong to say that the aim itself was *unthinkable* in the 60s and 50s.[45] That is to commit the hegemony-into-empire error once again.

The question, in sum, is not when or whether the 'closed sea'
was thinkable but when and how Athens was able to close the sea to
suit herself. And why. As we shall see in a moment, Athenian purposes did not require total control, even if that were within their
reach. The Corinthian warning, in 432, that inland states would
soon learn what maritime states already knew, that Athens was able
to prevent them from bringing their produce to the sea and from
buying what they required in turn (Thuc. 1.120.2), is meaningful
but must be understood correctly in practical terms. So is the
'Megarian decree'. Not even the most monumental special pleading
has succeeded in diluting the plain words, repeated three times by
Thucydides (1.67.4, 1.139, 1.144.2), that a decree, moved by Pericles in 432, among other provisions excluded the Megarians 'from
the harbours of the Athenian empire'. All the elaborate arguments
about the impossibility of blockade by triremes and about the ease
of 'sanction-busting', founded in fact though they are, are irrelevant.[46] The Athenians claimed the right to exclude the Megarians
from all harbours, and they could have enforced that claim *had they
wished*. The long story that began with Eion and Skyros was known
to every state which had a harbour, and there were Athenian officials (as well as *proxenoi* and other Athenian friends) in every
important harbour-town.

That Athens did not wish to *destroy* Megara is patent, and significant. What she wished, and accomplished, was to *hurt* Megara
and at the same time to declare openly and forcefully that she was
prepared to employ the 'closed sea' ruthlessly as an instrument of
power. The coinage decree, whenever one dates it, was precisely
the same kind of declaration.[47] Both were expressions of *Machtpolitik* - but not, in the normal sense of that term, of *Handelspolitik*. At this point, we must introduce into the discussion the
distinction first formulated clearly in the field of Greek history
by Hasebroek, the distinction between 'commercial interests' and
'import interests' (specifically food, shipbuilding materials,
metals).[48] Athens could not survive as a great power, or indeed
as any kind of large autonomous *polis*, without a regular import on
a considerable scale of grain, metals and shipbuilding materials,
and she could now guarantee that through her control of the sea.
In not a single action, however, did Athens show the slightest

concern for private Athenian profits in this field: there were no
Navigation Acts, no preferential treatment for Athenian shippers,
importers or manufacturers, no efforts to reduce the large, perhaps
preponderant, share of the trade in the hands of non-Athenians.[49]
Without such moves, there can be no *Handelspolitik*, no 'monopolization of trade and traffic'.[50] And on this score there was no difference between the landowner Cimon and the tanner Cleon.

Many Greek *poleis*, and especially most larger and ambitious
ones, had a comparable need to import. Athens could now block
them, partially if not completely, and that was the other use of
the 'closed sea' instrument. When the Athenians sent a fleet in
427 B.C. to support Leontini against Syracuse, their real aim, explains Thucydides (3.86.4), 'was to prevent corn from being ex-
ported from there to the Peloponnese'. How often and under what
circumstances Athens used her fleet in this way in the course of
the half-century after 478 cannot be determined from the pitiful
evidence. The very existence of her navy normally made an open
display of force unnecessary, and there is no reason to think that
Athens blockaded other states merely for practice or sadistic
amusement. In the absence of genuinely commercial and competitive
motives, interference in the sailing and trading activities of
other states was restricted to specific situations, as they arose
ad hoc in the growth of the empire. Only during the Peloponnesian
War (or so it seems), which radically altered the scale of operations and the stakes, did it become necessary to make massive use
of the 'closed sea' instrument. And even then the volume of traffic in the Aegean was considerable enough for the Athenians in 413
B.C. to abandon the tribute for a five per cent harbour tax (Thuc.
7.28.4) *in an attempt to increase their revenue*.[51]

Obviously a steady flow of food and other materials was a
benefit to many Athenians individually. But to include such a
gain under the rubric, 'other forms of economic subordination or
exploitation', would strain the sense unduly.

V

'Athens' is of course an abstraction. Concretely, who in Athens
benefited (or suffered) from the empire, how and to what extent?
In what follows, I shall remain within my narrow framework,

restricting 'benefits', 'profits', to their material sense, excluding the 'benefits' (not unimportant) arising from glory, prestige,
the sheer pleasure of power. I shall also ignore such side-benefits
as the tourist attraction of every great imperial city.

The traditional Greek view is well enough known, as it was
'quantified' by Aristotle (*Const of Ath*. 24.3): the common people
of Athens, the poorer classes, were both the driving force behind,
and the beneficiaries of, the empire. Their benefits are easily
enumerated. At the head of the list is the extensive land confiscated from subjects and distributed in some fashion among Athenians. Perhaps as important is the navy: Athens maintained a
standing fleet of 100 triremes, with another 200 in drydock for
emergencies. Even 100 required 20,000 men, and, though we do not
know how many ships were kept at sea regularly on patrol duty and
for practice,[52] or how many ships campaigned for how long through
all the fighting of the periods 478-431 and 431-404, there seems
little doubt that thousands of Athenians earned their pay for row-
ing in the fleet through the sailing-season annually, and that tens
of thousands (including many non-Athenians) were engaged for longer
or shorter periods on campaigns in many years. Add the work in the
dockyards alone and the total cash benefit to poorer Athenians was
substantial though not measurable; to a large percentage of all the
poor, furthermore.

To be sure, Athens maintained a navy before she had an empire,
and continued to do so after the loss of the empire, but the later
experience demonstrates that, without the imperial income, it was
impossible to pay so large a body of crewmen regularly. Similarly
with the corn supply: Athens succeeded in maintaining imports in
the fourth century, too, but in the fifth century everyone knew
how imperial power guaranteed those imports (as it supported the
navy), even if not everyone knew the text of the Methone decree or
had heard of the *Hellespontophylakes*. And it is always the poor
who are most threatened by shortages and famines.

Finally, there was pay for office, on which Aristotle laid
his greatest stress in his attempt at quantification. No other
Greek state, so far as we know, made it a regular practice to pay
for holding public office or distributed the offices so widely.[53]
That was a radical innovation in political life, the capstone of

'Periclean' democracy, for which there was no precedent anywhere.
Fundamental radical measures require powerful stimuli and unpre-
cedented necessary conditions. I believe that the empire provided
both, the necessary cash and the political motivation.[54] 'Those
who drive the ships are those who possess the power in the state',
wrote Pseudo-Xenophon (1.2), and I have already indicated that
this unpleasant writer did not always miss the mark with his gnomic
propaganda statements.

What, then, of the more prosperous Athenians in the upper
classes, the *kaloi kagathoi*? The paradox, in modern eyes, is that
they both paid the bulk of the domestic taxes (in which I include
the liturgies) and constituted the armed forces. Yet, as we have
already seen, they also supported the imperial advance of Athens,
surely not out of idealistic or political interest in the benefits
to the lower classes. How did they benefit? Did they? There is
total silence in the literary sources on this question, save for a
remarkable passage in Thucydides (8.48.5-6).[55] During the ma-
noeuvres leading to the oligarchic coup of 411, Phrynichus spoke
against the proposal to recall Alcibiades and replace the democracy. It is false, he said (in Thucydides' summary), to think
that the subjects of Athens would welcome an oligarchy, for 'they
saw no reason to suppose that they would be any better off under
the *kaloi kagathoi*, considering that when the democracy had per-
petrated evils it had been under the instigation and guidance of
the *kaloi kagathoi*, who were the chief beneficiaries'.

Phrynichus was a slippery character and we are not obliged
to believe everything (or anything) he said in a policy debate.
However, Thucydides went out of his way, to an unusual degree, to
stress the acuity and correctness of Phrynichus' judgements,[56]
and that puts a different light on his assertion about upper-class
benefits from the empire. It at least suggests something more
than glory and power-as-such as the aims of the long line of *kaloi
kagathoi* beginning with Cimon who built, defended and fought for
the empire. The puzzle is that we are unable to specify how the
upper classes could have been the chief beneficiaries. Apart from
the acquisition of property in subject territories, I can think of
nothing other than negative benefits. That is to say, the imperial income enabled the Athenians to construct splendid public

buildings and to float the largest navy of the day without adding
to the taxpayers' financial burdens. How much of a burden the navy
could impose became clear in the fourth century. That is something, but it is hardly enough to resolve the puzzle Phrynichus
has left us with.

Be that as it may, the conclusion seems to me compelling that
the empire directly profited the poorer half of the Athenian population to an extent unknown in the Roman empire, or in modern empires. There was a price, of course, the costs of constant warfare. Men were lost in naval engagements and sometimes in land
battles, most shatteringly in the Sicilian disaster. Athenian farmers suffered from periodic Spartan raids in the first stage of the
Peloponnesian War, and even more from the permanent Spartan garrison at Decelea in the final decade of the war. The connexion between those evils and the empire was obvious, but what conclusions
were drawn? War was endemic: everyone accepted that as fact, and
therefore no one seriously argued, or believed, that surrender of
the empire would relieve Athens of the miseries of war. It would
merely relieve them of certain particular wars, and the loss of
empire and its benefits did not seem worth that dubious gain.
Athenian morale remained buoyant to the bitter end, reflecting
their calculus of the profits and the losses.

VI

No doubt the subject states would have preferred freedom from
Athens to subjection, other things being equal. But the desire
for freedom is often a weak weapon, and other things are rarely
equal in real life. I am referring not merely to the staggering
difficulties of staging a successful revolt - Naxos tried and was
crushed, Thasos tried and was crushed, later Mytilene tried and
was crushed - but to the more complex relationships inherent in
all situations of subjection and domination. 'The allies (or
subjects)' are as much an abstraction as 'Athens'. Athens had
friends in every subject city.[57] In 413, before the final battle
at Syracuse, when the position of the Athenian army had become
hopeless, the Syracusans offered the allied contingents their
freedom and a safe-conduct if they deserted. They refused and
accepted the Athenian fate. Two years later, the people of Samos

reaffirmed their loyalty to Athens and remained faithful to the
bitter end.

We do not know why the Samians reacted in this way in 411, the
Mytileneans in the opposite direction in 428. We lack the necessary information. The history of empire reveals a similarly diver-
gent pattern everywhere: the view from the imperial state is more
or less unitary, whereas the view from the receiving end varies
from community to community, and within each community from group
to group. Among some of Athens' subjects, the common people preferred democracy backed by Athenian power to oligarchy in an autonomous state. That would be one explanation of a particular reaction (though Athens did not always oppose oligarchies). In this
connexion, it is worth remembering that we are never told how the
tribute was collected *within the tributary state*. If the normal
Greek system of taxation prevailed - and there is no reason to believe that it did not - then the tribute for Athens was paid by
the rich, not by the common people. That burden would therefore
not have caused the latter any concern. In sum, the material
costs borne by the subjects were uneven, and by and large their
weight and impact elude us.

In Thucydides' account of the debates at Sparta that ended
with a declaration of war against Athens, the historian attributes the following words to an Athenian spokesman (1.76.2):

'We have done nothing extraordinary, nothing contrary to human practice, in accepting an empire when it was offered to us and
then in refusing to give it up. Three very powerful motives prevent us from doing so - honour, fear and self-interest. And we
were not the first to act in this way. It has already been a rule
that the weak should be subject to the strong; besides, we consider that we are worthy of our power.'

There is no programme of imperialism here, no theory, merely
a reassertion of the universal ancient belief in the naturalness
of domination. Looking back, the historian is free to make his
own moral judgements; he is not free to confuse them with practical judgements. Too much of the modern literature is concerned,
even obsessed, with trying to determine whether Athens 'exploited
her allies in any extensive way', 'how much exploitation and oppression took place', whether or not '*Ausbeutung*' is an applicable

epithet.   Such questions are unanswerable, when they are not meaningless.   Athenian imperialism employed all the forms of material
exploitation that were available and possible in that society.
The choices and the limits were determined by experience and by
practical judgements, sometimes by miscalculations.

6: ATHENS IN THE FOURTH CENTURY

G.T.Griffith (Gonville and Caius College, Cambridge)

In the fifth century the *arche* stands for the imperialism of Athens
in all its strength (and its weaknesses). In the fourth century
one might expect the Second Confederacy to perform a like service,
of offering the aids (*tekmeria*) through which to interpret the imperialism of this later generation of Athenians. Have they learned
something? Have they forgotten anything? In the scope of this essay there would be no point, clearly, in trying to summarize the
history of the Confederacy or its institutions, which have been
well served by studies in detail whether of the whole or of various parts.[1] It is a matter of focusing on one or two points of
interest and of querying one or two orthodoxies, even if there is
no hard evidence which refutes them. Especially, can it really be
true that the Athenians not only tried but in large part contrived
to repeat the 'confederacy-to-empire' *tour de force* for a few
years?

The most prevalent opinion seems to be that the Athenians at
heart changed little. Of Demos one could say, as of the poor
prince in another context, 'He is no better, he is much the same'.
Though *arche* had been a thing unknown in the Greek experience before the subjugation of Naxos (*para to kathestekos*), and though it
could be seen as at best an impropriety and at the worst a crime,
still it had been a crime to be proud of, not ashamed. (So 'Pericles' in 430, so 'the Mantineans' in 418.[2]) In 395, according to
the contemporary Xenophon, the Theban ambassadors at Athens, whose
mission persuaded the Athenians into alliance and started the
Corinthian War, said, 'We all know that you would like to recover
the *arche* which you had before' (*HG* 3.5.10). Xenophon was not in
Athens at the time, and his report has been discredited as unreliable, and obviously it may well be that, for several reasons;
but it is still good evidence of what Xenophon thought the Thebans
could have said (or should have said?) on this occasion. It tells
us that *arche* was still nothing to be ashamed of (if you could get

away with it). The Spartans were getting away with it at that moment, as it happened - having marched out 'to liberate the Greeks'
in 431, and again in 414. Seager, in his good study of the Athenians in the 390s, goes forward from Xenophon's proposition here to
interpret the Athenian policy from 395 onwards as aimed at a re-
gaining of the *arche*. Indeed he believes that the Athenians thought
now of their whole alliance-system of the *arche* as still in existence: when the Aegean allies were liberated by Conon in 394, 'the
unfortunate break in Athenian domination was now at an end and
could henceforth be disregarded'.[3] True, Conon liberated them
for Persia not for Athens, as Seager rightly emphasized (ibid.);
but this did not stop the Athenians from basing their policies
abroad on an assumption that it had all been done for them. They
it was that the Greek world had been waiting for as leaders (again).
We hear of no Athenian in these years (as we do see Isocrates and
others forty years later) suggesting that times have changed,
fashions have changed, the first duty of leaders, now, is to the
led (and so on).[4] Thucydides had noted that in 411 the whole political ethos of the Athenians was moulded by 'the habit of ruling
others' (8.68.4). This 'habit' produced, too, some assumptions
about leadership, and helped to form the attitudes to it of the
politicians of the 390s and 380s; see especially (for example)
Andocides *On the Peace* and the *Epitaphios* of Lysias.[5]

The Athenians perhaps were ripe to take up the empire again
from where they had been forced to drop it. The material attrac-
tions of empire were just as seductive now as ever, and the
Athenians, though they were only about 30,000 now instead of 50,000
or nearly, were no less liable to be seduced by them. The 'mass of
the people and the common soldiers' (*ho polus homilos kai strati-
otes* of Thuc. 6.24.3) needed 'pay' no less in the 390s than in 415,
and could easily be talked into voting for war as a provider of
pay in the short term, and (with luck, and in the longer term) a
provider of goodies of several kinds (booty, and new colonies, the
most obvious) as well as all the benefits to all kinds of people
that were liable to accrue from an active foreign policy and a
vigorous use of naval power.[6] For a start, there were the places
overseas which in the course of a misspent youth (of naval hegemony and rule) Athens had actually annexed and came to count as

her own territory. Nobody (in the 390s) wanted to start saying anything that could be seen as speaking out of turn, this is self-evident. But there could be no harm in stating or restating an Athenian claim to any of these places which no longer had any of their original inhabitants left in them. The Athenians, relatively weak though they still were, did state their claim to Lemnos, Imbros and Scyros; and by the Peace of Antalcidas their claim was recognized by the King of Persia and by the Greeks in general.[7]

The mentality of *arche* does not appear in the actual terms of their alliances at this time of course. As it happens, no alliance-treaty survives from the years of the Athenian revival 394-387. Before Cnidus, with Athens still 'unfortified', with the fleet still a ghost of the past, with the hoplites still bleeding from the terrible encounter with the Spartans near Nemea (Xen. *HG* 4.21.19ff.), in the treaties of 395 (with Thebes and with the Locrians) and in that of July 394 with Eretria of the old allies, one would not expect butter to melt in anybody's mouth - and it does not.[8] And the same again after the King's Peace in 386, for obvious reasons (below). But after Cnidus (and before the King's Peace), it is not even clear how many new alliances Athens did make with old allies, though no one will doubt that she made some. Seager, whose extreme position on the Athenian view of their old allies I mentioned above, is equally extreme in his view of the Athenian revival of the 390s as including a revival of the *arche*.[9] Yet at a certain level of interpretation, I can see no ground for disagreeing with him. Though the evidence is very defective, some of the symptoms of *arche* as we learned to recognize them in the fifth century (the taxation of allies to meet the costs of war, the occasional introduction of a garrison, the occasional appointment of Athenians as 'archons in the cities'), do appear in these years, just enough to leave us unhappy if we try to explain everything away in terms of 'military necessity'. Significant, too, at this same level of interpretation, is the appearance occasionally in the language of the Athenian decrees of one or other of those cliché clauses that do betray what may be called an *arche*-mentality. 'If any man kills Archippus ... etc., he shall be an exile from the city of the Athenians and from the other cities that are allies of

the Athenians ...' (*IG* II^2 24(b).3ff.). The proposer or drafter
of this Athenian decree concerned with Thasos in 389 or soon after
was doing his best to remember his manners; but his best was still
not good enough. He knew better than to say 'from the other cities
whom the Athenians *rule*', as they used to say in the bad old days
of the fifth century (*IG* I^2 56.13ff.). But he still did not know
any better than to take it for granted, simply, that the Athenian
jurisdiction extended beyond the frontiers of Athenian territory
and into the territory of all the allies of Athens. Or again,
'And if the Eteocarpathians need anything, the Coans and the
Cnidians and the Rhodians and any of the allies that are able in
that vicinity, are to do them any service in their power.'[10] Not
only Ctesias who drafted this, but also the citizens who voted for
it and made it 'law', had been indeed for more than half a century
(as Thucydides had put it) 'in the habit of ruling others'. Likewise (or not so very differently), 'Her Britannic Majesty's Principal Secretary of State for Foreign Affairs Requests and Requires
in the name of her Majesty all those whom it may concern to allow
the bearer to pass freely without let or hindrance, and to afford
the bearer such assistance and protection as may be necessary.'

I mention this Secretary of State, and his pretensions expressed on the passport of British subjects, as a reminder that we
probably do need to be careful about the level on which we interpret our bits of evidence about Athens at this time. Since 1945
or not long after, no British Secretary of State has been in a
position to 'require' anything of any foreign government, not even
that it should do what it has undertaken to do by treaty. Since
the Suez fiasco of 1956, there is no excuse for anybody, anywhere,
taking the Secretary's 'require' seriously, and so far as one
knows nobody ever has. The Athenians, too, of the 390s had no
excuse for being deluded by a too-grand word or phrase. Aegina
stared them in the face across the Gulf, 'the eyesore of the
Piraeus': it was in the hands of the enemy, the base from which
he squeezed Athenian seaborne trade.[11] While this was so (and it
was always going to be so unless Athens could re-create the resources which had overpowered Aegina before), no Athenian citizen
could conceivably think that he was starting up an Empire again
when he made a few alliances with this city or that in the Aegean,

whatever nonsense borrowed from the vocabulary of *arche* the wind-
bag politician might have written in to his *psephisma* about it.
And not only the Athenians; 'the Greeks' too knew the difference
between Athens then and Athens now. We need to remind ourselves
of this perhaps, when we notice, fascinated, the former victims of
Athens re-entering into association with her. They will not have
seen Demos or his advisers as reformed characters now. But they
will have seen him as very much the worse for wear, and not in the
least capable of great crimes, however evil his hopes or intentions.

Even the old symptoms, then, if we detect them, are not telling us necessarily of the old disease. When we read of the Athenians in 389 levying money for the war from their allies, ten per
cent at the Bosporus, five per cent on seaborne cargoes,[12] when we
hear of a garrison, or even of an Athenian archon, in an allied
city, it is not enough to recognize these Greek nouns and instantly
congratulate ourselves on recognizing how quickly the Athenians
were back in business again. It is wiser to try to see the context
in these years as the Athenians themselves and 'the Greeks' could
see it; that is, to see Athens strong again as compared with her
years of impotence (403-394), but still impotent compared with her
years of strength. No Greeks in the 390s or 380s were put in a
panic by the name *eikoste* (five per cent), any more than mid-
nineteenth-century Europeans were panicked by the name Napoleon
Bonaparte popping up again as Emperor of the French. In the early
380s cities freed recently from Sparta were at war with Sparta now,
as was Athens. Those of them who turned again to Athens for alliance knew that this war would cost good money, like any other
naval war, and they knew that Athens, financially and fiscally the
merest ghost of her Periclean self, had no chance whatever of paying for it alone, and that the Persian money had dried up for the
time being. All allies would have to pay something; the *eikoste*
need have come neither as surprise nor grievance to anybody.

As to garrisons in cities, still more to Athenian archons in
cities, though the past Athenian record is an invitation to interpret any new instances strictly, the context of each case is still
important. For garrisons, the exigencies of war do provide a
'blanket' cover in all the years before 386, for what that is
worth; but as it happens the only two Athenian garrisons that we

hear of before 386 prove to have almost impeccable credentials.
The one is a garrison (for Clazomenae) discussed at Athens in the
Assembly, which decided against it (below, p.133). This garrison,
then, never happened. The other is a garrison on Carpathus which
we know of only from the record of the Athenian decision to withdraw it (its installation at some time in the years 394-390 was
pretty well justified by exigencies of war, it may be thought).[13]
Much more equivocal is the instance at Thasos, the only one known
in these pre-386 years, of an Athenian archon appointed to an allied city. The decree which includes this appointment is the one
quoted above (p.129) for its use of a phrase betraying '*arche*-
mentality' in its proposer. Presumably 'an archon to Thasos' *was*
'appointed right now' (*autika mala*) (*IG* II^2 24(b).12ff.); and by
any standards this must be counted a serious matter. Juridically
speaking, 'an archon to Thasos' is indefensible, incompatible
with Thasian sovereignty and autonomy. Pragmatically speaking,
the functions and character of Athenian 'archons in the cities'
will have varied greatly from place to place, from case to case.
At worst, an Athenian archon in a punitive context can have been
an autocrat like a Spartan harmost. At best, he may have been
more like an agent or a consul (in the modern sense) than like a
governor; and especially (depending on personalities) his presence in a city may have been a positive advantage to it on occasions when an Athenian general stormed in, needing money desperately to pay his crews.[14] Above all, the general context is
vital for interpreting what the appointment of an archon really
meant. Juridically indefensible at any time, and genuinely a
sign of subjection (*douleia*) when Pericles proposed it, was it
still a sign of *douleia* if a Thrasybulus or an Agyrrhius proposed it in the dicey 390s or 380s, when it was manifest to all
that Athens was no more capable of 'enslaving' Thasos than she
was capable of facing Spartan hoplites and making them run, or
of manning 200 triremes and paying their crews? I doubt it.
I can see the Thasians irritated by this appointment, but I do
not see them shaking in their shoes. It was ham-fisted perhaps,
but to call it tyrannical might be to dignify it unduly.

By contrast at Clazomenae (where, again, the question of an
archon was raised) the Athenians will have been seen in 387 as

veritable models of correct deportment. 'Concerning an archon and
a garrison the [Athenian] *demos* is to decide by vote at this meeting whether to put them in at Clazomenae, or whether the *demos* of
Clazomenae is to be free to decide whether it is willing to receive
them or not.' And concluding the same long record, 'The *demos* voted
that they pay no additional taxation [beyond the five per cent tax
mentioned earlier], that they receive no garrison and no archon, and
they are to be free just like the Athenians.' The worst that can be
said against this exemplary decision is that in an ideal world such
decisions ought to be unnecessary, their purport taken for granted.[15]
But let there be no mistake about the sensitive nature of Clazomenae's place in the scheme of things, an offshore island of Asia
and right in the front line of current operations of war. And when
a few months after this the King's Peace is made, it is in the front
line of that too. 'King Artaxerxes considers it just that the cities in Asia should belong to him, and of the islands Clazomenae and
Cyprus; the remainder ...' (Xen. *HG* 5.1.31). Certainly there were
several good reasons why the Athenian *demos* should watch its next
step where Clazomenae was concerned.

As to all this, the King's Peace itself came as an excellent
rule of thumb, no doubt. The decree of Aristoteles reinforced it.
From this time forth *arche* is outlawed, in general by the keywords
'free and autonomous', in particular by the prohibiting of its more
obvious symptoms; tribute (*phoros*), garrisons, governors (*archontes*).
Sparta had accepted the rule of thumb, conveyed as it was from the
King by their own Antalcidas; but the Spartans did not immediately
choose to comprehend all its implications, or they were able to
give a passable imitation of people who had not yet comprehended it
all (so the antics of Phoebidas and Sphodrias seem to be saying,
and their condoning by the Spartan 'establishment' does nothing to
contradict them (Xen. *HG* 5.2.25-35, 5.4.20-33, etc.)). This gave
the opportunity to Athens, 'in order that the Lacedaemonians may
allow the Greeks, free and autonomous, to live at peace and in full
and secure possession of their own territory' (Tod 123.9-12), to
advertise their own new alliance system now (378-377); no *arche*,
this, but a genuine and respectable hegemony, in which each ally
shall be 'free and autonomous, under the form of government of its
own choice, admitting no garrison, accepting no *archon*, paying no

phoros, but on the same terms as Chios and Thebes and the other allies' (Tod 123.19-25).[16] The rules were all here, written in; and
in addition there was that very popular rule forbidding Athenians
to own land or property in the territory of allied states (Tod.
123.25-31, 35-46). In this way a repetition of the fifth-century
cleruchies was ruled out. At the moment of its foundation the new
confederacy offered both to Athens and to the Aegean cities the
thing that they most wanted and needed and at a reasonable cost,
security against Sparta. Was it reasonable to think that, taking
a much longer view too, these people could reckon that their best
hopes for the future lay in holding together?

The answer to this question seems clearly 'Yes', they did
reckon this. Alliances of this nature, in which a group of allies
gathered round a *hegemon*, had always started from a tacit assumption
(if no more) of permanence, if only because the *hegemon* assumed it
if nobody else did.[17] But it is interesting to see that still in
384, when cities forming alliances needed very much to mind their
Ps and Qs (because of the King's Peace with all its implications),
Athens and Chios write in to their alliance the clause 'and the alliance is to be for all time'.[18] Surprising that these allies, who
are being so careful about the terms of their alliance,[19] do not
see *this* as one of the things that they need to be careful about?
Perhaps because this was an alliance between two individuals, of
equal status, and not a corporate arrangement or part of one? Between individuals of equal status, 'for all time' meant 'for the
foreseeable future and so long as the general background of things
remains as it is'? Men of sense in Athens, and in Chios, would
always know this? Yes indeed (let us say). But this same clause
in the treaty's solemn undertaking did become built in to the corporate agreement of the Second Confederacy in a few years' time
('free and autonomous ... and on the same terms as the Chians and
Thebans and the other allies', Tod 123.23-5). The states that
joined joined 'for ever', as the surviving alliance document of
Corcyra confirms (headed 'Alliance of the Corcyraeans and the
Athenians for all time', Tod 127.1-2). How solemn was this, we
wonder? There was room for disagreement, obviously, or for interpretation at different levels.

Meanwhile, however, the Confederacy seems well designed to

give Athens a hegemony while denying her an *arche*. Especially, the Council of allies (*sunhedrion*) underlined the difference between the two things. The 'allies' under the *arche* had had no voice or vote in the taking of decisions. But there is no reason to think that this *sunhedrion* now was a mere formality or a rubber stamp.[20] Its existence is not an absolute insurance against *douleia*, but it must have been quite a strong deterrent, in the sense that the Athenians could be sure that nothing that happened now would go unremarked. Every move in the busy relationships of *hegemon* with each of the allies, each difference of opinion on policy, every quarrel about money, could now (and this means would, now) achieve a publicity loud and clear in the Council's debates. It is this that helps to make academic, largely, some of the questions that are the natural questions for us now (as for the principals then, in the earliest days of the alliance). The taxation, for instance, that raised the money which year after year needed to be raised while war went on. It was called, we see, *suntaxis* now, and we remember that the well-hated *phoros* had been banned by the treaty.[21] Was this, then, just a cynical joke (as Theopompus seems to imply), or a bureaucratic reluctance to call a spade a spade? Ignorant as we are of most of the details of *suntaxis*, it still seems clear that the rate of this taxation was not very high (comparable to the fifth-century rate under Pericles, probably, rather than under Cleon), and that there was no prospect whatever of the Athenians being able to use it to build up a reserve fund.[22] On the contrary, their war finances were always hand to mouth at this time.[23] The *phoros* of the fifth-century *arche*, a novelty then and in some ways a sort of miracle, had been prize-money on a scale quite unrepeatable now. Athens was not in it now for the money: the money was chickenfeed compared with the great days of old.

This Confederacy of seventy or more states in the twenty years of its period of success (377-357) cannot truly be said to have become an Athenian *arche* in the same sense as the Delian Confederacy a century before. The well-known symbols of 'subjection' (*douleia*), the garrisons in cities, the Athenian 'governors' (*archontes*, *epimeletai*), do appear, but the number of instances known is very small compared with the fifth-century record, and most of them seem well justified by a state of war and emergency at the time.[24] Only at

Ceos, and perhaps at Naxos, can we see an interference with the
city's autonomy which looks sinister.[25] Ceos, we see, had tried
to secede from the alliance.[26] Secession was not allowed, any
more than it was allowed to Megara by Sparta in 460. No *hegemon*
was going to allow it unless obliged, for the obvious reasons.[27]
On the other hand member-states of the Confederacy (or at least
important ones) were allowed to 'answer back' now and to complain
in public. This seems a necessary inference from the inscription
which preserves part of an Athenian reply (proposed by Callistratus) to messages from Mytilene, in which Athenian policy *vis-à-
vis* Sparta evidently had been criticized.[28] This in 369-368 B.C.,
when Sparta, so recently the aggressor against whom this confederacy for mutual protection had been formed, became now an ally
in great need of care and protection itself. The allies of a
hegemon always might expect to find themselves fighting in quar-
rels which meant much more to the *hegemon* than to them; and in
this instance neither the Mytilenaeans nor any single one of the
allies was shocked by the Theban victory at Leuctra in the way
that the Athenians had been shocked by it, or shared the Athenian
determination not to let Sparta go under, or the Boeotians go
top.[29]

     This was one factor making for trouble between *hegemon* and
allies, the wider interests and involvements of the *hegemon*, for-
ever acting or reacting to developments in central Greece or in
the Peloponnese for which most of the allies cared not at all.
Another factor (which is really an extension of the first) was an
Athenian practice of making separate alliances on the side, with
states or potentates who became allies without becoming members
of the Confederacy. Such were (almost certainly) Amyntas III of
Macedonia perhaps as early as 375, Jason of Pherae by 373, Dionysius I of Syracuse in 367, to say nothing of a number of kings in
Thrace, Paeonia and Illyria, and presently Philip of Macedon himself.[30] The more important the potentate, obviously, the more
unthinkable that he would have accepted Athenian hegemony by
joining the confederacy; but even with the less important kings
of the north, there were reasons of instability and incompati-
bility that made them inappropriate as members while still acceptable as allies. These alliances could still be of use and benefit

to the Confederacy as a whole, and probably there is no need to see anything sinister in them, or objectionable.

More questionable however was the making of separate alliances with individual *cities*, especially when it is recalled that so far as we know no new members at all were ever admitted to the Confederacy after 371 (though the Euboean cities were readmitted when they reverted from the Boeotian alliance to the Athenian in 357).[31] These new acquisitions of Athens in the 360s included the northern cities Methone, Pydna and Potidaea, besides Samos, the Thracian Chersonese except Cardia; and after the Peace of 362 they formed alliances with Arcadians, Achaeans, Elis and Phleious, and with the Thessalian League. The last two need not delay us, for the Athenian motives here represent most obviously an insurance against the Boeotians and their allies and against Alexander of Pherae, while the Peloponnesians and the Thessalians on their side had no need at all to accept Athenian hegemony by joining the Confederacy. In each case they became the allies 'of the Athenians and their allies';[32] and they were capable of looking after themselves, if Athens had had designs on them of some improper kind. Vigilant critics have sought reasons, and rightly, for what seems to be a 'closing of the list' by Athens (the list of the decree of Aristoteles, where every one of the fifty-three or so member-allies whose names survive belongs to the very first few years after 378).[33] But these two instances of the Peloponnesians and the Thessalians are not the ones that are to show us Athens behaving like an imperial power. Rather the reverse: if these people would not join as members anyway - and nothing would make them: why should they? - the form of the two treaties as they stand is a sign of 'correctness' on the part of the *hegemon* acting in consultation and cooperation with 'the allies'.

It is the single cities which associate with Athens but without becoming members, that rouse our suspicions (aided as we are by hindsight). Something does seem to be going on, we see; and it may be by design. The decree of Aristoteles, by its clause prohibiting land ownership by Athenian citizens in the territory of any member-state of the Confederacy (p.134 above), purported to rule out this the most attractive and worth-while of all the material rewards of empire, colonization on land belonging to somebody else. So far as we know, the Athenians honoured this undertaking scrupulously, at least till after the great war of secession that ended in 355. Before that date we know of no cleruchy, or colonization in any form, on the territory of allies who were members of the Confederacy. Our information admittedly is not fully complete: only fifty-three or so names survive on the 'Aristoteles' stone out of the seventy or more members (D.S. 15.30.2, Aeschin. 2.70). And the very earliest (fourth-century) Athenian cleruchy that we learn of, belonging almost certainly to the year 370-69, was bound for a destination unknown to us.[34] But all the identifiable Athenian cleruchs went to places which became associated with Athens after 371, and most probably without their ever becoming Confederacy members. This was the generation in which Athens in most years had about two-and-a-half quite good generals simultaneously. In the 360s especially were some notable successes. In 365 Timotheus took possession of the island of Samos after a blockade and siege. A year or two later, in the north, Methone and Pydna and Potidaea came over to Athens. In 353 Chares had recovered Sestos, whence followed a reoccupation of the Chersonese. We see cleruchies go out presently to Samos, Potidaea, and the Chersonese. Samos and Potidaea certainly were not members of the Confederacy: the Chersonese cities may have been, but it seems far from certain.[35]

If there was room now for more spacious moves in foreign policy, here or there, might it be a pity, perhaps, to deny oneself something interesting merely because the terms of the decree of Aristoteles ruled it out?[36] Unfortunately only once (so far as I know) are we favoured with a contemporary expression of opinion on just this question, of admitting a new ally to the Confederacy, or not admitting him, when the alliance is made. Aeschines in retrospect was indignant (or professed to be) because Demosthenes had connived with Callias of Chalcis that Chalcis and other Euboean cities should become allies without joining the Confederacy (in 341). As he put it, 'they quietly relieved you of the *suntaxis* of Oreus and of Eretria, the ten talents'; 'he proposed a motion that you elect ambassadors to go to Eretria and beg them ... to pay their *suntaxis* no longer to you, the five talents, but to Callias'; 'his motion that the ambassadors require the people of Oreus, too, to pay their five

talents not to you but to Callias' (Aeschin. 3.94 and 100; cf. 91
and 93). Naturally Aeschines makes much of the loss to Athens of
the *suntaxis* of cities which were allowed here to be allies without rejoining the Confederacy - thanks to Demosthenes! We would
not expect him to make much of any prospects of cleruchies in
Euboea which these arrangements might have opened up. But in
truth of course there were no prospects of cleruchies in Euboea
here and now. The Euboeans now were forming their own Euboean
Confederacy with Chalcis its *hegemon*, and were just as capable of
looking after themselves as the Peloponnesians in 362 and the
Thessalians in 361-360 (above p.137).[37]

But with the isolated cities of the north and the small cities of the Chersonese things could be different. If they became
allies without the safeguards of the decree of Aristoteles, they
could be thought to offer some temptation, perhaps, to the Athenians. Their *suntaxis* payments individually were modest enough,
and could not compare as an attraction with a colonial prospect.
To provide permanently for some hundreds, perhaps thousands, of
poor citizens as cleruchs was unquestionably the most substantial
and direct economic gain that the Athenian state could possibly
hope for at this date. If it could be done, it was emphatically
worth doing, unless the moral or political consequences of doing
it were going to be disastrous.

Most intriguing in this context is the case of Samos. Samos
was not a small, weak island or one geographically in Athens'
pocket (like Andros or Ceos). But in the long siege which won
Samos the Athenians were overcoming virtually a Persian or pro-
Persian garrison and a government of oligarchs (a tyrant and his
circle); they were not fighting the Samian *demos* (Isoc. 15.111;
Dem. 15.9f.). Nor had they any business to fight the Samian
demos of course, now or ever, if they remembered their love affair of 405, and its renewal in 403. No other allies (except
the Plataean remnant) had ever been honoured and cherished like
the Samian *demos* in 405, granted the Athenian citizenship *en masse*
(at the one moment in the history of Athens when to possess it
was a real and deadly danger to all possessors).[38] In 403 the
grant was confirmed (and when the danger was over); but with no
discernible effect on the political behaviour or standing of

Samos in the years after.[39] When both cities free themselves from Sparta (in 395 and 394 respectively) they do not come together, and so far as can be seen the Athenian gesture was as abortive in reality as Churchill's corresponding gesture to the French in 1940.

Presumably there can be no question, then, (attractive though the notion might be) that the Athenian annexation of Samos in or after 365, and the sending of Athenian cleruchs, was no more than a marriage of true minds and a fusion by consent of good democrats with good democrats, fused as they were already in law, by the decrees of 405 and 403. The union was a more earthy affair, we may be sure, though there is no need to doubt that the Samian *demos* may perhaps have welcomed an Athenian 'presence' now which got their own upper class off their backs. The lands for the. cleruchs will have been found from the estates of these newly-exiled and unpopular Samians. All good democrats, Samians, Athenians, and Athenian cleruchs at Samos, shared a common interest in continuing always to make absolutely sure that not one of those exiles ever came back.

This is how it could be in 365 at least, and while the honeymoon was still on. But as is well known, this is a sad and a cautionary tale which even ended by 'winning out into mythology' (the *muthos* of an Aesop rather than a Herodotus). It was Samos, alas, that made of 'the Attic neighbour' the Greek counterpart to our 'cuckoo in the nest'.[40] The details of the colonization are still not wholly established, but the first cleruchy certainly was sent there in 365/364.[41] There may have been a second in 361-360 (Aeschin. 1.53 and Schol.). But it was the sending of 2,000 cleruchs in 352/1, evidently, that really made Samos an Athenian possession, and reduced 'the Samians' to exiles.[42] Whether or no we believe the writer (Heraclides) who wrote 'They expelled them all', it is clear enough that in the end most of the Samians did find themselves exiles, whether they had quitted Samos by compulsion or by their own choice. The rich and desirable island ended firmly in Athenian hands, with some thousands of former Athenian thetes now comfortably settled as farmers there. This was really the biggest imperialist coup since the colonizing on Lesbos by the cleruchs sent there after the revolt of Mytilene (Thuc. 3.50.2).

The opening up of this policy in Samos in 365 was followed

quickly, we have noticed, by a second enterprise of the same kind
in the north, at Potidaea. It will have been a smaller affair
than Samos, no doubt; but it still looks as if 'the cleruchs of
Potidaea' of the Athenian decree of 361 may be a second batch,
sent now by request of a first batch already there.[43] These are
the years, too, when Athenian generals repeatedly tried to get
possession of Amphipolis, that genuine *apoikia* of the fifth century, offering full scope for the sending of new colonists, in
this place quite outside the safeguards of the decree of Aristoteles. An adventurous foreign policy, in the north especially,
but at Samos too by a piece of opportunism, could bring this of
solid advantage to the *demos* of Athens. The same adventurousness
and its results could have effects, perhaps, and repercussions on
the allies of Athens deeper than is at once obvious.

It has never been easy to explain just why the war of secession broke out in 357. When full weight has been given to the
occasional breaches of the decree of Aristoteles by Athens that
we know of, and to the occasional exuberances of Athenian foreign
policy to the advantage of Athens alone, it still seems clear
that in 360 there is no *arche*, no general *douleia*, in the sense
that there had been in 440; unless it is *douleia* to be unable to
make a free choice about seceding. This last is a very important
matter, obviously, and we see, still in the 360s, Byzantium and
Ceos and others being treated as enemies when they tried to secede - and of course again in 357 when Chios, Rhodes and others
tried and were successful. What made them try this time? Not
just as a matter of principle, one supposes (however unreasonable,
frustrating, maddening, to be forbidden). There was no tyranny
or terror. The *sunhedrion* still met and voted on what to do with
this year's *suntaxis*.[44] But is it fanciful to think that this
story of Samos, the story that was 'winning out into mythology'
before their eyes, might have been very influential?[45] True, it
was not till 352, or after, that the cuckoo finally cleared the
nest. But for the large, prosperous island-allies like Chios and
Rhodes the whole tale of Samos may have been seen as cautionary,
not just the end of it; the tale of how this large, prosperous
island could be besieged and won, its Persians and pro-Persians
sent packing, its good democrats jollied along by Athenian

democrats, and then the cleruchs arriving. However many or few
the cleruchs of the first wave, or first two waves (above, p.140),
they were, really and truly, that number too many; for no state or
people needs help from outside in making the best use (its own) of
its own territory. Samos had got into this mess by keeping bad
company, in a way that invited a 'liberation'. It is not surprising if Chios and Rhodes now saw Mausolus of Caria as (in this context) exceedingly good company, a man of real substance where the
meddler at Samos had been no more than a man of straw.

In 357, then, it could be a good time to have it out with
Athens. And then the second big surprise about this war of secession: it was really such a very small war when it came to it,
and when all was said and done. After only two summers and battles only mildly disastrous by the standards of Athenian fifth-
century disasters, Athens was financially crippled, we are told;
and quite certainly she has lost the will to fight. In 355 peace
is made. Those allies who want to secede, may secede now, and do.
(Samos, however, has come to no harm in the war, and still awaits
its final wave of cleruchs.) This is the peace and the policy
(we presume) of Eubulus, extricating Athens from the danger of a
long and unproductive struggle.[46] It was a waste of time and money
to carry on a war to stop unwilling allies from seceding; even
when they were willing, their *suntaxis* was not really a paying
proposition. Moreover if the war went on long enough, somebody
might liberate Samos again, this time from Athens; and Samos was
a paying proposition.

Presumably there were some hard-headed notions of this sort
behind the Athenian change of attitude in 355 towards their allies and their foreign policy in general, as well as the larger,
warmer notions which Demosthenes was to complain of a year or
two later, and which we see from time to time in the writings of
Isocrates.[47] Ten years later (341 B.C.) Demosthenes could tell
the Athenians (keeping a straight face), 'You are not well designed by nature to be imperialists: your talents lie in defending
victims of imperialism and thwarting the aggressor' (Dem. 8.42).
And (mellowing?), 'No leader of the Greeks was ever yet allowed
to please himself entirely' (9.23ff.). But Demosthenes need
never have feared that the *demos* was becoming altogether soft,

and 'wet'. It was not thus that the Samians found them in 352, when the 2,000 cleruchs were sent, and 'they expelled them all'. What provoked this drastic performance we do not know. Nor do we know the provocation at Sestos in the previous year to which the Athenians replied with their most disgusting atrocity since Melos: 'Chares the general of the Athenians sailed to the Helles- pont where he captured the city of Sestos: the men of military age he slaughtered, the rest of the population he sold as slaves' (D.S. 16.34.3). This single sentence represents the sum of our knowledge about Sestos at this time. What can the Athenians have thought they were doing? What can the world have thought of it? Naturally this savage act did not inhibit Demosthenes presently from complaining often of Philip of Macedon for his treatment of the Olynthians and others. But more surprisingly (and more de- pressingly) it did not stop other Greeks from associating just as freely with Athens as though it had never happened. Mytilene had no need to remain an ally of Athens when Chios and the rest had made their point and seceded. Euboea had no need to turn to Athens again, instead of to Boeotia again, in 341. And a few months later 'the Greeks' in general had no need to listen to Demosthenes when he told them to follow Athens' lead in a war to defend freedom against Philip. In spite of Sestos, and Samos, the Greeks were not all of a tremble now about what Athens would do to them next (and rightly not). Even the odious Speusippus, who was happy to back Philip's claim to Amphipolis against that of Athens and to tell the world that Philip could not have at- tacked Olynthus (Olynthus must have attacked Philip) - even Speusippus never thought of calling on Philip to liberate Greece from the horrors of Athenian new imperialism.[48]

It is no accident, I suppose, that the Greeks had no word for imperialism; no word, that is, corresponding to our word, developed out of 'empire', and echoing 'empire' easily, if eer- ily, through many an empty mind. It is no help, probably, to fancy that we see bits and pieces of fifth-century *arche* in the nursery-tea atmosphere of the Second Confederacy. *Polypragmosyne* for the Greeks contained most of the efficient and disagreeable characteristics that imperialists are made of. Isocrates sagely reminded the Athenians once (in 355) that behaving themselves ('peace', as he called it) actually paid better than *polypragmosyne*, justice than injustice, looking after their own possessions than wanting other people's (8.26). It may well be true to say that the Athenians still were just as beastly to people as they knew how, whenever they found themselves able; but their capacity for doing harm was so much less now. They were nowhere near capable, any more, of 'enslaving' everybody. They were lucky, now, if they could enslave anybody; and (paradoxically) when they can, it is not a sign that they have become all powerful, but a sign that they are less powerful than they were; this in spite of the great navy of the 350s and later.[49] To build and maintain this fleet served some purposes, material and moral. But its utility in the foreign field was limited by the Athenian will or capacity to pay for it on active service - as appeared in 355.

They could ill-treat Sestos, Samos, because no one feared Athens much now, and no one (alas) cared for the Sestians or the Samians enough, or for freedom enough, to start a row about them. Oddly enough, it fell to Philip, arch-equivocator with Greek freedom, to liberate Sestos and Samos in 338 if he chose. Characteristically he liberated the one but not the other. Athenian imperialists (and Greek) had met their master.

7: THE ANTIGONIDS AND THE GREEK STATES, 276-196 B.C.

J.Briscoe (University of Manchester)

Wars of liberation were well known in the ancient world. They go
back at least to the time at the beginning of the sixth century
when Cleisthenes of Sicyon undertook the First Sacred War to 'free'
Delphi from the control of Cirrha.[1] When states freed by such
conflicts are called *eleutheroi* or *autonomoi* it is clear enough
that these words by no means denote what we would mean by freedom
or independence. In concluding the Peace of Nicias in 421 Athens
and Sparta found no difficulty in agreeing that certain states
φερούσας τὸν φόρον τὸν ἐπ' Ἀριστείδου αὐτονόμους εἶναι (Thuc.
5.18.5). There is no doubt, too, that the freedom granted to the
Greek states of Asia Minor by Alexander was beset by a number of
conditions and that these cities were subject to a considerable
degree of interference from Alexander's officials.[2]

During the period of the Diadochi the 'freedom of the Greeks'
was simply a slogan in the wars of propaganda conducted by the
contenders for power. In 319 Polyperchon aimed to gain the support of the Greeks of the mainland against his rival Cassander by
declaring them free,[3] and in 315 Antigonus Monophthalmus proclaimed
that all Greeks, that is, both those on the mainland and those in
Asia, were to be *eleutherous*, *aphrouretous*, *autonomous*.[4]

Once Antigonus had made this move, his opponents had little
choice but to follow his lead and the freedom of the Greeks was one
of the provisions of the peace concluded between Antigonus and his
adversaries in 311 (Diod. 19.105.1), though it appears from a letter of Antigonus to the city of Scepsis that even then certain re-
strictions on Greek freedom were explicitly mentioned in the agreement.[5] A year later Ptolemy Soter was accusing Antigonus of maintaining garrisons in Greek states in violation of the terms of the
peace of 311 (Diod. 20.19.3). It is obvious enough that the freedom of the Greek states was, as it had been under Alexander, something limited, something very much at the disposal of the person
granting it, and that the prime motive behind the policy of the

Diadochi in this respect was to gain support for their respective causes. If at any moment such freedom, or any element of it, seemed to be against the interests of the dynast concerned, it was naturally those interests that came first. Rhodes, for instance, was not allowed to be free to continue its commercial relationships as it had in the past because such freedom endangered Antigonus' interests.[6] Another clear indication of the degree of sincerity in the successors' defence of Greek freedom is the fact that while it was the policy of Antigonus to establish democratic regimes in Greek states, in the years after the battle of Ipsus his son Demetrius Poliorcetes installed a harmost in Boeotia, and, though he had 'freed' Athens, in alliance with Athenian democrats, from the tyranny of Lachares, he proceeded to abolish two of the cornerstones of the democratic constitution – election of archons by sortition and prohibition of iteration of the archonship – and, a little later, restored the oligarchs whom he himself had exiled in 307.[7] The reason that Antigonus had chosen to support democracies was not, of course, that he had any particular attachment to that form of government, but simply that Cassander was following the usual Macedonian tradition of support for oligarchies. With Cassander dead Demetrius could revert to a more normal pattern.

Demetrius' policy towards the Greeks differed from that of his father in another way. While Antigonus had been subtle in his relations with the Greek cities and had resorted to military occupation only in extreme circumstances, Demetrius had no hesitation in throwing garrisons into places that came into his possession.[8]

When Demetrius' son, Antigonus Gonatas, took advantage of the confusion that followed Seleucus' victory over Lysimachus at the battle of Corupaedium in 281 – the assassination of Seleucus by Ptolemy Ceraunus and the death of the latter at the hands of the Gallic invaders – to establish himself on the throne of Macedonia in 276,[9] he had to take fresh decisions about his relations with the rest of the mainland. Thessaly, of course, was to all intents and purposes part of Macedon, even though Polybius could say that the Thessalians were in a different category from the Macedonians themselves.[10] Euboea, with the important garrison at Chalcis, was also under virtually direct Macedonian control.[11] Otherwise, in 276 there were Macedonian garrisons only at Corinth and, probably, the Piraeus.[12]

What, though, were the choices confronting Gonatas? Though the rulers of Macedon had never claimed direct rule over Greece as a whole, there had been, over the seventy years since the battle of Chaeronea, varying and shifting degrees of interference in Greek affairs. What mattered immediately to Gonatas was to preserve Antigonid rule in Macedon itself, together, of course, with control of Thessaly and Euboea. It is wrong, I think, to see Macedon as an imperial power consciously seeking to extend its control in Greece or with a carefully worked out idea of the degree of influence it should exercise over its neighbours. The period after 280 has often been described as one of equilibrium between the main successor kingdoms. Though he was not averse to taking such opportunities as arose to increase his power, Gonatas accepted this equilibrium as much as did the rulers of Egypt and Syria, and to have aimed at complete domination of Greece would certainly have been regarded by them as a threat to it.

It is tempting to assert that if the Antigonids had abstained completely from interfering in the mainland - their long-standing possessions of Thessaly and Euboea apart - and relied on the goodwill of genuinely independent Greek states, then Rome three-quarters of a century later would have had considerably more difficulty in finding allies to fight with her against Philip. It is very doubtful, though, whether Gonatas could ever have seriously considered such a policy. In part, no doubt, this is because it would simply never have occurred to him voluntarily to abandon such positions in Greece as he already held; that would have been regarded as an indication of weakness and an invitation to Thessaly and Euboea to attempt revolt. Pericles had warned the Athenians that to give up their empire could lead to the destruction of Athens itself (Thuc. 2.63.3). Gonatas may have feared that to give up such possessions as he had in the mainland would lead to the weakening of his basic position in Macedon itself.

But equally as important was the fact that the Greek states were continuing to behave in the way they had for so long. In disputes with other states they were always willing to call in an outside power, or, as Thucydides had noted (3.82.1), one faction in a state called for such help in order to gain the upper hand over its

rivals. If Macedon had declined all such invitations, the appeals
would have been directed elsewhere - primarily, no doubt, to Egypt,
and Gonatas would certainly have seen that as a threat to his position. But if the invitations were accepted, as they often were,
it was always likely that the opponents of those who had called on
Macedon would look elsewhere for help against Macedon. Macedon was
the nearest imperial power and so the one most available. But
equally it was the one of whose interference the Greeks had most
experience, and as a result there was never any lack of anti-
Macedonian sentiment in Greece, which Rome, in time, was able to
exploit.

The difficulty that confronted Gonatas, then, was inherent in
the situation. Rome faced the same difficulty later. In 194, the
senate, at the instance of Flamininus, decided that a free Greece,
loyal and grateful to Rome, was the best defence against the aggressive intentions of Antiochus III. One important unit, the·
Aetolian League, was dissatisfied, and little more than two years
after the withdrawal of Roman forces from Greece, amid scenes of
great emotion, Antiochus invaded the mainland, and Roman troops
had to return.[13]

The situation is exemplified in the events that led to the
failure of Pyrrhus' attempt to wrest control of Macedon from
Gonatas.[14] Pyrrhus had responded to an appeal by the Agiad pre-
tender Cleonymus for help in deposing the Spartan king Areus I.
Antigonus saved Sparta from Pyrrhus and might expect some genuine
gratitude - the Spartans' spirited defence of their city against
Pyrrhus certainly suggests that there was little enthusiasm there
for Cleonymus and Pyrrhus.[15] At Argos the situation is particularly clear: of the two rival leaders, Aristeas called on Pyrrhus
'because Aristippus appeared to have the support of Antigonus'.[16]
The result must have been to leave a pro-Macedonian government in
power. In Messene counsels may have been divided. We hear both
of a Messenian embassy welcoming Pyrrhus when he reached the
Peloponnese and of Messenians helping Sparta against him (Justin
25.4.6; Paus. 1.13.6, 4.29.6).

What is unfortunately not clear is what further measures
Gonatas took in the Peloponnese at this time. A very obscure passage of Justin seems to suggest that he had governments friendly

to him in a number of Peloponnesian states (26.1.3). At some point
he adopted a general policy of installing and supporting tyrants in
Greek states. It would make sense if this policy began after the
death of Pyrrhus, but this cannot be regarded as at all certain;
only two specific cases can be securely dated to this time.[17]

    The lack of any steadfast loyalty to Antigonus was made clear
by the events of what we call the Chremonidean war. Both the causes
and the course of the conflict are obscure, and this is not the place
to discuss them.[18] What is important is that the appeal of Ptolemy Philadelphus to the Greek states to make an alliance against
Gonatas was so readily and widely accepted. Even though Athens had
rid herself of the garrison at the Piraeus a few years previously,
without any retaliation from Gonatas, even though, as we have seen,
several of the governments in the Peloponnese had good reason to be
grateful to Gonatas, yet the degree of Antigonid control and influence exercised in the mainland after the defeat of Pyrrhus, and
fear of what might happen, was sufficient to ensure a ready response
to Philadelphus' rallying call of freedom from Macedon. The call
was accepted by Athens, Sparta, Elis, Achaea, Tegea, Mantinea,
Orchomenus, Aliphera, Caphyae, and Spartan allies in Crete (*Syll*.[3]
434-5, 11.25, 39-40). Areus had clearly quickly forgotten that he
owed his position to Gonatas.

    Gonatas won the war, though exactly how remains obscure. And
it is still uncertain whether, if he had not done so earlier, he
now instituted the policy of imposing pro-Macedonian tyrants in
Greek cities. What is certain is that his treatment of Athens was
severe. The reimposition of the garrison at the Piraeus must date
from this time, and troops were also placed at other strategic
places on the Attic coast.[19] Even more important, symbolically, a
garrison was installed in the city itself, at the Mouseion. Though
the form of the constitution was maintained, Macedonian nominees
held the magistracies and there was a Macedonian *epistates* (Apollo-
dorus, *FGH* 244 F 44; Paus. 3.6.6). In 256, according to Eusebius,
Antigonus 'freed Athens'. Quite what was involved is unclear – perhaps just the removal of the Mouseion garrison, which could be represented as 'freeing' the city.[20] But the other garrisons remained,
and Athens was not yet free to choose its own officials.[21] As elsewhere, the maintenance of a garrison was not incompatible with

'freedom'.[22]

This severe degree of control shows clearly that Gonatas was
not prepared to risk any further movement against him in Greece,
especially when it was organized by one of the other successor
kingdoms. But I doubt if Gonatas asked himself whether Athens was
now to be regarded as part of the Macedonian empire. His motives
for reacting as he did were doubtless mixed. Thucydides had made
the Athenian ambassadors at Sparta in 432 talk of Athens being
driven by three factors - *time*, *deos*, *ophelia* (1.76.2). Whether
Gonatas' possessions in Greece brought any material, economic advantage we may doubt. But *time* and *deos* can well be applied to
Gonatas. If Athens were left in complete independence, he would
be afraid of further movements against him. And Athens' actions
in the Chremonidean war were a blow to Gonatas' pride, his self-
esteem (particularly in view of his intellectual links with
Athens[23]). One could rationalize this factor by reducing it to a
fear that if such actions were left unpunished, others would act
likewise. But it is not necessary to do so - irrational motives
for political actions should never be discounted.

The troubles of the early part of the reign of Gonatas gave
the Aetolian League the opportunity to pursue its growth in central
Greece undisturbed.[24] In 251 came the decisive moment in the rise
of the second great power on the mainland, the Achaean League, when
Aratus seized power at Sicyon.[25] If the Aetolian League had risen
more or less independently of Macedon, there is no sign that Aratus
was planning to act independently of the great powers - indeed he
appealed, albeit unsuccessfully, to both Antigonus and Ptolemy for
help in getting rid of Nicocles, the tyrant of Sicyon.[26] It seems
that after first accepting financial help from Antigonus, and attacking Alexander, the son and successor of Craterus as governor
of Corinth, and now in revolt against Gonatas, Aratus then turned
to support Alexander, and sought and obtained financial help from
Egypt.[27] Aratus had chosen one side in a conflict. He did not
try and indeed could not have hoped to remain independent of the
contending powers. Aratus, in fact, made the most rational choice
he could in the circumstances in which he found himself. The
Aetolians, whose rise had been tolerated by Antigonus, doubtless
felt that they would be threatened if Alexander's rebellion

succeeded and took the opposite side.[28] They, too, could not remain
aloof from the conflicts of the time.

In the 240s, then, the Achaean and Aetolian Leagues were on opposite sides and the Antigonid ruler was aligned with one of them.
For the rest of the third century, and into the second, we have a
shifting pattern in the tripartite relationship between the two
Leagues and Macedon. For most of the time it is a question of any
two of the three powers finding themselves on one side of the fence
in opposition to the third. Alexander did not last long, and Antigonus was able to regain control over Corinth and Euboea,[29] but in
243 Aratus freed Corinth, perhaps with financial support from the
new Egyptian king, Ptolemy Euergetes.[30] Just before this the Aetolians had intervened in the Peloponnese to the disadvantage of the
Achaean League.[31] The battle lines were thus clearly drawn - Ptolemy and the Achaeans on one side, Antigonus and the Aetolians on
the other. Aratus was acting as independent agent within the
limits of some severe restraints.

In 239, though, Gonatas died. And under his son Demetrius II
there was a rapid change in the situation. For instead of the
Aetolians being on the side of Macedon against the Achaeans, the
two leagues were soon united against Macedon. It was, no doubt,
Demetrius' action in accepting an appeal for help from the Epi-
rotes, who were threatened by the Aetolians, that brought about
the change,[32] though we must always reckon with that aggressive,
almost irrational streak in Aetolian behaviour that made Polybius
so hostile towards them. As for Demetrius, not much can be deduced about his motives. He was cementing the marriage-link he
had formed with Epirus and acting to check the growing power of
the Aetolian league. But in so doing he was seeking to preserve
the existing situation, not to change it. What is important for
the future, I think, is that both the large confederations were
now in opposition to Macedon and both were very conscious of the
threat posed by Macedonian power. There was to be one more change
before Rome became involved, but we already have the situation
that made Rome's task so much easier. Moreover, faced with the
alliance of the two federations, Demetrius naturally moved into
central Greece, and Boeotia and Megara came into his possession.[33]
The more states had experience of more or less direct Macedonian

control, the more anti-Macedonian parties grew up in those states
and there arose the kind of internal dissension that Rome was later
able to exploit.[34]

The major change that came over the situation in the 220s, of
course, was the complete volte-face by Aratus and his success in
persuading the Achaean League to abandon its long-standing hostility to the Antigonids and seek an alliance with Macedon. This
was the only way he could see of countering the threat from Sparta
under Cleomenes III, a threat not just to the territorial integrity of the Achaean League but of the export of Cleomenes' social
reforms - increasing the number of Spartiates, redistribution of
land, abolition of debts, which can be not too inaccurately described as a left-wing revolution.[35] Whatever the force of the
arguments that drove Aratus to adopt this policy, the result was
clear enough. For the price that had to be paid was the reinstal-
lation of a Macedonian garrison in the Acrocorinthus, which meant
de facto control of Corinth itself.[36] At a stroke, one might say,
the most important of Aratus' achievements of the past twenty-
five years was undone. And, once again, the message is clear.
Even a relatively strong, undoubtedly independent state like the
Achaean League could look only to Macedon for help against threatening neighbours. And once again one state calls in an imperial
power for help against another.

Doson accepted the invitation when it came, but he had not
himself taken the initiative towards expanding Macedonian power.
He will have welcomed the fact that he was being accepted as the
arbiter of Peloponnesian affairs - especially so soon after Athens
had finally expelled its Macedonian garrison (in 229).[37] Doson
was in a position to demand the restitution of the garrison on the
Acrocorinthus as his price for cooperation, and the events that
followed - the broadening of the alliance between Macedon and the
Achaean League into the new Hellenic symmachy[38] and the victory
of this organization over Cleomenes at Sellasia in 222[39] - meant
that Macedon now had a stronger position in the mainland than at
any previous time in the third century. But it would still be
wrong to think that Doson had any aim of continual expansion, or
any clearly defined idea of how far he wanted to expand and what
degree of control he wanted to exert.

But with the accession of Philip V in 221 the situation
changes considerably. It was the symmachy that in 220 entered on
the so-called Social War with the Aetolian League,[40] and to begin
with Philip appeared to be simply following the path of Doson.[41]
But it soon became clear that Philip was far more active in seeking new spheres of influence, and far less sensitive in his dealings with the Greeks than his predecessors. In the case of Philip
it becomes increasingly possible to talk of aggressive imperialism
- and not only in Greece, for by making an alliance with Hannibal
he forced Rome to intervene in Greece in the First Macedonian War.

Rome, indeed, had twice before sent an army across the Adriatic in what we call the First and Second Illyrian wars, in 229
and 219 respectively. But on neither occasion was her action directed against Macedon. The first war is best explained, with
Polybius, as being motivated simply by the need to protect Italian
traders against Illyrian piracy.[42] The second was a pre-emptive
strike, to ensure that there was no danger from east of the Adriatic at a time when war with Carthage was imminent. The senate
must have been aware that Demetrius of Pharos, whom they had left
in charge of a considerable part of Illyria, had allied himself
with Doson, and may have been afraid that Demetrius' actions
against the Roman protectorate in Illyria had Macedonian support,
but its sole motive was to secure the Adriatic for the duration
of the war against Hannibal.[43] As for the Macedonian attitude
towards Rome, it is by no means clear that the Illyrian protectorate particularly worried Doson. It marched with Macedon only at
Antipatreia, and throughout the 220s Doson took no action against
it. In any case the protectorate represented only a diplomatic,
not a military foothold in Greece.[44]

But, of course, the action Rome took in 219 will have worried
Philip. Demetrius of Pharos fled to him, and tried to persuade
him not only to eradicate Roman influence in the Greek mainland,
but even to invade Italy.[45] It was Philip, not Hannibal, who took
the initiative in making the alliance which led to the First Macedonian War, and forced Rome to fight on two fronts.[46] Although
Philip's first aim was the eradication of the Illyrian protectorate, it is wrong to think that he did not envisage an ultimate invasion of Italy. That is what the sources say, and it is reasonable

to interpret the clause in the treaty with Hannibal providing that Philip should aid Hannibal ὡς ἂν χρεία ᾖ καὶ ὡς ἂν συμφωνήσωμεν (Polyb. 7.9.11) as looking to Philip's eventual coming to Italy.

Clearly the war was not of Rome's choosing and her aim in it was purely defensive. The mandate given to M. Valerius Laevinus, the first Roman commander in the war, was *ut Philippum in regno contineret* (Livy 23.38.11). Philip had to be prevented from crossing to Italy and aiding Hannibal. Naturally Rome found her allies in states with a history of antipathy to Macedon - the Aetolians, Sparta, Elis (an ally of Aetolia in the Social War), and Messene, formerly a member of the symmachy, but completely alienated by Philip's two extraordinary attacks on her in 215 and 214.[47] Philip neither got a great deal of help from his allies in the symmachy, nor was able to give them much. The Achaeans were fully involved in dealing with Rome's Peloponnesian allies, and Philip was fully involved in coping with the Roman and Aetolian forces in the north.[48] Livy makes the Achaean *strategos* Aristaenus, arguing in 198 for alliance between the Achaean League and Rome, point to the lack of Macedonian help.[49] Epirus, nominally a member of the symmachy, in fact adopted a position of neutrality,[50] and Boeotia was more threatened by Aetolia than a threat to her.[51]

The hostility to Macedon among those who threw in their lot with Rome evidently ran deep. Pro-Macedonians, like an Acarnanian speaker in 210, attempting to dissuade the Spartans from joining the Romano-Aetolian alliance, might describe the Romans as barbarians, and appeal to feelings of Hellenism.[52] But the memories of Philip's behaviour, the sacking of Thermos in the Social War[53] and the two attacks on Messene[54] rankled a great deal. It is also significant that one of the results of the Social War was that Philip assumed direct control of Phocis (as, during the First Macedonian War, he did of Eastern Locris[55]). It was far from clear that if Greek states had to throw in their lot with an imperial power Rome was a very much worse bet than Macedon. For the Aetolians, of course, their hostility to the Achaean League was now such that the mere fact of the Achaeans remaining allied to Philip was enough to predispose them in favour of Philip's opponents.

In the event Rome's performance in the First Macedonian War

did little to win friends. The second commander, P. Sulpicius
Galba, behaved in a cruel and insensitive way that left bitter memories - he plundered captured towns ruthlessly, and in the case of
Aegina refused to allow prisoners of war to send representatives to
friendly states to arrange a ransom, and wanted to sell them all
into slavery.[56] And Rome made it clear that she was motivated by
nothing more than her own self-interest. Once the defeat of the
Carthaginian fleet off Sicily had removed the danger of an imminent
invasion by Philip - who would have had to rely on Carthaginian
ships for transporting his troops - the senate lost interest in
Greece and the Aetolians were forced to negotiate their own peace
with Philip. The Romans, with a typically superior disregard for
the facts, chose to portray the Aetolians as having broken the
terms of their treaty with Rome by making peace; technically they
had done so, but in fact they had no alternative.[57]

If Philip had played his cards differently he might still
have secured some goodwill from the Greeks and given Rome a far
more difficult task. But immediately after his making peace with
Rome, at Phoenice in 205, he embarked on a series of actions which
it is hard to describe as anything but sheer and unashamed aggressive imperialism.[58] The previous history of his reign, I believe, justifies this description, and it is over-rationalization
to think that Philip's purpose was only to improve his position in
order to defend himself against Antiochus, or Rome. After some
covert support from his henchmen making trouble for Rhodes and attacking states in the Aegean and Hellespont, in 202 Philip himself
launched a major expedition in the Aegean and captured several
states - Lysimacheia, Chalcedon, Cius - which were allied to the
Aetolians. The latter, despite their disenchantment with Rome, appealed to the senate for help. They were turned down, perhaps more
because the senate was not yet sure of peace with Carthage than because they really felt angry with the Aetolians for having made
peace with Philip.[59] Philip proceeded to even more aggressions,
and in 201 he captured many of the Aegean islands, now under de
facto Rhodian protection following the decline of Ptolemaic power,
and attacked a number of states in Asia Minor. Naturally he was
opposed by Rhodes and Pergamum, both of whom already had friendly
relations with Rome. Rhodes had been an *amicus* since the end of

the fourth century – if I may take a dogmatic view on a controversial matter[60] – and Attalus I had fought on Rome's side in the
First Macedonian War, though, like Rhodes, he did not have a formal treaty with Rome.[61]

        Philip made the position even worse by returning to Greece
and invading Attica on a pretty flimsy pretext. Not only did he
invade it, he caused great offence by his wanton destruction of
cemeteries and temples.[62] Rome's initial campaign, though not an
outstanding success (and diplomatically the fact that P. Sulpicius
Galba, the insensitive commander of the First Macedonian War, was
again in charge was not helpful) was impressive enough to bring
the Aetolians back into the fold (Livy 31.41.1), and in the following year (198) the initial successes of Flamininus, and the
diplomacy of his brother Lucius, produced the most important
change: the Achaean League was detached from its alliance with
Philip (Livy 32.23). The latter had foreseen the danger and attempted to forestall it by offering the League certain towns that
he still held in the Peloponnese (Livy 32.5.4-5). It seems that
he had promised to return the towns in 208 and failed to fulfil
his promise.[63] What swayed the Achaeans was first, awareness of
what Philip had done, and second, the realization that if they
refused alliance with Rome, they would be attacked by the forces
of Rome and her allies and Philip would be able to do nothing to
help them.

        These decisions of the Aetolian and Achaean Leagues, like
those made by Rome's allies in the First Macedonian War, were
taken when Roman forces were already in Greece. The critical
steps were the appeals to Rome for intervention against Philip
made in 201 by Rhodes, Attalus, and Athens. It might perhaps be
thought that these invitations represented nothing new. As I
have stressed, appeals for outside intervention had long been a
feature of disputes between Greek states – and not only appeals
to other Greeks. It was Persian gold that finally settled the
outcome of the Peloponnesian War, and the Great King was able
to pose as arbiter of Greek affairs for the first third of the
fourth century. But to open the door to a new and close-at-hand
non-Greek power, whose growth in the western Mediterranean was
well known, was very different from calling on Antigonus Doson

to defeat Sparta. We have seen the appeal to Hellenic sentiment
made by the Acarnanian speaker in 210 - and similar views were
expressed on other occasions.[64] What I have tried to emphasize
is that the grounds for Roman intervention were well-prepared.
From the battle of Chaeronea onwards the rulers of Macedon had
been interfering in the affairs of the Greek mainland, whether
directly or indirectly. As the nearest of the Hellenistic monarchs the Antigonids were obviously more of a threat to Greek
independence than the Seleucids or the Ptolemies. Philip acted
with far more open aggression than any of his ancestors since
Demetrius Poliorcetes. If he behaved like a barbarian there
could be no qualms for Greeks in inviting a non-Greek people to
defend them against him. Whether the senate was really motivated *ob iniurias armaque illata sociis populi Romani* (Livy
31.6.1) we may doubt. What is important is that three quarters
of a century of continuous Antigonid rule made Athens, the
Aetolians, Rhodes, and Pergamum quite ready to bring their complaints to a non-Greek power. If Philip had restrained himself
from his quite unnecessary aggressions in the last few years of
the third century, Rome would not have had the opportunity to
take the decisive step of intervention in 200. How long that
would have delayed Rome in the process of achieving control of
the Hellenistic world, however, is a question about Roman motives and Roman imperialism: which is not the subject of this
paper.

8: LAUS IMPERII[1]

P.A.Brunt (Brasenose College, Oxford)

I THE NATURE OF THE EVIDENCE

My purpose in this paper is to explore the conceptions of empire
prevalent in Cicero's day. What Romans thought is often best ascertained from their institutions and actions, and some use will be
made of this kind of evidence; it is necessarily inferential, and
there is always a danger of reading into the actions of Greeks and
Romans motives of too modern a kind. However this may be, I pro-
pose to draw principally on actual statements by Romans, as the
clearest indications of what was most explicit in their own consciousness; how far this reveals the true driving forces in their
imperial conduct is another matter, which may be left to bolder
inquiry.

Only two authors supply much material: Cicero and Caesar. It
may indeed be remembered that Virgil, Horace and Livy all matured
in Cicero's lifetime, and that Livy may often reflect the views of
annalists of this or of a still earlier period; moreover I believe
that the imperial ideals of the Augustan age were much the same as
those of the late republic.[2] Still, citations of these writers
will be subsidiary. It remains, however, to ask how far the utterances of Cicero and Caesar can be regarded as representative of
their time. Any assumption that they actually held typical views
themselves may appear unwarranted and indeed implausible.

Cicero's own personal opinions can only be properly elicited
from his intimate letters and those theoretical writings in which
he speaks *in propria persona* (as in *de officiis*) or through an
interlocutor in a dialogue who can be identified as his own mouthpiece, like Scipio and Laelius in his *de republica*, or Cotta in
de natura deorum. It is astonishing that certain scholars freely
quote from speeches, or from his exposition of those Stoic theories, which he may have been inclined to adopt but could never
quite accept,[3] as if they are sufficient to attest his true beliefs. Even the grand statement of a political programme in his

defence of Sestius (96-139) can only be safely taken as sincere because it agrees so closely with what he says in other works, where
he had no reason to veil or distort his real views. But for our
present purposes the speeches are actually of prime value. The
skilled and successful orator, such as he was, had to persuade his
audience and, therefore, to play on their beliefs and feelings.[4]
We know that Cicero could for this end express views he was far
from sharing, for instance in the ridicule he cast on the study of
civil law and on Stoic tenets in his speech for Murena (26-9,
60-7). His appeals to religion may in some degree be comparable
(see below). Whereas his own genuine beliefs about the empire
might in principle be treated as unique or unusual, his public
utterances should tell us by implication what was widely thought
by those who heard him. Orations delivered before the senate or
upper-class juries would have mirrored the opinions of senators and
equites, and *contiones* those prevalent in other strata of society.

Unfortunately we cannot overhear Cicero on the *rostra*; with
one exception the published versions of the speeches we have were
not verbally identical with those he delivered, and may sometimes
have differed significantly in substance; some indeed had no spoken
prototypes.[5] But it may surely be assumed that when Cicero published speeches he had delivered, as well as those he had not, his
purpose was either to influence opinion or to immortalize his eloquence,[6] if not to do both. In the former case his speeches are
evidently indicative of what others thought. The reading public
must indeed have consisted only of men of education and therefore
of wealth. It might then seem that the published versions of
speeches delivered to the people *may* tell us little of what he
said to them and consequently can provide no certain evidence of
their sentiments. But this need not be true. In so far as his
aim was to give permanence to specimens of his oratorical skill,
he had good reason not to omit any of the sophistries of per-
suasion that he had actually employed and that connoisseurs of the
art would enjoy. Although Cicero sometimes equated the perfect
orator with the wise statesman,[7] statesmanship was to be judged by
the ends pursued and the adoption of means appropriate to those
ends, and he had no reason to fear that his readers would think
less well of him as a politician, if it appeared that he had

pandered in words to the mob for such laudable purposes as defeating Rullus' land-bill or Catiline's conspiracy.[8] Such speeches in fact 'ring true', and surely reveal the popular sentiments on which Cicero found it expedient to play.

As for Caesar's *Commentaries*, I take it for granted that, however truthful they may be as a record of events, they were written partly at least in order to depict Caesar's conduct in a way that would win the approval of his readers. Thus Caesar too betrays the attitudes common in the whole upper class, to whom he is addressing an apologia.

II ROMAN AND ATHENIAN VIEWS OF THEIR EMPIRES

It will appear that the Romans themselves liked to believe that they had acquired their dominions justly, by fighting for their own security or for the protection of their allies. Victory had conferred on them the right to rule over the conquered, and they were naturally conscious that this right was profitable to them, nor were they ashamed of the booty and tribute they exacted. However, they preferred to dwell on the sheer glory of empire, which made Rome specially worthy of the devotion of her citizens (*de orat.* 1.156). Much of this thinking is reminiscent of the interpretation Thucydides put on Athenian imperialism, in the speeches he ascribes to Athens' spokesmen. Like all other peoples, the Athenians had been led to acquire their empire by considerations of security, profit and prestige (1.76), but it is on the undying fame that Athens had won by reducing the greatest number of Greeks to subjection (2.64) that he seems to lay the greatest weight, and it was the power of the city that should inspire the affection of her citizens and make them glad to sacrifice themselves in her service (2.43). To Romans the glory of their empire was even greater than that which Pericles could claim for Athens, because they had come to think that it properly embraced the whole world. Moreover, this dominion was ordained by the gods, whose favour Rome had deserved by piety and justice, and it was exercised in the interest of the subjects. It needs no proof that Thucydides did not look on Athenian policy in the same light. But less impartial or less cynical observers could go almost as far in justifying her imperialism. We can see this from Isocrates' *Panegyricus*, which certainly reflects ideas already current

in the fifth century, though it would take me too far afield to
demonstrate this here. The Athenians too had liked to see themselves as protectors of peoples unjustly threatened or oppressed,
and as benefactors of their subjects; it seems very doubtful if
many of them acknowledged publicly or in their own hearts that
their empire was a tyranny and unjustly acquired. What was most
novel in the Roman attitude to their empire was the belief that
it was universal and willed by the gods.

III THE GLORY OF IMPERIAL EXPANSION

In the political programme Cicero sketched in his defence of Sestius
(96ff.) he maintained that all good men should seek *otium cum dignitate*. *Otium* must have included security from external attack (*de
orat*. 1.14), and *dignitas* suggests, among other things, the glory of
the whole state (*pro Sest*. 104); *provinciae*, *socii*, *imperii laus*,
res militaris are expressly named among the *fundamenta otiosae dignitatis*. Much of Cicero's programme can have had no appeal to the
poor either in Rome or in the country, but the urban plebs at least
could apparently be moved by the glamour of imperial glory; in his
speech for the Manilian law Cicero enlarges on the dishonour Rome
had suffered from the pirates and from Mithridates, and on the
necessity of entrusting the eastern command to Pompey, in order to
restore 'the prestige of the Roman people which has been transmitted
to you by our ancestors and whose greatness appears in every way and
above all in the military domain' (6; cf. 7-11, 53ff.). No other
people, he says there, had ever had such an appetite for glory, and
we know that in his own judgement this had been a dominant motive
for the old Romans (*de rep*. 5.9). He can argue for the propriety
or wisdom of any practices which have in the past served to aggrandize the empire (*pro Rosc*. *Am*. 50, *Phil*. 5.47), or which its long
existence in itself justifies. Both Pompey and Caesar are lauded
for making its boundaries coterminous with the *orbis terrarum*,[9] a
boast that Pompey made for himself on a monument recording his deeds
in Asia (Diod. 40.4). The speech *de provinciis consularibus* is particularly significant in this connexion. As an encomiast of Caesar
in 56, Cicero was in a delicate position. Both he and the majority
of the senate had recently been in opposition to Caesar. However,
he finds it plausible to assert that Caesar's achievements in Gaul

had changed their attitude, and rightly changed it, hence the extraordinary honours the senate had already voted to the conqueror (25;
cf. *in Pis.* 81). In the long letter he wrote to Lentulus in 54,
which was obviously intended as an apologia for a wider public, Cicero exculpates his own change of course in much the same way: it is
now, he claims, the triumvirs who are doing most to secure *otium cum
dignitate*, and Caesar's conquests are part of his case (*ad fam.*
1.9.12-18 and 21). It seems to me highly improbable that these sentiments, however insincere on the lips of Cicero, whose correspondence in the 50s, even with his brother Quintus in Gaul, betrays
little interest and no pride in the conquests, were not genuinely
felt by Romans, who had less than Cicero to lose from the dominance
of the triumvirs, or that Caesar himself was untruthful in recording
that in 49 the councillors of Auximum, from Pompey's homeland of
Picenum, declined to exclude from their town *C. Caesarem imperatorem,
bene de republica meritum, tantis rebus gestis* (*BC* 1.13).

There is abundant evidence for the value individual Romans set
on *gloria*,[10] but, as Cicero says in his defence of Archias, they
could win no greater renown than by victories in war, renown in
which the whole people shared (21ff.; cf. 30). In *de officiis* Cicero
admits that most men rank success in war above achievements in peace
(1.74), and that it had been the most natural and traditional objective for a young aristocrat (2.45); in public he declared that military talent had brought eternal glory to Rome and compelled the world
to obey her commands and that it was to be more highly valued than
the orator's eloquence (*pro Mur.* 21ff.). He scoffed at the Epicurean
Piso's professed disdain for a triumph as preposterous and incredible
(*in Pis.* 56ff.), and for all his own rational expectation to be im-
mortalized as the Roman Demosthenes (cf. n.6) and perhaps as the
Roman Plato, he magnified his own petty exploits in Mount Amanus in
hope of the honour.[11] The triumph, properly granted only to the
general who had slain 5,000 of the enemy in a single battle (Val.
Max. 2.8.1), was itself the institutional expression of Rome's military ideal. According to Cicero (*de rep.* 3.24) the words *finis
imperii propagavit* appeared on the monuments of her great generals;
in his speeches he takes it for granted that victory and the extension of empire are the objectives of any provincial governor (*de
prov. cons.* 29, *Phil.* 13.14), and at his most theoretical he

prescribes that wise statesmen should do their utmost in peace and war *ut rem publicam augeant imperio agris vectigalibus* (*de offic.* 2.85), thus accepting in 44 B.C. a principle of statecraft that no contemporary had done more to fulfil than Caesar, whom at this very time he was concerned to vilify (1.26, 2.23-8, 3.83 etc.). In *de oratore* 1.196 he roundly asserted that no fatherland deserved so much love as Rome, *quae una in omnibus terris domus est virtutis, imperii, dignitatis.*

IV VIRTUS, FORTUNA AND THE WILL OF THE GODS

Thus Cicero could not free himself from the militarism of the traditions he revered, which appeared in the old prayer of the censors for the aggrandizement of Rome (Val. Max. 4.1.10), in the rule that the *pomerium* might be extended only by those *qui protulere imperium* (Tac. *Ann.* 12.23) - among them was Sulla - and perhaps in the alleged predictions of *haruspices* that the wars with Philip V, Antiochus and Perseus would advance *terminos populi Romani*. If these predictions recorded by Livy (21.5.7, 36.1.3, 42.30.9) are not annalistic fabrications, they cast doubt on the view that any of these wars were merely defensive in motivation, but even if they were invented by Valerius Antias or Claudius Quadrigarius (if not earlier), they still illustrate the imperialistic conceptions dominant in the time of their invention, and accepted by Livy, in whose work *belli gloria* is naturally a pervasive theme. In particular, the legend of Marcus Curtius, for which our earliest source is a contemporary of Cicero, Procilius, enshrined the truth that it was *arma virtusque* that guaranteed Rome's perpetuity (7.6.3). In Livy's view it was the number and valour of Rome's soldiers and the talents of her generals - elsewhere he also stresses military discipline, to which Cicero only once alludes (*Tusc. disp.* 1.2) - which with the help of fortune had made Rome unconquerable.[12]

It was, however, not only military qualities that were thought to have made Rome great. Wise policy was another factor (*de rep.* 2.30). Like Polybius, Cicero clearly laid great weight on Rome's balanced constitution.[13] Most Romans were not political theorists, but traditions counted heavily with them; as Cicero's innumerable allusions in speeches to ancestral wisdom[14] indicate; in his defence of Murena (75) he casually refers to *instituta maiorum quae*

diuturnitas imperi comprobat, and we may conjecture that a widely
shared conviction that these institutions had contributed to the
acquisition of empire was one reason why Augustus felt it necessary
to veil the extent to which he had subverted them.[15] In one speech
Cicero suggested that Rome's readiness to share political rights
with other peoples, even with defeated enemies, had been of the
highest importance in her aggrandizement (*pro Balb.* 31); more was
to be made of this theme by Livy, and by Dionysius who doubtless
drew the idea from Romans he met or from the annals he read.[16]
Posidonius too was obviously following Roman mentors when he extolled the frugality, simplicity, good faith and piety of the old
Romans in a passage in which he is accounting for Rome's rise to
power:[17] *moribus antiquis res stat Romana virisque.* Sallust and
others apprehended danger to Rome from the degeneration from those
pristine standards which they detected in their own day.[18]

Romans themselves acknowledged that fortune as well as virtue
had assisted them; for instance the situation of the city, and the
centrality of Italy within the Mediterranean world, had favoured
expansion, and Italy's natural resources were actually exaggerated.[19]
But the Roman conception of fortune tended to be that of which Cicero speaks: *divinitus adiuncta fortuna* (*de imp. Cn. Pomp.* 47). The
gods were the guardians of city and empire.[20] It was Roman piety
that had earned their goodwill. In Propertius' words (3.22.21),
quantum ferro tantum pietate potentes stamus. Virgil's Aeneas,
pietate insignis et armis, was the prototype of the people aided
and destined by the gods to conquer. In public Cicero gave the
most eloquent expression to the notion, which we can trace from a
praetor's letter of 193 B.C. to the time of Augustine, that 'it was
by our scrupulous attention to religion and by our wise grasp of a
single truth, that all things are ruled and directed by the will of
the gods, that we have overcome all peoples and nations'.[21]

It may be doubted if Cicero himself had firm religious convictions. There is no hint of personal devotion in his intimate
letters; above all, he never expresses hope of assistance from the
gods in moments of the deepest distress or anxiety.[22] But he held
that it was expedient to imbue the citizens with religious faith,
in order that they might be deterred by the fear of divine retribution from infringing oaths and treaties, and from crimes in

general. If men ceased to think that the gods took no care for mankind and to pay them due honour, good faith, social cooperation and
justice would surely be extinguished. Polybius had already traced
the high moral standards of old Rome to the prevalence of a scrupulous fear of the gods.[23] The ideal system of sacred law Cicero
sketches in the second book of *de legibus* is expressly modelled on
the Roman (2.23). He lays great emphasis on the powers of the aristocratic priesthoods, 'for it helps to hold the state together that
the people should always need the advice and authority of the *optimates*' (2.30). Cicero unhesitatingly approved the abuse of priestly
authority for obstructing 'seditious' proposals.[24] The truth of beliefs implicit in the ancestral rituals was irrelevant to their
utility. In the same way Varro adopted the view of Q.Mucius Scaevola
that philosophic views on religion were unsuited to the masses and
that traditional rites should be kept up for their benefit. Varro
indeed held that there was a basis of truth in the old religion,
which he reconciled with Stoic pantheism.[25] In *de legibus* Cicero
adopted a similar standpoint.

    In this work he accepted the Stoic justification of divination;
it was at least credible in principle, though Cicero already denied
that the augurs of his own day (he was one himself) any longer enjoyed knowledge of the future,[26] and insisted above all on their
political importance. By the end of his life he had come to reject
every kind of divination. Yet in the very treatise, *de divinatione*,
in which he discredits belief in the supernatural power of *haruspices*
and augurs as mere superstition, he reiterates that for political
reasons the old practices should be maintained.[27] This work is a
sequel to his *de natura deorum*, in which his mouthpiece, Cotta, refutes all Stoic teaching on divine providence in a way which could
be said *deos funditos tollere* (*de div*. 1.9). Cotta is actually made
to say that experience throws doubt on the very existence of gods,
though as a pontiff, bound to maintain the cults, he would never
avow this *in contione* (*de nat. deor*. 1.61). It is true that at the
end Cicero makes Cotta indicate that he would like to be convinced
that the Stoics were in the right (3.95), and declare that no philosophic reasoning could induce him to question the truth of ancestral
beliefs on the worship of the gods, and that Rome could never have
achieved such greatness but for her supreme care in placating them

(3.5ff.; cf. 14). Strictly this means that Cotta accepts on authority all the traditional *beliefs* including those which Cicero was
to ridicule in *de divinatione*. I suspect that Cicero has gone further than he really intended here, and that he should have made
Cotta say merely that all the ancient *practices* were to be preserved, irrespective of their truth.

Whatever Cicero's personal convictions may have been, they are
primarily of biographical interest; we cannot properly generalize
from a single individual. But the cynical manipulation of the official religion for political ends is itself one piece of evidence
for the decay of belief in it among the controlling aristocracy.
Of course it does not stand alone: at this time many cults were
neglected, the calendar was often in disarray, priesthoods were un-
filled, temples were falling into disrepair, the pontifical law was
no longer studied, and in public and private life auspices were not
duly observed.[28] Can we then suppose that the conception that the
empire depended on divine favour really had much influence on men's
minds?

The answer is surely that Cicero and other highly educated aristocrats were not representative figures. It is significant that
Cicero in his speech *de haruspicum responsis* (18) finds it necessary to deny that his philosophical studies have alienated him from
the old religion. The frequency of his public appeals to religion
is surely proof that belief was still widespread.[29] There can be
no doubt that superstition was rife among the ignorant masses.[30]
But Cicero was just as apt to play on religious sentiment when
addressing members of the higher orders. To take only one example,
religiones and *auspicia* come first in the *fundamenta otiosae dignitatis* as a part of the programme that was to enlist the support of
all *boni et locupletes* throughout Italy (*pro Sest.* 98). I do not
suppose that they were meant to think only of the opportunities for
political obstruction which the old religion furnished. The so-
called religious revival that Augustus was to attempt may well have
appealed to the old-fashioned municipal gentry, who were already
playing a larger part in the political life of Cicero's time and
whose support he sought, like Augustus after him.[31] It may be
noted that the incest of Clodius in 62 aroused indignation first
among the lower ranks in the senate, a body of which probably under

thirty per cent belonged to noble houses.[32]   Most Romans may well
have retained the conviction that it was to the gods that they owed
their empire, an empire that was said to be coterminous with the
orbis terrarum.

V   THE CONCEPTION OF WORLD EMPIRE

Virgil's Jupiter was to bestow on Rome a dominion without limits in
space or time (*Aen*. 1.277ff.).   Cicero and his contemporaries, and
perhaps Virgil's, were somewhat less confident.   More than once
Cicero avers that Rome had no external enemies to fear, but that
her eternity could only be assured if she remained faithful to the
institutions and customs that had made her great.[33]   On the other
hand he constantly speaks, and sometimes in quite casual ways with
no rhetorical inflation (e.g. *de orat*. 1.14), as if Rome already
ruled all peoples or the whole *orbis terrarum*.[34]   This conception
also appears in an admittedly rather grandiloquent preamble to a
consular law of 58: *imperio amplificato pace per orbem terrarum*.
A century earlier, Polybius had held that by 167 B.C. the whole, or
virtually the whole *oikoumene*, or its known parts, had come under
Roman dominion.   His true meaning is better conveyed in other texts
in which he ascribes to Rome mastery over land and sea *kath'hemas*,
or of those which had fallen under inquiry (*historian*); evidently
these did not embrace all the parts of the world that geographers
had described but only those which formed Polybius' political universe.[35]   *Orbis terrarum* was often used in the same restricted
sense (cf. n.34).

Even so, it is obvious that in the time both of Polybius and
of Cicero Rome did not herself administer the whole of this political universe.   Both must then have conceived that her dominion extended beyond the provinces to the kings, tribes and cities who
were bound to Rome by alliances, even if the terms of the treaty,
as with little Astypalaea,[36] affected a formal equality between
the High Contracting Parties which harsh reality rendered meaningless, or who were linked by the looser tie of *amicitia*, which
within Rome's own society was often a courteous synonym for client-
age.[37]   In form the status of such allies and friends of Rome beyond provincial frontiers was no different from that of others
like Massilia whose territories constituted enclaves within a

province. In reality the degree of their dependence was determined
by the advantages or disadvantages that might induce Rome to punish
or overlook disobedience to her will.

Augustus was to regard all *reges socios* as *membra partisque
imperii* (Suet. *Aug.* 48). Owing their thrones to recognition, if not
to appointment, by Rome, they were not necessarily scions of an established royal house nor even drawn from the people they ruled;
normally they now enjoyed Roman citizenship, a symbol of their function as creatures and agents of the suzerain. Augustus naturally
included his dealings with them in his record of the deeds *quibus
orbem terrarum imperio populi Romani subiecit*. In his view Armenia
was in revolt when it rejected the princes he named. He justified
by ancestral practice his decision not to annex that country; Lucullus and Pompey had in fact already reduced it to vassalage.[38]

Under his more efficient regime 'client' states were perhaps
more closely controlled than in the republic, but Cicero had already
included all kingdoms and *liberae civitates* in the *orbis terrarum*,
where every Roman in virtue of his citizenship should be safe from
arbitrary punishment (II *Verr.* 5.168), and in 47 B.C. an attack on
king Deiotarus could be construed as a violation of *populi Romani
ius maiestatemque* (*B. Alex.* 34). In Cicero's phrase Rome was *dominus
regum* (*de dom.* 90), and when Tacitus declared it to be an ancient
and long-approved practice of the republic to make kings *instrumenta
servitutis* (*Agr.* 14), he was echoing Sallust, who represents Mithridates as telling how Eumenes of Pergamum had been reduced by Rome
to the most wretched slavery (*ep. Mith.* 8; cf. *BJ* 31.9). Sallust
too makes Adherbal recall to the senate that his father, Micipsa,
had enjoined on him *uti regni Numidiae tantummodo procurationem
existumarem meam, ceterum ius et imperium eius penes vos esse.*[39]
From the second century such rulers had had to look to Rome for
recognition, and like free cities and friendly tribes, they were
expected to conform their policy to Rome's will, to furnish military aid and money or supplies, when occasion demanded; some were
actually tributary. In return they had a moral claim to Rome's
protection (e.g. *BJ* 14, *B. Alex.* 34). In 51 B.C. king Ariobarzanes
of Cappadocia plainly depended wholly on Rome to defend him against
Parthian attack or internal discontent, fostered no doubt by the
exactions required to meet the usurious demands of Pompey and

Brutus. Modern descriptions of such client kingdoms or peoples as 'buffer states' is never adequate and often quite misleading. Analogies with the princedoms of British India or the system of 'indirect rule' in British Nigeria would be more to the point.[40] A recent writer has drawn a distinction between the Roman empire *stricto* and *lato sensu*, the former comprising only territory under Rome's own administration and the latter the subordinate states as well. This is clearly a useful tool of analysis, but it does not correspond to Roman usage.[41]

VI UNLIMITED EXPANSION

The duty acknowledged by the Romans (but not invariably performed) of protecting their friends and allies could involve them in wars with peoples who had hitherto lain beyond their orbit. Victory made these peoples in turn Rome's subjects. Thus the limits of the *orbis terrarum* within which she claimed dominion were continually advancing. There was no point at which such expansion could halt, so long as any independent people remained. Indeed, as P.Veyne has recently argued, the very existence of a truly independent power was viewed at Rome as a potential threat to her own security.[42]

The early treaties with Carthage, and perhaps one with Tarentum, had bound Rome to keep out of certain lands or seas.[43] There is no certain evidence that she ever accepted such a restriction after the war with Pyrrhus. Livy indeed says that under the pact with Hasdrubal the Ebro became *finis utriusque imperii* (21.2.7), but Polybius that it simply forbade the Carthaginians to cross that river, and there is no hint that Hannibal argued that Rome had infringed its terms by intervening on behalf of Saguntum.[44] At one time Flamininus offered Antiochus III a line of demarcation between his sphere of authority and Rome's, but the treaty of Apamea certainly set bounds for Antiochus, without debarring Rome from interfering beyond them.[45] Caesar would not accept either Rhine or Channel as limits to Roman power. Whatever the practice of earlier ages, his attitude was characteristic for his own time.

It is true that according to Orosius (6.13.2) the Parthian king complained that Crassus' crossing of the Euphrates was an infringement of 'treaties' made by Lucullus and Pompey; Florus (3.11.4) refers instead to 'treaties' made with Sulla and Pompey.

Many scholars suppose that one or more of these generals had in fact recognized the Euphrates as a boundary delimiting the Roman and Parthian spheres of influence or at least as one which neither party was to cross in arms. Yet, since Crassus was patently launching an offensive against Parthia, the Parthian king was perhaps merely reminding him of previous pacts of friendship, which need have comprised no such precise stipulation. Certainly none is recorded in the other texts, admittedly meagre, which relate to the negotiations between these generals and the Parthians.[46] Lucullus was actually quartered far east of the Euphrates at the time, having overrun much of Armenia. Pompey too invaded Armenia, reduced king Tigranes to vassalage, and sent troops into Gordyene. According to Plutarch (*Pomp*. 33.6) Phraates then proposed the Euphrates as a frontier, but Pompey merely replied that he would adopt the just boundary. That was manifestly an evasion. In his monument he claimed to have 'given protection to' not only Armenia but Mesopotamia, Sophene and Gordyene (Diod. 40.4), and if he was unwilling to fight the Parthians, who did indeed forbid him to cross the Euphrates again (Dio 37.6), for Tigranes' right to Gordyene, he successfully offered Roman arbitration between the rival claims there of Tigranes and Phraates (Dio 37.6f.). It is significant that he denied Phraates the title of 'king of kings' (Dio 37.5; Plut. *Pomp*. 38), which might have suggested that his state was on a parity with Rome. He entered into friendly relations with the rulers of Osrhoene, Media Atropatene and even Elymaitis,[47] as well as Armenia; when and if it suited Rome, she could intervene to defend her friends beyond the Euphrates against Parthia.

When Crassus did cross the river, he was received as a liberator from Parthian oppression at least by many Greek cities (Dio 40.13, Plut. *Cr*. 17), and he had the support of the vassal king of Armenia (Dio 40.19), while the ruler of Osrhoene pretended to be friendly (ibid. 20).

Although Cicero denied that Crassus had any justification for war (*de fin*. 3.75), and our authorities all represent him as the aggressor, perhaps condemning him, as Plutarch suggested (*comp. Nic. et Cr*. 4), only because he failed, we can easily surmise that he had excuses for intervention, on behalf of peoples with whom Rome had already entered into friendly relations, as plausible as

Caesar for his Gallic offensives. It is, moreover, significant that
even though Romans could see the disaster at Carrhae as divine retribution for an unjust and undeclared war, just as Cicero ascribes the
destruction of Piso's army by pestilence to the judgement of heaven
on Piso's alleged aggressions (*in Pis*. 85), they continued to assume
down to 20 B.C. that it was right for them to punish the Parthians
and even to conquer them, in order to vindicate Rome's honour and
secure her eastern dominions.

Whatever the provocation they had received, foreign peoples
which attacked Rome could at best be said to wage a *bellum prope
iustum* (*de prov. cons*. 4). It would be hard to say how far the conviction that the gods had destined them to rule the world predisposed
Romans to treat as legitimate *casus belli* which the uncommitted observer would have thought nugatory.

VII   RELUCTANCE TO ANNEX TERRITORY
It is then quite mistaken to deny that Roman policy was imperialistic
whenever it did not result in outright annexation. Until the first
century B.C. Rome was notoriously slow to annex territory.

Gelzer explained this on the ground that the Roman state absolutely lacked an organ for carrying through far-reaching plans of expansion, with annual magistrates whose choice rested on the caprice
of the electorate, who were often incapable, and who in any event
could not assure continuity in policy, and a senate which met only
when summoned by a magistrate to consider such matters as he referred to it.[48] It seems to me that he unduly depreciated the real
power of the senate to make decisions, and that the fluctuations in
its policy did not differ significantly from those we find in the
policy of imperial states governed either by absolute rulers or by
parliamentary democracies; for instance, no change in senatorial
foreign policy was more marked than that which occurred when Hadrian
succeeded Trajan.

Badian, while rightly insisting that at any rate after 200 Rome
was determined 'to dominate whatever was within reach and to build
up strength to extend that reach' and practised what he calls 'hegemonial imperialism', argues that the Roman governing class was reluctant to resort to annexation, because it early became conscious
'that large increases of territory could not easily be administered

within the existing city-state constitution'. I know of no evidence
for such consciousness, and I doubt if it be true that 'under the
Roman Republic no real system of administering overseas territories
was ever evolved'.[49]

As Gelzer observed, we must not think in terms of a modern
bureaucracy when we speak of Roman government. But this applies almost as much to government in the Principate as in the republic.
Pliny actually had not so many high officials to assist him in
governing Bithynia and Pontus under Trajan as Cicero in Cilicia.[50]
The activities of government were far fewer than they are today, and
they were largely left to local authorities; at most these were
gradually subjected by the emperors to somewhat closer supervision.
It was only rarely under the Principate that even barbarous tribes
were directly governed by Roman military officers; the centralized
administration of Roman Egypt was always exceptional.

Nor was there anything unusual by ancient standards in Roman
practice. In the Persian empire Greek and Phoenician cities had
been left to manage their own affairs; so had the Jews, and doubtless most other unurbanized peoples of whom we know nothing; it is
immaterial that the Persian kings, like Rome, sometimes installed
local rulers on whose loyalty they could count. Athens and the
Hellenistic kings (except again in Egypt) had followed the same
practice. The Romans had no reason to think that they were less
able than other ruling powers to administer subjects in this loose
way. The only puzzle is that they did not always choose to demand
tribute (as distinct from heavy war indemnities, which could ultimately be paid off), outside the frontiers of a province; the first
known cases are those of Macedon and Illyria in 167 (Livy 45.18.7f.).

In the republic the tasks of provincial government may be
classified under four heads.

(a) *Taxation*. Collection of taxes was left to publicans or to local
authorities; a host of officials employed by the central government
was not needed. This long remained true under the Principate.[51]

(b) *Jurisdiction*. The governor was omnicompetent, outside privileged communities, but we need not assume that he as yet possessed
that monopoly of jurisdiction over serious crimes which may be inferred from evidence of later centuries, and in civil cases he may
generally have limited himself to suits in which Romans were

concerned. A *lex provinciae* might actually reserve many types of
case to local courts. In Cilicia such rules evidently did not exist,
and Cicero makes out that it was his innovation to let the Greeks
settle their own disputes in local courts under local laws, but I
suggest that he did no more than *guarantee* this 'autonomy' to them,
whereas his predecessors had been ready to assume jurisdiction if
ever they saw fit, perhaps to the advantage of influential magnates
and to their own pecuniary gain.[52]

(c) *Supervision of local government*. Cicero praised his brother for
ensuring that the Asian cities were administered by the *optimates*.
This was no doubt normal policy, though in Asia, for instance, popular assemblies were allowed to retain some power,[53] and Caesar on
occasion installed kings in Gallic *civitates*.[54] In general local
rulers, whether or not Rome had placed them in control, were left to
administer their own communities with little interference. Cicero
indeed must have spent much time in checking municipal accounts and
unveiling corruption, but the mere fact that he examined accounts
for the past ten years indicates that within that period no proconsul had thought this a task necessary to perform.[55]

(d) *Internal order and defence*. Here lay the governor's inescapable
obligation. Spain, Gaul, Macedon and some parts of the east nearly
always required legionary garrisons. As Badian saw,[56] this was
costly to the treasury and burdensome to the Italian peasantry.[57]
Generations of war in Spain might well have made the senate appre-
hensive of assuming military responsibilities that could be shifted
on to reliable vassals. Even with the threat of a Parthian invasion
in 51, the worthy consul, Servius Sulpicius, vetoed a *supplementum*
for the weak forces in Syria and Cilicia.[58] The elder Cato is said
to have opposed annexation of Macedon in 168 because Rome could not
afford protection (*HA Hadr.* 5.3).

It may be thought that this aversion to assuming the task of
military defence ill fits the Roman passion for military glory. But
we have to reckon, as Badian argued (cf. n.56), with the prevalence
of mutual jealousy among the Roman aristocracy. Provincial commands
gave particular individuals better than average chances of augment-
ing their personal glory and wealth, and their influence at home.
This jealousy is manifest in the *leges annales*, in the normal restriction of provincial commands to a single year, and in the

strength of the objection in the late republic to extraordinary commands. In 57-56 no agreement could be reached on the restoration of
Ptolemy Auletes to the Egyptian throne, whether by Pompey or any one
else; success would bring too much honour even to such a respectable
figure of the second order as Lentulus Spinther. Moreover, once a
commander was in the field, it was hard for the senate to exercise
any control over him. For over two years (57-55) the proconsul L.
Piso did not so much as send a single despatch to Rome, though Cicero
claims that this was abnormal. The provisions that appeared in
Sulla's law on *maiestas* and in Caesar's on *repetundae*, and in many
older enactments, forbidding governors *exire de provincia, educere
exercitum, bellum sua sponte gerere, in regnum iniussu populi Romani
ac senatus accedere* (*in Pis.* 50) were clearly unenforceable.[59] Both
in order to restrict the opportunities for individuals to attain
pre-eminence and to preserve its own authority, the senate had good
reason to frown on annexations. And that was not all. Just because
annual commands were preferred, there was always the danger that in-
competent nonentities would sustain ignominious defeats, and it became hard for generals to carry through a systematic course of expansion or pacification; hence it was not until Augustus' time that
order could be established throughout Spain, though it is hard to
believe that the complete conquest of that country can ever have
seemed undesirable.

VIII THE THEORY OF THE JUST WAR
Following Panaetius, Cicero implied that states as well as individuals should respect the just principle of *suum cuique*. Men should
not only abstain from doing wrong themselves but so far as possible
prevent wrong-doing by others (*de offic.* 1.20-4). Wars should therefore be fought only *ut sine iniuria in pace vivatur* and as a last
resort, if diplomacy failed; they were, however, justified not only
in self-defence but also for the protection of friends and allies
against injury.

Cicero claimed that Numa had implanted in the Romans a 'love of
peace and tranquillity, which enable justice and good faith most
easily to flourish', and in rebutting an argument, which had been
advanced by Carneades on his visit to Rome in 155, that all men
necessarily followed their own interests without regard to justice,

and that Rome had naturally pursued a policy of aggrandizing her own
wealth and power, he maintained that her wars had been just: in particular, it was by defending her allies that Rome had secured world
dominion. (Sallust propounds a similar view.) According to Cicero,
by strict observance of the old fetial procedure, or of a procedure
modelled on it, under which war had to be formally declared, and was
to be declared only when reparation had been sought and refused,
with the gods invoked to punish unjust demands, Rome had demonstrated
her respect for the rights of others. Cicero's insistence that every
war must have a *iusta causa* was certainly not peculiar to himself,
but corresponded to Roman practice or propaganda since at least the
third century.[60] Nor, despite lamentations on the supposed decay of
moral standards, had it been abandoned in Cicero's own time. Caesar
followed it with as much, or rather as little, scrupulosity as the
senate had done in the second century. Augustus was later to boast
that he had pacified the Alps *nulli genti bello per iniuriam inlato*
(*RG* 26).

     In fact the primitive fetial procedure was certainly formal-
istic and permitted the enforcement in arms of demands that had no
equitable basis. Livy, to whom we owe the preservation of what he
took to be the ancient ritual (1.32), put into the mouth of the
Alban dictator the cynical observation that though both Romans and
Albans were putting forward claims for reparation *ex foedere*, 'if
we are to say what is true rather than what is plausible, it is lust
for empire that rouses two kindred and neighbouring peoples to arms'
(1.23.7). For Livy himself the two cities were contending for *imperium servitiumque* (1.25.3); as Drexler observed, we are in a world
where there can only be rulers and subjects, not equal independent
powers. It was particularly hard for others to concede that Rome
was merely fighting in defence of her friends and allies if (as was
sometimes the case) she admitted states to her friendship and offered them protection at a time when they were already threatened
or under attack; it was all too obvious that she was then acting
for her own interest,[61] and of course victory would give her control
of the conquered *iure belli*, and justify mass-enslavements, heavy
indemnities or annexation, at her own discretion. Moreover, even
Cicero adopted a wide formulation of the rights of a state to defend
itself and its friends: 'we may ward off any disadvantage that may

be brought to us' (*si quid importetur nobis incommodi propulsemus*,
de offic. 2.18).

   To an enemy like Perseus (Livy 42.52.16), and even to so sympathetic an interpreter of Roman policy as Polybius (1.10.6), it
could appear that Rome took the mere existence of a powerful and
potentially dangerous neighbour as such a disadvantage, and Cicero's
principles were quite compatible with Cato's argument for finishing
Carthage off: 'the Carthaginians are our enemies already; for who-
ever is directing all his preparations against me, so that he may
make war on me at the time of his own choice, is already my enemy,
even if he is not yet taking armed action' (*ORF*^{2} fr. 195). In all
cases the Romans were in Hobbes' words 'judges of the justness of
their own fears'. In retrospect Lactantius could aver that 'it was
by using fetials to declare war, inflicting injuries under cover of
law and unceasingly coveting and carrying off what belonged to
others that Rome obtained possession of the world' (*de div. inst.*
6.9.4). Roman reactions to the possibility of a threat resembled
those of a nervous tiger, disturbed when feeding. It is hardly
surprising that Polybius, although in his analysis of the origins
of many particular wars Rome's policy appears to be defensive, concluded that Rome had persistently and deliberately aimed at extending her dominion.[62]

   Cicero himself casually refers to Roman wars like those waged
with Italian peoples, Pyrrhus and Carthage, the purpose of which
was empire or glory. Such a purpose was hardly consistent with
Panaetius' general account of justice, and I take it that it was
Cicero who inserted the reference to them, half-conscious that
Panaetius' doctrine did not after all permit the justification of
all Rome's wars. He does indeed hasten to add that just causes
must be found even in such cases.[63] But a just cause is now nothing
but the 'decent pretext' that Polybius (36.2) thought the Romans
were right to look for, after deciding on war for reasons of self-
interest; it might be as legalistic and inequitable as those adduced
for the Third Punic War.

   Polybius thought that Rome needed them to impress the world,
i.e. the Greek world, and it may be that as late as c. 150 the
senate still had some regard for Greek public opinion, such as it
had shown in the previous generation. This sort of consideration

is certainly ascribed to the Romans on other occasions,[64] and their
propagandist assumption of the role of protector of Greek liberty
finds an analogy in Caesar's attempt to parade himself in 58 as the
champion of the freedom of Gallic peoples against German invaders
(*BG* 1.33 and 45); indeed his relations with the Gauls in a single
decade offer a sort of telescoped parallel to those of Rome with
the Greek cities between 200 and 146.

But Polybius may have been both too cynical and too inclined
to overrate the importance in Roman eyes of his own fellow-Greeks.
We must not forget that for Romans a just war was one in which the
gods were on their side. The very formalism of Roman religion made
it possible for them to believe that this divine favour could be
secured, provided only that all the necessary ceremonies and procedures had been duly followed. Drexler (p.110) suggested that the
Romans fought better because they were convinced in this way of the
rightness of the cause, even in cases when it does not seem morally
defensible to us.[65] However Machiavellian the *principes* may have
been in directing policy, they had perhaps to think of the morale
of the common soldiers. Dio at least supposed that the near-mutiny
at Vesontio in 58 was inspired not only by fear of Ariovistus but
also by the suspicion that Caesar was entering on a campaign out of
personal ambition without a just cause (38.35).

IX CAESAR IN GAUL

The most remarkable document of Roman imperialism is Caesar's *de
bello Gallico*. Sallust thought that he hankered for a new war in
which his *virtus* would shine out (*Cat.* 54.4). Suetonius was later
to write of his shameless aggressions and ascribe them principally
to greed (cf. n.81). Conquest was clearly bound to fill his purse
and enhance his fame.

Plutarch said that by crossing the Channel he carried Roman
supremacy beyond the *oikoumene* (*Caes.* 23.2), just as Claudius later
boasted of extending the empire beyond the Ocean (*ILS* 212.1.40),
that encompassing stream which Alexander had done no more than reach.
According to Sallust (*Hist.* 3.88), Pompey had sought to emulate
Alexander from his youth; his assumption of the *cognomen* 'Magnus'
suggests this, and Cicero could refer to him as 'invictissimus' (*in
Pis.* 34), just as Alexander had been honoured as the 'unconquered

god' (Hyperides, *c. Dem.* 32). There is indeed little reason to believe that Alexander was much in Caesar's mind,[66] and even Pompey
had had no such freedom as the autocratic king to carry his arms
whithersoever he would. Still it was Alexander who had first conceived, or so it was generally supposed, the ideal of world conquest, which figured in the contemporary appearance of the globe on
Roman coins, a symbol that became more common under Caesar's rule,[67]
and which was voiced in the imperialist language of Cicero; he extolled Pompey for making the Roman empire coterminous with the
limits of the earth and sky, and found it necessary to praise Caesar
in almost similar terms (cf. n.9). A writer so friendly to Caesar
as Nicolaus held that at the end of his life he was bent on subduing
not only the Parthian empire but India and all lands up to the marge
of the Ocean.[68]

However that may be, before Caesar had attained absolute power,
he could, like Pompey whom he was no doubt intent on rivalling, pursue only limited objectives. He did not even start with the project
of conquering Gaul. His original purpose must have been to operate
in Illyricum; he was diverted by the accident of the Helvetian migration.[69] But he seized every opportunity to extend Roman dominion. He assumes the sympathy of his readers. Every forward step
he took could be said to conform with the peculiar Roman conception
of defensive war, which covered the prevention and elimination of
any *potential* menace to Roman power. The *Commentaries* candidly reveal that *casus belli* were subsidiary at least to that end. Though
they voice no grandiose aspirations for world conquest, world conquest, if attainable at all, could be attained only by stages, and
as opportunities offered. It would be unwise to affirm that belief
in Rome's mission to rule the world did not underlie Caesar's own
attitude, and that which he expected in his readers.

Beyond the narrow confines of the province it is convenient
to call Narbonensis, Rome had recognized the freedom of Gallic
peoples such as the Arverni, whom she had defeated c. 120 B.C., and
had established ties of friendship with some of them, for instance
the Aedui. Her policy had, however, been largely one of non-
intervention. She had not sought to arbitrate in wars in which her
own friends were involved. The Sequani had called in bands of Germans under Ariovistus to aid them against the Aedui, apparently in

72, and inflicted a heavy defeat on that people, only to find themselves gradually reduced to submission by their own *condottieri*. So
far from answering an Aeduan appeal for protection in 61, Rome at
Caesar's own instance honoured Ariovistus with the name of friend in
59 allegedly at his own request.[70] None the less, the ties of
friendship formed outside the province gave the Romans what they
could regard as a just cause for intervention, whenever it suited
them.[71]

   In 58 the Helvetii sought to migrate from Switzerland to
Saintonge. Very naturally, Caesar refused them passage through Nar-
bonesis (*BG* 1.5-8). But he was also resolved to resist their movement by any route. They were (he claims) a fierce, warlike, people,
who had destroyed a Roman army in 107, an event Caesar harps on,[72]
and who evidently had no peaceful relationship with Rome. He con-
tends that whereas they were useful in their old home, as a buffer
between north Italy and the Germans, their presence in Saintonge
would endanger the security of Narbonensis (*BG* 1.10). They designed to march through the lands of the Aedui, whose appeals
gave Caesar a *iusta causa* to fight and hinder or punish their
depredations.[73] But he leaves no room for doubt that he had
decided to bar their migration simply because of the danger so
strong a people might constitute in Gaul to Roman interests.

   Meantime Ariovistus had been bringing more Germans into
Sequanian territory. Not only the Aedui but the Sequani were encouraged by Caesar's victory over the Helvetii to seek his aid
against the German intruders (*BG* 1.30-2). Caesar says that, re-
calling the Cimbric invasion of Gaul, he thought the presence of
this growing German power there a threat to Rome, and considered
it disgraceful *in tanto imperio populi Romani* that the Aedui, as
friends and brothers of the Roman people, should be in servitude
to them (*BG* 1.33). Yet their plight must have been well known to
him when he had procured Ariovistus' recognition as king and
friend of Rome. He presented Ariovistus with the demands that he
should settle no more Germans across the Rhine, restore the Aeduan
hostages and make no wrongful attack on the Aedui and their allies. Ariovistus, on Caesar's own showing, found these demands
inconsistent with Rome's previous neutrality and his own position
as her friend. He retorted that Caesar had no better right to

interfere in his part of Gaul than he in the Roman province; both
had acquired legitimate dominions *iure belli* (*BG* 1.34.4; cf. 44).
Caesar obviously intended his readers to find here proof of what he
calls the German's insolence. Ariovistus was told that Rome expected from her friends dutiful compliance with her will. Of course
compliance would have dissipated his own prestige and power. War
inevitably followed. It was clearly not the consequence of Aeduan
appeals which had hitherto been disregarded, nor of any German aggression – Caesar lays no stress on the fact that the Germans actually struck the first blow (*BG* 1.46) – but of Caesar's decision to
destroy a potential menace to Rome, and to aggrandize Roman dominion.[74]

He claims that by his success in 58 he pacified all Gaul, evidently in the restricted sense of that term, excluding Aquitania
and Belgica.[75] This meant in effect that its peoples had become
subjects. Like so many others who had sought Roman protection,
they had become *subiecti atque obnoxii* to the Romans (Livy 7.30.2).
The legions wintered in Sequanian lands (*BG* 1.54), and henceforth
even the Aedui were bound to obey Caesar's directions, to submit
like other friendly peoples to interference in their internal affairs, and to send contingents to his army.[76] In his reply to
Ariovistus Caesar had said that the victory over the Arverni in 121
had already given Rome the best title to rule over the Gauls, and
that it was an act of grace on her part to allow them freedom, an
act that also debarred any one else from taking it away from them
(*BG* 1.45). It soon appeared that Rome rather than the Germans
would deprive them of liberty.

In 57 the Belgae already feared attack and 'conspired' to an-
ticipate it. Caesar took this as a justification for striking
first. He does not bother to suggest that a Belgic raid on the
territory of the Remi, who had voluntarily submitted to him, was
the warrant for his offensive operations.[77] One by one the
Belgae were forced to surrender. If such peoples took up arms
again, it was rebellion and a breach of faith.[78] In 56, without
so much as an allegation that any attack on Roman territory was
brewing, Roman troops invaded Aquitania, where the people could
be treated as hostile because they had assailed Roman forces in
the Sertorian war (*BG* 3.20).

In 55 Caesar first crossed the Channel on the plea that Britons
had assisted his Gallic enemies in almost every war; this hitherto
unmentioned assistance cannot have been significant. Some *civitates*
were forced, or induced, to promise obedience to Roman orders, and
the second invasion could then be justified, either to hold them to
their undertakings or to protect them against still independent
neighbours.[79] Tribute was imposed (*BG* 5.22.4); this must have been
Caesar's general practice in Gaul, whenever he had met and subdued
resistance (cf. *BG* 7.76.1); in 51/50 he was careful to impose no
new burdens (*BG* 8.49). Even peoples which had voluntarily submitted were required to send military contingents and in general to
obey Caesar's will.[80]

Again in 55, after refusing to allow some German tribes to
settle peacefully west of the Rhine, in the fear that they would
combine with disloyal Gauls against him (*BG* 4.5f.), Caesar attacked
and massacred those who had crossed. The preventive action he took
was no different in principle from his previous offensives, of which
his enemies at Rome do not seem to have complained, and he no doubt
expects his readers to infer that his Machiavellian detention of the
German chiefs who had come to him as ambassadors, while he cut their
leaderless followers to pieces in time of truce, was warranted by an
earlier violation of the truce on the part of the Germans (*BG* 4.11-
14; cf. 8.23.3). At Rome, as usual, supplications were voted for
his victory, though Cato urged that for his perfidy he should be delivered up to the Germans.[81] Both in 55 and 54 Caesar went further,
crossing the Rhine himself, to punish German inroads and spread the
terror of the Roman name. Once again he had clients (the Ubii) to
protect beyond the river, whom he characteristically treats as subject to his orders - and that made it absurd in Roman eyes if the
Sugambri claimed that the Rhine was the frontier of the Roman empire. But Caesar does not conceal the fact that his German campaigns
were essentially designed for the security of Roman dominion in
Gaul.[82]

Caesar's account of these transactions is self-exculpatory only
in a certain sense. He undoubtedly intends his readers to think that
it was not for personal greed or glory that he undertook his campaigns, but he has no need to insist on their justice. Though he
never claims to have planned the conquest of Gaul, it is implicit in

the *Commentaries*, from the very first sentence, that this was what
he had achieved. Few Romans besides Cato needed to be convinced of
the propriety of any measures he took to this end. In his speech
of 56 *de provinciis consularibus*, without troubling himself about
the niceties of Caesar's treatment of this or that individual Gallic
people, Cicero argues flatly that Caesar was performing the highest
service to the state by conquering the whole country, since there
was no other way of providing permanently for Italy's security; it
made no difference that Caesar had mastered peoples whose very
names had never been heard at Rome before.[83] On this sort of principle no war that Rome could fight against foreign peoples who might
some day be strong enough to attack her could be other than defensive. There is no indication in the speech that this view was contested. Those who wished to relieve Caesar of his command evidently
argued not that his campaigns had been unjust or unnecessary, but
that the war was already over.

Of course this was far from true. Caesar's greatest crises
were yet to come. In 52 he had to contend with an almost pan-Gallic
rebellion. It may be that he actually exaggerated Gallic unity on
sundry occasions (n.75); and made it plausible that Rome could not
stop short of subduing the whole nation and implicitly excused operations against any one *civitas* whose offence was solely that of not
having submitted. Caesar himself allows that his opponents were
fighting for liberty, 'for which all men naturally strive'. Roman
writers were never reluctant to recognize this motive for resistance
and revolt.[84] But they did not concede that their subjects or de-
pendants had any right to be free of Roman rule. Liberty was the
privilege of the imperial people, as Cicero boasted to the Quirites:
*populum Romanum servire fas non est, quem di immortales omnibus
gentibus imperare voluerunt.*[85] Caesar's admiration for Vercingeto-
rix is easily to be discerned, but as the great rebel, he still merited death.[86]

X ROMAN 'CLEMENCY'
Wherever necessary, the most brutal methods of repression were therefore in order. Death or enslavement was the common penalty for free-
dom-fighters. Caesar was alleged to have made a million slaves in
Gaul;[87] he himself casually refers to a load of captives he shipped

back from Britain in 55 (*BG* 5.23.2), the only kind of booty, Cicero
had heard (*ad Att.* 4.16.7), that could be expected from this poor
island; he was delighted at Quintus' promise to send him some of
them (*ad QF.* 3.7.4). Caesar did all he could to extirpate the Ebu-
rones (*BG* 6.34 and 43). On one occasion, like Scipio Aemilianus,
that paragon of Roman *humanitas* (App. *Iber.* 94), he had the right
hands of all his prisoners cut off (8.44). Yet he speaks, as does
Hirtius, of his clemency.[88]

It was characteristic of Romans as early as Cato (Gell. 6.3.52)
to boast of what Livy calls their *vetustissimum morem victis parcendi*
(33.12.7). Once again Cicero held that Roman practice conformed to
Panaetian laws of war; especially when wars were fought for glory,
the conquered were to be treated with mercy. Only the destruction
of Corinth had perhaps marred Rome's record. Not indeed that Cicero
considered that mercy was always proper; it was not due to enemies
who were themselves cruel or who were guilty of violating treaties,
Rome naturally being the judge, nor when Rome's own survival was at
stake. He does not make it clear how he would have justified the
destruction of Numantia, which he approves.[89] But Numantia had re-
belled; to Romans rebellion was in itself proof of perfidy. Polybius reports Flamininus as saying in 197 that the Romans were 'moderate, placable and humane', since they did not utterly destroy a
people the first time they fought them (18.37). By implication repeated resistance might call for severity, which was also regarded
as a virtue. When Virgil defined Rome's mission as *parcere sub-
iectis et debellare superbos*, he was in effect dividing mankind
into two categories, those too insolent to accept her god-given
dominion, and those who submitted to it. The latter were to be
spared: what of the former? Germanicus was to set up a monument
boasting that he had 'warred down' the Germans, after exterminating
one community with no distinction of age or sex (Tac. *Ann.* 2.21f.).

Naturally this was not the practice Romans preferred. We may
readily believe Augustus' claim that it was his policy to preserve
foreign peoples who could safely be spared rather than extirpate
them (*RG* 3). After all, the dead paid no taxes. Moreover it was
usually more expedient to accept the surrender of an enemy, offered
in the hope or expectation of mercy, rather than to incur the expense of time, money and blood in further military operations, and

then to fulfil that expectation, if only to encourage others not to
prolong their own resistance. Hampl found a precedent for Rome's
normal conduct in Hittite inscriptions. It was not motivated primarily by humanity, but by rational consideration of self-interest.[90]

    It is true that Cicero connected with Rome's supposed clemency
to the vanquished her liberality with the franchise. In degree, if
not in kind, this was undoubtedly a practice for which we can find
no parallel in the policy of other city states. But for Cicero himself it was not altruistic generosity, but a device by which Rome
had extended her empire (see p.165). In early days it must have
been prompted by self-interest, however enlightened, and it was not
always welcome to beneficiaries such as the Capuans, if they did not
attain to full equality of rights in the Roman state. By the time
that Roman citizenship had come to be an object of the subjects' aspirations, it was a privilege granted reluctantly and sparingly. In
Cicero's youth the Italians had had to wrest it from Rome by force
of arms. Few now wished to go further and add to the numbers of
Romanos rerum dominos gentemque togatam. All efforts to enfranchise
the Transpadani failed until Caesar could carry the measure by military power in 49.[91] It was Caesar too who began to extend citizenship to provincial communities. More often he was content to bestow
the Latin right, as to the Sicilians. They were Cicero's old
clients, whose loyalty to Rome he had extolled in fulsome terms in
70; none the less, he regarded this grant as 'insufferable'.[92]

XI JUSTICE FOR THE SUBJECTS
In general Cicero speaks with contempt of provincials. Thus the
most eminent of Gauls is not to be compared with the meanest of
Romans; they were an arrogant and faithless people, bound by no religious scruples, the true descendants of those who had burned down
the Capitol (*pro Font*. 27-36). Conceivably there might be Sardin-
ians whose testimony a Roman court might believe, but most of them
were mere barbarian half-breeds, more mendacious than their Punic
forebears, and not one community in the island had earned the privileges of friendship with Rome and liberty (*pro Scaur*. 38-45). Even
the Greeks, to whom Rome owed her culture, as Cicero often allowed,[93]
were now for the most part degenerate,[94] yet they stood at a far
higher level than such peoples as Mysians and Phrygians (*ad QF*.

1.1.19), who constituted most of the population of the province of
Asia. Jews and Syrians were 'nations born for servitude' (de prov.
cons. 10). Admittedly in most of the passages cited Cicero was
trying to discredit witnesses hostile to his clients, and he could
speak, when it suited him, honorifically of provincial magnates and
communities, but none the less such statements are eloquent of the
prejudice he could easily arouse, and some of his private remarks
even on Greeks are disdainful (e.g. ad QF. 1.2.4).

The 'ideal of inclusiveness' which Last treats as an 'outstanding feature of the political technique devised by the Roman
Republic' had not in fact emerged.[95] The third book of Cicero's
de republica preserves traces of an argument in which imperial dominion seems to have been defended as just in much the same way as
the rule of soul over body or masters over slaves; men who were incapable of governing themselves were actually better off as the
slaves or subjects of others.[96] The theory naturally did not imply
that any actual slaves or subjects belonged to this category, but a
Roman could easily persuade himself that experience showed the subjects to be unfitted for independence.

Under Roman private law the master was entitled to exploit his
slaves as he pleased, and the iura belli, accepted throughout antiquity, allowed similar rights to the victor in war. Beyond doubt
Romans took it for granted that Rome was justified in profiting
from her empire. Yet in Panaetius' theory, which Cicero adopted,
just as masters were bound to give slaves just treatment (de offic.
1.41), so an imperial power had a duty to care for the ruled, which
Rome had faithfully discharged in the 'good, old days' before Sulla
(2.27). Good government was due even to Africans, Spaniards and
Gauls, 'savage and barbarous nations' (ad QF. 1.1.27).

Many or most of Rome's subjects had come under her sway, not
always after defeat, by deditio, which involved the surrender of
divina humanaque omnia (Livy 1.38) and the extinction of the community concerned, but Rome regularly restored to the dediti their
cities, lands and laws, often recognized them as her friends and
sometimes concluded treaties with them; they thus acquired rights
that fides or religio bound Rome to respect. In practice Rome left
them all to manage their own internal affairs, at most ensuring
that they were administered by persons loyal to the sovereign.[97]

Indemnities or taxes might be demanded from defeated enemies as *quasi victoriae praemium ac poena belli* (II *Verr*. 3.12), and provinces could be described as virtual estates of the Roman people (ibid. 2.7), yet Cicero at least felt it necessary to argue that taxation was in the interest of the provincials themselves: armies were required for their protection, and revenue was indispensable to pay them (*ad QF*. 1.1.34). Thus taxation of the subjects was justified by the benefits conferred on them. Precisely the same argument was to be advanced by Tacitus.[98] There was not even anything new in Tiberius' celebrated dictum that he would have his subjects sheared, not shaved (Suet. *Tib*. 32): Cicero rebutted Verres' claim that he had acted in the public interest by selling the Sicilian tithes at unprecedentedly high amounts, by observing that neither senate nor people had intended him to act in such a way as to ruin the farmers and jeopardize future returns (II *Verr*. 3.48). This, however, is only a question of rational exploitation of the subjects, not of justice towards them.

We may indeed ask how far Cicero spoke for many more than himself in advocating justice to the subjects. Here I attach some significance to his denunciations of the misgovernment prevalent in his time, in the Verrines written for an upper-class audience, in his speech before the people on the Manilian law, and even in a despatch from Cilicia to the senate.[99] He assumes that his own sentiments are generally shared. He actually tells the senate that because of the oppressive and unjust character of Roman government the *socii* are too weak or too disloyal to contribute much to defence against Parthia. About the same time he wrote to Cato that it was his principal object, given the lack of adequate military resources, to provide for the protection of his province by his own mild and upright conduct that would ensure the fidelity of the *socii*, and he later claims that he had reconciled the provincials to Roman rule by the excellence of his own administration.[100] It was indeed a commonplace of ancient political thinking, doubtless based on oft-repeated experience, that in Livy's words *certe id firmissimum longe imperium est quo oboedientes gaudent*;[101] it recurs, for instance, in discussions of absolute monarchy, which teach the king to show justice not only for its own sake but in order to secure the affection of his subjects and make his rule more secure.[102]

However, Cicero's letters from Cilicia and his advice to his
brother in Asia (*ad QF*. 1.1) do not suggest that good government was
to be practised purely for this prudential reason. Cicero tells
Atticus, for instance, that his integrity as a governor afforded him
the greatest intrinsic satisfaction of his life. It mattered to him,
he says, more than the fame it brought (*ad Att*. 5.20.6). But the
allusion to fame should also be marked. 'Fame' he says in the first
Philippic (29) 'is demonstrated by the testimony not only of all the
best men but by that of the multitude.' It was in this sense that
he expected his reputation to be enhanced by his virtues as a
governor. So too he surely supposed that denunciations of misrule
would evoke indignation - Pompey in 71, he tells us (I *Verr*. 45),
had actually roused the people in this way - and equally that there
would be a popular response to his laudation of Pompey, not only as
a great general but as one whose upright behaviour won the hearts of
the subjects (*de imp. Cn. Pomp.* 36-42); he does not add in this en-
comium that his behaviour would strengthen Roman rule. In the same
way Caesar in his *Civil War* digresses to excoriate the cruelty and
rapacity of Metellus Scipio and his officers in the east (*BC* 3.31-3);
this was in part a propagandist work, and Caesar evidently hoped
that his readers would condemn his enemies for their ill-treatment
of provincials. The author of the *Bellum Africum* also contrasts
Caesar's care for African provincials (3.1, 7.2) with the depredations, and worse, of his adversaries (26).

Perhaps the constant use of the term *socii* to describe provincials in itself indicates something about Roman attitudes to them;
it could hardly have been totally divested of the nuance imparted
by its other senses. Much more striking, however, is the history
of *repetundae* legislation. At least from the late third century
the senate had been ready to hear compaints from the *socii* against
Roman officials and to provide for reparation or punishment.[103]
The statutes on this subject passed between 149 and 59 were the
work of politicians of varying complexion, but according to Cicero
(*de offic.* 2.75) each enactment made the law stricter. It is
notable that the clause authorizing recovery of money from third
parties who had benefited from the governor's extortions, a clause
that could affect equites and was apparently often invoked, was
introduced by Glaucia, who sought their political backing, and was

simply adopted in later statutes (*Rab. post.* 8-10). Cicero briefly
characterizes Sulla's law as *lex socialis* (*div. in Caec.* 18).
Caesar's statute, comprising no less than 101 clauses (*ad fam.*
8.8.3), and approved by Cicero (*pro Sest.* 135; *in Pis.* 37), remained
in force until Justinian's time and formed the basis of the law
throughout the imperial period.[104] Our accounts of the eventful
year in which it was passed are fairly full, yet they do not allude
to its enactment. It was probably uncontroversial. Like earlier
repetundae laws, it was concerned only with the wrong-doing of senatorial officials. The governor himself was supposed to protect subjects in his courts against publicans and usurers. On paper even
Verres promised heavy damages against the former, if they were
guilty of illicit exactions (II *Verr.* 3.26), and some governors gave
the provincials real protection.[105]

No proof is needed that provincials found insufficient aid in
the *repetundae* laws, *quae vi, ambitu, postremo pecunia turbabantur*
(Tac. *Ann.* 1.2), or that many governors, for prudence or profit,
connived at or participated in the rapacity of tax-gatherers and
moneylenders. Personal or political connexions could also distort
the conduct of senators who, like Cicero, had no wish for their own
part to pillage the subjects.[106] In practice the provincials were
usually at the mercy of the proconsul, who was virtually absolute
in his province, *ubi nullum auxilium est, nulla conquestio, nullus
senatus, nulla contio* (Cic. *ad QF.* 1.1.22). Their best hope lay in
his probity and courage. In general he was restrained from indulg-
ing in or permitting extortion only by his conscience, or regard
for his own reputation. Cicero enjoins upon Quintus and claims for
himself, and for Pompey, such virtues as justice, mercy, accessibility and diligence. No quality is more often commended than that
elementary honesty for which the most revealing Latin term is
abstinentia.[107] The very frequency with which it is ascribed,
whether truly or falsely, to individuals shows how little it could
be assumed as a common characteristic of officials (cf. n.110).
Still, we must not too lightly treat a Verres or an Appius as typical of republican governors. Others are known to have been men of
personal integrity, or, like Scaevola, Lucullus and perhaps Gabinius
(n.105), to have protected the subjects against usurers and publicans. Scaevola remained an exemplar; Cicero took his edict as the

model for his own (cf. n.105). In 50 Cicero tells Atticus that he
had heard only good reports of all but one of the eastern governors;
they were behaving in conformity with the high principles of Cato,
a quo uno omnium sociorum querelae audiuntur,[108] and, incidentally,
with those which Atticus had himself repeatedly recommended to
Cicero.[109] The standards of good government were already recognized
and approved in the republic, and the only change that came about in
the Principate in this regard was that they were somewhat better observed, an improvement that it is easy to exaggerate.[110]

When Cicero included *provinciae, socii* among the *fundamenta
otiosae dignitatis*, I feel sure that he meant among other things
care for their welfare (cf. *de leg.* 3.9). But *aerarium* is another of
the *fundamenta*, and in his day it was the provinces which supplied
most of the revenue. It was probably not until the nineteenth century that any imperial power scrupled to tax subjects for its own
benefit; the Romans were not ashamed to do so, and I imagine that
most of them would have thought Cicero's justification of the practice, which I cited earlier, as superfluous. In one way or another
senators and equites, soldiers and grain recipients at Rome all
profited from the empire. In addressing the people Cicero can refer
to 'your taxes' and 'your lands'.[111] He did not forget in advocating the Manilian law to argue that it served the interests of the
treasury and of Romans with business in the east (*de imp. Cn. Pomp.*
14-19). Pompey boasted of the enormous accretion of revenue his
conquests had brought (Plut. *Pomp.* 45). Nor must we overlook what
Romans seldom mentioned, that victorious wars stocked Italian estates with cheap slaves.

I will add only one further point. Under the Principate the
worst features of republican misrule were obliterated; above all
peace and order were better preserved. But exploitation did not
end. Italy benefited as much as the provinces from the Roman peace,
yet until Diocletian the land there was immune from tax.[112] While
contributing less than the provinces to the common needs for expenditure, Italians continued, as late as the third century, to enjoy
a share of the higher posts disproportionate to that of provincials,
if we simply equate Italy with an area in the provinces of like size
and population.[113] Moreover provincial revenues were spent lavishly
on feeding and amusing the inhabitants of Rome and beautifying the

city, to say nothing of court expenditure. These privileges were
not challenged by provincials in the senate or on the throne.
Equality as between Italians and provincials was not attained, until all were sunk in equal misery.

9: GREEK INTELLECTUALS AND THE ROMAN ARISTOCRACY IN THE FIRST CENTURY B.C.

M.H.Crawford (Christ's College, Cambridge)

Roman attitudes to the Greek world and Greek attitudes to Rome in the first century B.C. were alike complex.[1] The development of Roman hegemony and the intermittent occurrence of brutality had long provoked both protests and attempts to throw off the Roman yoke; yet the first century B.C. saw the final consolidation of Roman rule in spite of the efforts of Mithridates VI and the increasing incidence at Rome of civil strife; the demands of the opposing sides in the civil wars actually increased the pressures on the Greek cities and encouraged acts of brutality culminating in the sack of Rhodes in 42 B.C. Recognition, however, of the futility of armed resistance to Rome did not prevent the continued voicing of opposition to Roman rule or to particular aspects of it.

One thinks at one level of Timagenes,[2] brought to Rome as a captive by A.Gabinius, bought by Faustus Sulla, who followed the profession of *sophistes* at Rome; he was notorious for the claim that Theophanes persuaded Ptolemy Auletes to leave Egypt in order to provide a command for Pompeius and publicized the story of Caepio and the gold of Tolosa; he was described as *felicitati urbis inimicus*, jealous of the well-being of the city, who regretted fires at Rome because the city always rose more glorious than before; he may be one of the *levissimi ex Graecis qui Parthorum quoque contra nomen Romanum gloriae favent*, 'frivolous Greeks who rate the glory of Parthia above the reputation of Rome', who stimulated Livy to an angry refutation of their view that Rome would have been no match for Alexander.[3] One thinks also of the anti-Roman historians who favoured barbarian kings attacked by Dionysius of Halicarnassus, some of whom perhaps belonged to the end of the republic.[4] One thinks of the critique of Rome reproduced by Pompeius Trogus.[5] On another level, there is the 'oracle of Hystaspes' and the later portions of the third book of the Sibylline oracles.[6]

At the same time, numerous Greek individuals and communities not only attempted to avoid the possible unfortunate consequences

of Roman rule, but actively sought the benefits which could be won
from Roman notables or the Roman senate; in their struggles the
still undiminished and ever more widely acknowledged cultural superiority of the Greek world provided an important weapon; at the
same time there developed in the late republic 'the open conspiracy
in which Greek and Roman aristocracies found a bond of sympathy and
material interest' and which formed the basis of Roman rule in the
Greek world under Augustus and his successors.[7]

Increased acceptance by the Greek world of Roman rule, indeed,
did not lead to any decline in the value attached to traditional
Greek institutions or to any reluctance to assert Greek cultural superiority; one reaction to the early stages of the Roman conquest of
the Greek world had been the defensive one of claiming superiority
in matters other than military, combined with the naive belief that
the Romans only needed to have things explained to them in order to
appreciate the Greek point of view; so too in the first century B.C.
Greek communities consciously sought to preserve their Greekness and
Greeks continued to claim the right to set cultural standards. A
Roman acceptance, even if hesitant and only occurring in some quarters, of Greek cultural standards of course lies behind the early
stages of the Hellenization of Rome; by the first century B.C. the
Greek orientation of certain aspects of Roman culture is, I think,
strong enough not only to provide a stimulus to Greek intellectual
activity, but even to influence its nature. The mediating factor
is the existence on a scale previously unknown of links between
Roman notables and Greek intellectuals, which may be taken as a
special form of the links in any case existing between Greek and
Roman aristocrats. But in order to understand this state of
affairs, some discussion is necessary of the vitality of Greek
institutions and of the Greek assumption of cultural superiority.

The persistence, despite the decline of Magna Graecia, of Greek
customs and institutions in those Greek cities of Italy which survived until the coming of the Romans is well known. The Tarentini,
a miserable and poverty-stricken community in the second century,[8]
regarded by Lucilius as on a par with Cosentini and Siculi,[9] in 102
welcomed Archias, Greeks welcoming a Greek, along with Rhegium and
Neapolis.[10] Neapolis, along with Heraclea, where also Archias had
been honoured by being given citizenship (Cic. *pro Arch.* 6),

hesitated over whether to accept Roman citizenship after the Social
War (Cic. *pro Balb.* 21), no doubt in part because of a fear of being
swallowed up in Roman Italy.[11]   Neapolis, along with Velia, provided
Rome with priestesses of Ceres, who had to be Greek (Cic. *pro Balb.*
55).   Neapolis, along with Dicaearchia (Puteoli), offered prayers in
the manner of the Greeks when Cn. Pompeius was ill in 50 (Cic. *Tusc.*
disp. 1.86; cf. Festus 109 L).   Tarentum, Rhegium, Velia and Neapolis
remained Greek in character in the early empire, an attribute perhaps
shared by the Hellenized native community of Canusium.[12]

The reluctance of Neapolis and Heraclea to accept Roman citizenship is paralleled by a clear, though diminishing, reluctance to become Roman citizens among Greeks in general.   No firm conclusion can
be drawn from a list of such individual enfranchisements as are attested; but it is striking that when Asclepiades and his two associ-
ates were lavishly rewarded in 78 for their services to Rome they
were not granted citizenship (Sherk 22).   With interesting forth-
rightness, a Cretan serving on the Italian side in the Social War
had already rejected citizenship as a reward for betraying his com-
panions with the remark that 'in the eyes of Cretans citizenship is
high-sounding claptrap' (Diod. 27.18).   It is also striking that although Theophanes of Mytilene was enfranchised by Pompeius, another
great friend, Pythodorus of Tralles, did not acquire citizenship.   A
changing attitude is perhaps implied by the fact that Lyso of Patras,
a friend of Cicero, allowed his son (perhaps in about 50), to be
adopted by a Roman, albeit exiled (*ad fam.* 13.19.2).   The Civil Wars
after 49 brought large-scale enfranchisement in the Greek east and
Octavian's navarch Seleucus was granted citizenship *ad hominem*
(Sherk 58); when T.Statilius Lamprias of Epidaurus died between A.D.
40 and 42, the Athenians described him, in marked contrast to the
earlier Cretan viewpoint, as honoured by possession of 'that great
gift, renowned among all men, Roman citizenship'.[13]

Reluctant to accept Roman citizenship, the Greeks of the east
in the late republic are also attested as acting to preserve the
traditional limitation of land-holding to members of their own communities.   We hear of clashes over *enktesis* at Parium and at Colo-
phon, with Cicero writing to get support from the provincial governor
for the intending Roman in each case, also of preposterous manoeuvres
by Decianus at Apollonis to get possession of land against the wishes

of the community.[14]

On the whole content with their own citizenship and sometimes
attested as resisting *more maiorum* the holding of land by outsiders,
the Greeks of the first century B.C. in religious matters also normally kept to their own ways. The dedication of the Lycian Aichmon,
who served with P.Servilius Isauricus against the pirates in 78, to
Mars (Ares) instead of to Jupiter is conspicuous for its isolation
(*OGIS* 553). Agonistic festivals in the Greek world continued to follow the traditional pattern, of which participation by Greek com-
petitors was a conspicuous feature; gladiatorial contests were of course
imported into the Greek world, but remained an alien excrescence,
without attracting Greek participation.[15] The use of aromatic plants
in funeral rites remained an almost purely Roman custom, unattested
in the Greek world except for isolated introductions (in the context
of Roman settlement) in the early empire.[16]

Normal Greek practice in dedicating a statue was to name the
honorand in the accusative, Roman practice to name him in the dative;
the Greek usage persisted, with only four imperial dedications in
the Greek world in the dative (from Mytilene, Athens, Sparta and
Asia, this last Hadrianic).[17] There is one isolated republican
example of a private dedication in Greek in the dative,[18] a few more
from Augustus onwards. The Greek place of honour was on one's right,
the Roman on one's left;[19] the Gytheum inscription shows Livia on
Augustus' right, the more honoured in Greek usage than Tiberius on
Augustus' left.[20]

The imperviousness of the Greek world to Roman customs is attested also by archaeological evidence. Even in Sicily, Roman styles
and techniques of architecture are rare.[21] The Roman urban pattern of
insulae with shops around continues to contrast with the Greek pattern of small housing units with separate shops.[22] The Roman *vicus*
organization is unknown in the east, except in a colonial context.[23]
In Cyrenaica the Greek (and native) population in a sense took over,
but metamorphosed almost out of recognition, Roman funerary art.[24]

The vitality of Greek institutions, then, is amply attested;
the Greek assumption of cultural superiority is no less clear. There
is still little trace of any interest in Latin literature in any Greek
author and not even the grudging admission of some Athenians of the
early second century A.D. that *some* of the poetry of Catullus and

Calvus was up to the standard of Anacreon and other Greek lyric
poets.[25] Assertion or reassertion by a Greek community in the east
of the value of its past and of its culture is attested by the re-
inscription at Miletus around 100 of the decree of the *molpoi* of
450/49 and of the third and early second-century list of *aisymnetai*.[26]
The Greek world in general and Greek intellectuals in particular
also expected to set standards. The trio of adjectives applied, we
do not know on what grounds, by Posidonius to Marcellus is significant[27] – despite his military ability, moderate, benevolent and lov-
ing *Hellenike paideia* and Greek learning, admiring those who engaged
in intellectual activity though he had not time enough for it; the
expectations of Posidonius emerge clearly from the improving tale,
for which he is the sole source, of the successful intercession of
Nicias of Engyion with Marcellus for his city. It is also clear
from what Cicero tells us of Cato the Younger and from what Nepos
tells us of Atticus that the Greek ideal was for Greek philosophical precepts to govern Roman conduct.[28] The implausibility of the
notion is evidence of the obsession with the ideal. Evidence for
Greek standards of behaviour may also be drawn from the account
in Dionysius of Halicarnassus of the opposing Roman and Tarentine
claims to Neapolitan friendship in 327, presumably reflecting attitudes of the first century B.C. and cast in terms of what Greeks
should or should not do.[29] And the story in Strabo of Demetrius'
protest to Rome over Antiate piracy, again presumably in a first
century B.C. dress even if the essence of the story is authentic,
is a perfect example of Greek didactic moralizing (5.3.5 (232)).

Greek cultural claims in the first century B.C. are therefore
clear enough; what is less immediately clear is the nature of the
relationship between these Greek intellectual claims and their
Roman addressees and the nature of the hold which Greek intellectuals had over members of the Roman aristocracy. I shall suggest,
first, that in the first century B.C. the cultural interests of the
Roman aristocracy were more Greek oriented than before, despite the
persistence of certain readily intelligible ambiguities; second,
that men who were never able like Cicero, or for that matter Catullus
or Lucretius, to pursue whatever cultural interests they had acted
as patrons of the arts instead; third, that the availability of
patronage for Greek men of letters and the form which it sometimes

took of lightening the burden of Roman rule for the communities of
the men concerned provided a possible stimulus to intellectual activity which was not directly beneficial to the patron. I suggest
that not all Greek men of letters were wholly honest in the way they
went about their business; if some Romans wished first and foremost
to be seen to be men of Hellenic culture, not all Greeks lived up to
the tenets of the *paideia* which they professed.

Even in private, Cicero found little to admire in the Greeks of
his own day;[30] in public, there was a rich vein of prejudice to be
exploited. It was easy to equate Epicurean philosophy with the immorality for which the Greeks were notorious (*in Pis*. 68-72). Jews
and Syrians, that is, the Greeks of Syria, could be described as
nationes natae servituti, peoples born to slavery; the Greeks, despite their culture, were hopeless liars as witnesses;[31] they were
easily led into passing decrees against Roman magistrates, indeed
irresponsibility was the dominant feature of their assemblies, which
actually *sat* to deliberate.[32] Allied to the Roman view, that when
it came to running a state the Romans were incomparably better than
the Greeks, was the clearly held belief that Roman civil law was
superior to anything which the Greek world had to offer;[33] it is
amazing, remarks Cicero, how all *ius civile* apart from our own is
crude and almost absurd.[34]

But in a famous passage in a letter to his brother, Cicero
characterized his debt to Greek culture: even if his brother were in
charge of Africans, Spaniards or Gauls, *immanes ac barbarae nationes*,
'wild and barbarous peoples', he should look after them; but since
he is in charge of Greeks, from whom *humanitas* has spread to others,
he must show it to them.[35] Cicero goes on to say that his achievements are due to what he has learnt from the Greeks. But even here
there is a reservation: the story of Cicero's life does not allow
what might otherwise be a possible inference, namely that an interest
in Greek learning is a sign of *inertia* or *levitas*. Too great a knowledge of Greek culture could be misunderstood; Cicero had been re-
proached for speaking Greek in Syracuse and in attacking C.Verres
was careful to apologize for knowing the names of Greek artists,
even an artist such as Praxiteles.[36] There is in fact a fundamental
ambiguity in the attitude of Cicero and his contemporaries, an ambiguity which echoes that of the elder Cato and his contemporaries a

century earlier and which cannot be adequately explained in terms of
the difference between contemporary and classical Greece or between
intellectual and immoral Greeks.

Despite the dangers, Cicero and his peers sometimes seem to
have behaved as if Greek culture was the only culture which mattered.
Education by Greeks and through the medium of Greek was taken for
granted by the upper classes. Although Cicero learnt from the Roman
speech-writer and antiquarian, L.Aelius, *eruditissimus et Graecis
litteris et Latinis*, 'an outstanding Greek and Latin scholar', and
naturally listened to Roman orators and studied the *ius civile*, most
of his education was at the hands of Greeks, beginning with the Epicurean Phaedrus.[37]

When Philo, the head of the Academy at Athens, came to Rome in
88 as a refugee from Mithridates, Cicero spent all the time he could
with him.[38] He went on to devote himself to philosophy and rhetoric,
under the guidance of the Stoic Diodotus, who lived for a time under
Cicero's roof and in his company;[39] the oratorical exercises undertaken by Cicero were in Greek rather than in Latin;[40] the visit of
Apollonius Molo to Rome in 82-81 provided Cicero with an opportunity
to broaden his education still further.[41] Finally a trip to the
east saw Cicero studying for six months under Antiochus of the Academy and also under Phaedrus once more and under Zeno, another Epicurean philosopher; he also studied with Demetrius, a teacher of
rhetoric; he then went to Asia and travelled round in the company of
a number of great orators, Menippus of Stratonicea, Dionysius of
Magnesia, Aeschylus of Cnidus, Xenocles of Adramyttium; then on to
Rhodes to study again under Molo.[42]

Nor was Cicero untypical; C.Aurelius Cotta had set the fashion
(Cic. *ND* 1.59); Caesar also sailed to Rhodes to study under Molo,
though he was diverted by the outbreak of the Third Mithridatic
War.[43] And when Sertorius set out to educate the Spaniards, he provided teachers in Greek and Roman learning (Plut. *Sert.* 14). The
three nonentities, P. and C.Selius and Tetrilius Rogus, in Alexandria
with Lucullus, had listened to Philo in Rome with some attention
(Cic. *Acad.pr.* 2.11). A generation later, Cicero's son and nephew
went through the same educational process as he had himself.[44] Caesar
had Octavian given a rhetorical education in Greek and Latin (Zonaras
10.13). Massalia was able to profit from the Roman desire for a

Greek education by setting itself up as a rival to Athens (and
thereby perhaps recovering some of the prosperity lost as a result
of backing Pompeius) (Strabo 4.1.5 (181)). Things had progressed
so far that the Greek education of Juba II actually took place in
Italy.[45]

It comes as no surprise to discover that it is for the period
of Cicero's youth that there is recorded the first occasion on which
a Greek ambassador addressed the senate without an interpreter,
Apollonius Molo in 82-81.[46] Twenty years later, in 62, Cicero asserted that Greek literature was read in almost all countries (in
contrast to Latin), Italy clearly included (*pro Arch.* 23). Within
Cicero's lifetime, there apparently emerged the catchphrase *utraque
lingua*, automatically understood as referring to the two languages
available to an educated Roman.[47]

But the Roman aristocracy in the generation after Sulla was
not only Greek educated and Greek speaking; for them apparently
only Greek culture was good enough. There was a ready market in
Rome for the library of Aristotle;[48] L.Gellius, censor in 70,
equipped himself with a Greek mythological ancestress in the shape
of Lamia-Gello, daughter of Neptune and queen of the Laestrygonians,
and probably used the Palazzo Santa Croce reliefs to illustrate the
claim;[49] early contacts between Greece and Rome in the shape of
Delphic oracles were recklessly invented;[50] Caesar felt himself
obliged to include 500 Greeks among the 5,000 new colonists of
Comum (Strabo 5.1.6 (213)); the future triumvir M.Lepidus advertised
on his coinage the at best exaggerated claim that an ancestor had
been tutor to Ptolemy V.[51] Greek fashions in everything from metal
ware to perfume were all the rage.[52]

Some Romans even seem to have gone so far as to ignore most
contemporary developments in the field of Latin literature, aping
the Greeks thereby. This attitude is both exemplified by and
particularly striking in Cicero, himself both outstandingly cre-
ative in one branch of Latin literature and clearly aware of his
oratorical achievements; Latin literature is apparently of almost
no interest to him before the last decade of his life and only a
Greek is thought suitable as the author of a monograph on his consulship.

To take history first, Claudius Quadrigarius, writing a history

of Rome from the Gallic sack down to his own day in the decade after
Sulla, is mentioned neither by Cicero nor by any other writer before
Livy; Cn.Cornelius Sisenna, a perhaps younger contemporary, praetor
in 78,[53] writing a monograph on the wars of 91 to 82, is quoted once
by Cicero in connexion with dreams and omens (*de div.* 1.99), once by
Varro on a point of grammar (*LL* 8.73); this despite the favourable
judgement by Sallust (*BJ* 95.2). C.Licinius Macer, tribune in 73 and
praetor perhaps in 68, author of a history of Rome probably down to
his own day,[54] appears to have been almost wholly ignored by the age
of Cicero; but Sisenna and Macer were at least discussed by Cicero
when he came to reflect on Roman historiography towards the end of
his life. The unfortunate Valerius Antias is mentioned by no one
before Dionysius and Livy, although he may have been used by Varro.[55]

Cicero's critique of Roman historiography, placed in the mouth
of Atticus, is indeed remarkable (*de leg.* 1.5-7). A request to
Cicero to write a history of Rome comes first, *ut in hoc etiam genere
Graeciae nihil cedamus*, 'so that in this genre also we may not be inferior to Greece'; the concern is characteristic of Cicero's later
years. Brief and derogatory remarks about Pictor and other early
writers are followed by savage attacks on Macer and Sisenna, the
former for learning nothing from the Greeks,[56] the latter for learning
only from Cleitarchus and thereby ruining his style.[57]

I find it hard to believe, however, that Cicero's contempt for
the efforts of contemporary Latin historians can be explained solely
by reference to their stylistic inadequacies or by reference to their
regrettable mendacity, castigated by Cicero in general terms (*Brut.*
62), or in terms of the accepted convention whereby all historians
denigrated their predecessors. His attitude is not dissimilar to
the view apparently widespread among his contemporaries that only
Greek culture was good enough. It was for this reason that Cicero's
commentarius on his consulship was in Greek[58] and that Atticus' piece
on the same subject was in the same language;[59] more significantly,
Cicero sent copies to Posidonius and others, with a request to work
the *commentarius* up into something grander.[60] (He appears to have
believed their polite protestations that they could not possibly
improve on his work.)

Nor does Latin poetry of the age of Cicero attract any more
attention than Latin historiography from Cicero and his friends.[61]

Cicero's admiration for Varro can be readily explained in terms of
his interest in those aspects of Roman history and institutions
where her greatness was most apparent.[62]

The dominance of Greek culture in the minds of Cicero and his
contemporaries in the period between the Sullan settlement and the
outbreak of war between Caesar and Pompeius can best be explained,
I think, in terms of a whole-hearted acceptance of Greek cultural
values, of the attitude against which the elder Cato had protested,
that all except Greeks were barbarians: all that a Roman could do
was to seek admission to the magic circle. In the same passage in
which Cicero apologized for knowing the name of Praxiteles, he remarked of a 'Greek' of Messana, the owner of the work by Praxiteles
under discussion, that he regarded Romans as ignoramuses in artistic
matters; it would be hard to think of a more striking expression of
the Roman inferiority complex.[63] This complex is apparent also in
the urge which Cicero and other Romans evinced to defend their cultural backwardness.[64]

Cicero's pathetic desire for Greek approbation for his Greek
literary efforts is also relevant; in 60 he instructed Atticus to
distribute copies of his *commentarius* on his consulship to Athens
and the other cities of Greece (*ad Att.* 2.1.2). His angry letter
to Pelops of Byzantium should be interpreted in the light of this
instruction; it was, according to Plutarch (*Cic.* 24), one of the
only two angry letters which he wrote to Greeks (the other one was
to Gorgias, accused of miseducating his son) and complained of
failure to get Cicero certain honorific decrees at Byzantium.
Honorific decrees for Greeks were part of Greek city life; they
must now be conferred on Cicero, as on other Romans before him.

Equally revealing of the Roman attitude as a whole is the context of Cicero's remarks about Piso's Epicurean leanings; they are
prefaced by careful flattery of his audience: he is talking *in
hominum eruditissimorum et humanissimorum coetu*, in a gathering of
learned and educated men; the flattery continues with Cicero (following a basic precept of ancient rhetoric) careful to appear not
to know more than his audience, but to be citing facts well known
to them and to all men of culture (*in Pis.* 68). Similar flattery
appears before Cicero's discussion of Cato's Stoic views, in his
defence of Murena, prosecuted by Cato.[65] At the beginning of the

pro Archia, Cicero talks about being in a gathering *hominum litter-
atissimorum*, of well-read men (*pro Arch.* 3). Greek intellectuals
were in business, I think, in part in order to provide flattery of
the same kind.[66]

It is of course true that from the earliest days of Roman involvement in the Greek East prominent members of the Greek cities
used their friendship with the commanders sent out by the Romans to
ensure the safety or the advancement of their own or other communities and that Greeks often performed real and tangible services for
Romans. Despite the warning which Cicero gave to his brother while
governor of Asia about trusting the Greeks of that province, Cicero
himself made use in Cilicia of one Apollonius, a former freedman of
P.Crassus, whom Caesar also used in Egypt (*ad QF.* 1.1.15-16; *ad fam.*
13.16).

It is also true that the abilities of intellectuals as per-
suaders were early harnessed by Greek cities in their dealings with
Rome, as they had been harnessed in dealings with the Hellenistic
monarchs.[67] One has only to think of the Athenian embassy of the
three philosophers of 155, of the missions of Posidonius and Molo.
But it seems to me that for the period after Sulla one can document
a relationship between Greek intellectuals and republican *principes*
(which may indeed be surmised earlier), in which flattery of Roman
cultural pretensions was one service which was provided in antici-
pation of rewards for the individuals concerned and their own or
other communities.

The central and for my purposes paradigmatic figure is Pompeius.
In no meaningful sense a man of culture, Hellenic or otherwise,[68] he
clearly had pretensions to Hellenic culture. He was accused of re-
taining for his own use hunting-nets and books from the booty of
Asculum; if the accusation was just, Pompeius was clearly imitating
L.Aemilius Paullus, who introduced the Greek, or perhaps rather Macedonian, recreation of hunting to Rome and retained for his own use
the library of Perseus (Plut. *Pomp.* 4). Pompeius' last words to his
family before disembarking to meet his end in Egypt were two lines
of Sophocles, yet he had to write down beforehand the Greek speech he
proposed to deliver to Ptolemy XIII.[69]

The pretensions of Pompeius chiefly took the form of surrounding
himself with Greeks, of whom Theophanes of Mytilene was only the most

notable.[70] Theophanes' willingness to involve himself in Roman politics meant that he was able to perform certain services for Pompeius;[71]
he claimed in his history and no doubt made it clear from an early
stage of Pompeius' presence in the east that he was going to claim
that the archives of Mithridates included a *logos* of P.Rutilius Rufus
urging the massacre of the Romans in Asia which Mithridates insti-
gated in 88 (Plut. *Pomp.* 37); this slander, Plutarch surmises, was a
response to Rufus' criticism of Pompeius' father. I am, however, not
persuaded by Strabo's assertion that Theophanes, although a historian,
became a friend of Pompeius primarily because of his political skill
and was responsible for his successes, whence great benefits for
Mytilene (13.2.3 (617-18)). Cicero speaks of Theophanes only as the
author of an account of Pompeius' deeds in discussing his grant of
citizenship to him (*pro Arch.* 24); the period of his influence on
Pompeius in the sphere of politics, such as it was, comes only in
and after 51.[72]

   The rewards for Theophanes and Mytilene, however, belong at the
end of the Mithridatic War; the latter are explicitly dated there by
Plutarch. Theophanes' acquisition of Roman citizenship antedates
the *pro Archia* of 62, where it is explicitly described as conferred
militia, on active service. And the account of Pompeius at Mytilene
in Plutarch makes it quite clear that what Theophanes provided for
Pompeius in return for the freedom of Mytilene was a cultural ego-
trip (*Pomp.* 42). His achievements provided the only subject matter
for the poets competing at the traditional festival that year; his
reaction to the theatre was a decision to build a similar one at
Rome, but bigger. That Pompeius did not simply want an account of
his achievements in Greek by Theophanes and the poets competing at
Mytilene is clear from his next moves; he went on to Rhodes and
listened to all the teachers of philosophy, including Posidonius
(who later published the piece he delivered), giving them a talent
each, and then to Athens where he behaved similarly towards the
philosophers and in addition gave the city fifty talents for building works.[73] His deeds recorded by a Greek historian, sung by
Greek poets, himself conversant with the philosophers of Rhodes and
Athens, patron of the centre of Greek civilization - how could
Pompeius not be a man of deep Hellenic culture? I do not doubt that
it was an illusion which Theophanes carefully fostered.

A similar figure to Pompeius and no doubt a model was L.Licinius
Lucullus; he is described by Plutarch as possessed of an adequate
knowledge of Greek and Latin; Sulla's dedication to him of his *Memoirs*
tells us nothing of his intellectual abilities, any more than does
the polite remark accompanying the dedication that Lucullus was someone who would improve the history by editing and arranging it.[74] The
unusual story of a literary competition, involving an impromptu composition in Greek or Latin between Lucullus, Hortensius and Sisenna,
is equally unrevealing for our purposes.[75] Lucullus' real philistin-
ism can be inferred from Cicero's desperate protestations to the contrary in the *Academica priora* (2.4; cf. 7 and 1), even without the
benefit of the letters in which he explained that Lucullus, Catulus
and Hortensius were wildly unsuitable interlocutors in a philosophical dialogue (*ad Att.* 13.12.3, 16.1, 19.5).

Yet Lucullus collected works of art, including a globe and a
statue of Autolycus by Sthenis chosen from the booty from Sinope,
and a library, which he ostentatiously opened to all and took care
to frequent.[76] He also had the Greek Eupolemus of Caleacte with him
during the Third Mithridatic War (II *Verr*. 4.49), Archias of Antioch
in Syria, who had travelled with him in 102 and attached himself to
the Luculli, with him in both the First and the Third Mithridatic
War (*pro Arch*. 11). The result was a poem celebrating Lucullus and
the Mithridatic War.[77] Archias' native city had no serious contact
with Rome until Pompeius annexed Syria, in circumstances in which
Archias, as a protégé of Lucullus, could be of little help. His own
reward for aiding and abetting Lucullus' cultural pretensions were
material gifts from Sulla as proconsul and protection when citizenship was challenged (*pro Arch*. 11).

Lucullus, however, also associated with Antiochus of Ascalon,
resident for most of his working life in Athens; like Archias,
Antiochus accompanied Lucullus both in the First and in the Third
Mithridatic War and referred to one of Lucullus' brothers in a
treatise on the gods.[78] Lucullus took care to advertise his refusal
to billet troops in a friendly Greek city (Plut. *Luc*. 33) and it is,
I think, a legitimate surmise that the two inscriptions in honour of
Lucullus at Athens reflect benefactions to that city, requested by
Antiochus in return for his association with Lucullus (*IG* II-III[2]
4104-5).

A clear example of a benefaction to a Greek city through the mediation of a Greek intellectual involves Caesar. Herodes, who wrote badly on Cicero's consulship and complained to Cicero and Atticus about the lack of appreciation for his work (*ad Att.* 2.2.2), is plausibly to be identified with the Herodes who in 51 got a gift of fifty talents from Caesar for Athens.[79] The amount and the timing are both significant: the amount is the same as that given by Pompeius after the Mithridatic War (see above); the gift occurs at the end of the war in Gaul, which provided Caesar with glory and resources to match those of Pompeius.

The role of Greek intellectuals who possessed links with members of the Roman governing class was of course crucial at moments of crisis. Caesar spared Athens despite her aid to Pompeius, because of the glory of her citizens of the past and, no doubt, because of her present reputation as a centre of learning;[80] the teacher of Cassius pleaded with him for the safety of Rhodes; Areius saved Alexandria from revenge by Octavian.[81]

I conclude therefore that by being or appearing to be an intellectual a Greek of the right social class could in the generation after Sulla and probably earlier attract the attention of Roman *principes* and by flattering their pretensions acquire a hold over them which enabled them to win benefits for themselves and for communities whose claims they chose to advance, whether their own or others. It is reasonable to suppose that Roman rule in the Greek world actually provided a stimulus to Greek intellectual activity.

There is, however, another way in which the lives of Greek intellectuals became bound up with the destinies of their rulers; the efforts of Mithridates VI and the just hatred for Rome of her eastern subjects had come close to ending Roman rule in the east; many who called themselves philosophers had supported Mithridates; thus Diodorus had been his general at Adramyttium, Athenion had held Athens for him.[82]

To a Greek, intellectual activity was possible either within the framework of a city or at the court of a monarch; while one Hellenistic monarchy after another crumbled, only partially replaced by the emergence of Roman *principes* as patrons, the former mode remained important; but the survival even of that now depended increasingly on the survival of Roman rule. It was not only that

Roman magnates acted as patrons to Greek intellectuals (and facilitated scientific exploration); Rome underwrote the society in which alone such as Posidonius who had thrown in their lot with Rome could exist and pursue their *métiers*.[83] It is not surprising that Posidonius was deeply worried about the quality of Roman rule; his vitriolic account of Athenion is equally a measure of his insecurity.

In retrospect, all seemed simple; the *Geography* of Strabo breathes a serene nonchalance about the inevitability of Roman rule and its cultural underpinning (9.2.2 (401)); to Dionysius of Halicarnassus, the emergence of Rome as ruler of the world and the qualities of her leaders had resulted in the spread of worthwhile cultural activity, both Greek and Roman, and in the revival of Atticism (*de orat. ant.* 3); to Plutarch, despite the views of the elder Cato, 'during the period in which the city was most successful in her affairs (i.e. the years in which her empire was created), she became much attached to every form of Greek learning and culture' (*Cato Mai.* 23.3). But to the embattled Greek intellectual of the last generation of the Roman republic, desperately deploying his skills to ward off the effects of the Roman revolution, such sanguine views were surely impossible.

10: THE BENEFICIAL IDEOLOGY

V.Nutton (Selwyn College, Cambridge)

It was the great eighteenth-century classic and orientalist, Johann
Jakob Reiske, who remarked that of all the authors he had read - and
he had read many - the orations of Aelius Aristeides came second only
to the speeches of Thucydides in difficulty of comprehension; and
that their substance was of major importance for the understanding
of the Roman empire in the second century, with the exception of the
'Sacred Tales', which he dismissed as woeful superstition and absurd-
ity.[1] Today it is the 'Sacred Tales' that are most fascinating and
revealing, and in their turn the political discourses are left un-
read, with the regrettable consequence that despite the volume of ink
outpoured on the speech 'To Rome' there is still no satisfactory
study of Aristeides' political ideas in the context of other literature of the period.[2] On the one hand, while individual snippets of
information given by him have been subjected to the closest of scru-
tiny to discover their truth,[3] his general themes and major ideas
have been largely neglected: on the other hand, the frequent condem-
nation of him as a declaimer uttering commonplaces,[4] even if it is
acknowledged that in his day the main criterion of literary excellence was an ability to express in beautiful and striking language
traditional themes and concepts, obscures the fact that for him and
his audience the commonplaces themselves had some value. The general
categories in which he and his contemporaries described the benefits
of Roman rule, however vague they may be, can be used neutrally to
define provincial attitudes to the Roman empire and to construct an
ideology in which both orator and audience shared.[5]

The traditional Roman explanations and justifications of their
supremacy in the theological or moralistic terms of their *fortuna*,
constantia, *fides* and so on,[6] although accepted to some extent by
the Greeks,[7] do not figure prominently in their writings, and we
have little means of telling the effectiveness of the propaganda
that stressed the emperor's *providentia*, *liberalitas* and similar
virtues.[8] But some practical benefits were acknowledged by both

ruler and ruled and became part of the common stock of ideas on the
merits and duties of an emperor and governor towards their subjects.

   The sophists, rhetoricians and litterateurs who furnish the evidence for such theories come from similar backgrounds in the wealthy
local aristocracy of the eastern provinces. Plutarch was high priest
at Delphi;[9] Dio's affluence involved him in contentious litigation
with his fellow townsmen of Prusa;[10] Aristeides had property at
Hadriani, Hadrianoutherae and Smyrna;[11] Galen's father, an amateur
architect, owned at least two estates and a town house at Pergamum,
which, when bequeathed to Galen, effectively freed him from the normal economic constraints of a doctor's life;[12] and whatever the truth
that lies behind Lucian's 'Dream', his family was not one of agricultural peasants, *oreitupoi*, who only occasionally visited the city,[13]
and even if he had a hard struggle to survive in the world of the
great sophists – and Galen's evidence suggests that this notion is
exaggerated[14] – he nevertheless had several friends and acquaintances
among the governors and leading provincials of the East.[15] As
Bowersock has shown,[16] the links between litterati and the government
in Rome were many and strong, and it is enough here to emphasize that
only Aristeides of the authors so far mentioned had no close connexion
with the court and emperor in Rome itself, and that more from ill-
health than from reasons of political ideology. Dio was an adviser
to Trajan, Galen doctor to several emperors, while Lucian and possibly Plutarch held office as procurators.[17] In short, they were just
the sort of men whose learning and culture would be expected to advance them in the mandarin society of the second century; domestic
wealth provided them with an entry, their literary talents made them
especially valuable guests. Thus it is not surprising that their
assessment of the merits of the Roman empire is generally favourable,
for they were prime beneficiaries, yet they are often doing little
more than expressing in more ornate phrases opinions widely held and
found in many less prestigious authors.

   Of their broad themes, the most prominent is that of peace,
established and maintained by the emperor throughout the whole world
and bringing an end to *stasis* and civil war, which also develops into
a recognition that the empire provides its inhabitants with *asphaleia*,
security against external attack.[18] Dio in his second oration
stresses the martial virtues of the emperor, and both Aristeides and

the author of the *eis basilea* welcome the fact that thanks to the
emperors dangerous barbarians are kept beyond the frontiers of the
empire.[19] But of the economic consequences of the peace, much less
is said: peace for the Greek sophists is primarily interpreted in
terms of its effect on the internal politics of the cities. True
there are exceptions: thanks to the Roman peace Galen could draw on
larger stocks of drugs from all over the world (Gal. 14.7-9, 12.216-17),
and Aristeides talks of ships sailing freely, of cargoes coming to
Rome from the whole world, of travellers no longer in danger of brig-
ands in the mountains, and of universal prosperity.[20] But Aristeides
was too rich to appreciate the Alexandrian sailors' reaction to
Augustus, *per illum se vivere, per illum navigare, libertate atque
fortunis per illum frui* (Suetonius, *Aug.* 98), and it seems to have
been among the Christians that the social and economic consequences
of the peace are emphasized. Origen believed, rightly, that the
spread of Christianity was facilitated by the imperial peace,[21] and
Tertullian, in a passage worthy of Aristeides,[22] noted the changes
that followed the peace:

> *omnia iam pervia, omnia nota, omnia negotiosa*; smiling farms
> have replaced famous wastes, fields have conquered forests, dom-
> esticated animals have driven out wild beasts, the deserts are
> sown, marshes are drained; there are now cities where once not
> even houses stood; neither lonely islands nor rocky crags deter
> us: *ubique domus, ubique populus, ubique respublica, ubique vita*.
> The world is over-populated; we should hope for plague, famine,
> war and earthquake to cut man down to size.

A second major theme developed by the Greek sophists is that
of the true freedom of the inhabitants of the Roman empire, for an
essential difference between it and other ancient empires is that
the Romans govern free men, not slaves;[23] no man is prevented by
law or fear of punishment from cherishing his ancestral ways
(Athenagoras, *Leg.* 1.1). The cities have an equal share in honour
according to their merit; they govern themselves without reference
to Rome; and the tribute that they pay is in no way excessive
(Athenagoras, *Leg.* 1.2; Arist. 26.36, 36.16). But Dio, Plutarch
and the Ephesian magistrate of Acts 19 knew the reality behind the
facade. Their energies and advice are directed to preventing local
disorder or at least restraining it lest the Romans be led to

intervene. The stress in speeches and on coins on the importance of
concord between cities and citizens has a twofold purpose, to emphasize what little remains of a city's independence, its ability to
enter into agreements with other cities, and apotropaically to an-
nounce to the governor and the emperor that police action is unnecessary.[24] Plutarch's *Precepts of statesmanship*, so informative
on the possibilities open to a local provincial politician, aim to
keep the Romans out of local politics, for the intervention of the
proconsul is a sign of a failure of the polis.

Yet the Roman empire to which Dio advocated loyalty and whose
merits Aristeides extolled at length was over and above the polis,
and Aristeides' formulation of the relationship between the two requires some elucidation, for of all the adjectives he used to describe it, the most prominent, *koinos*, is also at the same time the
most vague and elusive. Far from indicating, as Oliver argued,[25]
that the sophist saw the Roman empire as a Greek league, *koinon*,
with Rome as its hegemon, the frequent usage of the word elsewhere
in his speeches suggests that it denotes something in which the
speaker shares, although it was not his originally. Corinth is
the *koine agora*, the *koine panton kataphuge*, and the *koinon astu*;
Pergamum is the *koine tis koruphe tou ethnous*; Ephesus the
tamieion koinon of Asia, as well as its *patris* (Arist. 46.23-4,
23.13, 23.24). Significantly, only Smyrna, where Aristeides is an
insider, is not qualified by this adjective – except that its destruction by an earthquake is a *koinon ptoma*, for Aristeides was
willing to share his lamentations, if not his privileges, with the
rest of the world.[26] The fact that this adjective appears so often
in the *eis Romen* indicates that Aristeides, and presumably at least
some of his audience, found something in the Roman empire in which
they could share and which they acknowledged not to have been
theirs from the beginning. But in which of all the many *koina
agatha* given by the emperors were the Greeks most interested?[27]

For the upper classes the Roman empire was indeed a *koine arche*,
for they could pass easily from the leadership of their polis into
imperial service, as *advocatus fisci* perhaps, or into the senate, and
Hippolytus acknowledged that Rome collected *tous gennaiotatous ton
ethnon* and made them Romans (Arist. 27.32; Hippolytus, *Comm. in Dan.*
4.9). Those who stayed at home might gain authority by attaching

themselves like ivy to the growing power and influence of a senator or emperor, while residence abroad at the very least enabled the un-political to escape the daily troubles and turmoil of life in their native city (Plut. 805E, 605B-C). For the politically ambitious the prospects were even brighter: a man from Chios or Bithynia might even become *consul ordinarius* (Plut. 470C). A traditionalist such as Plutarch regarded this flight from the city to the senate and to lush procuratorships with horror as both time-consuming and unprofitable, but his strictures appear to have had no effect.[28]

Aristeides also refers twice to *koinoi nomoi*. At 26.102 he says that the Romans assigned common laws to all, and at 24.31 he asks, 'Is not all the land *koine*? Is there not one emperor, common laws for all, and a freedom to act and participate in politics or not as one thinks fit?'. Oliver suggested that every man would recognize in this an echo of Aristotle's universal law, the *koinos nomos* of *Rhetoric* 1.10-15,[29] but Aristeides is clearly thinking of something far more specific and relevant, the commonplace in Roman propaganda that it is Rome's duty and privilege to give laws to all nations, even to the races of the East.[30] The equity and fairness of Roman justice is accepted by many Greeks, and Roman *eunomia* is a fit subject for a loyal epigram,[31] but, granted that these laws are just, in what ways are they common? Oliver is here on stronger ground when interpreting *koinoi nomoi* to refer to the gradual assimi-lation of Greek law codes to Roman practice in various ways.[32] Roman citizens resident in the provinces may well have exercised their right to have their cases tried under Roman rather than local law; the decisions of a governor applied equally to Greek and Roman, and the justice of the emperor consisted in administering the law im-partially to all (Athenagoras, *Leg.* 1.2; Arist. 26.37-9); and there is some evidence that the Greeks themselves were modifying their local law codes in the direction of Roman law, and, especially in public law, were unlikely to pass a municipal decree hostile to Rome's interests.

Aristeides, it is agreed, is speaking about public law, for until the universal grant of citizenship by Caracalla the private affairs of non-Roman citizens, one with another, were unaffected by Roman law, but whether Caracalla's edict put an end to peculiar non-Roman private law has been hotly debated.[33] General statements by

clerics that Rome on conquest abolished all the laws of the Arabians,
including circumcision, or that all the inhabitants of the empire
were under one and the same law can be easily dismissed as idle rhetoric,[34] but the more detailed comments of Menander of Laodicea demand
greater respect. In his handbook of oratory, written about 270,
Menander lays down instructions on how to praise a city: one should
stress the *sophrosune* and *phronesis* of its laws, and explain how they
stand out from the generality in their treatment of, for example,
widows and orphans, marriage and *ta akosma* - some cities expressly
forbade women to engage in trade, others prevented them from appearing in a full agora, others kept them indoors until late afternoon.[35]
But twice Menander has to say, a little sadly, that this argument
about the merits of an individual city's laws is now obsolete because
all are now governed according to the common laws of Rome (202, 205):
the justice of the emperor is administered to all by impartial
governors (227), with the result that marriages are more lawful and
contracts juster, the rights of inheritance are better protected, the
pleas of the poor do not fail, and the proud boasts of the wealthy
cease.

It may very well be doubted whether this glorious age of legal
rectitude that succeeded Caracalla's edict was ever more than a fig-
ment of rhetorical exaggeration, yet the examples that Menander uses
of *koinoi nomoi*, marriage and inheritance, certainly imply that in
his opinion there was now a universal (Roman) law which embraced
both public and private law throughout the empire.[36] Local law was
now suppressed, everywhere there was uniformity. Yet, despite the
vigorous advocacy of Professor Talamanca on his behalf, Menander is
either badly informed or exaggerating from his own limited experience.[37] In his favour can be set the gradual assimilation of Greek
law to that of Rome, a process undoubtedly accelerated by the edict
of Caracalla and the change in attitude towards local practice,
consuetudo and *mos*, that can be seen in the third century. At the
beginning, *longa consuetudo* is allowed some validity, especially
where no specific enactment has been made, and in A.D. 224 governors
were encouraged to see that nothing was done against ancient custom:[38] Ulpian (D. 43.24.3.4) accepts that additional rights could be
given to a *curator civitatis* by a *lex municipalis*, and Gordian (CJ.
7.9.1) recognized a grant of freedom made in accordance with a *lex*

municipalis. But ever tighter limits were laid down for the operation
of non-Roman rules and ideas. According to Ulpian (D. 47.12.3.5)
burial was forbidden within the city walls even if local law had permitted it; Decius in 250 (CJ. 6.58.3) confirmed the right of a woman
to inherit from an intestate brother as greater than that of the sons
of a second brother, thereby rejecting the Greek law of inheritance;
a decision of 285 (CJ. 5.5.2) forbade any man *sub dicione Romani
nominis* to have more than one wife; *abdicatio* of a son was prohibited
by Diocletian in 288 (CJ. 8.46.6) although it was a Greek institution;
and in 290 it was declared that a will written in local customary
form was invalid unless *speciali privilegio patriae tuae*.[39] No customary law was adjudged so strong as to vanquish reason or the law
(CJ. 8.52.2 (319)) and not even *mos provinciae* was to be taken into
account in deciding a man's *origo*, the place where he was primarily
eligible for *munera*.[40]

One of the most striking assertions by Aristeides in the *eis
Romen* is that the Romans have best proved that earth is the *patris
koine panton*.[42] From this Sherwin-White concluded that the orator
was looking at the Roman or Ciceronian ideal of *communis patria* and
adapting an argument that dealt primarily with individual citizens
to one concerned with the relationship between Rome and the cities

Yet local law and custom continue to find a place in Roman law,
even in family matters where Menander implies they had disappeared.
Emancipation according to *lex municipii* was accepted by Diocletian
(CJ. 8.48.1) and an emperor might restrain a governor from acting
against *lex civitatis* in certain property cases (CJ. 11.30.4). A
guardian might have to pay interest on his ward's property 'according to the custom of the province' (D. 26.7.7.10) and *mos regionis*
had a part to play both in determining security against eviction (D.
21.2.6) and in deciding who paid for losses in a contract that were
occasioned by the vagaries of the weather (CJ. 4.65.8). The fact
also that Decius and Diocletian decided against certain non-Roman
legal practices indicates that these practices were current in some
provinces at least until then. At best, however, even when it survives, local law and custom are always subsidiary and ancillary,[41]
and never override Roman law, which as the third century progressed
became ever more universal in its penetration, without attaining the
complete uniformity of domination that Menander implies.

of the provinces.[43] But it is the earth that is the *patris koine*,
not Rome, and Aristeides is merely repeating the unexceptionable
philosophical commonplace of the unity of mankind on the earth[44] in
a context that suggests that, thanks to Roman rule, a man may travel
wherever he wishes and that Roman citizens are to be found everywhere. Although he refers elsewhere to other cities as *patrides*,
implicitly at 26.100, where the traveller goes *ek patridos eis
patrida*, and explicitly at 23.24, where he declares that all men are
brought to Ephesus *hos eis patrida*, he does not go so far as to assert
that Rome is the *patris* of all citizens. For that formulation we
must wait another generation until the lawyers Callistratus and Mo-
destinus, both jurists with strong links with the Eastern provinces
(D. 48.22.18 pr., 27.1.6.11).

Yet there is a possible connexion between the idea of earth as
the *communis patria* and that of Rome, through the theme of *urbs Roma*
as a microcosm of the *orbs*, which can be found in poets and orators
from all over the empire:[45] and it cannot be doubted that Polemo's
famous description of Rome as the epitome of the whole world was
largely true (Gal. 18A.347; Athenaeus 1.20B-C). All races and creeds
of the known world could be found there, and most of the major Greek
authors visited it at some point. Galen, who describes so well the
terrifying anonymity of the big city and who fiercely accuses provincial doctors of fleeing thither to avoid detection and punishment
for their crimes[46] - even he, a provincial from Pergamum, spent over
thirty years there. And Lucian's belief (*Nigrinus* 15) that Rome was
not the place for the pure philosopher but only for the avaricious,
the debauched, the gluttonous and the devotee of the bangings,
scrapings and dreadful wailings of modern music, did not prevent him
from visiting the city. In Rome, and possibly also for a time in the
army, there was a real *epimixia andron*,[47] and the city could with
justice be described as the *communis patria* of the whole world.

My catalogue of *agatha* has so far been confined almost entirely
to vague generalities - peace, freedom, common laws and a common
fatherland - which may indeed support A.H.M.Jones' contention that
on the whole the Greeks were passive and indifferent to Roman rule.[48]
But they undoubtedly appreciated that the Romans, and especially the
emperor, could be of practical advantage to them, and the imperial
propaganda that the emperor was accessible to all his subjects,

responsive to their needs and effective in action would have confirmed them in their view that in him was a sure source of help and
assistance.[49] The only enthusiastic comment relating to Rome in
Plutarch's *Precepts* (814C) is that they are always most eager to
promote the interests of their friends in the provinces; Dio (47.13)
claimed that all emperors were interested in the prosperity of cities; and Galen (14.217) believed that they regarded the welfare and
safety of their subjects as the greatest duty of kingship. Mene-
machus is advised by Plutarch to attach himself to a leading Roman,
whose friendship he may use to benefit his city by turning away
wrath or by securing an emperor's interest in its problems.[50]

For a local politician the favour of the emperor was a strong
card to play. Dio defended his conduct towards his native Prusa by
enumerating Trajan's services to him at his request (Dio 40.15,
45.3). How munificent imperial gifts might be imagined, or even expected, to be, is clear from Dio's description (40.14) of the rumours
that Trajan had given the Smyrniote envoys many presents and untold
wealth for the city, and that a river of gold was now flowing from
the emperor to Smyrna. When disaster struck, the emperor was the obvious saviour.[51] When an earthquake destroyed Tralles in 26 B.C.,
Chaeremon rushed to Spain to appeal to Augustus, who restored the
city in response to his plea;[52] and the moving letter of Aristeides
to Marcus Aurelius and Commodus on the earthquake at Smyrna brought
both tears and results.[53] But even in normal times the emperor was
besieged with requests, and his friends could use their influence
with him to secure titles and privileges for their home towns.
Statilius Criton, the doctor and historian of Trajan, was responsible for the appellation, *Ulpia*, given to his native city of Heraclea.[54] Alexander of Cotiaeum, the tutor of Marcus Aurelius,
brought only happiness for his kinsmen, his friends, his city and
for the eastern cities in general; and although he charged a fee
for his services as a teacher of rhetoric, he secured these benefits
for others without demanding any payment.[55]

In general it is true that Greek writers regard the empire from
the point of view of people receiving rather than distributing benefits - apart from their *paideia*.[56] Aristeides mentions Greeks serving in the army - in contrast to Menander a century later, who remarks that the army of the emperor gives better protection than city

walls and that the Greeks have now no need to fight for themselves[57] - but on the whole the Greeks' perception of the imperial qualities of the Roman empire are few indeed. It may be only Galen, an acute observer of society in Rome and the provinces, who praises an imperial achievement that has nothing to do with the East, the road-building programme of Trajan in Italy.[58]

> He laid stone causeways over marshy and swampy ground, hacked through thorny jungles and rough ground, bridged dangerous rivers: where possible he shortened the route or took it on an easier way than over a high and difficult crag, abandoning a lonely road infested by wild beasts in favour of a broad highway, and making the rough places plain.

In Latin there is a parallel in Statius (*Silvae* IV 3), a poem on the Via Domitiana, which contains, as well as the memorable conceit of the river god Volturnus peering over his new bridge to congratulate Domitian and to express his loyal thanks (67-94), a considerable amount of technical detail.[59] The new road speeds up the journey from Sinuessa to Baiae from a day to just over two hours (36-7); it takes the Puteoli and Baiae traffic from the slower Via Appia (102-4); and lines 40-55 describe the methods of road construction. 'Some workers are cutting down woods and mountain forests; others are prising out rocks and beams; others are laying the road surface; others are draining ponds or diverting streams.' In Greek, Cassius Dio (68.7.1) notes in passing Trajan's many necessary repairs to roads, harbours and public buildings, and there are several references in other writers to the ease and freedom of travel as a result of the Roman peace,[60] but, with one exception, they differ in both tone and precision from Galen's eulogy. The exception is Plutarch, who in his life of Caius Gracchus, ch.7, notes his zeal for road building, combining practical utility and graceful beauty:

> For his roads were carried straight through the country without deviation, and had pavements of quarried stone, and substructures of tight-rammed masses of sand. Depressions were filled up, all intersecting torrents or ravines were bridged over, and both sides of the roads were of equal and corresponding height, so that the work had everywhere an even and beautiful appearance. In addition to all this, he measured off every road by miles ... and planted stone pillars in the

ground to mark the distances.

This passage, however, does not say where Gracchus' roads led, and it may be that Plutarch is describing the roads of his own day rather than of the Gracchi's, and, like Galen, developing a commonplace about the stone roads that marched straight, bridging hollows and streams and letting no obstacle defy them.

Epigraphy and archaeology confirm the truth of Galen's observation: Trajan built the Via Traiana Nova, and possibly two others, in Etruria; he repaired the Via Aemilia near Rimini; he continued the repaving of the Via Appia *ex glarea silice* and cut through a projecting cliff at Terracina; and his construction of the Via Traiana and some new access roads, complete with bridges and causeways, shortened the journey from Beneventum to Brundisium by a day.[61] Which of these new roads struck Galen so forcefully is an idle question, but they left a tremendous impression on him, for I know of no other example of a Greek describing his own achievements in terms of a Roman one. Hippocrates discovered and planned the road; Galen, like Trajan, swept aside the tangled confusion, repairing and re-aligning the old ways of Hippocrates; and his implicit claim was that the Galenic system of medicine would be as impressive and enduring as the road system of Trajan.[62]

I have deliberately excluded epigraphic evidence from the discussion so far, because, while a long list could be made of imperial gifts of buildings, endowments, corn for starving cities and so on, it would merely exemplify the banal conclusion that the emperor was often and in various ways a great benefactor of the eastern cities, and would reveal very little about the attitude of the provincials to the gifts and the giver.[63] But an overall consideration of eastern inscriptions set up in honour of provincial governors suggests a significant change in the relationship between the cities and the central government from the mid-third century.

Thirty years ago, Louis Robert assembled a long series of Greek epigrams in favour of provincial governors, dating from about A.D. 250 until the sixth century, praising them in the most florid language for their services and their gifts of buildings, and extolling their virtues of justice, incorruptibility and so on.[64] Previously the governor, unless himself a local man, is a remote figure, whose achievements and merits are briefly and plainly

recorded. In part this change can be ascribed to a preference for
verse instead of prose – although the grandest prose eulogies are for
local magnates, scholars and officials, not for governors[65] – and in
part also to a general tendency towards a more contrived and recherché
style, but many of the themes and epithets can be found in the first
century, and earlier,[66] applied to local magistrates. The virtues
of the small-town bigwigs of the East, from Paros to Petra, from
Crete to Bithynia,[67] are commemorated in the same ornate phrases and
conceits, and justice, prudence and wisdom are seen to prevail among
the leading families of all the East. But from about A.D. 250, before the Diocletianic reforms, the governor begins to displace the
city magistrate as the object of such praises,[68] and even a governor's
servant can receive a laudatory epigram for his supervision of the
Phrygian gold mines (GVI 1170).

This transfer of interest from local to imperial officials, evident from these late epigrams, can be confirmed from other sources.
Firmicus Maternus regards civic magistrates of the early fourth century as mere extensions of the central government and subservient to
higher, imperial authority;[69] and Menander of Laodicea emphasizes
that it is the governor who is the mediator between city and emperor,
who transmits the complaints and requests of provincials to the
emperor, who executes imperial decisions, and who guards the laws
and the emperor's justice.[70]

This growing dependence of the cities on the emperor and his
officials may be a direct result of the financial and social crisis
of the third century,[71] when in some areas traditional ties of
patronage and dependence were shaken and destroyed, and when new
forms of relationship, both formal and informal, grew up between
the central government and its subjects. In the West the power of
the great landlords was gradually recognized by the emperor at the
expense of the free tenant;[72] and in the East, imperial officials
(and, later on, the bishop and the holy man[73]) took on the role
formerly occupied by the local aristocracy. In the Precepts of
Plutarch, the governor is involved in the affairs of the city only
in emergencies; in the orations of Aristeides, the governor dis-
penses justice, but is inferior to the mighty provincials who are
on the most intimate terms with the emperor and who might even
throw a proconsul out on the street.[74] It is some measure of the

decline of the city that a century and a half later this official
has become the arbiter and saviour of its fortunes.[75]

11: ROME'S AFRICAN EMPIRE UNDER THE PRINCIPATE

P.D.A.Garnsey (Jesus College, Cambridge)

With the inauguration of the Principate of Augustus, the history of
Roman imperialism entered a new phase. Augustus' long reign was
marked by conquest, pacification, colonization and administrative
reorganization designed to secure the provinces and make possible
their rational exploitation.

In this paper I analyse the character of Roman rule in North
Africa in the period of the Principate and the nature of the society it produced.[1] My original purpose was to assess the material
benefits of Roman rule for provincials, and especially for Africans.
This theme is not lost sight of here, but I have thought it necessary to set it against the background of the interests of the imperial power and the methods of Roman imperialism in Africa. Just
as in the context of Roman social relations *beneficia* were given
for services rendered, so the most tangible benefits[2] received by
subjects of Rome were granted in return for support of the imperialist enterprise. The main beneficiaries were those who cooperated in the work of pacification, political and social control, and
economic exploitation.

How far the mass of Africans benefited from membership of
Roman provincial society is uncertain. To the assertion that the
basic *beneficia*, security and order, were enjoyed by all sections
of African society, there is the rejoinder that the establishment
of the *pax Africana* was accompanied by physical coercion, expropri-
ation, and social dislocation; and that the continuation of peaceful conditions was contingent on the docility of an exploited
peasantry.[3] Whether or how far the rural population gained from
the expansion of the economy is similarly a matter for dispute.
Such issues will not be easily resolved, given the difficulty, or
impossibility, of estimating the net gains and losses of incorpor-
ation in the Roman imperial system for those at the lower levels
of African society. But there is a chance that they will be con-
structively debated, if the aims and policies of the imperial

power are properly understood.

I THE LAND

Africa Vetus was won by conquest from Rome's traditional and most
hated enemy. Africa Nova was annexed by Caesar following the defeat
of the Numidian king Juba I and the Pompeian forces in the civil war.
Bocchus, who backed the winning side, and later Juba II, were presented with the Mauretanian littoral down to the Atlantic coast, an
arrangement suspended temporarily when Bocchus died, bequeathing the
kingdom to Rome, and permanently when Gaius brought the house of
Juba to a violent end. Such of the interior of Africa as was occupied after the initial annexations (in South Numidia, for example,
the Romans penetrated as far as Castellum Dimmidi, about 700 kilometres east-south-east of Carthage) was taken by force of arms.

     This background largely explains the dominant feature of the
pattern of landownership in Roman North Africa, which is the frequency and the extensiveness of large estates. The bulk of African
land was classed as *ager publicus* of the Roman people, to be disposed of as they saw fit. By the lex Rubria of 121 B.C., 200 *iugera*
(120 acres, 50 hectares) of choice land near the site of Carthage
were set aside for each of 6,000 colonists; these allotments were
many times larger than those customarily awarded to communities of
colonists whether of Roman or Latin status, or in viritane assig-
nations. The law was subsequently cancelled, but some of the 6,000
took up their land and were confirmed in possession of it by the
agrarian law of 111 B.C. This law, which in the section relating
to Africa (*FIRA* I^2 no.8, 52ff.) provided for the sale or lease of
land, offered security of tenure not only to the seven loyal cities
and the Carthaginian deserters, but also to the ordinary subject
communities whose land was held on usufruct. But in practice the
large holdings of senators, equestrians and wealthy men of lower
status must have been built up to some extent at the expense of
existing African landholders. Meanwhile, grateful generals, most
conspicuously Caesar, freely awarded generous land-grants to their
followers. In time the emperors entered the field, assigning land
to discharged soldiers, and acquiring it for themselves.

     An early fifth-century constitution of Honorius and Theodosius
II (CTh. 11.28.13, 422) gives the sum of imperial property in

Proconsularis and Byzacena as 15,152 square kilometres at that time, or about one-sixth of the total area of the two late imperial provinces.[4] This figure obviously cannot serve as the basis of a calculation of the size of imperial holdings in an earlier age. The emperor's stake in Africa, initially modest, became substantial after Nero sequestered the properties of six senatorial landowners (Pliny, *NH* 18.35).[5] Thereafter the imperial properties grew more or less continuously through confiscations, gifts, legacies, inheritance and other methods. The largest concentration of imperial properties lay in the rich Medjerda (Bagradas) valley south-west of Carthage, and in the region of Sitifis in Mauretania Caesariensis.[6]

The imperial estates grew mainly at the expense of wealthy private landowners, who had been permitted to carve out *saltus* in areas once held by Carthaginian magnates and Libyan kings. However, an authority quoted by one of the Agrimensores and writing under the Principate considered the private estates in Africa to be comparable in dimension with the rural territories subject to cities, and remarked on the frequent litigation between *privati* and *res publicae* on the issue of jurisdiction over the countryside. The passage ends with an acknowledgement of the 'not inconsiderable' possessions of the emperor (who was also caught up in controversies with municipal authorities), but it was the *saltus* of the *privati*, with their 'substantial population of common people and villages like cities grouped around the villa' which impressed the writer.[7] Recent archaeological investigation in a relatively un-Romanized area of Mauretania Caesariensis has shown that the largest farmhouses in the countryside dependent on Caesarea, the administrative capital, were flanked by villages, the whole forming sizeable agglomerations.[8] Such settlements when fortified could provide protection for their inhabitants in unsettled times, and in a different age could serve as focal points for rebellion mounted by native chieftains against the Roman power.[9] Across the Numidian border at 'Aïn Mechira, which lies between Cirta and Diana Veteranorum, an inscription records the 'foundation' of a village and a twice-monthly market by Antonia Saturnina, aunt of *clarissimi viri*, and presumably a large landowner in the locality.[10] It may be suggested that a large number of villages in North Africa were closely linked to, if not fully integrated with, villa-based estates.

As to the relative significance of imperial and private estates, the implied judgement of the source of the Agrimensor cannot
be tested in detail, but at least areas can be pointed to which
were relatively unencumbered by imperial possessions. Cirta, second
only to Carthage among the cities of Roman Africa, had a dependent
rural territory of immense size, covering perhaps 10,000 square kilometres, in which there are few traces of imperial estates.[11]

At all times, therefore, large tracts of African land were in
the hands of wealthy *privati*. Among them, members of the Roman upper classes must have been prominent, although in the early empire
we have also to reckon with a group of beneficiaries of the civil-
war period and their descendants, of whom the most familiar examples
are P.Sittius and his followers in the territory of Cirta, and a
certain C.Julius, another supporter of Caesar along with his father
Masinissa, Vitruvius' friend and companion in philosophical discussion, and proprietor of the *oppidum* Ismuc thirty-two kilometres
from Zama.[12] The senatorial and equestrian property-owners were in
the early period predominantly non-African by birth, but decreasingly
so after the turn of the first century A.D. In the Antonine and
Severan periods numerous Africans, whether descended from colonial
(largely Italian) or purely local families, or of mixed stock, acquired senatorial rank or followed equestrian careers.[13] The basis
of their wealth and the foundation of their careers was rural property in Africa accumulated sometimes over generations. Cirta and
its environs provided the first African-born consuls, probably
descended from an Italian family, and many of those who followed.[14]
It can be no accident that a city with such an extensive rural territory, the bulk of it apparently in private hands, was particularly
productive of senators. It therefore becomes important to decide
whether in the case of Cirtenses, and other successful Africans,
promotion into a higher order which necessitated a change of residence was accompanied by the liquidation of their African assets.

On this point the information provided by the sources is limited in quality as well as quantity. So Septimius Severus, the
first African emperor, is said to have owned only a modest house in
Rome and a single farm (*fundus*) for much of his earlier career as
senator (*HA* Sev. 4.5).[15] I assume that Severus also owned estates
in the region of his native Leptis Magna and retained them when he

embarked on a senatorial career. I would expect most African senators to have been similarly placed and to have behaved in a similar
way.

Senatorial ownership of land outside Italy was never questioned
by the emperors, themselves owners of provincial property. On the
contrary, Augustus gave senators an automatic right to visit their
properties in Sicily, and Claudius extended the dispensation to
cover Gallia Narbonensis.[16] 'Exeats' must have been freely available to senators who wished to travel further afield for the same
purpose. No province was subsequently put on a level with Sicily
and Narbonensis, but this does not reflect any growing appetite
among senators for Italian investments. Trajan endeavoured to com-
pel senators, many of whom were by now of non-Italian origin, to
invest one-third of their resources in Italian land (Pliny, *Ep.*
6.19.4). The measure was ineffective. Marcus revived it, setting
the less ambitious target of one-quarter (*HA Marc.* 11.8).

Moreover, there are indications that the residence rule was
relaxed in just this period (from Trajan to Marcus), so that some
senators are found re-establishing domicile in their native or
adopted cities after careers of moderate length.[17] This development is a reflection of the senate's loss of political power, but
it is also probably related to the influx into the senate of men
from the East. Thus far African senators do not figure among known
returning expatriates.[18] One factor may have been the relative accessibility of many African estates to their Rome-based proprietors.
A few days' journey from the imperial capital would have sufficed
to bring Marcus' urban prefect Lollius Urbicus to his family estates near Tiddis, within the territory of Cirta.[19] It may also
be conjectured that some African senators were consciously turning
their backs on a provincial culture.[20] Fronto, tutor of Marcus,
orator, born in Cirta and domiciled in Rome, compared himself with
the philosopher Anacharsis, 'Scythian of the nomadic Scythians',
who had settled at Athens. Fronto too was a barbarian, 'Libyan of
the nomadic Libyans', who had found his way to a centre of civilization and culture.[21] Behind the laboured joke lies a heart-felt
tribute to the city which was for Fronto the cultural centre of the
world. The Eastern senators, on the other hand, were not ashamed
of their heritage, whether or not they came from great cultural

capitals (as many of them did). Their cities commanded a level of
patriotism in their leading citizens unrivalled in the West.

Be that as it may, the inscription set up in Cirta in honour
of P.Iulius Proculus Celsinus on the occasion of his election as
consul at Rome exemplifies a common pattern: the senator is pursu-
ing his career at the capital, having entrusted his interests at
home and the celebration of his exploits there to an agent (*actor*)
of slave or freedman status.[22] In the same period the Antistii of
Thibilis, a *pagus* of Cirta, who provided a general of Marcus' wars
and shortly afterwards a colleague for Commodus in the ordinary
consulship and husband to a daughter of Marcus, committed their
house in Thibilis, and probably their land in the locality, to the
care of an equally dutiful freedman.[23] The most that could be hoped
for from expatriates of this kind was that they would favour the
city of their origin with benefactions, and use their influence to
gain benefits for it and promotion for its leading citizens. Some
had special opportunity to renew contact with their *patria*, when
their careers took them back to Africa.[24] Others like Fronto, who
appears to have kept his distance, may be supposed to have played
some part in the recruitment of senators from their home towns.
Whether the advancement of individuals was adequate compensation
to the community for land held by absentees and rents lost abroad
is another matter.

But there is a rival recurring pattern, which is illustrated
by an inscription from Bulla Regia.[25] An equestrian statue voted
at public expense for a newly appointed patrimonial procurator of
Narbonensis is paid for by the man's brother, who is shown to be at
home and in control of the family fortunes (*AE* 1962, 183). The
continued local residence of relations of successful men – and the
parents and brothers of Lollius Urbicus are another example (*ILAlg.*
II 3563) – demonstrates both that the family has maintained its
roots in Africa and that its estates have remained basically in-
tact. It is a matter for debate, or conjecture, how far in such
cases the senator or equestrian, once launched on his public career, continued to draw upon the revenues of those estates, which
had to sustain the political activities and social life of those
left behind.

There remain to be considered under the heading of large

landowners two categories, first, a group of equestrian officials
who were not permanently lost to their *patria* and province, and secondly, a class of wealthy men who never pursued a higher career. A
number of equestrians who had served the emperor in a military or
civil capacity, or in both capacities, returned home on completion
of their term of service.[26] Born into local aristocratic families,
and having in some cases held local offices and priesthoods, they
resumed their position as local aristocrats after a hiatus (usually
brief, for only a small minority had extended careers), with enhanced status and additional resources. For other local aristocrats, however, whether of equestrian status or not, the locality
or the region remained the centre of their activity and attention,
though they might like Apuleius or his wealthier friend and future
stepson Sicinius Pontianus (an equestrian) travel abroad for educational or other reasons (Apul. *Apol.* 62,72). A considerable number of inscriptions from Africa concern 'equestrians of status',
holding perhaps honorary membership of the jury courts at Rome, but
more often merely the rank of equestrian.[27] Of the thirty-odd
equestrians from Cirta and its dependencies the great majority had
no record of imperial service.[28] Apuleius' *Apologia* gives us a
glimpse of the level of wealth attained by 'local equestrian' families in Oea in the middle of the second century A.D.[29] Aemilia
Pudentilla the widow whom Apuleius married at the instigation (he
claimed) of Pontianus, her elder son, had a fortune of four million
sesterces at her disposal, almost four times the senatorial census
(*Apol.* 77), her own dowry came to 300,000 sesterces, a sum not far
below the equestrian census (*Apol.* 92), and she gave away in largesse one sixth of this sum on the occasion of Pontianus' marriage
(*Apol.* 87). Pontianus married the daughter of one Herennius
Rufinus, who, according to Apuleius, had squandered the inheritance
of three million sesterces received from his equestrian father
(*Apol.* 75). From Apuleius we learn also that she brought with her
into the marriage a dowry of 400,000 sesterces (borrowed the day
before according to our hardly impartial source), which compares
favourably with Pudentilla's own 'modest' dowry (*Apol.* 76-7).

Little in terms of wealth separated 'local equestrians' from
the richest non-equestrian city leaders. A member of the Gabinii
of Madauros, the home town of Apuleius, could claim only one

equestrian among his relations, a cousin, but the 375,000 sesterces
that he spent on a theatre about the end of the second century
points to a patrimony of several millions (*ILAlg.* I 286). Apuleius'
father, ex-duumvir and princeps at Madauros (*Apol.* 24), left two
million sesterces.

There is no way of comparing the value of the land held by, on
the one hand, African-born senators and procurators, and on the
other, the richest stratum of the curial class. In any case I have
suggested that absentee landowners resident abroad did not withdraw
all the Africa-originating revenues to which they might have been
entitled, and that a proportion of procurators returned to their
homeland. On the other side allowance must be made for African land
held by non-Africans, and especially by the emperor. The general
conclusion seems secure, that a substantial amount of African land
of good quality was owned by landlords residing outside Italy, and
that a sizeable proportion of the surplus was withdrawn, in the form
of rents, from the local economy. Moreover, we have not yet taken
into account the question of taxation.

Two important items are missing from this survey of landholding
in Africa, which has concentrated on the larger estates. They are,
the properties of moderate size belonging to the bulk of the members
of the curial class, or the class of local politicians and benefactors, and peasant tenures. These curial properties, though modest,
were numerous; they may indeed have exceeded in value the *saltus* of
the very few rich provincial notables.[30]

The best known but by no means the largest group of smallholders
in North Africa consisted of discharged soldiers.[31] It is not known
for certain how much land, or cash-equivalent, was given to those who
settled in Africa under the Principate, but 15 *iugera*, or 9 acres
(3.75 hectares) is a reasonable estimate.[32] In the fourth century
the retiring soldier received about 20 *iugera*, or 12 acres (4 hectares).[33] A farm of this size would have produced at best a small
surplus. By the middle of the first century A.D. something in the
region of thirty colonies had been planted in North Africa, largely
the work of Augustus; the only part of the empire which approaches
this tally is the Iberian peninsula with perhaps twenty-six, but
several Spanish colonies were old foundations, dating to the first
hundred years of Roman rule.[34] If the African colonies, which in

the early period were mainly on or near the coast, contained a nu-
cleus of 300-500 colonists each,[35] then about 10,000 smallholders
were established in formal colonies. To this total we must add the
pockets of veterans established in the territories of the peregrine
civitates, such as the cives Romani pagani veterani pagi Fortu-
nalis, who were given land by Augustus in the region of Sutunurca
in the Miliana valley not far from Carthage (ILAfr. 301),[36] and
farmer-veterans who set themselves up individually in an area of
their choice.

The next period of vigorous colonization extended from Vespasian's to Trajan's reign. Augustus had used the provinces, particularly Africa, as a dumping-ground for veterans to ease the
pressure on Italian land. For Vespasian and his successors, veteran colonies were a means of consolidating new conquests; colonies
like Ammaedara, Thelepte, Cillium, Theveste, Madauros, Thamugadi,
Diana Veteranorum, Cuicul and Sitifis, all cities with a central
core of veterans, were established in strategic areas: the interior
of Tunisia, southern Numidia, and eastern Mauretania.[37] After Trajan
there was a change in policy; no more veteran colonies were founded.
Many of the soldiers discharged in later reigns are likely to have
taken up residence in communities not far from the permanent military base at Lambaesis in Numidia. Verecunda, just east of Lambaesis, Lamasba, a neighbour of Lambaesis to the north-west, and
Lambaesis itself are conspicuous examples of communities in which
veterans participated to some degree. Verecunda and Lambaesis
evolved into municipia in the second half of the second century, and
Lambaesis had secured the higher rank of colony (by now a purely
honorific title) by the middle of the third century.[38]   There is no
sign that Lamasba was promoted. There is a little evidence, though
not from Africa, that frontier lands were being distributed to veterans as early as the first part of the third century (e.g. D.
21.2.11). The settling of serving members of regular units on the
limits of the empire as soldier-farmers is a late imperial development. In Africa, however, it appears that barbarian tribesmen
(gentiles) under Roman officers (praepositi limitis) rather than
regular troops guarded the frontier zone and received land as a reward. There are signs that this system was already in operation in
Tripolitania by the middle of the third century.[39]

The assignment of land to tribes or fragments of tribes by imperial functionaries is recorded as early as the reign of Tiberius
and was commonplace thereafter.[40] How far this policy resulted in
the conversion of tribesmen to a sedentary existence is obscure.
As Berthier, drawing on the work of Despois, has recently demonstrated, it is a mistake to imagine that the Roman authorities had
no other policy towards nomadic groups than 'sedentarization'. In
the Flavian period the Suburbures Regiani and the Nicives were
given rights over the plain of 'Aïn Abid south-east of Cirta; the
city lost some municipal land in the process.[41] It was once thought
that this exemplified an imperial policy of seeking to 'sedentarize'
tribes which might otherwise have imperilled the peace of the
countryside.[42] The location of a *res publica gentis Suburburum
colonorum* one hundred kilometres away in the region of Azziz ben-
Tellis, attested in an inscription of Severan date (*BAC* 1917, 342-3),
and the somewhat later evidence that N'gaous, which is twice as far
from 'Aïn Abid, and about fifty kilometres west of Lambaesis, was a
centre of the Nicives (the name apparently deriving from the loca-
tive Nicivibus), were considered to be evidence that the scene of
tribal sedentarization had shifted, following the adoption of a
'later' strategy of forcing the tribesmen further west and south towards the desert. Such a hypothesis, however, must give way before
the finding of Despois that the plain of 'Aïn Abid was one of the
terminal points of the transhumance route leading through the depression of N'gaous.[43] Here a Severan inscription from the area
south of the Chott el Hodna becomes relevant. A commission of three,
operating under the orders of the legate of the Third Augusta, assigned *agri et pascua et fontes* to persons unknown (*AE* 1946, 38).
The beneficiaries are likely to have been tribesmen.[44] The region
of the Chott el Hodna forms part of the waiting zone whence the nomads of Metkaouak and Barika drive their flocks in May or early
June into the high plains of Constantine. Despois explains the
land-allocations as aimed at regularizing and controlling nomadic
life.

There was no question of suppressing nomadism. Quite apart
from the military problems that a policy of sealing off the nomadic
routes would have created, there were sound economic reasons for
leaving them open.[45] The nomads carried commodities for which

there was demand in the north and further afield; and customs stations
set up on key points on the transhumant routes, as at Zarai, brought
the state useful revenues.[46] Moreover, the nomads (plus semi-nomads
and transhumants) doubtless filled out the ranks of the seasonal
workers, whose annual appearance en route to employment in the corn
fields 'around Cirta, the capital of the Numidians, or in the plains
dominated by the mountain of Jupiter' was the signal to the peasant
of Maktar to set about harvesting his own crop (CIL VIII 11824).
The triangular Bedouin tent on the mosaic of the house of the Laberii
at Uthina (a city which a rustic poet might well describe as dominated by Jupiter Balcarnensis) provides useful corroborative evidence of the extent of their penetration into the region of settled
agriculture.[47] The Romans could live with nomads, once they had
been tamed and their movements regulated.[48]

On the other hand, the participation of at least the tribal
leadership in cities such as Thubursicu Numidarum, Gigthis and
Turris Tamelleni (centres of the Numidae, Chinithi and Nybgenii, respectively), suggests that a policy of sedentarization had achieved
some success.[49] Again it is difficult to explain otherwise the
emergence of communities such as the res publica gentis Suburburum
colonorum. It is noteworthy, however, that the members of this particular community style themselves coloni rather than possessores.
It may be surmised that in some areas at least the tribesmen were
transformed not so much into peasant proprietors as into tenant-
farmers and agricultural labourers on the large estates.

Another group of smallholders is revealed by those inscriptions
referring to coloni or cultores or possessores awarded the ius possi-
dendi on subseciva or virgin land or land that had gone out of cul-
tivation on the fringe of imperial estates. A law of Hadrian, referring back to a lex Manciana of unknown origin, gave anyone who
undertook the farming of such lands the right to possess them, and
enjoy their produce, alienate them or transmit them to heirs, together with tax-exemption for an initial period.[50] Hadrian and
later emperors such as Septimius Severus who apparently attempted
to revive the law are often credited with a desire 'to improve the
lot of the peasantry', in Africa and in other provinces of the empire.[51] In the first place, however, one should always be on the
look-out for an essentially practical motive underlying any imperial

beneficium, here the extension of the cultivated area and the raising of agricultural output. Secondly, while it can be agreed that
several emperors had the general aim of bringing abandoned and uncultivated land into production, and that Hadrian at least may have
pursued this aim on an empire-wide scale, there is little sign that
they offered farmers outside Africa enhanced rights over the land.
Thus in Egypt Hadrian merely lowered rents on deserted or damaged
property belonging to the state.[52] Thirdly, as was noted long ago
by Leschi, capital was needed both to cover the planting of vines
and olive trees on virgin land and to tide the farmer over during
the years in which the trees were unproductive.[53] An ordinary landless peasant who sought to take advantage of the law would have been
a debtor from the start, with only a slight chance of establishing
his financial independence. Temporary tax-concessions would not
have sufficed. The farmer (*agricola*) who restored the *fundus Aufidianus* which lay in the region of Mateur (Matera) to the north of
the Bagradas valley, and improved the property by planting more olive
trees and vines, and adding an orchard and water-storing facilities,
proudly advertised his debt-free status as a *conductor pariator*.
We can be sure that he had accumulated some capital as well.[54]

Thus the Hadrianic law 'concerning virgin soil and fields that
have remained untilled for ten consecutive years' is unlikely to
have created a new race of independent farmers out of landless
peasants, although it may have enabled small and medium landowners
to widen the gap separating them from the mass of the rural population. This class of proprietors presumably had incomes and investments below those of decurions, for the most part. The *con-
ductores* of the imperial *saltus*, doubtless more important men than
the lessee of the *fundus Aufidianus* who belonged to an insignifi-
cant peregrine community, are probably to be found in the top
stratum of this sub-curial class, if they did not actually penetrate
into the local aristocracy. One of the wealthy Gabinii of Thugga is
thought by some to have been a *conductor* of the estates of the region, though the reading is disputed.[55] The many imperial laws of
the late empire which deal with the subject of deserted and uncultivated land are addressed principally to the large landowners, who
were best able to take up imperial land offered on perpetual or em-
phyteutic lease with favourable terms.[56] But the sublease, and

therefore the *conductor*, must have remained an essential feature of
estate management on the *saltus*.

The general impression I derive is one of fluidity, with land
being acquired under the supervision of Roman officials, sometimes
at the expense of existing possessors, and a social hierarchy emerging equally fashioned under imperial direction. Three main categories of beneficiaries can be identified. The first consisted of
members of the Rome-centred ruling elite. It is not unlikely that
the larger portion of the most fertile and productive land in Africa
was within their grasp. This land may have been removed from the
jurisdiction of cities, in practice if not in theory, and the
profits from its exploitation, or a good proportion of them, went
out of the region. The other privileged groups were members of the
local elite, and military men. In rewarding the African elite with
land and other material benefits, the Romans were following their
traditional policy of building up a network of families, groups and
communities with vested interests in the prolongation of Roman
rule.[57] What emerged in Africa, as elsewhere, was a highly strati-
fied society, reflecting an unequal distribution of the land. The
curiales made up a tiny percentage of the population,[58] yet a wide
social and economic gulf separated even the poorest of them from
the mass of the rural population. Among the *curiales* themselves
there were significant differences in wealth. The average small-
town decurion was no match in status and wealth for the Carthaginian grandee before whose carriage all other travellers withdrew
(Apul. *Flor*. 21). As for the military men, their land was granted
in return for a specific service. It is to be noted that Africans
made up a respectable portion of the beneficiaries in the first
category, and dominated the remaining categories.

It is difficult to assess the degree of dislocation and upheaval which accompanied the changes I have described. One relevant factor is the extent to which the Romans introduced new and
alien modes of production into rural Africa.

One specific question to be faced is, how far was the condition
of the *coloni* of the Principate, or, for that matter, the *coloni* of
the Late Empire, comparable with that of the *coloni* of the pre-
Roman period? It has been suggested that a tied colonate was a feature of Numidian royal estates.[59] The case rests on one passage of

Diodorus (32.16), which describes Masinissa's gift to his sons of
estates 'with all their *kataskeuai*' (or *instrumenta*, equipment), and
on another from Vitruvius (8.3.24) concerning an estate, part, it is
thought, of a royal domain, which included a whole *oppidum*. The
kataskeuai in Diodorus, if comparable with the Roman civil law definition of *instrumentum*, might or might not include 'human equipment'
(see e.g. D. 33.7.8), and if it did, we would have no means of telling whether slaves or tied workers of free status were meant. The
Vitruvius passage cannot resolve this problem for us, as it notes
only that the *agri* of the *oppidum* were in the possession of the
landlord (his friend C.Julius, son of Masinissa), without touching
on the relationship between landlord and *oppidum*-inhabitants or the
status of the latter. In short, a comparison of pre-Roman and Roman
colonates is hardly possible. It is open to us to hypothesize that
the position of the free tenant-farmer and agricultural worker
changed very little under the Principate, and that the major innovation lay in the fact that the Romans spelled out the obligations
of their tenants in laws (the lex Manciana and the lex Hadriana),
which also defined their rights over the land, in the case of those
undertaking to occupy uncultivated or abandoned land. The Carthaginians, for their part, drew taxes and military manpower from the
subject Libyan population, but as yet there is no evidence that
they employed them as rent-paying tenant-farmers and agricultural
labourers. It is normally accepted that they made extensive use of
slave-cultivators.[60]

This brings us to a second question, which is, how far did the
Romans introduce or extend the slave mode of production, which was
dominant at least in large areas of Italy and Sicily in the late
republic and early empire? Slaves were regularly utilized on the
farms of the wealthy in Roman Tripolitania, at least around the
middle of the second century.[61] This is the clear implication of a
statement of Apuleius, addressed to Aemilianus, that he neither
knew nor cared 'whether you have slaves to till your land, or work
on exchange with your neighbours' (*Apol.* 17). Apuleius' object in
making this apparently casual remark was to raise in the minds of
his audience the possibility that his enemy was hard-up. This is
confirmed a little later, when the information (true or false) is
released that Aemilianus had himself lately ploughed the *agellum*

which represented his entire inheritance from his father, with a
single donkey in three days (Apol. 23). Our interest is not so much
in Apuleius' (in the end) vain attempt to brand Aemilianus a pauper,
as in the disclosure that a substantial landowner would be expected
to have a labour force of slaves. Moreover, in due course Apuleius
furnishes an example. To allay the fears of her sons that her marriage with Apuleius would deprive them of their inheritance, Pudentilla made them the gift of some highly productive land, complete
with a luxury villa, a quantity of valuable flocks and produce, and
'hardly fewer than 400 slaves' (Apol. 93). What is unclear is
whether agricultural slavery in Tripolitania was an inheritance from
the Carthaginian period or a Roman implantation. Given the continued
dominance under the Romans of Punic families at Leptis Magna (the
only Tripolitanian city where we can study the membership and public
activities of the governing class and therefore of the landowning
class), and the evidence for the infiltration of Punic culture into
the countryside, the former alternative appears to be worthy of
serious consideration. The Punic background of Pudentilla's own
family is disclosed in a passage of Apuleius, where he charges her
younger son Pudens with speaking nothing but Punic plus a few words
of Greek learned from his mother, and having neither the desire nor
the ability to speak Latin (Apol. 98).

In other parts of Roman North Africa, including areas which had
seen slaves under the Carthaginians, the evidence for agricultural
slavery is much less convincing.[62] The crucial texts are usually
ambiguous or difficult to evaluate. We should resist the temptation
to find a parallel between Pudentilla's slave-run estate and the
fundus Cornelianus of another African lady, who legated it with all
instrumenta including both mancipia and reliqua colonorum (D. 33.7.
27.1). If these slaves included agricultural workers, which is
likely,[63] then they may have cultivated one part of the estate, perhaps 'the home farm', while the rest was leased to coloni.[64] Whether
this was a common pattern in rural Africa we cannot tell. That
slave-estates on the Italian model may have existed cannot be ruled
out altogether, considering the amount of land held by wealthy absentee landlords domiciled abroad, but evidence is lacking before
the late empire.[65] The agricultural work-force was largely free
in Africa,[66] as it was in Egypt, the other main grain-producing

province of the empire.[67]

II TRIBUTE

Tribute was as inevitable a concomitant of imperial rule as territorial expansion (cf. Cic. *de off.* 2.85).[68] It was imposed 'by
right of conquest' (*iure victoriae*). The words come from the well-
known speech attributed to the Roman commander Petilius Cerialis,
but are less often cited than the justification that follows: 'For
peace between nations cannot be maintained without armies, nor
armies without pay, nor pay without taxes' (Tac. *Hist.* 4.74). On
the whole, the Romans do not appear to have bothered to justify
themselves in this way; I know of no parallel passage in any writer
of the imperial period.

    Similarly, it would be hard to construct a 'provincial' point-
of-view on the basis of the surviving literature. A few short utterances emanating from wealthy easterners represent the level of
tribute as moderate (Athenag. 1.2; Arist. 26.36, 36.10). That is
nearly all, apart from Tertullian's charge that the land tax and
capitation tax were 'marks of captivity' (*notae captivitatis*, *Apol.*
13.6). This would be a startling comment if Tertullian had been an
orthodox spokesman for this same, basically loyal, class of local
aristocrats. But ordinary provincial subjects would have shared
his dislike of tribute, especially those for whom tribute-paying in
whatever form was an unfamiliar experience. In Tertullian's own
province, one of the wilder and more militant tribes, the Nasamones,
had massacred tax-collectors in the reign of Domitian (Dio 67.4.6).

    The specious logic of the argument of Cerialis is undermined
(in advance, as it were) by a provincial who lived under Augustus,
Strabo. In discussing the decision of the Romans, that is, of
Augustus, not to occupy Britain and turn it into a province, Strabo
writes as follows: 'For it seems that at present more revenue is
derived from the duty on their province than tribute would bring
in, if we deduct the expense involved in the maintenance of an army
for the purposes of guarding the island and *collecting the tribute*;
and the unprofitableness of an occupation will be still greater in
the case of the other islands about Britain' (C 115-16). In a later
section Strabo estimates that at least one legion and some cavalry
would be needed 'in order to carry off the tribute from them' (C 200).

In fact three legions and numerous auxiliaries held down the province of Britain under the Principate;[69] and when Appian was writing a century and a half after Strabo, the Romans still regarded Britain as unprofitable (App. pref. 5; cf. 7).

In the event it was Africa not Britain which received the one legion and auxiliaries from Augustus. The decision to provincialize Africa had of course been taken long before, in 146 B.C. Appian records the imposition of direct taxes on persons and on property from that date (*Lib*. 135). But it was left to Augustus to take a census, here as elsewhere in the empire, with the aim of putting the tax-system on a sound footing and extending the circle of tribute-payers. Taking our cue from Strabo, we can see that the introduction of a military garrison was part of this same strategy. *Publicani* or civil officials could not be expected to collect taxes beyond the relatively settled area in the heart of the province. The barbarian tribes of the interior, unused to paying tribute in any form, would have to be compelled to do so by soldiers. This lesson had been learned in other settings, notably in Spain in the middle Republic.[70] We can perhaps assume that the *praktores* who were victims of the Nasamones were soldiers (Dio 67.4.6); as for the tax-collectors gibbeted by the Frisians in Lower Germany in A.D. 28, they are expressly said to have been soldiers, under the command of the senior centurion Olennius (Tac. *Ann.* 4.72). It is a fair assumption that the *praefecti gentium*[71] who were put over partially subjugated tribes in Africa from the late Julio-Claudian period, if not before, had fiscal responsibilities parallel to those of Olennius *regendis Frisiis impositus*. In short, the army, in addition to its more obvious functions, acted as an agent of exploitation.

There is little unambiguous evidence concerning the tax-system in Africa. The rate of the poll-tax is known only for Syria: one per cent of assessed capital (App. *Syr*. 50; cf. Mark 12.14). In the African section of the agrarian law of 111 B.C. reference is made to *vectigalia*, *scriptura* (fees for grazing livestock) and tithes, this last perhaps representing the *stipendium* which is early mentioned as levied on land (*FIRA* i^2 no.8, ℓ.78; cf. 82,85). This evidence is hard to reconcile with a passage in the *Verrines* (3.12-13) where Cicero states that 'most of the Poeni', like the Spaniards, pay a fixed tax (*vectigal certum*), in contrast with Asia, where the tax-system is regulated by the censor's contracts, and with Sicily, where the ordinary unprivileged Sicilian cities are subjected to a tithe on produce.

The next reference to rates of direct taxation is from the second century A.D., and concerns the great imperial estates. The *coloni* of the estate of Villa Magna Variana were required to pay a fixed percentage of the crop in most cases, a third of wheat, barley, wine and oil, and a fourth of beans (*CIL* VIII 25902, Hr.Mettich, I 20ff.). (In addition, six days' work were due each year at peak periods on the estate (IV 23ff.).) The same inscription refers to *ager octonarius*, apparently land adjacent that paid one eighth in kind. The payments of the imperial tenants are presumably higher than this because they represent rent plus tax. How far these tax-rates were notional, what percentage of the produce was actually taken from the threshing-floor, vat or press, what percentage of the produce, or its equivalent in cash, reached the city of Rome or other officially designated destinations, what was the total volume or value of commodities (or their cash-equivalent) exacted as land-tax from the North African provinces – these are matters for speculation.[72] We have Josephus' statement that Africa fed the people of Rome for eight months of the year and paid taxes of many other kinds besides (*Bell.Jud.* 2.383). This is an exaggerated figure, no doubt, but at least it can be agreed that Africa was Rome's largest corn-supplier under the Principate. If Cicero's figures for Sicily are any guide (*Verr.* 3.163),[73] then it is possible that as little as one third of the African corn that found its way to Rome was tribute-corn.

Rome had other needs, for example, oil. Septimius Severus is said to have added a daily distribution of oil to the traditional monthly distribution of corn to the urban plebs of Rome (*HA Sev*. 18.3; cf. 23.2). It is now recognized that Africa had supplanted Spain as the main supplier of oil to the capital by the middle of the third century.[74] A certain proportion of it, perhaps one third, was exacted as tribute.

To the direct taxes on persons and property we must add the miscellaneous taxes referred to by Josephus, such as customs dues, sales taxes, death duties, and the various irregular imposts, one of which, the periodic requisition of provisions and equipment for the Roman army, became more and more regular in the course of the third century.[75]

Shortage of information makes impossible any close comparison between the tax-burdens of the various provinces in the period of the Principate.[76] Egypt was certainly more heavily taxed than Africa - the Egyptian peasant surrendered one half of his crop. Meanwhile Italy (not of course a province) paid no direct tax except the death duty until the time of Diocletian. Despite the influx of provincials into the senate and civil service, the empire was run chiefly in the interests of Rome and Italy throughout the Principate.

III MILITARY MANPOWER

It has been suggested that Africans were regularly conscripted for service abroad, at least up to the time of Hadrian.[77] If true, this might mean, at worst, that Africans were used as cannon fodder in wars that did not concern them, at best, that under Roman management, considerable numbers of Africans were lost to their fatherland. Tacitus (*Ann.* 16.13.4) mentions a levy held in Gallia Narbonensis, Africa and Asia at the end of Nero's reign with the aim of filling up the Illyrian legions. There is little other evidence.[78] Africans do not appear to have been used on the Rhine in the first century,[79] nor in significant numbers in Egypt in the same period. In the second and third centuries, about 8% of the Egyptian garrison (of which we possess only a small sample) came from Africa, Egypt itself supplying two thirds.[80] The Nicopolis inscription is an aberration: of 133 soldiers recruited into legio II Trajana in A.D. 132-3, apparently to meet the great Jewish rebellion under Bar Kochbar, 89%, or 66% of those who survived to be discharged in A.D. 157, came from Africa (34 from Carthage, 16 from Utica, and 4 only from Numidia), and not one from Egypt.[81] Other evidence for the II Trajana shows 5% of its recruits drawn from Africa, and 75% from Egypt (*CIL* III 6580 = *ILS* 2034). The Nicopolis inscription, then, merely shows that Africa was a favoured recruiting ground in emergencies, because of its reserve of manpower and the quality of its troops. We must therefore conclude that, as far as the legions were concerned, recruitment for service abroad was only a modest drain on African manpower.[82]

The thesis we have been considering might, however, apply to
auxiliary troops, within a fairly restricted period.[83] Spaniards
and Gauls had frequently served abroad as auxiliaries in the republican period.[84] As for Africans, Moors were certainly conscripted and probably fought abroad as early as the Flavian period,
at which time one or more cohorts of Musulamii and at least one cohort of Numidae were put together for service in Syria. Probably
also under the Flavians six Gaetulian tribes, described as located
in Numidia, were led in some unknown arena of war by Pliny the
younger's maternal grandfather. Further Gaetuli are recorded as
soldiers at Cemenelum (Cimiez) in the Maritime Alps, in Judaea and
in Lower Moesia, as early as Vespasian's reign.[85]

It has been suggested that for the Musulamii, for example, to
have contributed soldiers on this scale, they must have 'accepted
Romanization'.[86] Yet formidable opponents of Rome such as Arminius
and Tacfarinas served in the Roman army, and the loyalty of auxiliary brigades was far from assured, as the *cohors Usiporum* demonstrated dramatically in Britain (Tac. *Agric.* 28). So unsure were
the Flavian emperors of the Musulamii, that they established a tri-
angle of two military colonies (Ammaedara, Madauros) and a legionary camp (Theveste) on their territory, which was much reduced in
size. Trajan moved the legion from Theveste to Lambaesis, but
Theveste was transformed into a third military colony, further cutting into tribal land, while Trajan's legates finished the job of
delimiting Musulamian territory. It was standard practice (again
there are numerous parallels from the republican period) to demand
auxilia from a native tribe;[87] the men conscripted would be virtual
hostages and the tribe itself less capable of organizing or sus-
taining resistance against the occupying power. Thus the Romans
are likely to have pressed Musulamii into service abroad as part
of the continuing process of pacification in the interior of
Tunisia and eastern Algeria. The strategy was no doubt effective.
No Musulamian cohorts are known after the reign of Trajan.

We must next consider the military needs of North Africa itself
and the way in which they were met. Africa was served under the
Principate by one legion, the Third Augusta, and a variable number
of auxiliary brigades (plus an urban cohort based in Carthage).
There could not have been a demand for more than two- to three-

hundred new recruits each year in normal circumstances. From what
sources were they drawn?

We no longer believe as did Cagnat that in the first century
soldiers for the Third Augusta were chosen exclusively from Italy
and the Romanized provinces of the West.[88] This, if true, would
have constituted a signal vote of no-confidence in the trustworthi-
ness of Africans. In fact, the origins of only eleven soldiers were
known to Cagnat. Since his day the number of inscriptions of soldiers of known origin from the first century has been doubled (but
only doubled);[89] we can see that at least some Africans entered the
legion (less than twenty per cent of our tiny sample are Africans),
probably conscripted in the main from established cities like Carthage and Cirta and their hinterlands, and that the Tres Galliae
were drawn upon more heavily than Gallia Narbonensis.

There is more information available for the Antonine and
Severan periods, and a new pattern has arisen. By the second quar-
ter of the second century, local and regional recruitment was becoming common throughout the empire. The army lists at Lambaesis
from the second half of the century show a considerable proportion,
up to about fifty per cent, of men of camp origin, that is, sons of
legionaries.[90] Since Hadrian, men born in the camp (*castris*) were
permitted to inherit by will from their fathers, though they were
not legitimate heirs (*BGU* 140 = *W.Chrest.* II 373). The proportion
of Berber blood in the Roman army of Africa must have increased
with each generation. This was now, moreover, an army largely of
volunteers, not conscripts.[91]

The significance of this is as follows. Veterans were a privileged group. We need think only of the economic benefits that accrued to them and the status improvement that could result from the
award of land on discharge.[92] The Caesarian and Augustan colonies
had established foreigners on African soil. The veterans set up in
colonies by emperors from Vespasian to Trajan, however, at least
included Africans, men who had joined the army in the second half
of the first century. The same can be said of the veterans of the
Third Augusta or an auxiliary brigade who settled in groups or as
individuals in other areas in the early empire. In contrast, most
of the leading citizens as well as the smaller landowners of Lambaesis when it was promoted to municipal status were not recent

immigrants from outside Africa, but families already settled in the area. They were Africans by birth not adoption; their families had provided soldiers in the past and would continue to do so in the future. Imperial policy was now working in favour of Africans, but in this, as in most cases, Africans who had done service for Rome.

With the military men who became landowners and socially and politically prominent in their localities, we have reached the fringe of the group which most obviously benefited from Roman rule, the city-based aristocracy or curial class. But before we consider the composition of this group, its accessibility to Africans and the opportunities it afforded for further advancement, it is appropriate to discuss the role of the cities themselves, as seen by the central government.

IV   THE FUNCTION OF CITIES

Africa is acknowledged to have been, outside Italy, the most heavily urbanized region of the empire in the west. The phenomenon of urban growth, and the process by which peregrine *civitates* and *vici* gained promotion into fully fledged *municipia* and *coloniae*, have been much studied.[93] One theme that has received stress has been the progress of Romanization in the urban centres of Africa. Two other factors which form an essential part of the background of the drive for status promotion among the urban communities of Africa have been less generally recognized: the role of the self-governing city within the imperial administrative system, and the exploitation by the city of the rural communities dependent on them.

For the furnishing of taxes and military manpower, which were the most crucial needs of the empire, the central authorities depended on local administrative units, principally urban communities, which had responsibility for their adjacent rural territory (*pertica* or *territorium*).[94] A passage in a work of one of the Agrimensores shows that city officials in Africa characteristically exacted, or tried to exact, from the rural population unspecified compulsory services (*munera*), recruits, transport and supplies.[95] There were, to be sure, large tracts of Roman Africa where the writ of city officials did not run. In the tribal reserves responsibility rested with the *praefectus gentium* where he existed, or other officials, usually military, who collected taxes in kind and raised recruits with the cooperation of the leading tribesmen. The large estates, whether under imperial or non-imperial ownership, appear to have been largely independent of the city authorities, although it is doubtful whether the legal position on this subject was clear. The Agrimensor indicates that city officials frequently came into collision with agents of both imperial and private landowners in a judicial setting, and it is improbable that all such disputes concerned merely the precise territorial limits of estate and city territory, especially as it is indicated that the initiative for litigation came from the cities. Be that as it may, there can be no doubt that there were substantial areas of Africa which fell within the jurisdiction of the cities.

The *territorium* of a city was divided into *pagi*, territorial units which were likely to contain one or more nucleated settlements, or *vici*. In raising the tax-revenues and recruits that were needed for the central government, the city authorities worked through the *pagus* and *vicus* officials. It was an unequal relationship, which the former were no doubt able to exploit to their own and their city's advantage.[96] It is clear that financial contributions and services were regularly exacted from dependent communities for the benefit of the city itself.[97] The cities prospered through their exploitation of the countryside.

It follows that in the upgrading of urban centres the interests of local community and central government might well coincide. There were clear material advantages to be gained by a community and its leadership which managed to free itself from the territorial jurisdiction of another community (or the supervision of a prefect or other official imposed from outside); for that community was in a position to milk the resources of its dependencies for its own purposes, and unfairly distribute the burdens imposed on it by the imperial power. Thus the Galatian village of Orcistus sought city status from Constantine in order to escape the oppressive rule of the neighbouring city of Nacola (*ILS* 6099). Again, insofar as the central authorities were concerned to increase (or maintain) the level of tax-revenue and the supply of military manpower, and to impose effective law and order on the countryside, they would have had positive reason to favour the multiplication of self-governing administrative units. Africa, it is agreed, was relatively well stocked with cities.

　　Imperial policy was not in practice so coldly rational, or not
continuously so, at least prior to the third century. It was left
to individual cities to strive for improved status, and inevitably
some were more successful than others. The progress of city-
promotion was uneven, and the result of any particular request for
upgrading not always predictable. Antoninus Pius favoured only
Gigthis, among African cities. His reasons are unknown. The fact
that Orcistus was a community of Christians prejudiced Constantine
in its favour. The person, status and relation to the emperor of
the representative or patron of the petitioning community, the effect of the arguments he adduced (concerning, for example, the
community's loyalty, its level of Latin culture, its economic resources), the emperor's character, background and attitudes (including any personal connection he might have had with the relevant
city, region or province) - any of these matters might be decisive.
Nor should the possibility be overlooked that vested interests
might stand against change and oppose it successfully. I suspect
that a coalition between the many influential senators from Cirta
and the local leadership was able to prevent the carving up of the
city's vast territories and the loss of revenues and services this
would have entailed, well into the third century.[98] The mediation
of high-placed patrons was not entirely disinterested, if they were
major landowners in the region.[99] Again, the immense *pertica* of
Carthage was only slowly broken up through the award of municipal
status to individual *pagi et civitates* or *vici*, and to explain this
the influence of the grandees of Carthage and their allies in the
capital should be invoked.[100] An additional reason for the failure
of the Romans to municipalize this, the heartland of Africa Proconsularis, for so long was the scale of imperial interest and presence in the area, which included the grain-producing Medjerda valley. Administration and control, the traditional functions of self-
governing communities, were to some extent accounted for by the imperial authorities in Carthage and on the extensive imperial domains in the region. When the pace of municipalization eventually
quickened, under Septimius Severus, the size of the imperial estates, the number of communities and their proximity to one another
ensured that the new *municipia* would have exiguous territories and

little opportunity for growth.

The municipal policy of Septimius Severus and some later emperors should be set against the background of the gradual transformation of the whole system of provincial administration in the
course of the second century. Indirect rule, resting on the voluntary cooperation of the local elite, was giving way, and a regime
of compulsion replacing it, as the central authorities strove to
control more closely the process of tapping the resources of the
provinces.[101] The key to the performance of the various tasks imposed on the cities lay in the liturgical system. There was bound
to be conflict between the patriotic, but not altogether altruistic,
desire of the local magnate to spend his surplus funds on something
tangible and relevant to the life of his city, and the obligation
to perform expensive and time-consuming tasks for the central government. The central government showed an increasing tendency to divert or direct the energies and funds of the wealthy from the former
to the latter, and to increase the total burden on the wealthy. The
interventionist inclinations of the central administration are very
much in evidence in the reign of Septimius Severus. It was during
his rule that municipal or quasi-municipal government came to Egypt,
as a way of spreading more widely the burdens of administration
among the better-off members of the subject population. The newly
promoted African *municipia* had more to gain than the Egyptian *metro-
poleis*, but to interpret the stepping-up of the municipalization of
the *pertica* of Carthage as a demonstration of liberality is to overlook the ambivalent attitude which the central authorities had long
displayed towards city-foundations and -promotion.[102]

V THE AFRICAN ELITE

In this section I outline some of the ways in which social advancement and recognition were available to Africans. My examples of
successful Africans will be drawn from cases where social background
or ethnic origin is indicated more or less overtly. Some indigenous
Africans and their descendants give themselves away by their adopted
family names or their *cognomina*, or by the Berber or Punic names
which they or their relations bear.[103] Again, some are designated
tribal chieftains. I will not attempt to calculate the proportion
of local aristocrats belonging to various social or ethnic groups.

Even if this were a fruitful enterprise, for my purposes it is unnecessary. If social and political promotion was possible for
Africans in the several ways that are outlined below, then it is
difficult to avoid the conclusion that membership of local government was predominantly African - given that the level of immigration
was not high.[104]

There are several points to be made concerning indigenous
Africans and their mobility chances.

(1) The success of the peasant of Maktar in entering the council
    of his city and becoming censor (*CIL* VIII 11824) is mislead-
    ing.[105] Ordinary Africans had little hope of social advance-
    ment unless they joined the army. If they survived twenty-five
    years of military service, they had a chance of obtaining curial
    office for themselves or their descendants, especially in stra-
    tegic areas near the frontiers. Social prominence was all but
    guaranteed in the case of those who rose in the ranks.

(2) Indigenous Africans may be found with Roman citizenship and
    holding public office in areas where they have not been pushed
    off the land by immigrants from abroad or by aristocratic Roman
    landowners, emperors included.

(3) Such men tend to be already possessed of high status in their
    communities by virtue of their wealth, birth and military
    prowess.

(4) Under Roman rule, the gap between native leaders and their fol-
    lowers probably widened.

(5) Some citizens and office-holders can be shown to have been pro-
    moted by Roman commanders or emperors for services rendered.

(6) Some natives gained *beneficia* not so much as a reward for ser-
    vices rendered, as an incentive to future obedience or acqui-
    escence in Roman rule.

(7) Romanization or cultural assimilation was by no means a necess-
    ary prelude to the promotion of individuals or, for that matter,
    of cities.

(8) For a privileged few, local politics was a springboard to
    higher status and a public career outside the locality and the
    province.

The military men may conveniently be dealt with first. Given
that the Roman army in Africa was increasingly African in terms of

the ethnic origin of its members, we can take it that the governing
class of the cities where military men were prominent had a strong
indigenous element. With veterans and their descendants, however,
we have only penetrated the outer fringe of the class of successful
Africans. Military men were not prominent everywhere. As in the
empire at large, so in Africa, ordinary veterans were apparently
influential mainly in the smaller cities in the interior, such as
Verecunda, Madauros and Diana Veteranorum in southern Numidia.[106]
However, ex-officers are found in prominent positions in local society and government in other areas as well.[107]

Under points (2)-(4) I maintain that there was continuity of
leadership under the Romans in some areas, and if anything an en-
hancement of the distinction between leaders and followers. One
thinks of heavily Punic Leptis Magna, and its pre-colonial rulers
with names like Iddibal (*IRT* 319) and Anobal (*IRT* 324 a-c), or
heavily Berber Gigthis, with its Memmii, Messii, Servaei, Servilii,
many or most of native stock, most obviously Memmius Pacatus, described as *Chinithius*, and celebrated by the Chinithi in words
implying that he was their *princeps*: *ob merita eius et singularem
pietatem qua nationi suae praestat* (*CIL* VIII 22729 = *ILS* 9394).
His selection as juryman at Rome by Hadrian antedates the city's
promotion to municipal status by the successor of Hadrian, and the
award of citizenship to an ancestor may go back to Flavian times.
Although the Chinithi had formed part of the coalition of Tacfarinas in the first decades of the century, the tribe itself was not
displaced or dispossessed. Its leadership, however, was perhaps
reshuffled. The accentuation of the natural distance between
chiefs and rank-and-file tribesmen may also be illustrated from
Gigthis. Memmius Pacatus *princeps* was a juryman, and his family
produced senators by the Severan period, while the ordinary tribesmen remained non-citizens, both under Hadrian and under Pius *condi-
tor municipii*, whose charter for the city provided for the acquisition of citizenship only through entry into the local council
(*CIL* VIII 22737 = *ILS* 6780). Later in the second century, the
tribe, or a section of it, was still under the surveillance of a
praefectus (*CIL* VIII 10500 = *ILS* 1409).[108] Again, at Thubursicu
Numidarum, another tribal capital, the Numidian chieftain, A.Larcius
Macrinus, *princeps gentis Numidarum* (*ILAlg*. I 1297 = *ILS* 9392),

outstripped the mass of indigenous Africans in the city and in the
countryside, citizens in some cases, but with non-Roman names and
few prospects.[109]

Points (5)-(7), on the other hand, imply a background not of
continuity, but upheaval, engineered by the occupying power, which
is seen distributing rewards for signal service without respect for
status. An early case concerns the Marii.[100] Some of the 189 Marii
identified in African inscriptions, though not nearly as many as has
been suggested, were descendants of, or were linked with, Gaetuli
who fought for Marius and were rewarded with citizenship and land
(Bell.Afr. 56.3, 32.3, 35.4). The title Mariana is borne by Uchi
Maius and Thibaris, two cities in one pocket of the extensive
territory of Carthage, lying to the west of the Fossa Regia, and
the connexion of this area with C.Marius cos. VII seems assured.
The heaviest concentration of Marii, and the only Marii of any importance in Africa, were connected with cities such as Uchi Maius,
Thugga and Mustis. They held office at Carthage or had marriage
links with important Carthaginians. The one or two other municipal
magistrates among the African Marii were of recent Berber extrac-
tion, had been soldiers, and were significant individuals only in
southern Numidia. Most Marii are of no importance. One of them,
Marius Gaetulicus, son of Iulia Silleha of Theveste, provides a
bridging link to another group of Gaetuli of no importance, those
bearing the cognomen Gaetulus or a variant.[111] Out of seventy-four
one or two only shine through, such as Seia Gaetula of Cirta, whose
son-in-law was a senator of praetorian rank in the first half of
the third century (PIR[2] F 538). This is a small reminder of the
fact that the native populations were not excluded from positions
of influence even in this relatively cosmopolitan capital with its
strong immigrant element.[112] The same point can be made rather
more powerfully with reference to the numerous and important Sittii
and Iulii who owed their hold on Cirta and its environs to a whim
of Julius Caesar.[113]

Under the empire the promotion of individuals and cities continued. The most dramatic instance of an imperial beneficium for
services rendered is Claudius' in favour of Volubilis, a town in
Mauretania. The whole body of Volubitani received citizenship and
other privileges, and their city was awarded municipal status, in

return for their assistance in putting down the rebel Aedemon and his followers (*FIRA* I[2] no.70).[114] A more regular pattern is exemplified in the promotion of Gigthis - a local magistrate, an ancestor of whom had secured citizenship, gained for his town municipal status, but of a kind which benefited principally the elite. The arguments he used are unknown, but presumably he could have pointed to a certain level of Romanization among the beneficiaries (*CIL* VIII 22737 = *ILS* 6780). Volubilis, on the other hand, is a classic case of a promotion which preceded Romanization. The *principes* of the Baquates, a Mauretanian tribe whose relations with Rome can be followed to some extent for a century and a half, were sometimes awarded citizenship, but in quite different circumstances.[115] Aurelius Canatha is described as *princeps constitutus genti Baquatium* (*AE* 1957, 203), and the implication is that his position in the tribe has been strengthened with Roman assistance. This however was bribery, not the rewarding of services, and certainly not recognition of Romanization. Nor in the long run did this policy achieve positive results. A parallel is provided by the Banasa inscription from the reign of Marcus concerning the Zegrenses.[116] Julianus won promotion from one of the *primores* to *princeps*, and the new *princeps* and his family were awarded citizenship. These *beneficia* are dressed up as rewards for obedience, but the wording of the inscription conveys hope of future loyalty rather than gratitude for past performance. The initiative has come at least as much from the benefactor as the beneficiary.

There could be no greater contrast than that between tribal chieftains who were never integrated into the Roman provincial system and those members of the African aristocracy who passed into the imperial civil service and the senatorial order. By one estimate, by the later part of the second century about fifteen per cent of procurators[117] and about fifteen per cent of senators[118] originated in Africa. Precision is unattainable, but this matters less than the fundamental fact that Africans had access to the central administration and the highest status-group. The empire was still Rome-based, but the ruling class that directed it was cosmopolitan. 'You often command our legions in person, and in person govern these and other provinces. There is no question of segregation or exclusion' (Tac. *Hist.* 4.74). The words attributed to

Cerialis, inappropriate in their setting, Gaul in A.D. 70, had come
true. Whether the provincial established at the capital remembered
his native town and province and sought to advance their interests
is another matter.

VI CONCLUSION: ROMANIZATION AND RESISTANCE
In Roman North Africa the work of pacification was continuous and
long-lasting. The challenge represented by Tacfarinas and his formidable coalition of nomadic and semi-nomadic tribesmen, who maintained a destructive war for seven years, was never repeated in
Proconsularis and Numidia; but hostile encounters with tribal forces
occurred sporadically in certain areas, and in Mauretania they were
occasionally of a serious nature.[119] It has been forcefully argued
by Bénabou that this 'military resistance' was matched by 'cultural
resistance' among the people of Africa.

    This thesis is basically an attempt to account for the emerg-
ence of a particular and original Romano-African civilization, one
that was, moreover, town-centred, having little impact on a solidly
un-Romanized countryside. It makes much of the survival of indigenous cultural and religious traditions.[120] However, before accepting
the tenacity of local traditions as evidence of resistance, we must
enquire into the aims of the imperial power in the sphere of culture, and the prevalence of self-conscious opposition to the import-
ation of an alien civilization. The notion of resistance has limited explanatory power if it is used indiscriminately to describe
unconscious as well as overt opposition to a foreign culture.

    Upper-class Romans had little respect for the quality of life
of the peoples of the underdeveloped West.[121] For Cicero, Africans,
Spaniards and Gauls were 'savage and barbarous nations' (ad QF.
1.1.27); for Velleius, the Germans had voices and limbs but nothing
else in common with men (2.117.3). Treacherous conduct towards opponents of this nature merited no apology, while extermination and
enslavement were acceptable policies.

    Moreover, Roman or pro-Roman writers say nothing of any mission
civilatrice undertaken in the interests of the subject populations.
Nor was such a policy pursued by Roman administrators. Agricola,
whose attempt at 'civilizing the (British) barbarians' is described
by Tacitus in a well-known passage (Agric. 21), had strictly limited

aims. He did not, for example, impose a fully-fledged educational system on the Britons. This would not have been a practical proposition in Britain or anywhere else. But in any case Agricola would probably not have believed in it. Romanization for him was a means to an end, which was to turn a nation of warriors into peaceful subjects.[122] Moreover, his civilizing efforts were aimed at the British chieftains and their sons: it was they who were led to live a comfortable urban life, receive a Roman education and adopt Roman customs. He had no programme for the mass of the people, beyond administering justice equitably, moderating requests for taxes, supplies and military manpower, and maintaining a close supervision through the army (*Agric*. 19.3-4, 20.2). Again, the British leadership, according to Tacitus, quickly developed an appetite for Roman culture. Whether or not this is accurate in the case of the British, the Romans clearly believed, not without good grounds, that a native leadership would Romanize themselves, once shown the way. The attractiveness of Roman culture to less advanced peoples is not to be underrated.[123] There were additional incentives, on the subject of which Tacitus is silent. Within the Roman system, education was the key to social and political advancement. This was understood by one Seius Fundanus of Calama in Africa, who sent off his two sons to pursue their studies 'and thus assured them of honours' (*CIL* VIII 5770). Indeed Tacitus' assertion that the Britons 'instead of loathing the Latin language were eager to speak it eloquently' is more appropriately applied to the Africans. Africa produced both accomplished writers and orators and uninspired littérateurs in number. They came not only from the major cities but also from minor inland towns. Educational instruction was conducted in Latin and sometimes Greek, never Punic (cf. Apul. *Apol*. 98).[124]

In religion and cult a strong indigenous tradition survived throughout the period of Roman rule.[125] Given that the simple equation of survival with resistance cannot be accepted, one must again try to assess the Roman attitude to local practices, in this instance in the field of religion. To put it briefly, the Romans were on the whole tolerant of local cults as long as they did not become a focus of disturbance and rebellion. Thus a speaker in the *Octavius* of Minucius Felix (an African) can say:

Hence it is that throughout the wide empire, provinces and

> towns, we see each people having its own individual rites and
> worshipping its local gods, the Eleusinians Ceres, the Phryg-
> ians the Great Mother, the Epidaurians Aesculapius, the Chal-
> daeans Bel, the Syrians Astarte, the Taurians Diana, the Gauls
> Mercury, the Romans one and all. (6.1-2)

The only pagan cult practice in Africa to which hostility was shown
by the Roman authorities was the human sacrifice associated with the
worship of Saturn; its private performance, however, was tolerated.[126]
African Christianity was also subject to intermittent persecution.
It was this confrontation which provoked the only searching criticism of Roman imperialism and its theological underpinning which has
survived in the literature of the Principate.[127] It would be rash,
however, to assume that there was anything peculiarly African in the
arguments to be found in Tertullian and Minucius Felix,[128] while the
clash between state paganism and Christianity was of course empire
wide. On the other hand, the resistance mounted by the Donatists
against the imposition of Catholic orthodoxy by Christian emperors
was a specifically African phenomenon.[129]

    Roman rule in Africa produced a specific cultural complex, but
its individuality was not a threat to the imperial power, any more
than was the non-Roman character of the Hellenic civilization of
the East. Any attempt by the imperial government to eradicate a
local culture would have undermined its basic strategy of winning
the support and active cooperation of the local elite by offering
them material benefits. By choosing this course the Romans pro-
longed their rule. However, the loyalty of those Africans who accepted a certain level of cultural assimilation as a way of attaining more tangible rewards was likely to be undermined by the withdrawal or diminution of those rewards. In the event, long before
the *pax Africana* (the basic *beneficium*) broke down, the continued
and increased use of intervention and coercion, which were habits
the Romans could never break, had weakened the consensus supporting
Roman rule, because it upset the delicate balance between benefits
and burdens.

N.R.M. de Lange (Faculty of Oriental Studies, Cambridge)

I

In any attempt to understand the attitudes of subject peoples to Roman rule, the Jewish evidence cannot be ignored. The surviving literature is ample, and spans the whole period of Roman rule. Its authors were literate and articulate, and many of them played a leading part in political events. The result is, for him who has eyes to see, a vivid and intimate picture of provincial life and attitudes. But it is not an easy picture to interpret. Much of the material is fragmentary in form. It has an esoteric character, being written for initiates. It tends to avoid the explicit, to prefer the hint, the allegory. There is little straightforward historical writing; instead we have snatches of dark prophecies, of homilies, of commentaries on ancient texts. The overall effect is frequently frustrating, and it is small wonder that the material has been so little exploited.

Perhaps the very inwardness of the Jewish literature militates against its use as a guide to provincial attitudes to Roman rule. The Jews are a peculiar people; they have never been able to keep religion out of politics. The combination is sometimes bizarre and often bewildering to the sober political historian. Yet in a sense every people is a peculiar people, and the 'uniqueness' of Jewish-Roman relations can be exaggerated. The history of the Jews under Roman rule presents special features, especially when viewed in the long perspective; but the Judaeans were also Roman provincials, and shared many problems with provincials everywhere. Unlike others, they have left written records of their thoughts about the empire. The scarcity of such material makes it precious, even if its form is strange. It can be read as a specimen, not a typical sample, of attitudes to the Roman empire.

In what follows I shall try to sketch the main lines of Jewish response to the Roman empire as they are represented in the Jewish literature. This literature is of diverse kinds. Some of it is

written in Hebrew or Aramaic, some in Greek; some only survives in
Greek translation. Some, a very little, is Greek-style history,
but most of the writers accept a Semitic view of time in which past,
present and future are not easily distinguished. The rabbinic texts
take the form mostly of anonymous, ill-dated compilations of fragments of oral teaching, arranged around a common theme and often attributed to their authors. We are bound to have blind faith in the
soundness of these attributions: they are the only means we have of
making chronological sense of the material. What is known generally
of oral traditions justifies a measure of confidence. The fragmentary form entails a willingness in the reader to plunge, blindfolded
sometimes, into the heart of an aphorism or an anecdote: it is possible to be hopelessly wrong. Still, with the exercise of reasonable
precautions, the risk and effort are probably worthwhile.

       II

The Romans appeared over the Jewish horizon in the first half of
the second century B.C. They came from beyond the confines of the
traditional Jewish world, and this gave them a certain initial advantage. The Jews tended to judge other nations in terms of a
mythical history enshrined in their corpus of sacred writings. It
was hard for any of their neighbours to avoid being type-cast,
usually in an unenviable role. The Herodian family, for example,
suffered from their Edomite origins, and the source of antisemitism
can be located ultimately in the resentment felt by some Egyptians
at a hostile Jewish stereotype of Egypt. A total outsider started
on a more favourable footing, at least until the course of events
dictated a policy, and he came to be identified, in a typical sense,
with one of the ancient foes. The Greeks had benefited in this way:
Alexander receives a good press, but as time went on the image of
the Greeks progressively deteriorated, until they came to be cast as
archetypal enemies.

       It is as allies of the Jews against the Greek enemy that the
Romans first appear on the Jewish scene. In this guise they make
their solitary and shadowy appearance in the Greek Bible (Daniel
11.30, Septuagint), and a succession of treaties of alliance and
friendship between the Jews and Romans against the Greek menace is
recorded by Jewish writers.[1]

The first substantial Jewish account of the Romans and their
power is in a Greek translation of a work originally written in
Hebrew or Aramaic in the late second century B.C. They are powerful, but friendly to their allies. They have waged successful
wars against Greeks, Spaniards and others. Nearer home, they have
defeated a large army of Antiochus the Great.

> When the Greeks planned to attack and destroy them, they
> heard of it and sent a single general against them. Battle
> was joined, and many of the Greeks fell; the Romans took their
> women and children prisoner, plundered their territory and
> annexed it, razed their fortifications, and made them slaves,
> as they are to this day. The remaining kingdoms, the islands,
> and all who had ever opposed them, they destroyed or reduced
> to slavery. With their friends, however, and all who put
> themselves under their protection, they maintained firm friend-
> ship. They thus conquered kings near and far, and all who
> heard their fame went in fear of them. Those whom they wished
> to depose, they deposed; and thus they rose to great heights
> of power. For all this, not one of them made any personal
> claim to greatness by wearing the crown or donning the purple.
> They had established a senate where three hundred and twenty
> senators met daily to deliberate, giving constant thought to
> the proper ordering of the affairs of the common people. They
> entrusted their government and the ruling of all their terri-
> tory to one of their number every year, all obeying this one
> man without envy or jealousy among themselves. (I Macc.
> 8.(1-)9-16, New English Bible)

The references to Antiochus and the Greeks are not accidental. 'The
Greeks', or rather hellenized Syrians, were the principal enemy; the
conquerors of the Greeks would naturally be the friends of the Jews,
at least until Judaea was brought under the yoke of Roman rule. The
memory of the ancient alliance with Rome survived this change. As
late as the fourth century we have some reflections on the subject,
including the grandiose claim that it was only after the alliance
with the Jews that the Romans were able to defeat the Greeks (Dimi,
B 'Abodah Zarah 8^b).

The precise date of the establishment of Roman rule over the
Jews was a matter for dispute. Yose ben Halafta, the foremost rabbinic expert on chronology and the reputed source of the chronological work *Seder 'Olam Rabba*, stated (in the mid-second century
A.D.) that it took place 180 years before the destruction of the
Jerusalem temple, i.e. 110 B.C. (B 'Abodah Zarah 8[b], Shabbath 15[a]).
It is hard to see to what event this refers. Josephus, however,
unambiguously dates the subjection of the Jews to Roman rule to the
conquest of Jerusalem by Pompey in 63 B.C., in the course of a civil
war led by rival Hasmonean princes:

> The cause of this disaster for Jerusalem was the clash between
> Hyrkanos and Aristobulos. The consequences: we lost our lib-
> erty and became subject to the Romans; we were compelled to
> restore to the Syrians the territory we had won from them by
> force of arms; the Romans exacted more than 10,000 talents
> from us in a short period of time; and sovereignty, which had
> formerly been vested in the high-priestly family, became the
> preserve of laymen. (*Ant.* 14.77)

III

Pompey's conquest of Jerusalem is the subject of several contemporary Hebrew poems, preserved in Greek translation. In their analysis
of the rights and wrongs of the disaster they betray a blend of attitudes which became standard in subsequent Jewish explanations of
military defeats. For the Jews, it was axiomatic that historical
events affecting them bore the mark of divine intervention. If the
Jews won a war, God was on their side; if they lost, God was punishing them for their misdeeds. In the present case there is a strong
emphasis on the sins of the Jews:

> They incited God by lawbreaking in underground hideouts:
>   incest - son with mother, father with daughter;
>   adultery - wife-swapping sanctioned by solemn agreements;
>   plundering God's sanctuary with impunity,
>   trampling his altar with impurity.
> They left no sin undone, they were worse than the Gentiles.

God responded by pouring them an undiluted draught:
  he brought the mighty smiter from the end of the earth,
  he declared war on Jerusalem and her land.
The rulers of the land welcomed him with joy,
  saying, Welcome! Come in peace!
They smoothed the way before him,
  opened the gates to Jerusalem,
  garlanded her walls.
He entered in peace like a father visiting his children,
  in total security he planted his feet.
He captured her strongholds and the wall of Jerusalem;
  God brought him in safety because of their errors.[2]

The conqueror, even if he is led by God, is not described in
flattering terms: he is an alien, a sinner, an arrogant man (Ps.
Sol. 2.1-2, 29-30; 17.13, 15). One of the poems describes how he
himself is punished:

It was not long before God showed me his arrogance
  slain on the hills of Egypt,
  lower than the lowest on land or sea,
  his corpse unburied,
  arrogantly tossed by the waves,
because he scorned God contemptuously,
  not considering that he was a mere man,
  not considering the consequences,
  saying, I shall be Lord of land and sea,
  not recognizing that God alone is Great,
  mighty in his great strength (Ps. Sol. 2.30-3).

This, too, is God's justice. And the ultimate hope is for
national restoration under God's appointed ruler:

See, Lord, and raise them up their king, son of David,
  at the time you, God, choose
  for him to rule over Israel your child.
Gird him with strength to shatter unjust rulers,
  to purge Jerusalem of the destructive trampling of Gentiles,

wisely, justly to expel sinners from the Heritage,
to smash the sinner's arrogance like a pot.[3]

The picture which emerges is a complex one. The conquest is
a national disgrace, but it is a just punishment, and not a sign
that God has abandoned his people. This attitude, a relic no doubt
of the Babylonian exile, will reappear at later moments of national
calamity, and will prevent the nation from losing its self-confidence.
It contains little of specific judgement on Rome; on the contrary,
we see the Romans gradually being assimilated into the traditional
Jewish world-view.

A similar attitude can be discerned in other literary remains
of the period, accompanied by a growing and more specific hostility
to Rome. The most violent outbursts are to be found in the Third
Sibyl,[4] where the theme of sin and punishment is frequently repeated.
A strongly anti-Roman tract from Qumran insists that it is because
of the sins of their defenders that the fortresses are destroyed,
and contains the confident statement that 'God will not destroy his
people by the hand of the Gentiles; he will execute the judgement
of the Gentiles by the hand of his elect' (Habakkuk Comm. col.4).

It was in this early period of Roman hegemony, poorly documented
in comparison with the later period of direct rule, that the fundamental Jewish attitudes to Rome were moulded. We can detect a certain ambiguity: the might of Rome is still admired, particularly her
superiority over Greece (Nahum Comm. col.1; Orac. Sib. 3.520ff.),
but the image is changing to that of the 'devouring eagle' (Habakkuk
Comm. col.3). The nature of the surviving evidence probably distorts
the picture; still a striking feature is the steadfast belief that
God is in control, and the Romans are powerless to overrule his will.

IV

Roman-Jewish relations took a new turn after the death of the puppet-
king Herod in 4 B.C. In the midst of the in-fighting of the Herodian
princes, Josephus describes a popular embassy to Rome, appealing for
'autonomy' for the nation.[5] Autonomy is defined as freedom from the
(Herodian) monarchy and subjection to the legates of Syria. The appeal is refused, but something like it is granted in A.D. 6, after
the deposition of Archelaus. Judaea will be governed by Roman

prefects, under the eye of the Syrian legate. The Jews are left very largely in control of their own affairs, and in particular no attempt is made to interfere with the free practice of their religion. Roman rule is given concrete religious expression in the institution by Augustus of a regular daily sacrifice on behalf of the emperor in the Jerusalem temple.[6]

It might appear that the people have now achieved their desire: freedom from Herodian rule, and a powerful safeguard against Greek attacks and internal Jewish strife. 'Pray for the welfare of the empire', one priest declared, 'because but for the fear of it we would swallow one another alive.'[7] Philo gives a rapturous description of the world at the beginning of the reign of Gaius:

> Indeed, the life under Saturn, depicted by the poets, no longer seemed a fable, so great was the prosperity and well-being, the freedom from grief and fear, the joy which pervaded households and people, both by day and by night. (*Leg.* 13; cf. Jos. *Ant.* 16.38)

But, while some Jews were grateful for the blessings of Roman rule, the events of A.D. 6 also sparked off an extreme and militant anti-Roman reaction which eventually culminated in full-scale revolt. Throughout the period from 6 to 66 there were outbreaks of violence, and several of the zealot leaders are known to us by name. What is not entirely clear is the zealots' aim, if they had one. To throw off the Roman yoke, but then what? Probably they were motivated by extreme messianic fervour, such as we have already encountered in the Psalms of Solomon and other texts. Messianic feeling was certainly strong at this period. The messiah would restore the House of David and secure military supremacy for the Jews. It is hard to judge how much popular support there was for this extreme programme. Its proponents seem to have exploited a growing discontent provoked by the hardships of Roman rule, particularly the increased burden of taxation (e.g. Jos. *BJ* 2.118; Mark 12.15).

Whatever its popular appeal, it was a long time before the zealot movement received any official backing. Its propaganda has left few traces in the literature,[8] and it is only from its practical manifestations that it is known. It seems to have been stronger in

Galilee than in Judaea. In Jerusalem the priestly aristocracy is
generally thought to have been pro-Roman, and this is probably true,
although too little is known for us to enquire more deeply into its
thinking. The high priests were in the unenviable position of
having to appease both the Roman governors and an increasingly dissatisfied populace. In any case, the influence of the high priests
was waning at this time. Roman rule served to buttress it artifici-
ally for a while; after the destruction of the temple the high
priesthood disappeared without trace, and its loss does not seem to
have been regretted.

Between the two extremes of militant zealotry and fawning ap-
peasement we must imagine a whole gamut of attitudes to Roman rule.
Probably the majority of Jews grumblingly accepted the status quo.
Belief in messianic redemption was not inherently incompatible with
acceptance of Roman rule and even appreciation of its benefits.
Among the various popular movements which emerged at this time there
are hints of an attempt to separate religion from politics:

> Jesus said to them, Give to Caesar what is Caesar's and to God
> what is God's.[9]
> Rabbi Nehunia ben Hakkanah said: Whoever accepts the yoke of
> Torah is relieved of the yoke of the empire, but whoever shrugs
> off the yoke of Torah is subjected to the yoke of the empire.[10]

This last statement is admittedly ambiguous. It might mean
that the Roman burden is the result of neglect of Torah. More probably it means that each Jew is faced with a choice: religion or
politics, but not both. This was an attitude which was to become
more prominent later.

V

In A.D. 66 the militant tendency prevailed, and the Jews rose in revolt. The motives of the revolutionaries were not uniform; it is
clear that many who had previously been moderate or even pro-Roman
joined the revolt once it had started. Nor was the revolt purely
and simply a war between Jews and Romans. Josephus' title 'Jewish
War' is misleading. The Romans never declared war on the Jewish
people, or the Jewish religion. The war was entirely a local affair,

involving the large and prosperous communities of the rest of the
empire not at all. And, very significantly, it began with outbreaks
of violence between Jews and 'Greeks' in the Hellenistic cities surrounding Judaea (Jos. *BJ* 2.266-70, 284-8, 457-98). Civil commotion
on this scale could not but involve the Romans, and it was at this
point that the fighting took on the appearance of a revolt against
Rome. For Josephus, it was the abolition of the sacrifice for the
emperor which marked the change;[11] this was an act of zealotry.[12]
From now on the Jews of Judaea were plunged, whether they liked it
or not, into a head-on clash with Rome, in which even those who had
opposed the zealots were caught up.

Josephus gives a graphic description of attitudes in the towns
of Galilee on the outbreak of hostilities (Jos. *Vita* 30ff.; cf.
345ff.). In Sepphoris the inhabitants supported the Romans; they
were afraid of reprisals. In Tiberias there were three factions.
The first, consisting of 'respectable men', was pro-Roman; a second,
'made up of the basest elements', was bent on war; a third faction,
led by Justus, feigned hesitation, but were really in favour of revolution, hoping for personal advancement.[13] In Gischala, John tried
to quell the mounting revolutionary feeling and failed. (He later
became a leader of the war party in Jerusalem.) Finally, Gamala remained loyal to Rome, thanks to the efforts of Philip, an officer of
Agrippa II.

If we accept Josephus' account - and there seems no reason to
doubt its broad outline - the division was largely a social one: the
wealthier, more hellenized, more powerful men and those close to
Agrippa were against the war. Agrippa himself, according to Josephus,
was strongly opposed to it. Josephus puts a speech into his mouth
in Jerusalem in 66 which, while it agrees closely with Josephus' own
speeches, may well represent Agrippa's view. The more honest and
sincere elements of the people, he says, are in favour of peace. The
war party are motivated by their youthfulness, by an unreasoned hope
of liberty, and by the prospect of rich rewards. Many other nations
- even the Britons - have submitted to Roman rule. Finally, he argues that God himself is on the side of the Romans - otherwise they
could never have built up such a powerful empire (*BJ* 2.345-404).

Josephus, in his own speeches, makes similar points: The Romans
respect their enemies' religious monuments; they are masters of the

whole world; and it is wrong to resist them. In any case, it is not
Jewish to fight; Jews should put their trust in God's justice. The
zealots do not represent what is best in Judaism; they are sinners
who have polluted Jerusalem. And finally, again, God is on the side
of the Romans in this war (*BJ* 5.363–419, 6.99–110).

The accusation that the zealots are bringing disaster on the
city and have polluted it by their outrages is one that Josephus
often repeats (*BJ* 4.377–88, 5.562–6, 7.259–74). He was clearly no
lover of the zealots. It might be thought that, with his peculiar
life-history and especially his need to conciliate the Romans, his
attitude is uncharacteristic. Yet it is hardly different from the
image of the zealots projected in the rabbinic literature.

> When Vespasian came to destroy Jerusalem he said to them [sc.
> the zealot leaders]:
> 'Fools, why are you trying to destroy this city and to burn
> the temple? All I ask of you is that you send me one bow or
> one arrow, and I shall leave you alone.'
> They replied:
> 'Just as we attacked and killed both your predecessors, so
> we shall attack and kill you.'
> When Rabban Yohanan ben Zakkai heard this he sent word to the
> men of Jerusalem:
> 'My sons, why are you trying to destroy this city and to
> burn the temple? After all, what is it he asks of you? All
> he is asking for is one bow or one arrow, and he will leave
> you alone.'
> They replied:
> 'Just as we attacked and killed both his predecessors, so we
> shall attack and kill him.'
> Vespasian had men stationed near the walls who wrote every-
> thing they heard on arrows and shot them over the wall. They
> informed him that Yohanan ben Zakkai was one of Caesar's sup-
> porters.[14]

Yohanan ben Zakkai was the most influential Pharisee leader,
and after the war he became, with Roman support, the undisputed
head of the Jewish community in Judaea. The passage just quoted

introduces the oldest account of his escape from the besieged city.[15]
According to another version,[16] Yohanan had a nephew who was a zealot
leader in Jerusalem. The rabbis tried to persuade the zealots to
make peace with the Romans, but they refused and deliberately burned
the stores of wheat and barley. It was this act which decided
Yohanan to leave the city.

However much or little historical fact there may be in these
anecdotes it is clear that the later tradition was hostile to the
zealots, and saw them as determined to fight to the death against
the advice of the rabbis. The tradition also represents Yohanan ben
Zakkai as the leading advocate of conciliation. Admittedly the tradition has the benefit of hindsight, and is also influenced by considerations similar to those which must have weighed on Josephus
after the war. But if the legend of Yohanan was elaborated in the
years after the war, it is not likely that it would have done crude
violence to the attitude held by Yohanan and others before and during the fighting.

VI

The war of 66-73 marked the high point of the popularity of the
zealot cause in Judaea. The zealots never enjoyed such widespread
support before or after as they did at the time of the revolt. The
Jewish leadership which prevailed after the war in the shadow of
Roman rule repudiated them, and blamed them rather than the Romans
for the destruction of the temple. The 'official view' which
emerged was similar to that found in the Psalms of Solomon: it was
because of the sins of the Jews that Jerusalem was destroyed.[17]

The non-rabbinic literature of the period following the war
echoes the same theme:

> The Lord our God is just, but we are shamefaced - men of Judaea
> and Jerusalem, our kings and rulers, our priests and prophets,
> and our forefathers: we have sinned against the Lord and dis-
> obeyed him.[18]

These sentiments can be matched by any number of passages in
the apocalyptic writings of this period, mingled with visions of
the messianic age to come at a time of God's choice. And then

Rome's destruction will come:

> You have wielded power over the whole world with great terror,
>   and over the inhabited earth with fierce oppression;
> you have dwelt so long in the civilised world with fraud,
>   you have judged the earth, but not with righteousness.
> You have oppressed the weak and afflicted the peaceful,
>   hated the upright and loved liars;
> you have destroyed the houses of the prosperous
>   and razed the walls of those who did you no harm;
> and so your insolence has risen to the Most High,
>   your arrogance to the Mighty One...
>
> Therefore you shall totally disappear, O Eagle,
>   with your horrible wings and your hideous pinions,
> your harmful heads and your terrible talons,
>   and all your worthless body. (4 Ezra 11.40-3, 45)

Yet side by side with such fiery invective we find evidence of a different attitude:

> Pray for Nebuchadnezzar king of Babylon, and for his son
> Belshazzar, that their life on earth may last as long as the
> heavens; so the Lord will give us strength, and light to walk
> by, and we shall live under the protection of Nebuchadnezzar
> king of Babylon and of Belshazzar his son; we shall give them
> long service and gain their favour.[19]

The tension between pro-Roman and anti-Roman sentiment comes to be characteristic of Jewish attitudes in the following years. Prayers for the welfare of the empire stand side by side with prayers for its overthrow and the establishment of the messianic empire. Jewish messianism could tolerate Roman rule, but it could also erupt in savage violence, as it did in the second Jewish revolt, at the end of the reign of Trajan. Like the first revolt, this began as a conflict between Jews and Greeks; unlike the first revolt, it hardly affected Judaea, if at all.[20] Its battlegrounds were Libya, Egypt, Cyprus, Mesopotamia. Being a revolt of the diaspora, it has left barely a trace in the Jewish tradition,[21] despite its vast scale, and we lack the means to judge clearly its motives and aims.[22] It could not avoid taking on the character of a revolt against Roman rule, and it appears to have had messianic overtones (we even hear of a Jewish 'king' in Cyrene).

With the revolt crushed and Trajan dead, a new era seemed to be dawning, perhaps the age of the messiah. So at least it appeared to an apocalyptic poet, chronicling the Roman emperors of this period:

> ...Then shall come a great destroyer of godly men, displaying the letter of seventy.
> His son, who has the initial of 300, will succeed him and take over his power.
> After him will come an emperor of the letter four, a ?cursed man. Next a venerable man of the number of fifty.
> After him, one whose initial signifies 300, a Celtic mountaineer. Hot-footed for eastern war, he will not escape an ignoble fate, but shall succumb. Foreign dust will cover his corpse, bearing the name of the Nemean flower.[23]
> After him another shall reign, a silver-helmed man, bearing the name of a sea, an excellent man who understands all things. And in your time, most excellent, most noble, dark-haired prince, and in the time of your successors, all these days shall come. (Orac.Sib. 5.36-50)

VII

Hadrian's reign did not bring redemption, it brought another bloody revolt in Judaea, the messianic character of which is evident from the title 'Son of the Star' given to its leader by his supporters, among whom was one of the leading rabbinic authorities of the time, Akiba.[24]

But Akiba's support for Bar Kosiba should not lead us to suppose that all the rabbis shared his enthusiasm. The tradition preserves two interesting discussions of the time which present both sides of the argument. Both bear the stamp of authenticity, and they involve prominent Jewish figures.

Rabbi Judah (bar Ilai), Rabbi Yose (ben Halafta) and Rabbi
Simeon (bar Yohai) were sitting talking...
Rabbi Judah began:
'How splendid are the works of this people! They have built
market-places, baths and bridges.'
Rabbi Yose said nothing.
Rabbi Simeon bar Yohai answered him:
'Everything they have made they have made only for them-
selves: market-places, for whores; baths, to wallow in; bridges,
to levy tolls.' (B Shabbath 33^b; cf. 'Abodah Zarah 2^b)

Simeon bar Yohai is known as an opponent of Roman rule. He is
quoted as saying, 'If you see a Persian horse tethered in Palestine,
look for the feet of the messiah' (Lamentations Rabba 1.13.41). According to tradition he was condemned to death by the Romans and went
underground - literally - during the persecution.

Judah bar Ilai expresses an enthusiasm for the benefits of the
empire which cannot have been entirely isolated.

Yose ben Halafta, whom we have already met as an historian, evidently took a middle position. To him are attributed the statements
that the Romans and the Jews are brothers (B Pesahim 118^b), and that
Rome only persecutes the Jews on God's instructions, to punish them
for neglecting their religion (Genesis Rabba 67.7).

The second discussion involves Yose ben Kisma, who had survived
the fall of Jerusalem in 70 as a young man, and died, honoured by
the Roman authorities in Caesarea Philippi, during the third war, and
Hananiah ben Teradion, who died as a martyr not long afterwards.

When Rabbi Yose ben Kisma lay dying, Rabbi Hananiah ben Teradion went to visit him.
'Brother Hananiah', he said to him, 'do you not realize that
it is Heaven who has ordained this nation to rule? For even
though they have laid waste his home, burnt down his temple,
slain his saints and persecuted his servants, still (the empire) is firmly established.' (B 'Abodah Zarah 18^a)

We have encountered this argument before, in Josephus, and no
doubt it grew stronger, not weaker, as time went on. Another speech

of the dying Rabbi Yose, however, shows that in the long term he
shared the view of Simeon bar Yohai, who looked to the east for redemption:

> His disciples asked him, 'When will the messiah come?'
> He said:
>   'When that gate (perhaps the gate of Caesarea Philippi)
> falls, is rebuilt, falls, is rebuilt, and then falls a third
> time - before it is rebuilt again the Son of David will have
> come'...
> When he lay dying he said to them:
>   'Bury my coffin deep, for there is not a palm tree in Babylon
> to which a Persian horse will not be tethered, nor a coffin in
> Palestine out of which a Median horse will not eat hay.'[25]

The reign of Hadrian marks a clear turning-point in Jewish attitudes to Rome. For the first time, Romans are seen as persecutors
of the Jewish religion. It was remembered as a time of Roman brutality, and of heroic Jewish martyrdom reminiscent of the days of the
Maccabees. Hadrian earned a reputation similar to that of Antiochus
Epiphanes, and from now on it is conventional to refer to Rome as
'the evil empire'.

VIII

The image of Rome in the subsequent rabbinic literature is predominantly a negative one. Roman rule is increasingly accepted as a
fact, but it is generally referred to in hostile terms, frequently
derived from the sacred scriptures. The belief that these were a
repository of all wisdom for all time led the rabbis to scan them
carefully for guidance in their present situation, and to reinter-
pret the old texts to fit the new state of affairs. The image of
Rome was now fixed with reference to certain biblical figures, the
most constantly recurrent of which is Esau or Edom, already established as the type of the gentile, in opposition to Jacob-Israel,
the archetypal Jew:

> A (Roman) prefect once asked a member of the family of Sallu:
>   'Who will enjoy sovereignty after us?'

He took pen and paper and wrote:

And after that his brother emerged, his hand clasping Esau's
heel; and his name was called Jacob.

Of this it was said:

'See how ancient words become new in the mouth of a Sage!'
(Genesis Rabba 63.9, quoting Genesis 25.26)

The whole story of Jacob and his relations with his brother
Esau is opened up in this way as a prophetic document of the relationship between Jews and Romans. The amount of preaching on
this theme is enormous, but the lessons drawn from the texts are
by no means uniform. They cover the whole range of attitudes,
from the bitterly antagonistic to the positively enthusiastic, and
we are often presented with two or more interpretations side by
side:

Two nations are in thy womb   (Genesis 25.23)
Two proud rulers of nations are in thy womb: Hadrian for the
Gentiles and Solomon for Israel.
Another interpretation:
Two hated nations are in thy womb: all peoples hate Esau, and
all peoples hate Israel. (Anon. Genesis Rabba 63.7 = Midrash
Psalms 9.7)

The voice is Jacob's voice, but the hands are the hands of
Esau (Genesis 27.22)
Jacob's voice: This refers to the emperor Hadrian [sc. Trajan?],
who killed in Alexandria-by-Egypt sixty myriads on sixty myriads
(of Jews) - twice as many as came out from Egypt (under Moses).
  Or it refers to the cry caused by the emperor Vespasian [sc.
Hadrian?], who killed in the city of Bethar 400,000 myriads, or
some say 4,000 myriads.
the hands of Esau: This refers to the Roman empire which has
destroyed our shrine and burnt our temple and driven us out of
our land.
Another interpretation:
Jacob's voice: No prayer is effective unless the seed of Jacob
has a part in it.

the hands of Esau: no war is successful unless the seed of Esau has a share in it. (Anon. B Gittin 57^b)

Thus, while all interpreters agree that Esau represents Rome and Jacob the Jews, they can disagree about the moral of the story. While most commentators stress the irreconcilable hostility of the two brothers, there are always those who emphasize that 'even though he is Esau, he is still his brother' (Anon. Genesis Rabba 75.4; cf. Leviticus Rabba 15.9), and suggest that they have complementary roles to fulfil in the world.

The identification of Rome with Esau is only one instance of the tendency to apply biblical texts to the Roman empire. Other biblical enemies of Israel are identified with the Romans (e.g., Amalek, Pesikta Rabbati 12.4), and various texts are reinterpreted by various exegetical techniques to apply to the 'evil empire'. The famous prophecy of Isaiah, for example, 'watchman, what of the night?' (Isaiah 21.11f.), is ascribed to Rome by textual emendation.[26]

A particularly widely accepted interpretation is the identification with Rome of the 'fourth beast' of Daniel 7, 'whose teeth are of iron and his nails of brass', and also the 'little horn' which subdues three kings.[27] Many of the rabbis accept without question the apocalyptic view of world history, according to which the successive empires of Babylon, Persia, Greece are supplanted by Rome, which will eventually be overthrown and replaced by the world-domination of Israel, under God's messiah. Any number of texts speak of the violent punishment of Rome[28] and the hegemony of Israel in messianic times.[29] We may quote a striking example, one of many attributed to the third-century rabbi Samuel bar Nahman. It is an elaboration on Jacob's dream (Genesis 28.12). The angels ascending and descending are the guardian angels of the four empires. Each of the angels in turn ascends a number of rungs corresponding to the years of his empire's hegemony, and then descends, but the angel of Rome seems to be climbing for ever. Jacob is afraid. Is it possible, he asks, that this one will never be brought down? God reassures him with the prophecy of Jeremiah 30.10f., a powerful salve for national self-confidence.[30]

IX

The belief in the divinely assured destiny of the Jewish people is
a striking feature of the Jewish thought of our period, and one
which made an important contribution to the separate survival of the
people and the religion. It is hard to imagine any other nation so
powerless as the Jews maintaining so confidently, and in such an extreme form, the belief that they were destined ultimately to rule
the world. We shall see presently, and indeed we have already observed signs, that some leaders of Jewish opinion tried to moderate
the vigour of this grandiose ambition. But we should never lose
sight of the fact that the Jewish world-picture was centred firmly
on Israel. The Jews were unwilling to credit any foreign power
with an independent existence and purpose. Events were judged
solely in terms of their bearing on God's plan for his own people.
We are seriously told, for instance, that the barbarian invasions
were intended to distract Rome's unwelcome attention from Israel
(Hama bar Haninah, Genesis Rabba 75.9). Given this ideological
background, we should be less surprised by the persistence of apocalyptic visions of the destruction of the 'fourth empire' than by
the repeated insistence that Esau and Israel are brothers, and that
each has his allotted role to fill. The wealth and might of Rome,
the security and permanence of the empire, evidently made a formidable impression even on minds committed to the belief that all
human power is vanity, and that no foreign nation can rule for long
over God's own people.

It was consistent with the Jewish belief in God's intervention
in history to accept that the success of Rome was a sign of divine
support, even if it entailed the continued subjection of Israel.
This idea can be traced back, as we have seen, to the time of Vespasian and even Pompey. In the rabbinic period the Roman myth of
the foundation of the city was translated into Jewish terms, and
invested with divine sanction.

The Jewish myth runs as follows: God is the 'helper of the
fatherless' (Psalm 10.14). When Romulus and Remus were left orphans, God brought a she-wolf to suckle the infants, and in due
course they grew up and became great kings, and laid the foundations for the future city of Rome.[31]

Just as the various defeats of Israel were ascribed to the

sins of the people, so the emergence of Rome was linked to the sins
of Jewish kings:

> The day that Solomon married the daughter of Pharaoh Nekho,
> Michael the Great Prince came down from heaven and planted a
> great pole in the sea. A sandbank grew up on this spot, and
> it became a bed of reeds. This was the future site of Rome.
> The day that Jeroboam made the two calves of gold, Romulus and
> Remus came to the reed-bed and built two quarters of Rome.
> The day that Elijah ascended, a king was proclaimed in Rome.[32]

The city exercised a certain fascination, and legend exaggerated its wealth:

> The great city of Rome has 365 streets, and in each street
> there are 365 palaces. Each palace has 365 stories, and each
> story contains enough food to feed the whole world. (Ishmael,
> B Pesahim 118[b])

> The great city of Rome covers an area 300 parasangs square.
> It has 365 markets, one for every day of the year. The small-
> est, that of the poulterers, is sixteen miles square. Every
> day the emperor dines in one of them.
> Everyone who resides in the city, even if he was not born
> there, receives a regular portion of food from the emperor's
> household.
> So does everyone who was born there, even if he does not re-
> side in the city.
> There are three thousand baths in the city, with five hundred
> ducts to carry the smoke outside the walls.
> One side is bounded by the sea, one side by hills and moun-
> tains, one side by an iron fortification, and one side by
> pebbly ground and swamps.[33]

Finally, on the subject of the city of Rome, it is worth recording the belief that, just as Moses was brought up in Pharaoh's
palace, so the king messiah is living in Rome.[34]

X

Interspersed with the rabbinic commentary on Roman rule couched in typically Jewish language, there are many remarks about the benefits and burdens of the empire, such as one might expect to hear from any provincial.[35] The general verdict is not favourable. The rabbis adopted a high moral tone in castigating the immorality which they saw as characteristic of the empire: idolatry,[36] blasphemy,[37] sodomy,[38] rape and murder.[39] One preacher applies the words 'darkness on the face of the deep' (Genesis 1.2) to the unfathomable wickedness of Rome.[40] Another derives the word 'senator' from three Hebrew roots meaning hatred, vengeance and violence (Eleazar ben Yose, Genesis Rabba 67.8).

A common accusation against the empire is its rapacity and eagerness for gold. 'The eyes of Edom are never satisfied.'[41] In this context, the great wealth of Rome counts against her,[42] particularly since it was felt that the plundered Jerusalem temple had made a disproportionate contribution to this wealth (Hama bar Haninah, Genesis Rabba 70.8).

Taxation is mentioned frequently as a cause of discontent, coupled with conscription. Taxation had always been an issue, but the sources paint a desperate picture:

> Just as a bramble snatches at a man's clothing, so that even
> if he detaches itself on one side it sticks to the other, so
> the empire of Esau annually appropriates Israel's crops and
> herds. Even before that, it pricks them with its poll-tax.
> And even as this is being exacted, Esau's men come to the
> people of Israel to levy conscripts. (Pesikta Rabbati 10.1;
> cf. Midrash Psalms 10.6)

> You go into the country and you meet a bailiff; you come back
> to town and bump into a tax-collector; you go home and find
> your sons and daughters starving. (Simeon ben Lakish, B Sanhedrin 98[b])

Another aspect of the rapacity of the empire was the milking of wealthy men by promoting them to public office (?Yohanan, Genesis Rabba 76.6), a practice which was no less objectionable for having

been supposedly recommended to the emperor by a Jewish ethnarch
(Genesis Rabba 67.6). It was perhaps the son of this ethnarch who
coined the maxim:

> Beware of the government. They never recruit a man except to
> serve their own needs. They feign love when it suits them,
> but they do not stand by a man when he is in difficulties.
> (Mishnah Aboth 2.3)

A peculiarly Jewish image to convey the duplicity and greed of
the empire is that of the swine. The pig is technically an unclean
animal because it does not chew the cud, even though it has cloven
hoofs.

> Just as a pig lies down and sticks out its hoofs as though to
> say 'I am clean', so the evil empire robs and oppresses, while
> pretending to execute justice.[43]

The much-vaunted Roman justice was clearly felt by the rabbis,
who were also lawyers, to be the strong point of the empire. A
preacher whose view of Rome is normally far from complimentary pro-
duces the startling statement that the words 'God saw everything
that he had made, and, behold, it was very good' (Genesis 1.13) referred to the empire, 'because it attempts to establish justice for
mankind' (Simeon ben Lakish, Genesis Rabba 9.13). 'When you desired
to bring justice into the world', another rabbi apostrophizes God,
'you entrusted it to two men, Romulus and Remus, so that each could
veto what the other proposed', and he has praise for the Roman system of appeals.[44]

But if the theory is laudable, the practice might not always
follow suit. In particular there were complaints that Roman judges
asked leading questions of the 'when did you stop beating your wife?'
variety. 'Why did you murder him? How did you kill him - with a
sword, a spear or a dagger?' (Deuteronomy Rabba 1.17). 'You didn't
do it? Who was your accomplice?'[45]

XI

Despite the long tradition of apocalyptic prophecy of the overthrow

of the 'evil empire', and despite the predominantly negative tone
of much of the material we have considered, there is abundant evidence in the third-century sources of an attempt at reconciliation
with Rome on the part of the rabbis, or at least of resignation to
continued Roman rule.[46] The new attitude takes various forms in
the literature. One preacher may dwell on the brotherhood of Jacob
and Esau, another on the evident success of Rome, proof of divine
support, yet another on the idea of peaceful co-existence, and the
need to avoid confrontation. 'If you are for peace', Jacob is
imagined as saying to Esau, 'I am with you; if you are for war, I
am ready for you' (Anon. Genesis Rabba 75.11). Esau is God's sword,
'for with him you chastise the world' (Anon. Genesis Rabba 75.1).
'What must Israel do? They must open their hands to the Romans and
appease them with money' (Midrash Psalms 68.15). 'Esau's warriors
have wrested sovereignty from your hand... You [sc. God] gave them
power in this world. Such men are destined for lives of serenity
and prosperity, of peace and wealth in this world' (Midrash Psalms
17.12). The messianic vision of Rome's overthrow is not lost, but
it is tempered by a plea for patience, and submission to God's will.
Religion, to use modern parlance, should take the place of politics.
The Jews should accept Roman sovereignty, and challenge it not by
any show of force but by redoubled dedication to a life of goodness
and study of Torah.

As we have seen, these ideas are not entirely new. Traces of
them have been seen before, for instance in the teachings ascribed
to Yose ben Halafta.[47] But in the course of the third century they
assume a definite predominance, especially in the circle of the
leading Palestinian rabbi, Yohanan bar Nappaha. Although it is
never easy or safe to attempt to isolate the thought of individual
teachers from the rabbinic literature, we shall try in what follows
to trace the main lines of this quietistic approach to Rome in
statements attributed to the third-century Palestinian *amoraim*,
taking them in rough chronological order.

The period of the *amoraim* begins with the pupils of the ethnarch Judah I, the supposed editor of the Mishnah. Foremost among
them was Hiyya, a Mesopotamian by birth, who firmly believed in
the Babylonian diaspora and wished to see it grow as a centre of
Judaism independent of Palestinian supervision. Hiyya was one of

a series of easterners who came to study in the schools of Palestine, but whose loyalty was to the land of their birth, and during
this period there is a constant tension between the Land of Israel
and the diaspora. The ethnarch, like other Palestinian rabbis,
resented and opposed the pressure for Babylonian autonomy. On the
political plane Hiyya's feelings show themselves in remarks contrasting Rome and Babylonia. 'God knew that Israel would be unable to endure the cruelty of Edom, and that is why he exiled them
to Babylon' (B Pesahim 87[b]). It is rash to put all your eggs in
one basket: better for Jacob to divide his camps (cf. Genesis 32.7);
if Esau attacks one the other will escape unscathed (Genesis Rabba
76.3). Resistance is useless: if Esau attacks, the best plan is to
hide from him until his power has passed away (Deuteronomy Rabba
1.19).

Another pupil of Judah I in Sepphoris was Haninah bar Hama,
who, like Hiyya, became an important and influential teacher. He
disagreed with Hiyya about the reason for the Babylonian exile (B
Pesahim 87[b]), and was not in favour of emigration from Palestine to
Babylonia (J Mo'ed Katan 81[c]). While not being notably pro-Roman
(e.g. Midrash Psalms 52.4), he is credited with the teaching that
military might and political power are not for Israel. Other empires may enjoy world-domination; Israel 'enters in peace and de-
parts in peace' (Song of Songs Rabba 7.1).

Yannai was a pupil of Judah I and of Hiyya who, like Haninah
bar Hama, enjoyed something of a reputation for wealth. Owning or-
chards himself, he was sympathetic to the plight of farmers in
times of economic difficulty, and is the author of a ruling permitting crops to be sown in the sabbatical year, on account of the
hardship caused by taxation (B Sanhedrin 26[a]). He has left few remarks which can be interpreted in a political sense, but we may
deduce something of his attitude from the injunction 'Always display reverence towards the emperor' (B Menahoth 98[a] = Zebahim 102[a]),
and from the statement that the law forbids a man to incur danger
in expectation of a miracle (B Shabbath 32[a]). This is perhaps a
warning to those who were prepared to run any risk to hasten the
coming of the messianic revolution.

Such a view is expressed with greater precision by a contemporary, Joshua ben Levi of Lydda. Preaching on a prophetic verse

which was no doubt much used by messianic activists, 'Say to them
that are of a fearful heart, Be strong, fear not: behold, your God
will come with vengeance' (Isaiah 35.4), Joshua turns the text
against them by reading not 'those that are of a fearful heart' but
'those in a hurry', who try to force the end to come too soon (Leviticus Rabba 19.5). Joshua preaches patience and peaceful submission. The world is not big enough to contain the two contending
powers of Israel and Rome; Israel has yielded the purple voluntarily
to his elder brother (Genesis Rabba 75.4). Joshua had apparently
been to Rome (Genesis Rabba 33.1); he returned with the cryptic
message, 'If anyone says to you, "Where is your God?", reply, "In
the great city of Rome"' (J Ta'anith 64[a]).

   Yet another contemporary of Yannai and Haninah, Jonathan, expresses himself on the subject of those who are preoccupied with
the coming of the messiah: 'Blasted be the bones of those who calculate the end. They say that, since the calculated time has arrived and yet he has not come, he will never come. But you should
wait patiently for him, as it is written, "Though he tarry, wait
for him; he will surely come"' (B Sanhedrin 97[b]).

   This statement is quoted by a pupil of Jonathan and of Joshua
ben Levi, Samuel bar Nahman, whose sermon on Jacob's dream has already been quoted.[48] Samuel agrees that the day will eventually
come of which it is written, 'There shall come a Star out of Jacob,
and a Sceptre shall rise out of Israel' (Numbers 24.17),[49] and he
also reaffirms the traditional view that the Jews will overthrow
the power of Rome (Genesis Rabba 73.7 = 75.5). But, like other
rabbis of his time, he is opposed to active messianism. It is God
alone who rules all things. The Bible speaks of 'the redeemed of
the Lord' (Psalm 107.2, Isaiah 35.10), not 'the redeemed of Elijah'
or 'the redeemed of the king messiah' (Midrash Psalms 107.1; cf.
36.6).

   The outstanding Palestinian rabbi of the second half of the
second century was Yohanan bar Nappaha. Yohanan had studied as a
very young man under Judah I, but his main teachers were Yannai
and Haninah bar Hama.[50] He had made a special study of the traditions concerning the Roman destruction of the temple, and he
came to the conclusion that the Jews had brought destruction on
their own heads, by initiating the war (B Pesahim 118[b]). Although

he shares the common hostile view of the empire,[51] he does not believe in violence as a solution. Jews and Gentiles are both God's
handiwork; he will not destroy one side for the sake of the other
(B Sanhedrin 98[b]; cf. Megillah 10[b]). Of the messiah he says, 'Let
him come, but let me not see him' (B Sanhedrin 98[b]). The Jews can
rely on their ancient covenant with God (Leviticus Rabba 6.5); only
a preoccupation with religion can save them, not political flag-
waving (Midrash Psalms 4.10; Genesis Rabba 44.24). The whole course
of Jewish history shows that rebellion leads nowhere; at best it
provides only temporary relief from oppression. The only sure hope
is God:

> A man once tried to light a lamp, but every time he lit it it
> went out.
> Finally he exclaimed, 'How long shall I waste my effort on
> this lamp? I shall wait for the sun to shine, and then I
> shall have light.'
> So it is with the Jews. When they were enslaved in Egypt,
> Moses emerged to redeem them, but they were enslaved again by
> the Babylonians.
> Daniel, Hananiah, Mishael and Azariah emerged to redeem them,
> but they were enslaved again by the Elamites, Medes and Per-
> sians.
> Mordecai and Esther emerged to redeem them, but they were en-
> slaved again by the Greeks.
> The Hasmonean and his sons emerged to redeem them, but they
> were enslaved again by the evil Edomites.
> Finally the Jews exclaimed: 'We are tired of being continually
> enslaved and redeemed, only to be enslaved again. Let us pray
> for redemption not through any human agency, but through our
> Redeemer, the Lord of Hosts, the Holy One of Israel. Let us
> pray for light not from man, but from God.' (Midrash Psalms
> 36.6)

The name of Yohanan is inseparable from that of his colleague
and brother-in-law Simeon ben Lakish, a pupil of Haninah bar Hama
and Jonathan. Several of his remarks have been quoted here already.
Simeon may have been a zealot in his youth,[52] and he was certainly

no lover of Rome. He often challenges Yohanan's moderate statements[53] and expresses a more extreme view. He resented the strength
of the Babylonian diaspora because it weakened the defences of
Judaea. 'If the Jews had returned *en masse* under Zerubbabel, the
temple would never have fallen.'[54] Yet even he was apparently
capable of endorsing Yohanan's view of Israel's non-political destiny: the Jews have no wish to share power with the nations of the
world; they are satisfied with the rule of God's law (Midrash
Psalms 36.6).

Yohanan's attitude is reflected in the sayings attributed to
his pupils. Yose bar Haninah, for example, attempts to allay im-
patience at Roman rule. The success and prosperity of the empire,
despite its well-known oppression and rapacity, should be seen as
an aspect of God's justice (Ecclesiastes Rabba 5.7.1). It is part
of God's plan, too, that Rome and Israel should respect each other.
Israel should not rebel against the empire, and the empire in its
turn should not impose too heavy a burden on Israel (Song of Songs
Rabba 2.7.1). According to another version of this saying (B Ketu-
both 111[a]), Yose added that the Jews should not try to return to
the Land of Israel *en masse*. This is clearly a challenge to the
view of Simeon ben Lakish and other zealots. In its more fully
developed form this programme is attributed to a pupil of Samuel
bar Nahman, Helbo:

> The Jews should not rebel against their rulers,
>
> they should not seek to hasten the coming of the end,
>
> they should not reveal their mysteries to other nations,
>
> and they should not attempt to return from the dispersion *en*
> *masse* (otherwise why should the king messiah come to gather
> in the exiles of Israel?).[55]

A similar teaching is ascribed to another pupil of Yohanan,
Levi.[56] Although he insists on the mutual antagonism of Rome and
Israel[57] and is confident of the final violent overthrow of Rome,[58]
Levi is among those who are opposed to the hastening of the end.
Despite his grandiose claims, Jacob lacks the power to win Esau
over (Genesis Rabba 78.7). The tyranny of Rome is part of the
scheme of divine justice and retribution (Song of Songs Rabba 2.7.1).

Levi couches his quietism in language borrowed from Haimon's advice
to Kreon (Soph. *Ant.* 712-14): 'He who stands up to a wave will be
swept away by it; he who offers no resistance will survive' (Genesis
Rabba 44.18).

Similar statements to these could be quoted from other Palestinian *amoraim* of the late third and early fourth centuries who
likewise oppose violent resistance to Roman rule. The last word in
opposition to messianism, however, belongs to Hillel, the brother
of the ethnarch Judah II: all the messianic prophecies are irrelevant, because the messiah is not going to come (B Sanhedrin 99[a]).

XII

If there is any conclusion to be drawn from this survey, it is perhaps the persistence of certain typical attitudes over a long and
varied period of time. These attitudes reflect in most respects a
state of mind which is probably unique to the Jews, although to a
certain extent they may have been shared by Christians in the empire.

From the early fourth century on, the condition of the Jews
gradually changed. With the political triumph of Christianity they
lost their privileged position. They came be be discriminated
against and even singled out for persecution. Apart from a brief
upsurge of national hope under Julian, the vision of this-worldly
redemption receded ever further from view,[59] and at the same time
the main centre of Jewish population and cultural activity moved
outside the bounds of the empire, from Palestine to Persia. The
rest of the picture lies outside our scope.

Chapter 1. *Introduction*

1 For a study of the historiography of Roman imperialism see Flach (1976), who discusses the 'terminological struggle' and the problem of ideal types. In writing this introduction we have been influenced by A.P.Thornton, *Doctrines of imperialism* (New York, 1965), esp. 1-35.

2 E.g. Polyb. 1.63.9: 'On the contrary, it was perfectly natural that by training themselves in such vast and formidable enterprises, the Romans should have acquired the courage to aim at world dominion and also fulfilled their aim.' See Walbank (1964).

3 Holleaux (1920), 334.

4 M.Cary, *A history of Rome down to the reign of Constantine* (London, 1935), 145; Badian (1964), 21; R.M.Errington, *The dawn of empire: Rome's rise to world power* (London, 1971), 3. We might compare Tenney Frank's judgement in *Roman imperialism* (New York, 1914), 358: 'the free Roman people stumbled on falteringly and unwittingly into ever-increasing dominion', which recalls J.R.Seeley's famous remark that the British apparently acquired their empire 'in a fit of absence of mind'.

5 In 1.63.9 (quoted n.2) Polybius is countering the argument of certain unnamed Greeks, that Rome's acquisition of empire was merely 'accidental' or 'fortuitous'. But the debate is really about whether the Romans deserved to win their empire. If their success was unexpected, or actually belied all rational explanation, then any virtues they happened to possess, such as wisdom, courage and discipline, lacked causal significance. Polybius' view is echoed by Cicero: *non fortuito populum Romanum sed consilio et disciplina confirmatum esse* (de rep. 2.30). The debate has a modern parallel. Was it through luck or merit that the mid-Victorians were able to build up an empire?

6 Veyne (1975); the quotation is on p.796.

7 A.Lyall, *The rise of the British dominion in India* (London, 1893), 1; M.Kingsley, *West African Studies* (London, 1899), 280; Th. von Bethmann-Hollweg, *Reflections on the world war* (London, 1920), 20. These examples derive from Thornton (n.1).

8 Harris (1971). A book by the same author entitled *War and imperialism in republican Rome, 327-70 B.C.* is promised in the near future.

Chapter 2. Imperialism and empire in New Kingdom Egypt

Abbreviations used in this chapter

AJSL   *American Journal of Semitic Languages*

ANET   J.B.Pritchard, ed., *Ancient Near Eastern texts relating to the Old Testament* (Princeton, 1950; 2nd ed. 1955)

ASAE   *Annales du Service des Antiquités de l'Egypte*

Atlas   W.Wreszinski, *Atlas zur Altägyptischen Kulturgeschichte* (Leipzig, 1923-40)

BAR   J.H.Breasted, *Ancient Records of Egypt* (Chicago, 1906-7)

BASOR   *Bulletin of the American Schools of Oriental Research*

BIFAO   *Bulletin de l'Institut Français d'Archéologie Orientale*

CdE   *Chronique d'Egypte*

HRR   W.F.Edgerton and J.Wilson, *Historical records of Ramses III* (Chicago, 1936)

IEJ   *Israel Exploration Journal*

JARCE   *Journal of the American Research Center in Egypt*

JEA   *Journal of Egyptian Archaeology*

JEOL   *Jaarbericht van het Vooraziatisch-Egyptisch Genootschap, 'Ex Oriente Lux'*

JESHO   *Journal of the Economic and Social History of the Orient*

JNES   *Journal of Near Eastern Studies*

KRI   K.A.Kitchen, *Ramesside inscriptions, historical and bio-graphical* (Oxford, 1968-)

LD   C.R.Lepsius, *Denkmaeler aus Aegypten und Aethiopien* (Berlin, 1849-58)

Lexikon   W.Helck and E.Otto, *Lexikon der Ägyptologie* (Wiesbaden, 1972-)

Mat   W.Helck, *Materialien zur Wirtschaftsgeschichte des Neuen Reiches* (Wiesbaden, 1961-9)

MDAIK   *Mitteilungen des Deutschen Archäologischen Instituts, Abteilung Kairo*

PEQ   *Palestine Exploration Quarterly*

PM   B.Porter and R.L.B.Moss, *Topographical bibliography of ancient Egyptian hieroglyphic texts, reliefs, and paintings* (Oxford, 1927-)

RdE   *Revue d'Egyptologie*

SAK   *Studien zur Altägyptischen Kultur*

Urk IV   K.Sethe and W.Helck, *Urkunden der 18. Dynastie* (Leipzig, 1906-9; Berlin, 1955-8). Partial translation of the earlier parts by K.Sethe (Leipzig, 1914), and of all the later parts by W.Helck (Berlin, 1961)

VT   *Vetus Testamentum*

Wb	A.Erman and H.Grapow, *Wörterbuch der ägyptischen Sprache* (Leipzig, 1926-31)
ZÄS	*Zeitschrift für Ägyptische Sprache*
ZDPV	*Zeitschrift des Deutschen Palästina-Vereins*

1 Frankfort (1948), 7-9; Hornung (1966), 1-29.

2 Fairman (1958), 89-92.

3 *Lexikon* I, 67-9: 'Ächtungstexte'; A.Vila, 'Un dépot de textes d'envoûtement au Moyen Empire', *Journal des Savants* (1963), 135-60; A.Vila, 'Un rituel d'envoûtement au Moyen Empire égyptien', in *L'homme, hier et aujourd'hui; recueil d'études en hommage à André Leroi-Gourhan* (Paris, 1973), 625-39; Fairman (1958), 90-1.

4 A.M.Blackman and H.W.Fairman, 'The consecration of an Egyptian temple according to the use of Edfu', *JEA* XXXII (1946), 75-91.

5 E.g. *ANET*, 365-9; A.H.Gardiner, 'Hymns to Amon from a Leiden papyrus', *ZÄS* XLII (1905), 12-42.

6 E.g. *ANET* 366, stanza vii, 371; J.Zandee, 'Prayers to the sun-god from Theban tombs', *JEOL* VI, no.16 (1959-62), 48-71, at p.61. The god Thoth was credited with creating or separating languages, see J.Černy, 'Thoth as creator of languages', *JEA* XXXIV (1948), 121-2; S.Sauneron, 'La différenciation des langages d'après la tradition égyptienne', *BIFAO* LX (1960), 31-41; *Urk* IV 2098.7. A useful note on the epithet 'of foreign/desert lands' as applied to Egyptian deities is D.B.Redford, 'The Hyksos invasion in history and tradition', *Orientalia* XXXIX (1970), 1-51, at p.12, n.5.

7 R.Herzog, *Punt* (Glückstadt, 1968); K.A.Kitchen, 'Punt and how to get there', *Orientalia* XL (1971), 184-208.

8 H.Brunner, *Die Geburt des Gottkönigs* (Wiesbaden, 1964). In at least three temples the creator-god Ptah takes the place of Amen-Ra in a brief version of this myth, *HRR* 119-21, *KRI* II 263.5-264.7.

9 E.g. *Urk* IV 82.13, 283.16, *KRI* V 22.4 = *HRR* 23. The inheritance myth: e.g. *Urk* IV 368.13-15, 1276.13-20, 2118.18-19, 2123.3-4.

10 *Urk* IV 1652.2-8. On the 'Nine Bows' see E.Uphill, 'The Nine Bows', *JEOL* VI n.19 (1965-6), 393-420.

11 E.g. the Prophecy of Neferty of the early Middle Kingdom, *ANET* 444-6; the Speos Artemidos inscription of Hatshepsut, *ANET* 231; the prologue to Papyrus Harris I for the reign of Rameses III, *ANET* 260. The theme is expressed in terms reminiscent of Neferty in the much later Potter's Oracle, see L.Koenen, 'The prophecies of a potter: a prophecy of world renewal becomes an apocalypse', *American Studies in Papyrology* VII (1970), 249-54.

12 Ra-Horus of the Horizon: Atlas II 184a; *KRI* IV 20; Ptah: W.M.F.
    Petrie, *The palace of Apries (Memphis II)* (London, 1909), pl.
    XXI; *KRI* IV 23; Atum: W.M.F.Petrie, *Hyksos and Israelite cities*
    (London, 1906), pls. XXIX, XXX; Seth: te Velde (1967), pl. XI;
    G.Loukianoff, 'Stèle du pharaon Séti Ier trouvée à Tell-Nebi-
    Mendou en Syrie', *Ancient Egypt* 1924, 101-8.

13 *Urk* IV 2085.9-12. W.Helck, '"Vater der Väter"', *Nachrichten
    der Akademie der Wissenschaften zu Göttingen*. I. Phil.-hist.
    Klasse, Jahrgang 1965, Nr. 9, 173-6 concludes that the phrase
    refers to the principal gods of foreign countries. However,
    the key text is the speech referred to here which is apparently
    addressed, not to foreign princes as Helck assumes, but to
    Egyptian officials. See further, A.H.Gardiner, 'The Memphite
    tomb of the General Haremḥab', *JEA* XXXIX (1953), 3-12; R.Hari,
    Horemheb et la reine Moutnedjemet (Geneva, 1964), 121; *ANET*
    251 erroneously translates as 'their fathers' fathers'.
    Helck's other references are ambiguous.

14 te Velde (1967), ch.5.

15 *ANET* 200-1, cf. te Velde (1967), 119. E.Edel, 'Zur Schwur-
    götterliste des Hethitervertrags', *ZÄS* XC (1963), 31-5 dis-
    cusses occurrences in this same text where the names of Hittite
    deities have been turned into place names, as 'the god of N'.

16 Simons (1937), 5-11; Yadin (1963), 192-241, 332-50; Pritchard
    (1954), 101-18; Giveon (1971); *Atlas* II, 184a, whilst 34-53
    provides a good series of the chariot motif. See also D.
    Wildung, 'Der König Ägyptens als Herr der Welt? Ein seltener
    ikonographischer Typus der Königsplastik des Neuen Reiches',
    Archiv für Orientforschung XXIV (1973), 108-16.

17 E.g. W.M.F.Petrie, *Tell el Amarna* (London, 1894), pl. II; U.
    Hölscher, *The mortuary temple of Ramses III*, part I (Chicago,
    1941), fig.25, pls. 6, 7, 33, 35; W.C.Hayes, *Glazed tiles from
    a palace of Ramesses II at Ḳantīr* (New York, 1937).

18 J.D.Cooney, *Amarna reliefs from Hermopolis in American Collec-
    tions* (Brooklyn, 1965), 80-5; S.Schott, 'Ein ungewöhnliches
    Symbol des Triumphes über Feinde Aegyptens',*JNES* XIV (1955),
    96-9.

19 W.M.F.Petrie, *Buttons and design scarabs* (London, 1925), pl. XV,
    992-6; W.C.Hayes, *The Scepter of Egypt* II (New York, 1959),
    422, fig.268; C.R.Williams, *Gold and silver jewelry and related
    objects* (New York, 1924), pl. VIII, 26a-c.

20 *Urk* IV 370.9-10. Lorton (1974), 121-4 takes the word as a tech-
    nical term 'not to have relations with'. That any of the words
    used in these texts has precise juridical meaning is open to
    serious doubt, particularly since there is no obvious distinc-
    tion between texts dealing with Nubia and western Asia. In this
    particular case some contexts seem definitely to demand a more
    figurative meaning. Thus the sentence quoted next in the text
    (*Urk* IV 1866.18) is paired with another referring to the

'hidden' (presumably 'unintelligible') character of their speech
(line 13). The Hatshepsut Punt texts likewise enlarge on the
'unknown' character of the land, but here it is the Egyptians
who have not previously 'known' it (*Urk* IV 324.9, 344.8).

21 *Urk* IV 324.6-14; similarly with Rameses IV's quarrying ex-
    pedition to the Wadi Hammamat, *KRI* VI 13.11.

22 Simons (1937); Jirku (1937).

23 Edel (1966); also K.A.Kitchen, 'Theban topographical lists, old
    and new', *Orientalia* XXXIV (1965), 1-9; K.A.Kitchen, 'Aegean
    place names in a list of Amenophis III', *BASOR* CLXXXI (1966),
    23-4.

24 Thus foreign princes or envoys bring 'tribute' 'on their backs'
    in attitudes of obeisance, e.g. *Urk* IV 341.13-342.5, 1094-1102,
    and in some cases in return for the 'breath of life' from the
    king, e.g. *Urk* IV 2006.15-20.

25 Grapow (1947); *ANET* 234-8; Spalinger (1974).

26 Gardiner (1960); Schulman (1962); A.F.Rainey, 'Reflections on
    the Battle of Qedesh', *Ugarit-Forschungen* V (1973), 280-2.

27 In a Twentieth-Dynasty letter concerned with the administration
    of the gold mines worked for the benefit of the temple of Amen
    at Thebes, what must have been a minor local bout of hostilities
    with desert nomads, to be dealt with by an armed escort, is
    described in terms of 'the mighty arm of Pharaoh' casting the
    nomads to the ground, a clear example of the use of this figu-
    rative phraseology in polite everyday language: see W.Helck,
    'Eine Briefsammlung aus der Verwaltung des Amuntempels', *JARCE*
    VI (1967), 135-51, letter C.

28 E.g. Munn-Rankin (1956).

29 Lorton (1974), 3-4 provides a useful bibliography. Also
    Kestemont (1974); G.Kestemont, 'Le traité entre Mursil II de
    Hatti et Niqmepa d'Ugarit', *Ugarit-Forschungen* VI (1974), 85-127.

30 *ANET* 199-201; Théodoridès (1975), 115-40.

31 Edel (1974), (1976).

32 Knudtzon (1915); *ANET* 483-90; Oppenheim (1967), 119-34. For
    discussion see Edwards, Gadd, Hammond, and Sollberger (1975),
    ch.XX; Edwards, Gadd, Hammond, and Sollberger (1973), 483-93;
    Helck (1971), 168-87.

33 On relations with Cyprus see Y.L.Holmes, 'Egypt and Cyprus:
    Late Bronze Age trade and diplomacy', *Alter Orient und Altes
    Testament* XXII (1973) (Cyrus Gordon Festschrift 'Orient and
    Occident'), 91-8.

34 Kitchen (1962), 14. W.F.Albright and W.L.Moran, 'Rib-Adda of

Byblos and the affairs of Ty:e (EA 89)', J. *Cuneiform Studies* IV (1950), 163-8 studies a good example of the involved politics of the area; cf. also Liverani (1971).

35   E.g. E.F.Wente, 'A letter of complaint to the vizier To', *JNES* XX (1961), 252-7.

36   T.E.Peet, *The great tomb-robberies of the Twentieth Egyptian Dynasty* (Oxford, 1930), 28-45.

37   J.Černy, in R.A.Parker, *A Saite oracle papyrus from Thebes in the Brooklyn Museum* (Providence, Rhode Island, 1962), 35-48.

38   Peet (1930), see n.36 above; J.Capart, A.H.Gardiner and B. van de Walle, 'New light on the Ramesside tomb-robberies', *JEA* XXII (1936), 169-93; *ANET* 214-16.

39   Säve-Söderbergh (1941); Vercoutter (1959).

40   D.K.Fieldhouse, *The colonial empires, a comparative survey from the eighteenth century* (London, 1966), 380-94: 'The myth of economic exploitation'.

41   W.Decker, *Die physische Leistung Pharaos: Untersuchungen zu Heldentum, Jagd und Leibesübungen der ägyptischen Könige* (Cologne, 1971); Edwards, Gadd, Hammond, and Sollberger (1973), 333-8.

42   Helck (1939); Schulman (1964a).

43   Sauneron (1968); R.A.Caminos, *Late-Egyptian miscellanies* (London, 1954), 91-9, 168-70, 188-98, 229-31, 400-10.

44   Caminos (1954, see n.43 above), 51.

45   In general see Säve-Söderbergh (1941); Arkell (1961); Emery (1965); Trigger (1965), (1976).

46   A useful introduction to the geography of Upper Nubia is contained in K.M.Barbour, *The republic of the Sudan* (London, 1961). Count A.E.W.Gleichen, *The Anglo-Egyptian Sudan*, 2 vols. (London, 1905) is rich in detailed topographic information; interesting comments on Upper Nubia at the turn of the century can also be found in J.H.Breasted, 'Second preliminary report of the Egyptian Expedition', *AJSL* XXV (1908-9), 1-110.

47   Trigger (1976), ch.6.

48   *ANET* 555; L.Habachi, *The second stela of Kamose, and his struggle against the Hyksos ruler and his capital* (Glückstadt, 1972); H.S. Smith and A.Smith, 'A reconsideration of the Kamose texts', *ZÄS* CIII (1976), 48-76.

49   J.Vercoutter, *Mirgissa* I (Paris, 1970), 184-5; Vandersleyen (1971), 53-6.

50 H.S.Smith (1976), 8-9, no.488.

51 A.J.Arkell, 'Varia Sudanica', *JEA* XXXVI (1950), 24-40, at pp. 36-9; J.Vercoutter, 'New Egyptian texts from the Sudan', *Kush* IV (1956), 66-82, at pp.67-70.

52 Gebel Sahaba: T.Säve-Söderbergh, 'Preliminary report of the Scandinavian Joint Expedition', *Kush* XV (1967-8), 211-50, at pp.235-6; Sesebi: H.W.Fairman, 'Preliminary report on the excavations at Sesebi (Sudla) and 'Amārah West, Anglo-Egyptian Sudan, 1937-8', *JEA* XXIV (1938), 151-6: the so-called 'Trench'; another possible example is Dorginarti near the end of the Second Cataract, see J.Knudstad, 'Serra East and Dorginarti', *Kush* XIV (1966), 165-86.

53 To the sources listed in the standard text books add J.Vercoutter, 'Une campagne militaire de Séti I en Haute Nubie. Stèle de Saï S.579', *RdE* XXIV (1972), 201-8; H.S.Smith (1976), 124-9, no.1595, the latter from the reign of Akhenaten.

54 Both references cited in the previous note, for example, clearly involved desert peoples.

55 *Atlas* II, 168a.

56 E.g. Speos Artemidos, Gebel Silsila, Bir Hammamat, Wadi Abbad, Serabit el-Khadim in Sinai, Timna, see *PM* IV 163-5; V 208-13; VII 321-5, 345-57; G.Goyon, 'Le papyrus de Turin dit "des mines d'or" et le Wadi Hammamat', *ASAE* XLIX (1949), 337-92; B.Rothenberg, *Timna. Valley of the biblical copper mines* (London, 1972), ch.5. Even these temples had been built for the benefit of mining or quarrying expeditions.

57 Soleb: *LD* III, Blatt 85a; Faras: *Urk* IV 2068.17-20; Sai: Vercoutter (1956, as cited in n.51 above), p.75 and n.51; Sedinga: Breasted (1908-9, see n.46 above), 98; Amara West: H.W.Fairman, 'Preliminary report on the excavations at Amarah West, Anglo-Egyptian Sudan', *JEA* XXXIV (1948), 3-11, at pp.9-10; Gebel Barkal: *Urk* IV 1228.12.

58 Kemp (1972); also *Wb* IV, 82.6,7.

59 A.J.Mills, 'The reconnaissance survey from Gemai to Dal: a preliminary report for 1963-64', *Kush* XIII (1965), 1-12; A.J.Mills, 'The archaeological survey from Gemai to Dal - report on the 1965-1966 season', *Kush* XV (1967-8), 200-10.

60 *PM* VII 193 cites a granite column fragment of Merenptah probably from Old Dongola. But the current Polish expedition there seems so far not to have located any further Pharaonic material. Until more is found the provenance of the fragment should be regarded with some suspicion.

61 Gleichen (1905, see n.46 above), 35.

62 O.G.S.Crawford, *The Fung Kingdom of Sennar* (Gloucester, 1951),

218, 267, 290, 296, 300, 306; P.L.Shinnie, 'A note on Ast-
Raset', *JEA* XLI (1955), 128-9.

63   See n.51.

64   J.L.Burckhardt, *Travels in Nubia* (London, 1819), 209-53.

65   A recent brief discussion of the extent of Kerma remains is
B.Gratien, 'Les nécropoles Kerma de l'île de Saï' III, *Etudes
sur l'Egypte et le Soudan anciens* (Cahier de Recherches de
l'Institut de Papyrologie et d'Egyptologie de Lille, 3, 1975),
43-66.

66   A.M.A.Hakem, 'The city of Meroe and the myth of Napata', *Ādāb*
(Khartoum) II/III (1975) 119-33 is a recent treatment of the
background.

67   Implied in the parallelism of *Urk* IV 2064.8 and 19; see also
K.Zibelius, *Afrikanische Orts- und Völkernamen in hiero-
glyphischen und hieratischen Texten* (Wiesbaden, 1972), 162-3.

68   Cf. Priese (1974). If the Kurgus (Hager Merwa) incription of
Tuthmosis III, see n.51, is the same as the boundary inscription referred to in *Urk* IV 1246.3-5 (the Armant stele) then
presumably the important kingdom of Miu should be located in
the Berber-Shendi area.

69   For the economic background to temples in Egypt see B.J.Kemp,
'Temple and town in ancient Egypt', in P.J.Ucko, R.Tringham,
and G.W.Dimbleby, ed., *Man, settlement and urbanism* (London,
1972), 657-80. On Nubian administration see especially Säve-
Söderbergh (1941), 175-86; Habachi (1957), (1969); H.S.Smith
(1976), 198-217.

70   H.S.Smith (1976), 192 (no.963).

71   Simpson (1963), 37. Miam is the ancient name for Aniba.

72   G.Steindorff, *Aniba* II (Glückstadt, 1937), 25, no.47.

73   Mayors are attested at: Buhen: H.S.Smith (1976), 202; Aniba:
Steindorff (1937), 254 IXb; Simpson (1963), 32; Faras: *Urk* IV
2068.18; Soleb: *Urk* IV 2068.12; M.Schiff Giorgini, *Soleb* II
(Florence, 1971), 249, fig.484; Sai: P.Pierret, *Recueil d'inscriptions inédites du Musée Egyptien du Louvre*, II (Paris,
1878), 41; possibly also A.Minault and F.Thill, 'Tombes du
Nouvel-Empire à Saï (SA.C.5)', *Etudes sur l'Egypte et le
Soudan anciens* (Cahier de Recherches de l'Institut de Papyrologie et d'Egyptologie de Lille, 2, 1974), 75-102, pl. Va.

74   N. de G.Davies, *The tomb of Rekh-mi-rē' at Thebes* (New York,
1943), 32-6, 103-6; W.Helck, *Zur Verwaltung des Mittleren
und Neuen Reichs* (Leiden-Cologne, 1958), 212-17.

75   *BAR* IV, sect.474-83; *Mat* (295)-(297).

76 Griffith (1927); Säve-Söderbergh (1941), 199-200. That the basic form of the decree was itself not exceptional is suggested by the Elephantine parallel cited by Griffiths, and by another fragmentary one from Armant: R.Mond and O.H.Myers, *Temples of Armant* I (London, 1940), 161.

77 *Urk* IV 194.15-196.9; *Mat* (361)-(362). That the phrase 'The Head of the South: Elephantine' refers essentially to Lower Nubia can be deduced also from its use in the accession decree of Tuthmosis I to the viceroy of Kush, copies of which have been found at Buhen and Kubban, *Urk* IV 80.15. Cf. also G.Godron, 'L'Eléphantine-du-Sud', *CdE* XLIX, no.98 (1974), 238-53.

78 On the high price of cattle in Egypt see J.J.Janssen, *Commodity prices from the Ramessid period* (Leiden, 1975), 525-7.

79 Davies (1943): see n.74.

80 *Mat* (478).

81 *Mat* (196)-(199); (224)-(233); D.Kessler, 'Eine Landschenkung Ramses' III. zugunsten eines "Grossen der *thrw*" aus *Mr.mš'.f*', *SAK* II (1975), 103-34.

82 A.H.Gardiner, *The Wilbour Papyrus* (Brooklyn and Oxford, 1948); K.Baer, 'The low price of land in ancient Egypt', *JARCE* I (1962), 25-45 has a useful explanatory discussion.

83 Aul. Gell. XVI 13.9; E.T.Salmon, *Roman colonization under the Republic* (London, 1969), 18.

84 M.I.Finley (1976), 178.

85 Edzard (1970, see no.115), letters KL69: 277,279. For criticisms in general, see Ward (1972), 41-5. For the '*prw*, see below, p.55.

86 Cf. Säve-Söderbergh (1967-8), (1969).

87 Säve-Söderbergh (1960), (1963); E.Edel, 'Zur Familie des *Sn-msjj* nach seinen Grabinschriften auf der Qubbet el Hawa bei Assuan', *ZÄS* XC (1963), 28-31. For a statue of a prince of Teh-khet of very fine Egyptian workmanship, see B.V.Bothmer, 'Private sculpture of Dynasty XVIII in Brooklyn', *The Brooklyn Museum Annual* VIII (1966-7), 55-89, at pp.67-9.

88 Steindorff (1937, see n.72), 27, no.58, 187-9 (S66); for Pahul see p.221 (SA17).

89 Simpson (1963).

90 Helck (1971), 350-2. For the title in question see E.Reiser, *Der königliche Harim im alten Ägypten und seine Verwaltung* (Vienna, 1972), 91-3.

91 H.Ricke, G.R.Hughes, and E.F.Wente, *The Beit el-Wali temple of*

Ramesses II (Chicago, 1967), 18, 21, 25, 29; Steindorff (1937, see n.72), 26, 27, 28; A.M.Blackman, 'Preliminary report on the excavations at Sesebi, Northern Province, Anglo-Egyptian Sudan, 1936-7', *JEA* XXIII (1937), 145-51, at p.149, n.1 (Maat-Ra); *BAR* IV, sect.479; Säve-Söderbergh (1941), 201, n.5. See also L.Habachi, 'Divinities adored in the area of Kalabsha, with a special reference to the goddess Miket', *MDAIK* XXIV (1969), 169-83.

92 Säve-Söderbergh (1941), 201, n.6, 11.

93 R.Engelbach, 'The quarries of the western Nubian desert: a preliminary report', *ASAE* XXXIII (1933), 65-74; nos.7, 11; Simpson (1963), 51.

94 Säve-Söderbergh (1941), 201-2; J.Vercoutter, 'La stèle de Mirgissa IM.209 et la localisation d'Iken (Kor ou Mirgissa?)', *RdE* XVI (1964), 179-91; M.Dewachter, 'Nubie - notes diverses, sect.1 à 5', *BIFAO* LXX (1971), 83-117, at pp.100-9.

95 Säve-Söderbergh (1960), 30, pl. XV.

96 The king is one of the triad group statue carved at the back of the temple, H. el-Achiery, M.Aly and M.Dewachter, *Le speos d'El-Lessiya* II (Cairo, 1968), pl. XXXIX(E9).

97 Soleb: M.Schiff Giorgini, *Soleb* I (Florence, 1965), 119, 128; *LD* III, 83a, 85a; Faras: F.Ll.Griffith, 'Oxford excavations in Nubia', *Annals of Archaeology and Anthropology* (Liverpool) VIII (1921), 93; Rameses II: L.Habachi, *Features of the deification of Ramesses II* (Glückstadt, 1969); Fairman (1948, see n.57), 9-10.

98 Säve-Söderbergh (1941), 146.

99 Simpson (1963), 36-41.

100 P.L.Shinnie, 'Preliminary report on the excavations at 'Amārah West, 1948-49 and 1949-50', *JEA* XXXVII (1951), 5-11. For Renenutet in Nubia, see Steindorff (1937, see n.72), 34; J. Vercoutter, 'Excavations at Sai 1955-7. A preliminary report', *Kush* VI (1958), 144-169, at p.164; A.Rosenvasser, 'Preliminary report on the excavations at Aksha by the Franco-Argentine Archaeological Expedition, 1962-3', *Kush* XII (1964), 96-101, at p.98.

101 Adams (1964), 108.

102 Scientific data on ancient Nile levels and climate in Nubia are hard to find, but note should be taken of the geological findings at Aksha that the high Nile level in the time of Rameses II was more or less the same as the recent one, J. de Heinzelin, 'Le sous-sol du temple d'Aksha', *Kush* XII (1964), 102-10.

103 G.Brunton, *Qau and Badari* III (London, 1930), 23, sect.49,

pls. XXII, XXIII, where among 130 graves given a positive clear
date by the excavators, 104 belong to the Eighteenth Dynasty
(53 of them to the early part), 25 to the Nineteenth, and 1 to
the Twentieth. At Mostagedda and Matmar, neighbouring areas,
the New Kingdom material as a whole is evidently unrepresent-
ative, but note the comment of G.Brunton, *Matmar* (London,
1948), 80, sect.145 about the progressive disappearance of
pottery in graves during the New Kingdom.

104 The evidence of scarabs and other small inscribed objects published in G.Brunton and R.Engelbach, *Gurob* (London, 1927), the
same sort of evidence used for the Nubian conclusions, yields
the figures: Eighteenth Dynasty to Tuthmosis III: 13; later
Eighteenth: 1; Nineteenth: 2; Twentieth: 0.

105 E.g. Steindorff (1937, see n.72); Schiff Giorgini (1971, see
n.73).

106 At Soleb, the remains of 733 bodies were obtained from 49
tombs, Schiff Giorgini (1971, see n.73), with 41 in the shaft
of one tomb alone, pp.89-90, 311-13. Two chambers of a New
Kingdom tomb at Shellal contained 135 bodies, G.A.Reisner, *The
Archaeological Survey of Nubia, Report for 1907-1908* (Cairo,
1910), 69.

107 Burckhardt (1819, see n.64), 17.

108 S.Sauneron, 'Un village nubien fortifié sur la rive orientale
de Ouadi es-Sébou', *BIFAO* LXIII (1965), 161-7; M.Bietak,
Studien zur Chronologie der nubischen C-Gruppe (Vienna, 1968),
91-2.

109 L.Habachi, 'Five stelae from the temple of Amenophis III at
Es-Sebua'now in the Aswan Museum', *Kush* VIII (1960), 45-52.

110 Y.Yoyotte, 'Un document relatif aux rapports de la Libye et de
la Nubie', *Bulletin de la Société Francaise d'Egyptologie* VI
(1951), 9-14.

111 A.E.P.Weigall, *A report on the antiquities of Lower Nubia*
(Oxford, 1907), 98; F.Daumas, 'Ce que l'on peut entrevoir de
l'histoire de Ouadi es Sebouâ en Nubie', in *Nubie par divers
archéologues et historiens = Cahiers d'Histoire Egyptienne* X
(Cairo, 1967), 23-49, at p.28.

112 In general see Helck (1971), and the relevant chapters in
Edwards, Gadd, Hammond, and Sollberger (1973); Edwards, Gadd,
Hammond, and Sollberger (1975). The initial conquests of the
New Kingdom are dealt with in Vandersleyen (1971).

113 H.Klengel, 'Die neuentdeckten Tontafelarchive vom Tell Mardikh',
Das Altertum XXII (1976), 112-13; G.Pettinato, 'The royal archives of Tell Mardikh-Ebla', *Biblical Archeologist* XXXIX
(1976), 44-52; P.Matthiae, 'Ebla in the late Early Syrian
period: the royal palace and the State archives', *Biblical
Archeologist* XXXIX (1976), 94-113.

114   M.Bietak, 'Die Hauptstadt der Hyksos und die Ramsesstadt',
      Antike Welt VI (1975), 28-43; M.Bietak, Tell el-Dab'a II
      (Vienna, 1975), 165, 167 Abb.35.

115   Ta'anach: W.F.Albright, 'A prince of Taanach in the fifteenth
      century B.C.', BASOR XCIV (Apr. 1944), 12-27; Gezer: W.F.
      Albright, 'A tablet of the Amarna age from Gezer', BASOR XCII
      (Dec. 1943), 28-30; Tell el-Hesi: W.F.Albright, 'A case of
      lèse-majesté in pre-Israelite Lachish, with some remarks on
      the Israelite conquest', BASOR LXXXVII (Oct. 1942), 32-8;
      Kamid el-Loz: D.O.Edzard, 'Die Tontafeln von Kāmid el-Lōz',
      in D.O.Edzard, et al., Kamid el-Lōz - Kumidi; Schriftdokumente
      aus Kamid el-Loz (Bonn, 1970), 55-62; G.Wilhelm, 'Ein Brief
      der Amarna-Zeit aus Kāmid el-Lōz (KL72:600)', Z Assyriologie
      LXIII (1973-4), 69-75; D.O.Edzard, 'Ein Brief an den "Grossen"
      von Kumidi aus Kāmid al-Lōz', Z Assyriologie LXVI (1976), 62-7.

116   Helck (1960); (1971), 246-255; Mohammad (1959); Edwards, Gadd,
      Hammond, and Sollberger (1973), 467-83; Edwards, Gadd, Hammond,
      and Sollberger (1975), 102-7.

117   A.Alt, 'Hettitische und ägyptische Herrschaftsordnung in unter-
      worfenen Gebieten', Forschungen und Fortschritte XXV (1945),
      249-51 = Kleine Schriften zur Geschichte des Volkes Israel III
      (Munich, 1959), 99-106.

118   O.Tufnell, Lachish IV (London, 1958), 133.

119   The information is available only in brief preliminary form:
      S.Groll, [A note on the hieratic texts from Tel Sera'],
      Qadmoniot VI, no.2 (22) (1973), 56-7, in Hebrew; brief notes
      on the excavations are in R Biblique LXXX (1973), 401-5; IEJ
      XXIII (1973), 251-4; XXIV (1974), 264-6.

120   G.R.H.Wright, 'Pre-Israelite temples in the land of Canaan',
      PEQ (1971), 17-32. For an Iron Age example from Tell Qasile
      of similar type see A.Mazar, 'Excavations at Tell Qasîle,
      1971-72. (Preliminary report)', IEJ XXIII (1973), 65-71.

121   In general see Edwards, Gadd, Hammond, and Sollberger (1973),
      ch.X; Mazar (1970), (1971); also H.Reviv, 'Some comments on
      the maryannu', IEJ XXII (1972), 218-28; M.Heltzer, 'On tithe
      paid in grain in Ugarit', IEJ XXV (1975), 124-8.

122   Helck (1971), 252-3. The exact significance of a domain being
      royal is nowhere made clear, but presumably it was mainly a
      matter of the king being provided with revenues which were at
      his personal disposal.

123   Rothenberg (1972, see n.56), ch.5.

124   Edel (1976).

125   G.Loud, The Megiddo ivories (Chicago, 1939). On this topic
      generally see Smith (1965).

126 I.J.Winter, 'Phoenician and North Syrian ivory carving in
     historical context: questions of style and distribution',
     Iraq XXXVIII (1976), 1-22.

127 O.Tufnell, *Lachish* II (London, 1940). According to prelimi-
     nary reports similar material from a temple has been found at
     Tell esh-Sharia, see the references cited in n.119; Amman pro-
     vides a further example, V.Hankey, 'A Late Bronze Age temple
     at Amman: II', *Levant* VI (1974), 160-78.

128 R.Amiran, *Ancient pottery of the Holy Land* (New Brunswick,
     1970), 172. For Mycenaean pottery in the Near East, see V.
     Hankey, 'Mycenaean trade with the south-eastern Mediterranean',
     Mélanges Université Saint-Joseph XLVI (1970-1), 11-30; for
     Cypriote pottery in Egypt, see Merrillees (1968).

129 See Caminos (1954), cited in n.43, p.138.

130 E.Oren, [An Egyptian fort on the military route to Canaan],
     Qadmoniot VI nos.3-4 (23-4) (1973), 101-3; reports in *IEJ* XXIII
     (1973), 112-3; *R Biblique* LXXXI (1974), 87-9. For the military
     road itself see Gardiner (1920). Note also the cemetery of
     Deir el-Balah, near Gaza, whose burials contain much that is
     Egyptian, perhaps because they belonged to officials connected
     with the Egyptian presence in this strategically important
     area, T.Dothan, 'Anthropoid clay coffins from a Late Bronze
     Age cemetery near Deir el-Balah', two preliminary reports, *IEJ*
     XXII (1972), 65-72; XXIII (1973), 129-46.

131 W.M.F.Petrie, *Hyksos and Israelite cities* (London, 1906).

132 M.Avi-Yonah, *Encyclopedia of archaeological excavations in the
     Holy Land* I (London, 1975), 52-61 supplies references and dis-
     cussion for this difficult site.

133 A.Kempinski, 'Tell el'Ajjûl - Beth-Aglayim or Sharuḥen?', *IEJ*
     XXIV (1974), 145-52.

134 Stadelmann (1967).

135 Rowe (1930), (1940); James (1966); H.O.Thompson, *Mekal, the god
     of Beth-Shan* (Leiden, 1970); an important revision of the chro-
     nology of the site is by W.F.Albright in *Annual of the American
     Schools of Oriental Research* XVII (1936-7), 76-7. A convenient
     summary and bibliography is also in Avi-Yonah (1975, see n.131),
     207-29, although in the discussion on chronology the comparison
     between the temple plan and the el-Amarna shrine from Egypt
     should not be taken too seriously, particularly since, at Deir
     el-Medineh, similar designs were common in the Ramesside period,
     and in any case the resemblance in plan is much closer to other
     Canaanite temples.

136 H.R.Hall, 'A Ramesside royal statue from Palestine', *JEA* XIV
     (1928), 280.

137 *KRI* II 174.13-14 = *Atlas* II, pl. 78. The straightforward

translation of the text which produced this information was
challenged by K.Sethe, 'Missverstandene Inschriften', *ZÄS* XLIV
(1907), 35-41, at pp.36-9, but this was before the discovery
at Beth-Shan. The literal interpretation implies, of course,
that Rameses II was able to recapture and hold Tunip for a
while, cf. Edwards, Gadd, Hammond, and Sollberger (1975), 228.
A bronze statue base of Rameses VI found at Megiddo, *PM* VII
381, is, because of its late Ramesside date, of imponderable
significance. One might also note E.Gaál, 'Osiris-Amenophis
III in Ugarit (Nmry.mlk.ʿlm)', *Studia Aegyptiaca* (Budapest) I
(1974), 97-9.

138 A.Alt, 'Ägyptische Tempel in Palästina und die Landnahme der
     Philister', *ZDPV* LXVII (1944), 1-20; Helck (1971), 444-5.
     Doubts must linger over whether the epithet 'great prince of
     Askalon' on the Megiddo ivory of the 'songstress of Ptah'
     really does refer to the god Ptah, and thus imply a cult of
     Ptah there. The lady's title may belong to a period of up-
     bringing or education at the Egyptian court.

139 J.Černy, *The inscriptions of Sinai* II (London, 1955), 188-9,
     no.276 publishes a stele of Rameses IV commemorating the
     building of a 'mansion of millions of years' at the Hathor
     shrine in Sinai. Whatever it was, its architecture must have
     been very slight to judge from the site itself.

140 *Urk* IV 1443.19. Helck (1971), 444 argues that the following
     damaged line must refer to an Amen temple further north still.

141 Strongly worded by W.F.Albright, *The archaeology of Palestine*,
     revised ed. (Harmondsworth, 1960), 100-1; also in Edwards,
     Gadd, Hammond, and Sollberger (1975), 104-7.

142 Cf. M.W.Several, 'Reconsidering the Egyptian Empire in Pales-
     tine during the Amarna period', *PEQ* (1972), 123-33.

143 Brief report in *IEJ* XXVI (1976) 51.

144 Avi-Yonah (1975, see n.131), 23-5.

145 A convenient summary is by M.Greenberg in Mazar (1970), 188-200;
     and by W.F.Albright in Edwards, Gadd, Hammond, and Sollberger
     (1975), 110-16. Also Greenberg (1955).

146 Helck (1968); Giveon (1971); Ward (1972); M.Weippert, 'Semitische
     Nomaden des zweiten Jahrtausends. Über die Šꜣśw der ägyptischen
     Quellen', *Biblica* LV (1974), 265-80, 427-33; A.F.Rainey, 'Topo-
     nymic problems', *Tel Aviv* II (1975), 13-16.

147 Helck (1968).

148 On the archaeological aspects of possible 'Sea People' settle-
     ment in Palestine, see J.B.Pritchard, 'New evidence on the role
     of the Sea Peoples in Canaan at the beginning of the Iron Age',
     in W.A.Ward, ed., *The role of the Phoenicians in the interaction
     of Mediterranean civilizations* (Beirut, 1968), 99-112.

149 For this approach see Grover Clark, *The balance sheets of im-
     perialism: facts and figures on colonies* (New York, 1936).

     Chapter 3. *Carthaginian Imperialism in the fifth and fourth
                 centuries B.C.*

1   It is convenient here to acknowledge the help I have received
     in this paper from Mr P.Lomas. Details of this introductory
     section have been discussed and documented in Whittaker (1974).

2   For modern acceptance of Carthaginian imperialism, see most
     recently Hoffmann (1972).

3   Discussed by Merante (1972/3), esp. 78-89.

4   Badian (1968), 8; Veyne (1976), 813.

5   G.Vallet, *Rhégion et Zancle* (Paris, 1968), 328, suggests
     Phalaris of Acragas was the catalyst; Merante (1970) discounts
     a direct connexion between Phalaris and Malchus, but believes
     the rise of Acragas did provoke Himera's call for Carthaginian
     help c. 550-540 B.C.

6   Diod. 5.9.2-3, 4.23.3, and Hdt. 7.158 speak of Carthaginians;
     but Paus. 10.11.3, Hdt. 5.4.6 say Phoenicians only. Commented
     on by Finley (1968), 37. Merante (1970), 101, speaks of the
     'relative independence' of Phoenician cities at this period.

7   For 'Carthaginian' losses, see G.Ch.-Picard, *Carthage* (trans.
     M. and L.Kochan, London, 1964), 81, upon which is built the
     theory of recession. The size of the booty is not in doubt,
     but for the silver of Rhegium and Selinus see Vallet (n.5),
     86-7, 328, Merante (1970), 105-6, 112. The central importance
     of Motya's link with Himera is stressed by E.Manni, 'Tra Mozia
     ed Imera', *Mélanges Piganiol* (1966), esp. 702-6.

8   Ch.-Picard (e.g. see n.7) is the staunchest advocate of the
     Himera-decline theory; contradicted by L.Maurin, 'Himilco le
     Magonid: crises et mutations en Carthage au début du IVe
     siècle', *Semitica* XII (1962), 5-43, and A.R.Hands, 'The con-
     solidation of Carthaginian power in the fifth century' in L.
     Thompson and J.Ferguson, eds., *Africa in classical antiquity*
     (Ibadan, 1969), esp. 93. The most telling economic challenge
     is summarized by J.P.Morel, *Kokalos* XIV/XV (1968/9), 327.

9   It is unfortunate that the crucial passage on inter-city re-
     lations in Diod. 15.16.1 is so ambiguous. After a defeat and
     demand for the evacuation of Sicily by Dionysius I in 383,
     Carthage asked for a truce on the grounds that 'they them-
     selves were not empowered to hand over the cities', and they
     asked for time to consult *tois archousi*. Were these magis-
     trates in Carthage (as the imperial school argues) or in the
     allied cities, as seems to be more consistent with the other
     evidence? In the event no one was consulted; but Carthaginian

commanders frequently did negotiate terms in the field before
and after this without reference to Carthage. Maurin (n.8)
argues from this dubious passage for the advent of a new regime
of oligarchic control over kings and generals abroad, which is
methodologically unsound and historically difficult to sub-
stantiate.

10   Merante (1970), quoting earlier discussions.

11   Barreca (1974), 45-51.

12   In the Monte Sirai reports Barreca puts the destruction of the
     earlier archaic buildings somewhere from the seventh to the
     sixth centuries (Barreca (1971), 123, summarizes) and the second,
     classical phase as late as the fourth century (e.g. *Monte Sirai*
     III = *Studi Semitici* XX (1966), 43, n.1).

13   Moscati (1966), 243; although M. concedes it may not be 'dominio
     continuativo' but 'un controllo per capisalsi'. Barreca (1968),
     76, while accepting a new phase of Carthaginian domination says
     we should *not* stress the cultural aspects.

14   Barreca (1971), 16, 23 and in *Monte Sirai* III (n.9), 59.

15   For refs. see Warmington (1964), 114; Barreca (1974), 52, con-
     nects this with the rebellion in Diod. 15.24.2, although Diod.
     himself links the trouble to Carthaginian events. It may be
     the aftermath of this rebellion which has produced the extra-
     ordinary story in Arist. *de mirac.ausc.* 838b, that Carthage
     'ruled' the island and cut down 'all the produce needed for
     food and prescribed death for any inhabitant who replanted any-
     thing'. Manifestly not a permanent arrangement.

16   Note the wise scepticism of Garbini (1966), 140.

17   Garbini (1966) and Whittaker (1974).

18   For a general discussion, see J.P.Morel, 'Les Phocéens en occi-
     dent', *PP* XXI (1966), 378-420, esp. p.396; detailed refs. are
     given by P.Bosch-Gímpera, *CQ* XXXVIII (1944), 53-9, F.Villard,
     La céramique grecque de Marseille (Paris, 1960), 85-90.

19   I do not include here the vague and undatable ref. to Cartha-
     ginian attacks on Gades, which contradicts the notion of al-
     liance but could be in the third century B.C.; ref. Gsell (1928),
     I 444.

20   Toscanos and Trayamar - summary by Niemeyer and Schubart (1971),
     166. Tangiers - M.Ponsich, *Recherches archéologiques à Tanger*
     (Paris, 1970), 163-5, 169. For the Mogador gap, A.Jodin,
     'L'archéologie phénicienne au Mogador', *Hesperis* VII (1966),
     9-16; with which compare 'Fouilles puniques et romaines à
     Lixus', *Hesperis* VII (1966), 17, 22, for the break between ar-
     chaic building in the seventh century and later fifth-fourth
     century 'Punic'-style buildings.

21 Ponsich (n.20), 181.

22 Gsell (1928), II 287-330; M.G.G.Amadasi, *Le inscrizioni fenicie e puniche delle colonie in occidente* (= *Studi Semitici* XXVIII (1967)), *Sard.* 12, gives other examples of *scribae* (e.g. *CIS* I 86 in Crete).

23 Warmington (1964), 85; Gsell (1928), II 310.

24 480 B.C. - Diod. 11.20.4; 396 B.C. - Diod. 14.77.6; 291 B.C. - Diod. 21.16.1; 241 B.C. - Polyb. 1.82.6-7.

25 Warmington (1964), 118, 184, 188; but Heraclea went over freely to Pyrrhus in 277, *ibid.* 176.

26 Gsell (1928), II 295, n.3, 311, n.1.

27 E.LoCascio, 'La leggenda s.y.s. delle monete siculo-puniche e il concetto politico dell' ἐπικρατεια', *PP* CLXI (1975), 153-61, makes the ingenious suggestion that the initials *s.y.s.* are a semitic transliteration of the word Sicelia-Sicily, implying a geographic and political union that goes a good deal further than the evidence. For a more sceptical view, see G.K.Jenkins, 'Coins of Punic Sicily I and II', *SNR* L (1971), 25-78 and LIII (1974), 23-46; Jenkins is now reasonably sure that the 'Carthage type' coins began c. 410 B.C. before the fall of Acragas and were first struck during preparations in Carthage.

28 On the date of Motya, see V.Tusa, *Mozia* VII = *Studi Semitici* XL (1971), 54; A.M.Bisi, 'L'irradiazione semitica in Sicilia', *Kokalos* XIII (1967), 57, speculates on a second colonization based on cultural parallels. In addition to Motya, the archae-ological evidence from other sites such as Selinus, Eryx, etc. suggests Carthaginian colonization; it will be collected and discussed in a forthcoming article by P.Lomas.

29 Refs. in Gsell (1928), I 410, 427-8, although none is very convincing.

30 See n.39.

31 Mommsen's position is discussed by Gsell (1928), I 477, II 289; the ancient refs. to Libyphoenicians are in Gsell (1928), I 440, 427-8, 441, II 112-15, 288-98.

32 M.Weber, *Wirtschaft und Gesellschaft* (Tübingen, 4th ed. 1956), II 524. As far as I can follow it, this also seems to be the view of S.Moscati, *Problematica della civiltà fenicia* (Rome, 1974), ch.vi, 'La funzione delle colonie'.

33 Gsell (1928), II 240 interpreted the phrase *epi tas poleis* as 'put in charge of the cities'; but this seems extremely un-likely in the context.

34 Merante (1970), 129-30.

35 M.I.Finley, *The world of Odysseus* (new ed. London, 1977), 98-102; P.Gauthier, *Symbola* (Nancy, 1972), 17-22.

36 *magon* here is usually thought to be 'ein Mager', Gosser, *RE* s.v. 'Heracleides', 482; but the ref. to Libya makes it more plausibly a corruption of the Phoenician name Mago.

37 This was the basis of Maurin's argument, op.cit. (n.8).

38 See n.17.

39 The ancient refs. are collected by Gsell (1928), I 440-8, in addition to Ps. Scylax, *GGM* I, p.16 (51), p.91 (111).

40 Discussions of Hanno's and Himilco's voyages are legion - most recently by R.Mauny and G.Ch.-Picard, *Archéologia* 37 (1970), 76-80 and 40 (1971), 54-9. The silent gold trade of Hdt. 4.196 is enough to show the fifth- and fourth-century activity of Carthage. For recent studies of Carthaginian influence see the works of Jodin and Ponsich quoted in n.20.

41 Gsell (1928), I 457-8, IV 118-19; cf. F.Walbank, *A commentary on Polybius* (Oxford, 1970), I 341-2; although Gsell apparently subscribes to the theory of a trade embargo in eastern Libya by the second treaty of 348.

42 Timosthenes, although constantly denigrated by Strabo, had better geographical knowledge than Strabo about the Metagonian coast of Africa and the harbours of the Spanish coast; e.g. Strabo 17.3.6. Cf. M.Rostovtzeff, *Social and economic history of the Hellenistic world* (Oxford, 1941), 395-6. G. and C. Ch.-Picard, *The life and death of Carthage* (translated D.Collon, London, 1968), 136, explain away Pytheas' voyage as a special concession to a new, hypothetical, friendly relationship with Massilia and the Phoceans. But then Carthage's relations with Rome in 348 were also friendly - so what was the point of the treaty? Garbini (1966), 140-1, gives some archaeological reasons for believing Gades and Utica had more than simply nominal independence.

43 Whittaker (1974), 77-8.

44 For further refs. to piracy and the protection against pirates, see Gsell (1928), IV 126.

45 Cf. C.Lévi-Strauss, *The elementary structures of kinship* (Paris, 1969), 67, 'Exchanges are peacefully resolved wars, and wars are the result of unsuccessful transactions.' For a general exposition, see M.Sahlins, *Stone age economics* (Chicago, 1974), 298-302.

46 Polanyi (1957), 265 and elsewhere; Lepore (1972/3), 132-4; Humphries (1969), esp. 191-5.

47 Arist. *Pol.* 1280a says of Carthaginian-Etruscan relations, 'They have covenants (*synthekai*) about imports and trade

agreements (*symbola*) not to act dishonestly and treaties
(*graphai*) of alliance.' Evidence of this close rapport collected by M.Pallotino, 'Les relations entre les Etrusques et
Carthage du VIIe au IIIe siècle av. J.C.', *CT* XI (1963), no.44,
23-9, to which add, J.Ferron, *Latomus* XXV (1966), 689-709 and
Pallotino, 'La Sicilia fra l'Africa e l'Etruria', *Kokalos*
XVIII/XIX (1972/3), 48-76.

48 Discussed by Lepore (1972/3), 412, with earlier views that
this passage refers to either Sicily, Africa or Spain - the
last two most unlikely. For the historicity of Gelo's speech,
see the problem of Phoenicians and Carthaginians in n.6.

49 The most recent evidence of this Assyrian trade is published
by K.R.Veenhoff, *Aspects of old Assyrian trade and its terminology* (Leiden, 1972) and by a number of authors who comment on
an article by R.McC.Adams, 'Anthropological reflections on
ancient trade', *Current Anthropology* XV (1974). In spite of
attempts by Veenhoff and Adams to cast doubt on Polanyi's
model of state administered trade, only two texts out of the
several thousand can be produced to suggest loss trading, and
even they are highly dubious in context; see esp. the comments
by G.A.Wright on Adams.

50 *Encyclop. Brit.* (XIth ed. Cambridge, 1910), V 283-4, s.v.
'Capitulations'; Finley (1976), 177.

51 Unreasonably rejected by Walbank (n.41), 345.

53 Cf. Polanyi (1957), 165 and the study by A.Leeds, 'The port of
trade in pre-European India as an ecological and evolutionary
type', *Proc. of 1961 spring meeting of Amer.Ethn.Soc.* 26-48.
Carthage herself smuggled Cyrenaican sylphium out from an unauthorized *emporium* (Strabo 17.3.20).

53 Greek refs. collected by H.Knorringa, *Emporos; data on trade
and traders in Greek literature from Homer to Aristotle*
(Amsterdam, 1926), 71. Cf. the example given by Polanyi (1957),
256, in the fourteenth century, when the Sultan of Fakhanar
forced ships off the Malabar coast into his port to trade at
fixed prices.

54 The quotation is from Polanyi (1957), 7; I am here indebted
especially to P.S.Cohen, 'Economic analysis and economic man'
in R.W.Firth, ed., *Themes in economic anthropology* (London,
1967), 91-118.

55 M.Godelier, *Rationality and irrationality in economics* (translated B.Pearce, London, 1972), esp. 304-8.

56 Polanyi (1957), 96, 160; Humphries (1969), 95.

57 The fullest discussion is still that of Gsell (1928), II esp.
193-243. The inner council or *consilium sanctius* (Livy 30.16.3)
was probably a controlling elite of the noble 'order' of grandees; cf. *IRT* 318 for the Punic word *addire* translated as *ordo*
in Latin.

58 Gauthier (n.35), 200, although G. wrongly asserts that the
    Rome treaties were only extensions of rights of *asylon*.

59 R.Laqueur, 'Σύμβολα περὶ τοῦ μὴ ἀδικεῖν', *Hermes* LXXI (1936),
    469-72, with comments by Gauthier (n.35), 102.

60 J.Heurgon, 'The inscriptions of Pyrgi', *JRS* LVI (1966), 1-15;
    full modern refs. are collected by Amadasi (n-22), 159-60.

61 Kahrstedt's solution was to suggest that Tyrians in the treaty
    really meant 'Tyrians of Carthage'; accepted by Walbank (n.41),
    346-7, although it is inconceivable why such an odd form
    should be used.

62 See P.Xella, 'Sull'introduzione del culto di Demetra e Kore a
    Cartagine', *SMSR* XL (1969), 215-28, esp. 227.

63 I see no evidence to support Veyne's argument either that
    Carthage posed a threat to southern Italy or that Sicily was
    the only approach route if she had wished to invade; Veyne
    (1976), 827-8; I come much closer to the view of Heuss (1949),
    that Sicily was a Roman adventure.

64 The Libyan inscription from the Djebel Massaoudje has trans-
    formed our understanding of this new provincial system; dis-
    cussed by G.Ch.-Picard, 'L'administration territoriale de
    Carthage', *Mélanges Piganiol* (1966), III 1257-66.

Chapter 4. Spartan imperialism?

1 For instance, considerable argument would be needed to support
   any particular interpretation of Kleomenes' action at Plataia
   (Hdt. 6.108.2-4); and Herodotus' account of his motive might
   well be thought to depend on hindsight.

2 On the birth-dates of Pausanias and others of his family, see
   M.E.White, *JHS* LXXXIV (1964), 149-52.

3 προϊσχόμενοι indicates that the 'excuse' was to some extent
   spurious, and obviates argument about the meanings of πρόφασις.

4 Herodotus wrote in the knowledge of Pausanias' downfall, and we
   can fairly assume that he was familiar with the version given
   by Thucydides. C.W.Fornara, *Herodotus* (1971), 62-6, makes an
   attractive case for thinking that Herodotus expected his readers
   to grasp in full the unstated contrast with Pausanias' disgrace;
   but he did not need to deny (63) Herodotus' doubts about the
   degree of Pausanias' guilt.

5 Recently, C.W.Fornara, *Historia* XV (1966), 257-71; M.L.Lang, *CJ*
   LXIII (1967), 79-85; P.J.Rhodes, *Historia* XIX (1970), 387-400;
   Meiggs (1972), 465-6. H.D.Westlake, accepting many of these
   criticisms, suggests a written source, Ionic in manner and probably in dialect (*CQ* XXVII (1977), 95ff. I am grateful to him for
   allowing me to see this in advance). Fornara's chronological

objection is telling, that there was not enough time during
Pausanias' first period in Byzantium for the correspondence
and Xerxes' other measures; fuss about the *skytale* (Thuc.
1.131.1) is less helpful.

6   Xenophon does not mention Pausanias, but says that Gongylos
    was rewarded as the only Eretrian exiled for Medism; but were
    there no refugees after 490 (cf. Hdt. 6.101.2)? The letter
    which Gongylos carried to Xerxes may be spurious, but it would
    be too sceptical to deny the connexion with Pausanias entirely.

7   Lotze (1970), 274 thought in terms of a concession to the
    king's pride in return for recognition of the leading position
    of Sparta and Pausanias; M.L.Lang, *CJ* LXIII (1967), 82-5, of
    Pausanias as the agent of the Spartan government, disowned and
    made a scapegoat when their peace plan failed. Most refrain
    from precise definition.

8   On Gomme's belief that Thuc. 1.131.1 implies 'no long stay'
    see M.E.White, *JHS* LXXXIV (1964), 144. Pausanias' absence
    from Sparta would be lengthened if we accepted, with Meiggs
    (1972) and others, a confused passage of Justin (9.1.3) as
    serious evidence that he spent seven years in Byzantium; but
    there is no certainty what Trogus wrote, and I should find it
    hard to believe that he was left in control of this key pos-
    ition for several years, even if there were no evidence tending
    the other way.

9   According to Thucydides (1.132.2), his 'private' inscription
    on the tripod set up by the Greeks, for which the one we know
    (Meiggs and Lewis 27) was then substituted. But Thucydides'
    couplet is for a personal dedication, such as Pausanias is
    likely to have made from his large share of the booty (Hdt.
    9.81.2): did Thucydides' source confuse two dedications?

10 See the list in de Ste Croix (1972), app.xxvi 351-2; but I can-
    not agree with him (132) that none of these was held in the
    assembly. The most spectacular case in our period is that of
    Leotychidas (Hdt. 6.85). At 5.63 Thucydides maintains consist-
    ency by claiming that the Spartans' rough treatment of Agis in
    418 was 'against their custom'.

11 This is the controversial phrase τῷ μὲν λόγῳ ἐπὶ τὸν Ἑλληνικὸν
    πόλεμον (1.128.3). Wars are commonly named after the opponent
    (so for a Peloponnesian the 'Attic War', Thuc. 5.28.2, 31.5),
    some from the theatre (Dekeleian, Corinthian), a few from a
    leading personality (Archidamian, Chremonidean). Pausanias
    would then have said (sc. to his Spartan supporters), to put
    it at a minimum, that he was going out to hold what could still
    be held against Athens, i.e. Byzantium. The alternative is to
    understand, abnormally, a 'war on behalf of the Greeks', but a
    'private' war (ἰδίᾳ ... ἄνευ Λακεδαιμονίων) of Pausanias against
    Persia is not much less odd than one against Athens. The ob-
    jection to the latter is the obscurity of the phrase in a con-
    text of the Persian War where Thucydides has said nothing about
    fighting Greeks, whereas at 1.112.2 the sense of 'Greek war' is

plain when Athens turns from the Peloponnese to Cyprus. Geb-
hardt's emendation Μηδικόν is possible: for the type of psychological error supposed cf. the generally accepted emendation of
Λακεδαιμονίων to 'Αθηναίων in Philochoros, *FGH* 328 F 148.
Steup
and Gomme note that the Lamian War is called 'Hellenic' in Plut.
Phoc. 23.1, *IG* II² 505.17, and also in *IG* II² 448.43-5 (not
cited by Gomme), where ὑ]πὲρ τῶν 'Ελλήνων strongly supports
this sense; otherwise one might take this name geographically,
the war in Greece as opposed to others currently waged elsewhere, and in any case this may not be a safe guide to Thucydides' usage. Westlake (n.5) conjectures that we have here an
abnormal usage taken over from Thucydides' source, and he notes
another abnormality in τῆς 'Ελληνικῆς ἀρχῆς below in the sense
'rule over Greeks'. A shade of doubt remains: and if Pausanias
claimed that he was safeguarding Byzantium from the Persians,
that meant in effect holding it against Athens, which is how
the Athenians saw it.

12 See n.8.

13 Meiggs (1972), 38-9, 56-8, 482 stresses the importance of this
often neglected problem. If the intention was to safeguard
the Aegean against a Persian naval offensive, this called for
effective maintenance of a Greek position in Cyprus, which
might seem to be foreshadowed by Thucydides' strong phrase
(1.94.2) αὐτῆς τὰ πολλὰ κατεστρέψαντο, a verb he uses elsewhere only for the subjection by Athens of rebellious allies
and others, or for comparably complete conquests. It is not
easy to conjecture what Pausanias may have had in mind. The
problem would be sharply reduced if we could suppose that the
version of Diod. 11.44.1-2 had any solid base. Here Pausanias'
mission is to liberate the cities still garrisoned by the barbarians, and he does this in Cyprus.
    Herodotus presents a comparable problem, relevant to
Sparta's post-war intentions, at 6.72.1, where he uses of Leo-
tychidas in Thessaly the phrase παρεὸν δέ οἱ πάντα ὑποχείρια
ποιήσασθαι. That too is normally used of outright conquest or
the like; but at 5.91.2 it is used of the relationship that
the Peisistratids might have created between Athens and Sparta,
and this must be something less than total subjection. Herodotus also uses the verb καταστρέφεσθαι of total conquest and
subjection; but when at 1.68.6 he says that the bulk of the
Peloponnese was κατεστραμμένη to the Spartans this must, ex-
ceptionally, mean something milder than e.g. Kroisos' rule in
Asia Minor (1.28). Cf. de Ste Croix (1972), 109.

14 Gomme's note on Thuc. 5.105.2 was printed as he left it, in
spite of some obscurity, which is due to his insistence, both
here and in the passages of vol.I to which he refers back, on
the degree of autonomy which Athens left to her subjects. One
misses reference to the way in which the Athenian assembly
legislated for the empire without consultation, a massive
difference between the two leagues. See also de Ste Croix
(1972), 96-101: his full-scale examination of the Peloponnesian League (101ff.) is a most valuable contribution.

15 Gomme was certainly right to take Thuc. 3.93.2 καὶ ὧν ἐπὶ τῇ γῇ ἐκτίζετο as a reference to hostility from others besides the Thessalians; it is less clear that he was right to exclude the Trachinians themselves. Steup, who did take the passage as referring only to the Thessalians, understood it to mean 'those whose land the foundation threatened', comparing the ἐπί of 92.4 (and cf. e.g. 5.33.1); but 'those on whose land it was founded' would be at least as natural. Someone's land was surely annexed for the colonists, and the Trachinians are the likely victims.

16 Diod. 14.38.4-5, to be corrected from 82.7 and Polyaen. 2.21; cf. Andrewes (1971), 222-3. The date should be either 399 or 400.

17 On the usage of this word see D.J.Blackman, in J.S.Morrison and R.T.Williams, *Greek oared ships 900-322 B.C.* (Cambridge, 1968), 181 n. At the least some ship-sheds must have been built.

18 On the anomaly that the pass of Thermopylai was blocked to the east of the city, whereas its likely enemies were to the north, see Gomme's note to Thuc. 3.92.6.

19 On all this Parke (1930) is still the best guide, though some modification is by now needed. G.Bockisch, *Klio* XLVI (1965), 129-239, castigates Sparta unsystematically and adds nothing very useful.

20 Evidently not available to Brasidas in 424, they make their first appearance in 421 (Thuc. 5.34.1: see my note ad loc.).

21 Parke (1930), 55-6, with an estimate of Sparta's costs at n.35, argues that this is not greatly disproportionate to her commitments.

22 R.E.Smith, *CP* XLIII (1948), 150-3, argued that the dekarchies survived until 397; on this see Andrewes (1971), 206-16. The cities, at least till 394, will have had to take care that their 'ancestral constitutions' were suitable: Thuc. 1.19 is still relevant.

23 Beloch (*Gr.Gesch.* 3[2].1.11, n.3) assumed that these were the ephors of 403/2, newly entered into office; but this makes for a very tight chronology in autumn 403, and a change of ephors is not needed for a change in policy. I would under-stand Xenophon literally, that Pausanias 'persuaded' one or more of the ephors of 404/3 to take up a new stance. Pau-sanias was on friendly terms with the democratic leaders of Mantineia (Xen. *Hell.* 5.2.3, 6), and his sons are occasion-ally credited with a liberal outlook (Diod. 15.19.4, Polyb. 9.23.7), but this is mainly in contrast with Agesilaos. I make no attempt here to interpret the closing lines of Ephoros, *FGH* 70 F 118, or Arist. *Pol.* 1301b20: there is much that we do not know about King Pausanias.

24 Gauthier (1973), 163-78 cites the striking remark attributed
    to Phrynichos at Thuc. 8.48.6, which is not in all respects
    clear but certainly charges the Athenian upper class with ag-
    gravated oppression of the allies. See also de Ste Croix,
    Historia III (1954), 37-8.

25 The bad evidence is Plut. *Per*. 11-12, to which too much def-
    erence has been paid. I have analysed this in detail in an
    article to appear in a forthcoming *JHS*: meanwhile see W.G.
    Forrest in *The ancient historian and his materials*, ed. B.M.
    Levick (Farnborough, 1975), esp. 22-4.

Chapter 5 The fifth-century Athenian empire: a balance sheet

1   The ancient authorities and modern bibliography will be found
    in Schuller (1974), Meiggs (1972). I have kept both to a
    minimum.

2   A.P.Thornton, *Doctrines of imperialism* (New York, 1965), 47.

3   E.g. H.B.Mattingly in *Historia* X (1961), 184, 187; Erxleben
    in *APF* XXI (1971), 161.

4   See R.Folz, *L'Idée d'empire en Occident du Ve au XIVe siècle*
    (Paris, 1953).

5   E.Will, *Le monde grecque et l'orient: le Ve siècle (510-403)*
    (Paris, 1972), 171-3; cf. V.Ehrenberg, *L'état grec*, translated
    C.Picavet-Roos (Paris, 1976), 187-97.

6   As an outstanding illustration, note how the 454 'turning-
    point' dominates the analysis of Nesselhauf (1933). For an
    incisive brief critique, see E.Will, *Le monde grecque et
    l'orient*, 175-6. It is anyway far from certain that the trans-
    fer of the treasury occurred as late as 454; see W.K.Pritchett,
    'The transfer of the Delian treasury', *Historia* XVIII (1969),
    17-21.

7   J.A.O.Larsen, 'The constitution and original purpose of the
    Delian league', *HSPh* LI (1940), 175-213, at p.191.

8   Schuller (1974), 3. His central thesis of 'two layers'
    (*Schichte*) in the structure of the later empire and his list-
    ing of continuities and discontinuities, follow from his in-
    itial confusion between the psychological notion of 'eine
    Interesse am Beherrschtwerden' and the realities of power.

9   Even if one thinks, as I do not, that at the end of his life
    the historian came to believe, retrospectively, that the
    Athenian empire had been a mistake, that would not affect my
    argument.

10 Perlman (1976), 5.

11 Martin Wight, *British colonial constitutions 1947* (Oxford, 1952), 5. The parallel with Roman 'allies' in the third and second centuries B.C. comes immediately to mind.

12 I need hardly say that I find it both irrelevant and anachronistic to play with the notions of *de iure* and *de facto* exercise of power, as does e.g. Schuller (1974), 143-8.

13 Meiggs (1972), 215.

14 The fullest accounts will be found in Meiggs (1972), ch. 11; Schuller (1974), 36-48, 156-63. Neither includes the *Hellespontophylakes*, discussed below, sect. IV.

15 See Blackman (1969), 179-83.

16 Meyer (1960) weakens an otherwise sharp-eyed analysis by his insistence that there were never more than half a dozen or so ship-contributing states, and by treating ship construction solely as a privilege granted deliberately by the Athenians.

17 Meyer (1960), 499.

18 The most convincing discussion of this text seems to me to be M.Chambers, 'Four Hundred Sixty Talents', *CPh* LIII (1958), 26-32.

19 Throughout I shall ignore the temporary wartime reassessment of the tribute in 425, certainly an important indication of the strength and character of Athenian power but too much of an anomaly to be included in the analysis I am trying to make.

20 It does not trouble me that Thucydides calls the 600 talents *phoros*. Xenophon surely had the same figure in mind when he gave the total Athenian public revenue at the time as 1,000 talents 'from both domestic and external sources' (*Anab.* 7.1.27).

21 For what follows, the fullest collection and analysis of the evidence will be found in Amit (1965).

22 See L.Casson, *Ships and seamanship in the ancient world* (Princeton, 1971), 278-80.

23 Blackman (1969), 195.

24 R.S.Stanier, 'The cost of the Parthenon', *JHS* LXXIII (1953), 68-76.

25 Blackman (1969), 186.

26 I see no need to spend time on R.Sealey's view that the 'League of Delos was founded because of a dispute about booty and its purpose was to get more booty': 'The origin of the Delian league', *Ancient society and institutions. Studies ... Victor*

Ehrenberg (Oxford, 1966), 253; see A.H.Jackson, 'The original purpose of the Delian league', *Historia* XVIII (1969), 12-16; Meiggs (1972), 462-4.

27 On the ancient evidence for what follows, see Gomme's commentary on Thuc. 1.116-17.

28 See de Ste Croix (1972), 394-6.

29 Thuc. 1.101.3; Plut. *Cimon* 14.2 (presumably based on Stesimbrotus of Thasos, 107 F 5).

30 The list is conveniently set out in Jones (1957), 169-73. One need not accept the demographic argument in which the data are embedded.

31 It is unnecessary for me to embark on the unresolved difficulties faced in trying to sort out colonies and cleruchies; all earlier discussions have been replaced by Gauthier (1966) and Erxleben (1975).

32 See Finley (1976).

33 Gauthier (1973), 163. This article is fundamental for what follows.

34 For the texts of this block of inscriptions, now conventionally known as 'the Attic stelai', see W.K.Pritchett in *Hesperia* XXII (1953), 225-311, with full analysis in XXV (1956), 178-328.

35 Col. II, lines 311-14; cf. II 177. The figure is so large as to create the suspicion that there may be an error in the text.

36 J.K.Davies, *Athenian propertied families 600-300 B.C.* (Oxford, 1971), 431-5, estimates Pasion's total wealth at about 60 talents.

37 I am not persuaded by the argument of Erxleben (1975), 84-91, that the Euboean holdings, including that of Oionias, were built up through purchase of Athenian cleruchic estates on the island; or by the unsupported suggestion of de Ste Croix (1972), 245: 'I would suppose that the Athenian State claimed the right to dispose of land confiscated from the allies ... also by making grants *viritim* to individual Athenians, who would presumably purchase at public auction.' Such suggestions were effectively undercut in advance, in a few lines, by Gauthier (1973), 169. Nor do I understand how Erxleben, like many others, can accept as fact the statement of Andocides (3.9) that after the peace of Nicias, Athens acquired possession of two thirds of Euboea. The whole passage is demonstrably 'one of the worst examples we have of oratorical inaccuracy and misrepresentation': de Ste Croix (1972), 245.

38 On the excess phraseology see M.I.Finley, *Studies in land and*

credit in ancient Athens (New Brunswick, 1952), 75-6.

39 Finley (1965); (1973a), ch. 6. On the fiction of 'commercial wars' see also de Ste Croix (1972), 214-20.

40 *IG* I^2 57.18-21, 34-41 (Methone); 58.10-19 (Aphytis).

41 G.B.Grundy, *Thucydides and the history of his age* (London, 1911), 77. We have no idea of the duties of the *Hellesponto-phylakes* apart from this reference. Xen. *Hell.* 1.1.22 and Polyb. 4.44.4 say that Alcibiades introduced the first toll collection in 410, at Chrysopolis in the territory of Cal-chedon across the straits from Byzantium.

42 Correctly Schuller (1974), 6-7.

43 The best statement of this proposition is by Nesselhauf (1933), 58-68, though I shall indicate disagreement on two points.

44 An interesting example of 'rewarding friends' has been seen in the 24 small cities, most of them in the Thracian and Hellespontine districts, who 'volunteered' tribute in the years from 435, by Nesselhauf (1933), 58-62, and more fully by F.A.Lepper, 'Some rubrics in the Athenian quota-lists', *JHS* LXXXII (1962), 25-55, who take these instances as proof of the doctrine that tribute payment was a necessary con-dition of sailing the sea. The explanation is admittedly speculative; nothing more may be involved than local ma-noeuvres in a period of unstable relations between Athens and Macedon; see Meiggs (1972), 249-52.

45 Nesselhauf (1933), 64.

46 De Ste Croix (1972), ch. 7; see the judicious critique by Schuller (1974), 77-9.

47 I shall not repeat my reasons for holding the currency decree to be a political act without any commercial or financial advantage to Athenians; see Finley (1965), 22-4; (1973a), 166-9.

48 First formulated in a lecture (Hasebroek 1926), the analysis was then extended in a book (Hasebroek 1928); see Finley (1965).

49 See most recently E.Erxleben, 'Die Rolle der Bevölkerungs-klassen im Aussenhandel Athens im 4. Jahrhundert v.u.Z.', in *Hellenische Poleis*, ed. E.C.Welskopf (Berlin, 1974), I 460-520; more generally, de Ste Croix (1972), 214-20.

50 Nesselhauf (1933), 65.

51 I do not understand how some historians can seriously doubt that this tax was to be collected in all harbours within the Athenian sphere. At the end of the century, the 2% harbour-

tax, in the Piraeus only, was farmed for 39 talents (Andoc. 1.133-4), and no arithmetic can raise that figure to a sum, in 413 B.C., that would warrant the measure, when, as there is reason to believe, the tribute in the period 418-414 amounted to about 900 talents a year. I should add that I am prepared to leave open the possibility of a widespread toll system in the empire even earlier, as argued by Romstedt (1914) from the still unexplained reference to a *dekate* (tithe) in the 'Callias decree', *IG* I² 91.7. Romstedt's analysis is not convincing, but the possibility seems to me to deserve better than the neglect in all recent works on the empire.

52 I shall not become involved in the discussion about the reliability of the statement by Plutarch (*Pericles* 11.4) that 60 triremes were kept at sea annually for eight months. Meiggs (1972), 427, concludes: 'However dubious the details in Plutarch, his source ... is not likely to have invented the basic fact that routine patrols annually cruised in the Aegean.' That is surely right, and it is enough for my argument.

53 G.E.M. de Ste Croix, 'Political pay outside Athens', *CQ* XXV (1975), 48-52, has contested my argument on this point (see next note), but his evidence, that Rhodes occasionally paid for some offices in the late fourth century and perhaps in the Hellenistic period, and Hellenistic Iasos, too, and that Aristotle made some general remarks on the subject of pay in the *Politics*, completely misses the force of my argument.

54 See Finley (1973a), 172-4; (1973b), 48-50. Jones (1957), 5-10, tried to falsify this proposition by pointing to the survival of pay for office after the loss of empire, and he has been gleefully quoted by scores of writers. However, it is easily demonstrated that institutions often survive long after the conditions necessary for their introduction disappeared. Trial by jury is a sufficient example.

55 For what follows, I am grateful to A.Andrewes for an advance copy of his forthcoming commentary on the passage. I am also happy to thank him for several discussions of the relevant problems and for reading the text of this essay.

56 8.27.5, 48.4, 64.2-5. That Thucydides did not specifically endorse this particular argument of Phrynichus does not seem to me very important.

57 I see no need to enter into the debate over the 'popularity of the Athenian empire' initiated by de Ste Croix in *Historia* III (1954/5), 1-41; for the bibliography and a statement of his own most recent views, see de Ste Croix (1972), 34-43.

Chapter 6 Athens in the fourth century

1 Especially, Accame (1941); Gschnitzer (1958), 98-112; Perlman (1968); Seager (1967); Sealey (1957); Woodhead (1957 and 1962).

2 Thuc. 1.98.4 (Naxos); 1.124.3, 2.63.2, 3.37.2, etc. (impropriety, or crime; 'tyranny'); 2.64.3 ('Pericles'); 5.69.1 ('the Mantineans'); Xen. *HG* 2.2.3 and 10 (atrocities).

3 Cawkwell (1956), 72ff.; Seager (1967), 100ff., 115.

4 For Isocrates in 355 and Demosthenes on 'liberals', see below, p.142 and n.47.

5 Andoc. 3.1ff., 7-9, 12-16, 29-31, 37-40. Lysias 2.48-70; and see Seager (1967), 105-13, for many refs. of the contemporaries to matters pertaining to policies of *arche* or imperialism.

6 Aristoph. *Eccles.* 197ff. (of 392 B.C. probably): 'We must launch a fleet. The poor man votes in favour, the wealthy and the farmers vote against it.' Cf. Mossé (1962), 404ff. for a discriminating discussion of the moral and material motives for imperialism; and ibid. 110ff. and 124ff. for a certain decline of Athenian commerce in the fourth century.

7 Xen. *HG* 5.1.31 (cf. Andoc. 3.12 and 14); see Graham (1964), 174, 188.

8 Defensive alliances between contracting parties of equal status, and each containing a variant of a particularly pious thought on the reaching of decisions by joint consultation (Tod 101.11ff., 'Boeotia' – ἐὰν δέ τι δοκῆι ἢ προσθεῖναι ἢ ἀφελεῖν 'Αθηναίοις καὶ Βοιωτοῖς κοινῆι βουλευομένοις... Tod 102.9ff., 'Locrians' ὅ τι δ'ἂν ἄλλο δοκῆι 'Αθηναίοις καὶ Λοκροῖς συμβουλευομένοις, τοῦτο κύριον εἶναι. Tod 103.8ff., 'Eretria' ὅ τι δ'ἂν δοκῆι ἄμεινον εἶναι ταῖν πολέοιν κοινῆι βουλευομέναιν, τοῦτο κύριον εἶναι.

9 Seager (1967), 104ff.

10 Tod 110.28ff.

11 *Hell. Oxy.* (Bartoletti) 6.3, 8.1f.; Xen. *HG* 2.2.9, 5.1.1ff., 5.1.19ff. and 29, 6.2.1.

12 Xen. *HG* 4.8.27 and 31; Tod 114.8.

13 Tod 110.18-20. Tod's dating of it to these years follows from the internal evidence of the inscription, at ll. 28-31. (*Contra* Seager (1967), 109, but wrongly in my opinion.)

14 Allowance made for the language of compliments, it is hard to see Androtion, Athenian archon at Arcesine in 357-356, as anything other than a benefactor (Tod 152).

15 So e.g. Seager (1967), 114 considers this much more scandalous than I do.

16 For the alliance with Chios (384) see Tod 118.

17 One need only think of the origins of the Peloponnesian League

and of the Delian Confederacy. Cf. for the one, de Ste Croix (1972), 107ff.; for the other, Arist. *Ath. Pol.* 23.5.

18 Tod 118.35f.

19 Tod 118.6ff.

20 See esp., Accame (1941), 122ff.; Tod 127.12ff., 21ff., 31ff.; 144.12ff.; 152.25; 156.10ff.

21 Tod 123.23; Theopomp. F 98 (*FGH* 115).

22 For details see Accame (1941), 134ff.

23 Cf. Dem. 23.209, contrasting the fifth-century affluence with the present.

24 So Sealey (1957), 108: I agree. Instances at Cephallenia in 372 (*epimeletai*, and garrisons), Xen. *HG* 6.2.38, 6.4.1; *IG* II^2 98, 18-23 (= Bengtson (1962), no.267), cf. Tod p.86; at Arcesine and Andros in 356 (Tod 152 and 156).

25 For Ceos, Tod 142.45ff., 73ff. and see too perhaps idem 162; for Naxos, *IG* II^2 179, 7-16.

26 Tod 142.17ff., 27ff., 57ff. (And cf. Tod 141, belonging probably to a moment when Ceos was *not* allied to Athens.)

27 Cf. Tod 151.18f. (alliance of Athens with Thracian kings, 357 B.C.): 'if any of the cities [= of the Chersonese] secedes from Athens', the kings are to give military help to Athens on demand.

28 Tod 131.35ff. The Athenian reply seems distinctly defensive in tone.

29 For the Athenian reaction to the news of Leuctra, Xen. *HG* 6.4.19f.

30 Alcetas and Neoptolemus, father-and-son rulers of the Molossians, are the only potentates who appear in the 'Aristoteles' list (Tod 123.109f.). No one has ever seen Dionysius I or Philip as a member of the Confederacy. But for Jason, below, n.34.

31 This seems to follow for certain from Aeschin. 3.94f. and 100f., where the orator alludes to the *suntaxis* of Oreus and Eretria, in a context which requires that the *suntaxis* was still paid till 348, when these cities seceded again.

32 Tod 144.12ff., 17ff.; 147.12ff.

33 For a discussion of the dates of the new entries, Sealey (1957), 105ff., with Woodhead (1962), 265f.

34 *IG* II^2 1609.88ff.; cf. especially Sealey (1957), 95-9; I accept Sealey's date 370-369 for the cleruchy of *IG* II^2 1609, and his inferences of a harder Athenian policy drawn from the fact that

no new names are added to the list of allies after (I think) 373. His theory is not seriously undermined by the collapse of one of its supports, a belief in Jason of Pherae as a member of the Confederacy from 375. Woodhead (1957), 367ff., shows conclusively that there is really no good reason for thinking that the restoration of Jason as the deleted name of Tod 123.111 can possibly be right. Jason was never a member, though he did become an ally of Athens briefly and without being a member by 363: [Dem.] 49.10; Nep. *Timoth*. 4.2f.; with Xen. *HG* 6.1.10.

35 Of the Chersonese cities only Elaeus appears on the decree of Aristoteles list (Tod 123.123). The Athenian treaty of 357 with the three Odrysian kings (Tod 151) is heavily restored in every place that is concerned with the Chersonese cities. If the restorations are accepted, their '*suntaxis*' and the possibility of their 'secession', to say nothing of their (unrestored) 'freedom and autonomy' seem to make Confederacy members of them. Yet their names are not added to the 'Aristoteles' list, where there is still room for them (below line 130). Probably they are not protected by the 'Aristoteles' oath.
     Moreover, in spite of the Athenian claim to the cities, recognized by the Thracian kings in this treaty, it is not clear to me that the cities themselves recognized it at this date. See on this Dem. 23.173, 178ff., with Schäfer (1887), I 444, and especially Isoc. 8.22, where κομιούμεθα requires that the cities were not in Athenian hands in 355.

36 Sealey (1957), 108-9 puts this motive clearly.

37 For the Euboean Confederacy, Aeschin. 3.94.

38 Meiggs and Lewis 94.

39 Tod 97.3ff., 11ff.

40 Craterus, *FGH* 342 F 21; *ap.* Zenobius, *Prov*. 2.28, Ἀττικὸς πάροικος: 'Krateros says it comes from the Athenian *epoikoi* who were sent to Samos. For the Athenians who reinforced those already there in Samos settled and pushed out the native Samians.'

41 D.S. 18.8.9. For discussion, E.Schweigert (1940), 194-8; R.Sealey (1957), 95ff.

42 Heraclides, *FHG* II, p.216 (= Arist. F 611.35 Rose); Str. 14.639.18; D.S. 18.8.9.

43 Tod 146.9ff., with 4f.; cf. Dem. 6.20; [Dem.] 7.10. The extraordinary 'those who have come on the mission from those from Potidaea' of the inscription, alludes presumably not to the Potidaeates but to a first batch of cleruchs.

44 Tod 156.10ff. (356 B.C.).

45 It is not clear to me what Demosthenes meant when he wrote, 'The Chians and the Byzantians and the Rhodians complained that we had designs on them, and for that reason they started this latest war against us' (Dem. 15.3). If it is a specific allusion and not a purely general one, Samos fits it better than anything else we know of.

46 For the contemporary views on Eubulus, Aeschin. 3.25f.; Theopomp. *FGH* 115 F 99-100; and see in general G.L.Cawkwell (1963), 47ff.

47 Dem. 15.25 (351 B.C.): 'There are some people, gentlemen, who are marvellously good at arguing the rights of our neighbours, as against you, and I'd like to give them just this piece of advice: let them give their minds to stating your rights against the neighbours, so that we can see them practising what they preach. It's a queer thing for a man to start instructing you about "rights" when he's behaving quite wrongly himself. There is nothing "right" in a citizen mugging up the arguments against you and not those in your favour.' Isoc. 8.16, 8.20ff., 8.32f., 8.64ff., 8.75ff.

48 Speusippus, *Ep. Socrat.* 30.4-6 (early 342 B.C.), in R.Hercher, *Epistologr. Graeci* (Amsterdam 1965), 630.

49 *IG* II^2 1611.1-9, 283 triremes in 357/6; ibid. 1613.302, 349 triremes in 353/2; cf. Dem. 14.13 and 9.40.

Chapter 7. The Antigonids and the Greek states, 276-196 B.C.

Introductory note
There is no continuous ancient narrative of Greek history between the battle of Ipsus and the accession of Antigonus Doson, and in many cases the basic facts are in dispute. Hence it often happens that instead of quoting ancient evidence to support statements made in the text one can refer only to modern reconstructions. This, of course, is a fragile basis on which to build historical interpretation, and it is necessary to emphasize the provisional and hypothetical character of such interpretation. The best modern narrative, with references to both ancient sources and modern literature, is that of Will (1966). For more detailed citation of ancient evidence it is sometimes necessary to have recourse to the otherwise out-of-date accounts of Niese, *Geschichte der griechischen und makedonischen Staaten seit der Schlacht bei Chaeronea* (Gotha, 1893-1903), and Beloch, *Griechische Geschichte* IV (Berlin-Leipzig, 1925-7).

1 See W.G.Forrest, 'The First Sacred War', *BCH* LXXX (1956), 33-52.

2 Badian (1966) demolished Tarn's view that the Greeks of Asia Minor were genuinely free under Alexander.

3 Diod. 18.55.2, though there is no mention of 'freedom' in the actual edict of Polyperchon quoted by Diod. 18.56. What Polyperchon was in fact doing was replacing the oligarchic regimes set up by Antipater with democracies.

4 Diod. 19.61.2. Antigonus did not say, and did not mean, that they were to be free from tribute. Cf. Simpson (1959), 403-4.

5 Welles (1934), no.13, lines 18ff.

6 Cf. Wehrli (1969), 62ff., 120.

7 Boeotia: Plut. *Demetrius* 39.4-5; on the Boeotian constitution at this time, cf. P.Roesch, *Thespies et la confédération béotienne* (Paris, 1965), 125-6. On Athens at this period, cf. G. de Sanctis, *RFIC* LXIV (1936), esp. 256ff.; E.Manni, *Demetrio Poliorcete* (Rome, 1951), 89ff.; Wehrli (1969), 186.

8 For garrisons imposed by Demetrius, see Plut. *Demetrius* 33.1, 34.5, 39.2; *Pyrrhus* 10.5. On Antigonus' policy in this respect cf. Simpson (1959), 403ff.

9 On these events see Will (1966), 82-93.

10 Polyb. 4.76.2. Θετταλοὶ γὰρ ἐδόκουν μὲν κατὰ νόμους πολιτεύειν καὶ πολὺ διαφέρειν Μακεδόνων, διέφερον δ' οὐδέν, ἀλλὰ πᾶν ὁμοίως ἔπασχον Μακεδόσι καὶ πᾶν ἐποίουν τὸ προστατόμενον τοῖς βασιλικοῖς. A.H.M. Jones 'Civitates liberae et immunes in the East', *Anatolian studies presented to W.H.Buckler* (1939), 105, is wrong to take this as an indication that Thessaly 'was technically free from Macedonian rule'.

11 For the history of Euboea in the Hellenistic period, cf. Geyer, *RE*, Supp. IV 442ff.

12 Gonatas' brother Craterus was in charge of Corinth before 277; cf. Bengtson (1944), 347. The date of the expulsion of the Macedonian garrison from the Piraeus is uncertain, and even the fact of the expulsion has been challenged: cf. Will (1966), 189, 196. Macedonian garrisons may also have remained in Achaean towns for a few years after 276. Cf. W.W.Tarn, *Antigonus Gonatas* (Oxford, 1913), 205; F.W.Walbank, *A historical commentary on Polybius* (1956-), I 231, 233.

13 The senate's decision: Livy 34.43.8; cf. Briscoe (1972), 47. Aetolian disaffection: Polyb. 18.34, 18.45.1; Livy 33.11, 33.31.1, 34.23.5ff., 35.12. Withdrawal of Roman troops: Livy 34.48.2-51.6.

14 Sources in Will (1966), 190, 192.

15 Plut. *Pyrrhus* 26.8-29; Paus. 1.13.6-8; Justin 25.4.6-10.

16 Plut. *Pyrrhus* 30.1; for Argive help to Sparta, Paus. 1.13.6.

17 For Gonatas' policy of supporting tyrants in Greek states, see

Polyb. 2.41.10, 9.26.6; Trogus, prol. 26. For literature, see
Heinen (1973), 120, n.111. For Aristotimus of Elis and Aris-
todemus of Megalopolis, see H.Berve, *Die Tyrannis bei der
Griechen* (Munich, 1967), II 713.

18 For full discussion on all issues concerned with the Chre-
    monidean War, see Heinen (1973), 95ff. The only evidence for
    the outbreak of the war is the famous 'Decree of Chremonides'
    (*Syll.*³ 434-5).

19 See the literature quoted by Heinen (1973), 180, n.348.

20 Eusebius, *Chron.* (ed. Schöne), II p.237; cf. Paus. 3.6.6. See
    Bengtson (1944), 375-6.

21 Bengtson (1944), 376ff.; cf. J.Pouilloux, 'Antigone Gonatas
    et Athènes après la guerre de Chremonidès', *BCH* LXX (1946),
    488-96.

22 Samos and Caunus could both be described as free states in the
    alliance of Ptolemy (Livy 33.18.11-12, surely following Poly-
    bius here), yet they are known to have had garrisons (Samos:
    Polyb. 5.35.11, 16.2.9; Caunus: Polyb. 30.31.6).

23 On Gonatas' intellectual interests, see Tarn (op.cit. n.12),
    chs. 1 and 8, though Tarn exaggerates in saying that Gonatas
    'looked on Athens as his intellectual capital' (p.205).

24 On the rise of the Aetolian League, cf. Flacelière (1937),
    passim.

25 Polyb. 2.43.3; Plut. *Aratus* 5.9; Walbank (1933), 31-4; *Hist.
    Comm.* I 235-6.

26 Plut. *Aratus* 4.3; Walbank (1933), 32.

27 I follow, without any great degree of confidence, the chron-
    ology of Walbank (1933), 34ff.; Will (1966), 286ff. In *JHS*
    LVI (1936), 67, n.19 Walbank reverted to the view that the
    basileus of Plut. *Aratus* 11.2 is Ptolemy, not Antigonus, and
    that the revolt of Alexander followed, rather than preceded,
    Aratus' seizure of power at Sicyon. Aratus' attack on
    Corinth (Plut. *Aratus* 18.4) is seen by Walbank as an attack
    on Alexander as the representative of Gonatas, inspired by
    Ptolemy. For the alliance with Alexander, see Plut. *Aratus*
    18.1; for the support from Ptolemy, Plut. *Aratus* 12ff.

28 The only direct evidence for Aetolian action against Alex-
    ander is the attack on Nicocles (Plut. *Aratus* 4.1), and
    that is evidence only if one both accepts my chronology (cf.
    n.27) and assumes that Nicocles was a creature of Alexander
    (cf. Will (1966), 290). But there is no trace of any quar-
    rel between the Aetolians and Gonatas, and they fought
    against the Boeotians, who had allied themselves with the
    Achaeans (Plut. *Aratus* 16.1).

29 See Will (1966), 292-3.

30 Plut. *Aratus* 18-24; Walbank (1933), 45-7, *Hist.Comm.* I 236;
    Ptolemy only became an official ally of the Achaean League
    after the liberation of Corinth (Plut. *Aratus* 24.4).

31 Walbank (1933), 43-5; sources in Will (1966), 300.

32 Polyb. 2.44.1; Plut. *Aratus* 33.1; Justin 28.1.1-4; Walbank,
    Hist.Comm. I 237-8.

33 Polyb. 20.5.3; Feyel (1942), 83ff.; Will (1966), 316.

34 See particularly Polyb. 20.5ff. on the political situation
    in Boeotia; on its consequences in the Second Macedonian War
    see Livy 33.1-2, 27.5-29; Polyb. 18.40.1-4, 43.

35 On the reforms of Cleomenes, see B.Shimron, *CQ* n.s. XIV
    (1964), 232-9; *Historia* XIII (1964), 147-55; *Late Sparta* (New
    York, 1972), 39ff.; P.Oliva, *Sparta and her social problems*
    (Amsterdam-Prague, 1971), 230ff.

36 Polyb. 2.52.4. Aratus defended his action by claiming that
    a few years earlier Doson, the Aetolians and Cleomenes had
    formed an alliance against the Achaeans. This alleged al-
    liance is not to be accepted: cf. Walbank, *Hist.Comm.* I 239.
    The attempt by De Laix (*CSCA* II (1969), 65-83) to defend it
    is unconvincing.

37 Will (1966), 328ff.

38 On the formation of the symmachy, see Polyb. 2.54.4, 4.9.4;
    Walbank, *Hist.Comm.* I 256.

39 On the Sellasia campaign, see Polyb. 2.65.9; Plut. *Cleomenes*
    28; *Philopoemen* 6; Walbank, *Hist.Comm.* I 272ff.

40 For the Social War, see Walbank (1940), ch.2.

41 For Philip's initial good reputation, see Polyb. 4.27.10,
    7.11.8.

42 I make these statements about the Illyrian Wars dogmatically.
    For the First War, see Polyb. 2.11-12, to be preferred to
    App. *Illyrica* 7-8 and Dio, fr.49. For other views, see
    Holleaux (1920), 102, n.3, 109-12; Walser (1954); Badian
    (1964); Derow (1973); Levi (1973).

43 On the Second War, see Polyb. 3.16-19, 4.16.6-19.7; Livy,
    per. 20; App. *Illyrica* 8; Dio, fr.53.

44 The statement in the treaty between Philip and Hannibal that
    the Romans were *kurioi* of the protectorate (Polyb. 7.9.13)
    is simply propaganda. Whether we regard the protectorate as
    an area bounded by a line, or, as Badian (1964), 6ff. prefers,
    as only a collection of separate cities and peoples, makes

no difference to the argument.

45 Polyb. 3.19.8, 5.101.7ff., 105.1; cf. Walbank (1940), 64-5.

46 Polyb. 7.9; Livy 23.33.1-34.9, 38.1-39.4, 48.3; App. *Macedonica* 1.

47 Aetolia: H.H.Schmitt, *Die Staatsverträge des Altertums* (Munich, 1969), III, no.536. Sparta, Elis, Messene: Polyb. 9.28.39; Livy 26.24.9. Attalus of Pergamum also supported Rome, though without a formal treaty: cf. J.Briscoe, *A Commentary on Livy books xxxi-xxxiii* (Oxford, 1973), 56. Philip's attacks on Messene: Polyb. 3.19.11, 7.11.10, 7.12.9, 7.13.6-7, 7.14.2-5, 8.8a; Livy 32.21.23; Plut. *Aratus* 49, 51.

48 For the military events of the war from 210 to 208, see Polyb. 9.41-2, 10.26, 11.5.8, 22.11.9; Livy 27.29.9-32.5, 28.5-8; Strabo 9, p.435C.

49 Livy 32.21.16, 28; the speech has clearly been worked up by Livy, but there is no reason to doubt that Polybius had a speech at this point and that the basic material is Polybian: cf. Briscoe, *Comm.* 18-19.

50 Briscoe, *Comm.* 74.

51 On Boeotia in the First Macedonian War see Feyel (1942), 170ff.

52 Polyb. 9.37.6, and further references in Briscoe, *Comm.* 133. The Greek-barbarian dichotomy could still be used as a slogan for political purposes, but intelligent Greeks had come to realize that barbarism was a matter of culture, not of language, and accepted the Romans as *sui generis*. For Eratosthenes' criticism of the distinction, see Strabo 1, p.66C; H.C.Baldry, *Entretiens Fondation Hardt* VIII (1961), 191ff.; P.M.Fraser, *Ptolemaic Alexandria* (Oxford, 1972) I 530-1, and, for earlier expressions of the same view, II 761, n.87.

53 Polyb. 5.8-12; Walbank (1940), 54-5.

54 Cf. n.47.

55 Phocis: Walbank, *Hist.Comm.* I 558-9. Locris: Briscoe, *Comm.* 311.

56 Memories of Sulpicius: App. *Macedonica* 7. Plundering: Polyb. 11.5.6-8; Livy 27.31.1, 28.6.4, 28.7.4, 32.22.10; Paus. 7.17.5. Aegina: Polyb. 9.42.5-8. Cf. P.Meloni, *Il valore storico e le fonti del libro macedonico di Appiano* (Rome, 1955), 67.

57 Livy 29.12.1; the Aetolians had suffered a devastating attack by Philip (Polyb. 11.7.2; cf. Livy 36.31.11). On Roman representation of the Aetolians as treaty-breakers, cf. Briscoe, *Comm.* 52.

58 For the evidence for these events, see Briscoe, *Comm.* 36ff.

59 App. *Macedonica* 4. On the date of the Aetolian appeal, cf.
    Briscoe, *Comm.* 130.

60 Polyb. 31.5.6. See H.H.Schmitt, *Rom und Rhodos* (Munich, 1957),
    1-49.

61 Cf. n.47.

62 Polyb. 16.27; Livy 31.14.10, 16.2, 24.4-18, 26.

63 Briscoe, *Comm.* 175.

64 Cf. n.52. Similar views: Agelaus in 217 (Polyb. 5.104.1),
    Thrasycrates in 207 (Polyb. 11.7.5). See J.Deininger (1971),
    23ff.

Chapter 8. Laus imperii

1 This is an enlarged and revised version of the paper read to
   the seminar. References to modern works are necessarily
   sparse and often hardly reveal my debt to them.

2 Brunt (1963) on Meyer (1961); cf. also W.Schmitthenner, *Gnomon*
   XXXVII (1965), 152ff.; Wells (1972) - though the archaeological
   evidence he examines naturally cannot attest Augustus' ultimate intentions.

3 *de nat.deor.* 3.95. In *de offic.* he adopts the practical morality of the middle Stoa, but all his last philosophical works
   show that he could no longer accept the dogmatic basis for
   ethics and politics which he had taken over from the Stoa in
   de leg. book 1 with 2.15f.

4 See e.g. *de orat.* 1.219-23; 2.30, 131, 178 and 206. All these
   passages are put into the mouth of Antonius, whose conception
   of the orator's role certainly falls short of the ideal, expressed in the dialogue by Crassus, and by Cicero himself in
   his own person in his *Orator*, but Antonius' conception is only
   treated as inadequate, and the views cited are not contradicted
   elsewhere; cf. also *Brut.* 184-9; *pro Cluent.* 139.

5 On the relation between actual and published speeches see esp.
   L.Laurand, *Et. sur le style des discours de Ciceron*[2] (Paris,
   1925) I 1ff.

6 *ad Att.* 2.1.3 seems to me to show that when he sent his consular speeches to Atticus, surely for publication, his aim was
   to perpetuate the fame of the Roman Demosthenes, not to dis-
   seminate pamphlets relevant to the political situation in 60;
   cf. n.8.

7 This view is asserted, and repeated against objections, in

de orat. 1.29-34, 202; 3.55-60 and 133-42, but virtually abandoned in *Orator* (despite continued insistence on the need for
philosophic knowledge) and *Brutus.*

8   Contrast references to the Gracchi honorific in his *contiones*
    (*de leg.agr.* 2.11,31 and 81; *pro Rab. perd.* 14), hostile in
    speeches to the senate (*in Cat.* 1.3ff. and 29, 4.13; *de leg.agr.*
    1.21). In 60 he was engaged in protecting the interests of
    Sullan *possessores* by amendments to Flavius' bill without object-
    ing to the purchase of lands for distribution (*ad Att.* 1.19.4);
    in 63 he had shown his care for the former class in the senate
    (*de leg.agr.* 1.12), but railed at Rullus for protecting them
    before the people (*de leg.agr.* 3 passim), and he had protested
    against purchase of lands from willing sellers (1.14, 2.63-72).
    Knowing readers would have perceived the insincerity of his
    reproaching Rullus for speaking of the urban plebs *quasi de
    aliqua sentina* (ibid. 70; cf. *ad Att.* loc.cit.), and would
    have smiled at his pose as a true *popularis* and at his skill
    in representing the optimate ideals, of which in 60 he was an
    unashamed champion, as genuinely popular (1.23ff., 2.6-10; cf.
    pro Sest. 97ff.), and in invoking popular conceptions of
    libertas against the professedly popular tribunes, Rullus and
    Labienus (e.g. *de leg.agr.* 2.15-22; *pro Rab.perd.* 10-17), all
    in the interest of senatorial control.

9   E.g. *in Cat.* 3.26; *pro Sest.* 67; *de prov.cons.* 30, 33; *pro
    Balb.* 64.

10 *pro Arch.* 12-32 is the *locus classicus.* Much evidence in U.
    Knoche's paper, reprinted in H.Opperman (1967), 420-46. On
    the old Roman *virtus*, manifest in services to the state, see
    Earl (1961), ch.II.

11 See esp. *ad fam.* 15.4-6. Cicero retained the title of *imperator*
    at least till May 49 (ibid. 2.16).

12 Cf. Livy 1.16.7, 8.7.16: *disciplinam militarem, qua stetit ad
    hunc diem* (340 B.C.) *Romana res*; 9.17.3: *plurimum in bello
    pollere videntur militum copia et virtus, ingenia imperatorum,
    fortuna per omnia humana, maxima in res bellicas potens; ea et
    singula intuenti et universa sicut ab aliis regibus gentibusque,
    ita ab hoc quoque* (Alexander) *facile praestant invictum Romanum
    imperium*; 9.17.10 (discipline); praef. 7: *ea belli gloria est
    populo Romano ut cum suum conditorisque sui parentem Martem
    potissimum ferat, tam et hoc gentes humanae patiantur aequo
    animo quam imperium patiuntur.* (The idea that subjects accept
    an imperial power as 'deserving' to rule because of military
    prowess is in Thuc. 2.41.3.) Drexler (1959) cites many other
    texts from Livy on the concept of military glory.

13 *de rep.* 2 passim; cf. Polyb. 6.50.

14 See Roloff (1938).

15 F.Millar, *JRS* LXIII (1973), 50ff. and E.A.Judge in J.A.S.Evans,
    ed., *Polis and Imperium: Studies in honour of E.T.Salmon*

(Toronto, 1974), 279ff., may be right in denying that Augustus officially claimed to have 'restored the Republic' in so many words, but Vell. 2.89 (and much else) shows that such a claim would well have summarized the official view of his settlement; it is significant that Velleius, a new man himself, is so concerned to stress that *prisca illa et antiqua rei publicae forma revocata (est)*.

16 Livy 4.3ff. (whence Claudius' speech in *ILS* 212 and Tac. *Ann.* 11.24); 8.13 (*voltis exemplo maiorum augere rem Romanam victos in civitatem accipiendo? materia crescendi per summam gloriam suppeditat*); Dionys. *Ant.* 2.16ff.; 14.6; cf. Brunt (1971), 538f. Cf. Cic. *de offic.* 1.35 and p.185.

17 Jacoby, *FGH* 87 F 59. 111b (military discipline) and 112. I would ascribe Diod. 37.2-6 to Posidonius, who also deplored the decay of the old standards; cf. n.18.

18 E.g. Sall. *Cat.* 6-13; Cic. *pro Marc.* 23; *Tusc. disp.* 1.2; Hor. *Odes* 3.6 and 24, etc. Hampl (1959) cites further texts and argues that such complaints (cf. also n.17), which are just as common in classical Greece, have no basis in history and may actually betoken a heightened moral consciousness in the ages when they are made; I agree.

19 Cic. *de rep.* 2.5-11; Livy 5.54 (site of Rome); Vitruv. 6.1. 10ff.; Strabo 6.4.1 (strategic centrality of Italy). *Laudes Italiae*, a theme dear to Varro: Brunt (1971), 128ff.

20 E.g. *in Cat.* 2.29, 3.18-22 (a remarkable testimony to popular superstition); *de dom.* 143; *pro Sest.* 53; *in Vat.* 14; *pro Scaur.* 48; *pro Mil.* 83; Sall. *BJ* 14.19.

21 *de har. resp.* 18ff., with particular reference to the skill of the *haruspices* in advising on the placation of the gods. Cicero was bound, if he was to persuade senators who credited this nonsense, not to let his own scepticism appear. Cf. *de nat.deor.* 2.8 ('Stoic'); *SIG*³ 601; Hor. *Odes* 3.6.1ff.; *Mos. et Rom.Leg.Coll.* 6.4.8 (Diocletian); Aug. *Civ.Dei*, books 4 and 5 passim.

22 K.Latte (1960), 285f. Goar (1972) ascribes a more sincere religious belief to Cicero, but his candid analysis of the letters yields a similar result.

23 *de leg.* 2.15ff.; *de nat.deor.* 1.3ff., 77; Polyb. 6.56; cf. Posidonius (n.17). Cicero also suggests that Athenians and Romans were civilized respectively by the Eleusinian Mysteries and by Numa's rituals (*de leg.* 2.36; *de rep.* 2.26ff.). It is hard to see how Roman religion was ever thought to deter men from wrong-doing. Goar (1972) notes that Cicero only twice threatens his enemies with punishment after death (*in Cat.* 1.33; *Phil.* 14.32); see Latte (1960), 286ff., for lack of belief in an after-world, cf. esp. *pro Cluent.* 171. *de leg.* 2.25 suggests that religion makes men fear immediate punishment by the gods, but *de har. resp.* 39, *de leg.* 1.40 that they

merely afflict the wrongdoer with *furor*, to which *de leg.*
2.43ff. adds posthumous infamy.

24 *de leg.* 2.30-4, 3.27; *post red.sen.* 11, etc.; cf. Goar (1972),
48ff. Yet, as Latte (1960), 299, justly remarks, Bibulus'
obnuntiatio had no effect even on the masses.

25 Varro, who himself accepted Stoic theology (Tert. *ad Nat.* 2.2),
regarded it as superstition to fear the gods, disapproved of
images and thought sacrifices futile (Arnob. 7.1), none the
less followed Q. Mucius Scaevola in distinguishing three kinds
of theology, philosophic and political, and approved of the
last for the people, whom it was expedient to deceive; though
he would not have instituted the old Roman religion in a new
city, it was the duty of the priests to keep up the cults *ut
potius (deos) magis colere quam despicere vulgus velit* (Aug.
Civ.Dei 4.31; cf. 4.11.13 and 27; 6.5f.). Cf. Latte (1960),
291ff.

26 *de leg.* 2.32ff.; cf. *de div.* 2.75. On Appius Claudius see
Latte (1960), 291.

27 *de div.* 2.28.70 and 148.

28 Latte (1960), ch.X; F.Schulz, *Roman legal science* (Oxford,
1946), 80ff.

29 They are collected by Ursula Heibges, *Latomus* XXVIII (1969),
833-49. I do not accept her assumption that Cicero shared,
as well as adapted himself to, the vacillating beliefs of his
contemporaries.

30 See W.Kroll, *Kultur der ciceronischen Zeit* (Leipzig, 1933), I
ch.I, who in my view overestimates the continuing strength of
the traditional religion even in educated circles.

31 Tac. *Ann.* 3.55, 16.4; Pliny, *Ep.* 1.14.4 apply *a fortiori* to
this period, cf. Cic. *pro Rosc.Am.* 43-8; it is reasonable to
believe that piety was as much valued as other ancient virtues.

32 This is based on analysis of the list of senators in 55 in P.
Willems, *Le Sénat de la République rom.* (Paris, 1878), ch.XV,
which, though antiquated, will serve for a rough estimate; I
assume that *novi* preponderated among the *ignoti*. Clodius'
incestum: ad Att. 1.13.3; cf. 12.3, 14.1-5, 16.1-9. I can
see no evidence that Cicero or the other *principes* acted from
outraged religious feeling.

33 *in Cat.* 2.11; *pro Rab.perd.* 33; *pro Sest.* 50; *de rep.* 3.41.
Cf. Hor. *Epodes* 16; Livy 9.19.17.

34 Vogt (1960) assembles texts and interprets the meaning of the
phrase. *ad Her.* 4.13 is the earliest extant instance in
Latin. Alternatively, Cicero speaks of Rome's power over all
peoples, II *Verr.* 4.81; *de leg.agr.* 2.22; *de dom.* 90; *pro
Planc.* 11; *Phil.* 6.19. Cf. n.67.

35 *SEG* 1.335, cf. Cic. *ad Att.* 4.1.7 (consular law of 57 *de annona*); Polyb. 1.1.5, 1.3.10, 3.1.4, 6.50.6; for his true meaning 1.3.9, 15.9.5 with 2.14.7 and 4.2.2.   A gloss in Vell. 1.6.6 shows that Aemilius Sura dated Rome's world dominion to the defeat of Antiochus III; some hold that he wrote before 171, see Swain (1940). Polybius' conception was then perhaps shared by Romans in his own lifetime.

36 Sherk (1969), no.16.

37 Badian (1958), part I *passim*.

38 Cimma (1976) gives the fullest recent treatment of 'client' kings. Citizenship: *PIR*^{2} A 900; H 153; I 65, 131f., 149, 175ff., 274ff., 276ff., 472, 512-17, 541, 637, 644. Armenia: *RG* 27. Lucullus had overrun Armenia; Pompey received the humble submission of Tigranes and recognized him as king, friend and ally of Rome (Cic. *Sest.* 58ff.; Plut. *Pomp.* 53, etc.). When Corbulo proposed *parta olim a Lucullo Pompeioque recipere* (Tac. *Ann.* 13.34), he designed (as the context shows) to force the Parthian nominee on the throne to recognize, like Tigranes, the suzerainty of Rome: there was no thought of annexation.

39 *BJ* 14.1; cf. Livy 42.6.8 (Antiochus IV, see n.80); 45.44.19 (Prusias I); also the Rhodian speech in 37.54.

40 In 47 Caesar required the kings and dynasts near Syria to protect that province as friends of Rome (*B.Alex.* 65.4). But most of them had territories that did not lie *between* Syria and Parthia. Ariobarzanes: Cic. *ad fam.* 15.1-4 *passim; ad Att.* 6.3.5.   Tribute: Livy 45.18.7f.; Badian (1968), ch.VI.

41 Liebmann-Frankfort (1969), 7ff. and *passim*.

42 Veyne (1975) is no doubt right that in the third and early second centuries, with which he is concerned, 'Rome ne songe pas encore à dominer le monde, mais plûtot à être seule au monde', but 'defensive' wars fought for this purpose were bound to appear aggressive to others and to be interpreted in the light of the dominance Rome attained, which in turn created the ideal of world rule.

43 Polyb. 3.22-5 (the last renewal was in 279) for Carthage; App. *Bell.Samm.* 7.1 (Tarentum); the clause was perhaps ambiguous.

44 2.13.7 (cf. Walbank, ad loc., for varying views); 3.15, 3.20ff. and 28-30.

45 Livy 34.58; see Badian (1958), 76ff. Livy 38.38.

46 Ziegler (1964), 20ff.; Liebmann-Frankfort (1969), 171ff., 237ff., 263ff., 276ff., 296ff., 308ff. for evidence and discussion. Of course there was never any formal treaty ratified at Rome, and perhaps no more than a vague understanding; cf. Dio 37.5.

47 Plut. *Pomp.* 36; Dio 37.5-7; 40.20.1.

48 Gelzer (1963), 15ff. (first published in 1940).

49 Badian (1968), 9ff.

50 Cicero had a quaestor, four legates, a *praefectus fabrum* (*ad
    fam.* 3.7.4) and other equestrian prefects, of whom he sent
    one to do justice in Cyprus (*ad Att.* 5.21.6). Pliny had only
    one legate (*Ep.* 10.25); there were also an equestrian procu-
    rator with one or two freedmen assistants - Epimachus perhaps
    succeeded Maximus - and the prefect of the *ora Pontica* (21ff.,
    27ff., 83-6a). Both could call on a *cohors amicorum*, and on
    military officers, of whom there were far more in Cicero's
    province. No doubt the procurator had more clerical staff
    than Cicero and his quaestor.

51 A.H.M.Jones (1974), ch.VIII for a brief survey.

52 Cic. II *Verr.* 2.32; *ad Att.* 6.1.15, 6.2.4. I am not convinced
    by D.Kienast's rejection in *ZRE* LXXXV (1968), 330ff., of the
    orthodox view that grants of *libertas* did not give cities
    exemption from the governor's jurisdiction.

53 *ad QF* 1.1.25; cf. A.H.M.Jones (1940), 170ff.

54 *BG* 4.21, 5.25 and 54; but Commius (4.21) ultimately turned
    against the Romans, and the native leaders most dangerous to
    Rome were sometimes kings or aspirants to kingship backed by
    popular support (1.3ff., 7.4; cf. the case of Ambiorix, 5.27,
    6.31).

55 *ad Att.* 6.2.5.

56 Badian (1968), ch.I.

57 Brunt (1971), 432ff., 449. Conscription: ch.XXII.

58 Cic. *ad fam.* 3.3.1. Cicero's army: Brunt (1971), 689.

59 See also the Cnidus inscription published in *JRS* LXIV (1974),
    col.III 5ff. Despite Cicero's *plurimae leges veteres*, the
    prohibition might have been introduced first in Saturninus'
    maiestas law, as a result of recent disasters incurred by
    aggressive proconsuls. But were all provincial frontiers
    clearly defined? And was a proconsul debarred either from
    striking first at an enemy force mustering outside the prov-
    ince, or from pursuing it after repelling an incursion? In
    Cicero's Cilicia the land route from the Phrygian *conventus*
    to Cilicia Pedias actually passed through the Cappadocian
    kingdom; he went outside his province three times in a year.
    Caesar felt no inhibition in attacking Ariovistus, etc., and
    there is no indication that his apparent violations of his
    own rule was censured even by his enemies except in one in-
    stance (cf. n.81).

60 *Iustae causae* and fetial law: Cic. *de offic.* 1.34-6 and 80: *de rep.* 2.31 (cf. 26 on Numa), 3.34ff., part of the answer to Furius Philus' speech, 8ff., which derives from a discourse of Carneades (Lactant., *div.inst.* 5.14ff.), delivered at Rome in 155; cf. Capelle (1932) and Walbank (1965), 13; it is immaterial here whether Panaetius supplied the answer (*contra*, Strasburger (1965), 45). See also Sall. *Cat.* 6.5; *or. Lepidi* 4; Drexler (1959) collects much material from Livy. For adaptation of fetial procedure in the middle republic, see Dahlheim (1968), 171ff.; but see now J.W.Rich, *Declaring war in the Roman Republic period of transmarine expansion* (Collection Latomus CXLIX) (1976), ch.III. Neither its origins, cf. Hampl (1957), nor Roman practice, when documented, can warrant Cicero's claims that it embodied a distinctively high moral standard.

61 Witness the cases of Saguntum and of the Greek cities in Asia, whose freedom Rome professed to protect against Antiochus III, while perfectly willing to abandon it in her own interests, Badian (1958), 75ff.

62 1.3.6ff., 1.6, 1.10 with 20; 1.63.9, 2.31 with 21; 3.2.6, 3.3.8ff., 6.50.6, 9.10.11, 15.10.2. For Greek views of Roman imperialism, see also 5.104, 9.37.6, 11.5; Livy (P) 31.29.6. Polybius' general judgements deserve attention although they conflict with the details of his narrative perhaps derived from Roman informants, which fit a defensive interpretation of Roman policy (Walbank (1963) with a different explanation of the apparent inconsistency). See also Walbank (1965) on his cynicism in analysing many Roman actions after 168. Perhaps his experience of contemporary Roman conduct and knowledge of the actual consequences of earlier wars made it hard for Polybius to credit that Rome's policy had ever been so defensive as the information he accepted in his narrative naturally suggested.

63 *de offic.* 1.38, 3.87. On the Hannibalic war see Lucret. 3.836ff.; Livy 22.58.3, 27.39.9, 28.19.6ff., 29.17.6, 30.32.2. Unlike some Stoics (Cic. *de fin.* 3.57), Panaetius probably allowed some value to glory, but could hardly have regarded its pursuit as condoning injustice.

64 Polyb. 36.2 and 9, on which see Hoffmann (1960); for a parallel, 32.9 and 13. There is nothing peculiarly Roman in insistence on a *iusta causa* for a war prompted by very different motives, cf. Thuc. 6.93 and 105; 7.18 (Sparta); 6.6 and 8 (Athens); Polyb. 3.6 and Arr. *Anab.* 2.14 (Macedon). For public opinion, Drexler (1959) cited Livy 3.72.2ff., 30.16.8ff., 45.18.1.

65 Drexler (1959) cited Livy 5.51ff., 31.9.5, 45.39.10 and many other texts. Cf. Thuc. 7.18 (Sparta).

66 Weippert (1972) is exhaustive and judicious on imitation of Alexander in the republic.

67   M.H.Crawford (1974), index s.v. 'globe'.

68   Jacoby, *FGH* 90 F 130.95; cf. Plut. *Caes*. 58; Weippert (1972),
     171ff.; also 209ff. on Antony. Nicolaus in general views
     Augustus as Caesar's heir; so his conception of Caesar's aims
     may be relevant to his interpretation of Augustus' policy.
     Weippert, who admits that Augustus was at first influenced by
     Alexander, thinks that by 20 B.C. he had given up aspirations
     for world conquest (*contra* Brunt (1963), 170-6, which he had
     apparently not considered), but 257ff. shows persistence of
     the ideal with Drusus and Germanicus (esp. *P.Oxy.* 2435).
     Augustus' supposed criticism of Alexander for not giving pri-
     ority to organizing his conquests (Plut. 207D; Sen. *Suas.*
     1.8) is in character, but further conquests could be in order,
     following organization; in my judgement Augustus acted on
     that principle down to A.D. 6.

69   Illyricum, not Transalpina, was his province under the lex
     Vatinia. Early in 58 three of his four legions were at
     Aquileia (*BG* 1.10), a suitable base for an Illyrian offens-
     ive, for which such incidents as are described in 1.5.4 and
     5.1.5 would have provided pretexts. As late as 56 he still
     desired *eas quoque nationes adire et regiones cognoscere*
     (3.7); the same verbs are used of his plan to invade Britain
     (4.20). Cf. App. *Bell.Ill.* 12. The task had to be left to
     his adoptive son.

70   See generally *BG* 1.1-4 (cf. Cic. *ad Att.* 1.19.2 and 20.5),
     31 (cf. 6.12), 35, 36.7, 40.2.

71   Rome's *amici*: *BG* 1.33.2 and 35.4; probably too the peoples
     under Aeduan hegemony, cf. 43.7-9; I take it that the friend-
     ship with a former Sequanian king (1.3.4) did not mean that
     his people were still *amici* of Rome in 58. But the Arverni
     may have been: until 52 they took no known part in resistance,
     and retained a privileged position after their revolt (7.90.3;
     Pliny, *NH* 4.109).

72   1.7.4, 1.10.2, 1.12-14 and 30.

73   1.11; later Caesar told the Aedui that he had undertaken the
     war for their sake *magna ex parte*, 16.6.

74   1.34-6, 1.40, 1.42-5. Ariovistus' insolence: 1.33.5, 1.46.4
     (paralleled by similar Roman criticisms of the Aetolians and
     Rhodians in Livy 33.11.8, 37.49.2, 44.14.8; cf. Dahlheim
     (1968), 269ff.); his duty of respect as *amicus*: 42.2ff., 43.4
     (with his reply, 44.5). Dio makes Caesar answer the charge
     that he was bringing on the war for personal ambition by
     maintaining that it was Rome's tradition not only to protect
     subjects and allies but to seek aggrandizement (38.36-8),
     that she must anticipate inevitable attacks (38.40), and that
     Ariovistus' contumacious conduct proves his hostile intentions
     of which Caesar had been unaware in 59 (38.42-5). The speech
     is invention and often echoes imperialist speeches in Thucy-
     dides, but gives a perceptive interpretation of Roman

imperialism in general and of Caesar's conduct in 58, or
rather of his apologia for it.

75 2.2. 'Gallia' is used in contradictory senses here, as in
1.1.1 and 6, and often: the Remi are outside in 2.3 and inside in 6.12. K.Christ (1974) argues that Caesar exaggerates
the unity of Gaul, to justify his policy of subduing the
whole land. That policy is enunciated by Cicero (*de prov.
cons.* 32), not in the *Commentaries*. He had not conceived it
before early 58 (n.69 and text), but in retrospect he could
claim to have carried it out, and this representation of his
actual achievement is implicit throughout from the first
chapter of book 1.

76 2.14, 5.5-7, 7.32ff. Caesar also interfered in the internal
affairs of other peoples, before they had taken up arms
against him (5.3.25 and 54).

77 2.1-6. Sherwin-White (1957) notes an exact parallel in
Pompey's preventive war against the Iberians (Dio 37.1).

78 3.10.2, 4.30.2 and 38.1, 5.26.1, 6.8.8, etc. Livy 8.14.4
speaks of the *crimen rebellionis*. As Timpe (1972) shows,
Gallic peoples normally came under Caesar's control by *deditio*,
even if they had not previously been at war with him; for
earlier examples, see Dahlheim (1968), 52ff. For the consequences, cf. n.80. The *dediti* had a claim to protection
(2.28.3, 32.2, etc.). Timpe argues from 2.35 that Caesar
would not accept *deditio*, if he felt unable to guarantee this;
cf. also 4.21.6 and 27.5. In the last cases at least it seems
to me clear in the context that Caesar·did accept the offers
made. He is often less explicit about the settlements he made
than Timpe presumes. According to Timpe no Gallic *dediti* became *foederati* or *amici*. But Caesar does not mention the
foedus with the Helvetii (Cic. *pro Balb.* 32), and he does let
out that the Treveri were *amici* (5.3.3); cf. 4.16 (Ubii).

79 4.20.1, 21.5-8, 27.1, 30.2, 5.20-2.

80 3.11; 4.6; 6.5. Once the Ubii sought his protection, he considered them subject to his orders, though *amici* (4.8 and 16,
6.9). The Treveri, who had sought his aid (1.37) and sent
him cavalry (2.24), were treated as hostile in 54, because
neque ad concilia veniebant neque imperio parebant; such
obedience was part of the *officium* of *amici* (5.2-4); cf. n.74.
In 173 Antiochus IV had promised to obey Roman orders *quae
bono fidelique socio regi essent imperanda; se in nullo usquam
cessaturum officio* (Livy 42.6.8).

81 Plut. *Caes.* 22; *Cato Minor* 51; *comp.Nic. et Crassi* 4. Suetonius presumably reflects contemporary criticisms in asserting
that his campaigns were unjust and inspired by lust for glory
and wealth (*Caes.* 22, 24, 47, 54), but it was surely in 54
that the senate voted to send a commission to enquire into
charges of aggression (ibid. 24), if indeed it ever did; more
probably this was only a hostile proposal. There is no

evidence that his earlier offensiv̥es had been challenged at
Rome, and as noted by Timpe (1965), the supplications decreed
in his honour, e.g. in 57 (*BG* 2.35), gave them retroactive
approval.

82 *BG* 4.4-19; cf. 5.9.2, n.80.

83 *de prov.cons.* 19-36; *in Pis.* 81; *ad QF* 3.6(8).2. See Collins
    (1972).

84 *BG* 3.10.3; cf. 3.8.4, 4.34.5, 5.7.8, 5.27.6, 5.29.4, 5.38.2,
    and often in book 7 (1.5-8, 4.4, 14.10, 64.3, 76.2, 77.13-16,
    89.1), 8.1.3. Similarly he makes Gauls refer to Roman acts
    of injustice, 5.38.2, 7.38.10. Gelzer (1963), 7 gives other
    examples of Roman writers putting the anti-Roman views, e.g.
    Sall. *ep. Mithr.*; *BJ* 81.1; Tac. *Agr.* 30. The Romans could
    pretend to free subjects from the rule of kings - under whom
    they wished to live (Livy 45.18; Strabo 12.2.11).

85 *Phil.* 6.19.

86 Yet in 46 he no longer needed to satisfy his troops' lust for
    vengeance, as in the war itself (7.28.4, 8.38).

87 Plut. *Caes.* 15; App. *Celt.* 2, misinterpreted by Westermann
    (1955), 63, though naturally unreliable. Note *BG* 7.89.5.

88 *BG* 2.14.28 and 31ff., 8.3.5, 21.2. In 8.44.1 and 3.16 note
    apologies for special severity; but cf. Cic.*de offic* . 3.46.

89 Cic. II *Verr.* 5.115; *de offic.* 1.33-5, 1.82, 2.18, 3.46.
    Numantia: see Astin (1967), 153-5 on App. *Iber.* 98.

90 Hampl (1966) adduces early atrocities to disprove the fable
    that the Romans became less humane to enemies in the late
    republic. *Deditio*: Dahlheim (1968), ch.1. Especially sig-
    nificant on Roman motives for clemency: Livy 42.8.5ff.,
    44.7.5 and 31.1; Jos. *BJ* 5.372ff. Cf. generally Livy 30.42.7:
    plus paene parcendo victis quam vincendo imperium auxisse.

91 Cicero sought to arouse prejudice against L.Piso, *cos.* 58,
    because his mother was Insubrian, *in Pis.* fr. 9-12 (OCT);
    post red. sen. 15.

92 *ad Att.* 14.12.1. Contrast II *Verr.* 2.2-8.

93 *pro Flacc.* 62; *ad QF* 1.1.27ff.; *de rep.* 2.34; *Tusc. disp.*
    1.1-7 (but stressing Roman moral superiority).

94 *pro Flacc.* 9, 16, 57, 61; *ad QF* 1.1.16, 1.2.4; *pro Sest.* 141;
    pro Lig. 11. He found it necessary to differentiate the
    Sicilians (who were almost like old Romans!) from other
    Greeks, II *Verr.* 2.7.

95 *CAH* XI 437.

96   *de rep.* 3.37–41, whence Aug. *Civ. Dei* 19.21, cf. Capelle
     (1932), 93: note there *ideo iustum esse, quod talibus
     hominibus sit utilis servitus et pro utilitate eorum fieri,
     cum recte fit, id est cum improbis aufertur iniuriarum
     licentia, et domiti melius se habebunt, quia indomiti deter-
     ius se habuerunt.*

97   Dahlheim (1968), chs.I and II.

98   *Hist.* 4.74. Dio makes Maecenas add that taxation should be
     levied on all alike (52.28ff.). That was still not the case
     when he wrote.

99   See esp. II *Verr.* 3.207 (in 2.2–8, 5.8 he implausibly claims
     that the Sicilians loved their master, but treats them as
     exceptional); *de imp. Cn. Pomp.* 65; *ad fam.* 15.1.5.

100 *ad fam.* 15.3.2 and 4.14; *ad Att.* 5.18.2.

101 Cf. Polyb. 5.11, 10.36; Sall. *BJ* 102.6; Cic. II *Verr.* 3.14;
     Livy 8.13.16.

102 E.g. Sen. *Clem.* 1.3, 8.6ff., 11.4, etc., as in Polyb. 5.11.

103 Toynbee (1965), II 608ff. Particularly significant are the
     activities of the elder Cato in seeking to redress or punish
     wrongs done to subjects (*ORF*[2] frs.58ff., 154, 173, 196–9);
     note also the indignation that Gaius Gracchus tried to arouse
     at ill-treatment of the Italians (Gell. 10.3). Even if per-
     sonal or political feuds explain why some or most charges
     were brought, it would remain true that injustice to subjects
     was a suitable pretext for assailing personal adversaries.

104 Brunt (1961), part I.

105 On the duty of governors and its delicacy, Cic. *ad QF* 1.1.32–6;
     ad Att. 5.13.1. Posidonius held (with some anachronism) that
     equestrian control of the courts made governors too fearful
     to restrain Equites in the provinces (Jacoby, *FGH* 87 F 108d
     and 111b). There were certainly exceptions like Q.Mucius
     Scaevola and L.Sempronius Asellio (Diod. 37.5 and 8 from
     Posid.), Lucullus (Plut. *Luc.* 20) and perhaps Gabinius in Syria
     (Cic. *de prov. cons.* 10; *ad QF* 3.2.2); Cicero adopted Scaevola'
     edict on the publicans, while that of Bibulus in Syria was
     overtly still stricter (*ad Att.* 6.1.15, but see *ad fam.* 3.8.4),

106 From Cilicia Cicero pressed administrators of other provinces
     to comply with Roman moneylenders' demands (e.g. *ad fam.* 13.56
     and 61) in terms perhaps not very different from the pleas on
     Scaptius' behalf that he resented. Despite his condemnation
     of Appius Claudius' conduct as governor (e.g. *ad Att.* 5.15ff.
     and 6.1.2), he did what he could to hinder his conviction at
     Rome (*ad fam.* 3.10.1; *ad Att.* 6.2.10), and showed his dis-
     pleasure with hostile witnesses from Cilicia (*ad fam.* 3.11.3).
     Similarly in 70 L.Metellus had reversed Verres' *acta* in Sicily
     (II *Verr.* 2.62ff., 138–40, 3.43–6, 5.55) but obstructed his

prosecution (2.64ff., 160–4, 3.122, 152ff., 4.146–9).

107 *ad QF* 1.1 (a letter presumably intended for publication) com-
mends *aequitas, clementia, comitas, constantia, continentia,
facilitas* (for the meaning of which see *de imp. Cn. Pomp.* 41;
ad Att. 6.2.5), *gravitas, humanitas, integritas, lenitas,
mansuetudo, moderatio, severitas, temperantia*. Several of
these virtues (also *fides, innocentia*) recur in Cicero's
eulogy of Pompey (*de imp. Cn. Pomp.* 13,36–42) and in the
claims he makes on his own behalf in 51–50 B.C. (*ad Att.* 5.9.1,
15.2, 17.2, 18.2, 20.6, etc.; *ad fam.* 15.4.1 and 14), along
with *abstinentia* (for whose meaning see also *ad Att.* 5.10.2,
16.3, 21.5; *continentia, innocentia, integritas, temperantia*
are more or less synonymous), *iustitia* and *modestia*. See R.
Combès, *Imperator* (Paris, 1966), ch.VIII.

108 *ad Att.* 6.1.13; *ad fam.* 15.4.15.

109 *ad Att.* 5.9.1, 10.2, 13.1, 15.2, 21.5 and 7. Conceivably in
pressing Scaptius' case, Atticus did not know all the facts.

110 Brunt (1961), part II.

111 *de imp. Cn. Pomp.* 4ff., 7; *de leg. agr.* 2.80ff.

112 Aurelius Victor, *Caes.* 39.31.

113 G.Barbieri, *L'Albo senatorio da Severo a Carino* (Rome, 1952),
441, found that forty-three per cent of senators whose origins were known or probable were Italian. H.-G.Pflaum, *Les
Procurateurs équestres* (Paris, 1950), 193, assigned an Italian
origin to twenty-six out of ninety-one third-century procurators.

*Chapter 9. Greek intellectuals and the Roman aristocracy in
the first century B.C.*

1 This paper presents, at unseemly length, a hypothesis about
one aspect of Roman imperialism in the first century B.C.; I
am, *malgré tout*, grateful to Peter Garnsey and Dick Whittaker
for bullying me into finishing it.

2 Testimonia and fragments in *FGH* 88.

3 Livy 9.17–9 = *FGH* 88 T 9; despite Livy's efforts, Plut. *de
fort. Rom.* 326a–c implies that chance saved Rome from Alexander by reason of the latter's early death; compare Theo
Stoicus (*Rhet. Gr.* ii 110, 27) for speculation on what Alexander could have achieved; the saying attributed by Gellius
17.21.33, to Alexander of Molossus that he was going to Italy
to fight the Romans who were men, Alexander of Macedon was
going to fight the Persians who were women, is a piece of
Roman boasting cognate to that of Livy; there is little to
be learnt from A.Rapaport, *Eos* XXVII (1924), 26–7, alleging

a joint source for Livy and Plut. *Pyrrhus* 19.1-2; W.R.Breiten-
bach, *Mus. Helv.* XXVI (1969), 146-57, 'Der Alexanderexkurs bei
Livius'.

4   D.Hal. 1.4.4; E.Schwartz, *RE* IV 1886-91 (1901), discussing
Quintus Curtius, identifies the *bêtes noires* of Dionysius of
Halicarnassus with those of Livy and argues for the repro-
duction of their ideas by Pompeius Trogus, eliminating Timagenes; A.D.Momigliano, *Ath.* n.s. XII (1934), 45 = *Terzo con-
tributo* (Rome, 1966), 499, points out that the *bêtes noires* of
Dionysius of Halicarnassus and of Livy cannot be the same.

5   See O.Seel, *Eine römische Weltgeschichte* (Nuremberg, 1972).

6   Lactantius, *Inst.* 7.15 and 18; Lydus, *de mens* 2.4; Justin,
Apol. 1.20 and 44; Clement Alex. *Strom.* 6.5.43.1; see the discussions of H.Windisch, *Verhandelingen k. Akad. van Weten-
schappen, Afd. Letterkunde* XXVIII, 3 (Amsterdam, 1930); F.
Cumont, *Rev. Hist. Rel.* CIII (1931), 64; E.Benveniste, *Rev.
Hist. Rel.* CVI (1932), 337; the oracle perhaps emerged before
the achievement of a *modus vivendi* between Rome and Parthia;
E.Bikerman, *REL* XXIV (1946), 148 n.10; compare *Or. Sib.* 3.350
for a prophecy of the revenge of Asia on Rome (W.W.Tarn, *JRS*
XXII (1932), 137-8, conjectures Cleopatra as the vehicle,
doubted by V.Nikiprowetsky, *La troisième Sibylle* (Paris, 1970),
144-6).

    For Rome as a fourth empire, to be superseded by a fifth
empire, in Jewish and other works of the late republic and
early empire, see J.W.Swain, *CP* XXXV (1940), 15.

7   The quotation is from E.W.Gray, *JRS* XLII (1952), 123, reviewing
D.Magie (1950); for Augustus see Bowersock (1965), chs.2-11;
the principle is explicitly enunciated by Cic. *ad QF* 1.1.25,
which discusses 'your ensuring that the cities are governed by
the desires of the aristocracies'; whatever may be the truth
about the state of affairs in the first half of the second
century B.C., the hostility of the lower classes to Roman rule
is assumed without question by Livy, see Harris (1971a), 142-3.

8   Verbal information from F.Coarelli.

9   Cic. *de fin.* 1.7; compare *Brut.* 99; for the decline of Magna
Graecia in general, see *de amic.* 13.

10 Cic. *pro Arch.* 5; Archias was granted citizenship and other
praemia, also apparently by Locri (*pro Arch.* 10); note in the
latter passage that the Greeks are represented as unable to
shed their (to Cicero) distasteful habit of honouring actors
with their citizenship.

11 Compare the case of Emporiae, where the Spanish element in the
population achieved citizenship before the Greek, Livy 34.9.1-3.

12 *Tarentum*: Cic. II *Verr.* 4.135; *de fin.* 1.7; Strabo 6.1.2 (253);
for the survival of the *prohedria* in the first century A.D. see
NSc 1896, 100 = *ILS* 6462; *NSc* 1897, 68; L.Gasperini, in *Terza*

Miscellanea greca e romana, 162ff. *Rhegium*: Strabo 6.1.2 (253). *Velia*: *ILS* 6461; F.Sartori, *Problemi di storia costituzionale italiota* (Rome, 1953), 106; Velia produced a prolific Greek-type coinage well into the first century B.C. *Neapolis*: Varro, *LL* 6.15; Cic. *pro Rab. Post.* 26-7; Dio 55.10.9; Strabo 5.4.7 (246), 6.1.2 (253); Velleius 1.4.2; Suet. *Claud.* 11; *Nero* 20 and 25; Tac. *Ann.* 15.33; Dio 60.6.2; SHA, *Hadr.* 19.1; *CIL* X 1481; F. de Martino, *PdelP* VII (1952), 333-43. *Canusium*: Hor. *Sat.* 1.10.30, with Scholia. E.Keuls, *Atti Taranto* 1975 (forthcoming), documents the survival of Italiote religious art into the Roman period and its influence on Roman funerary art.

13 *SIG* 796B = *IG* IV 1^2, 84, lines 33-4; compare the ambitions of the officer who imprisoned Paul at Jerusalem, Acts 22.25-9, also of Opramoas, *TAM* II 906, with C.S.Walton, *JRS* XIX (1929), 38, 'Oriental senators in the service of Rome', at 55.

14 Cic. *ad fam.* 13.53.2, 69.2; *pro Flacc.* 70-83; *de offic.* 3.58, if a true story, suggests that at Syracuse there was no bar to a Roman acquiring land.

15 L.Robert, *Les gladiateurs dans l'Orient grec* (Paris, 1940).

16 L.Robert, *REA* LXII (1960), 332-42.

17 P.Veyne, *Latomus* XXI (1962), 68-75.

18 Veyne (n.17), 76-9; *IG* XIV 1121 = *CIL* XIV 2218 = *ILLRP* 372, a dedication in Latin and Greek to Naso at Nemi; the reverse process is also rare, *ILLRP* 194 (Delos), 337 (Delphi), 363 (Delos), 376 (Argos), all bilingual.

19 A.L.Frothingham, *AJA* XXI (1917), 187 and 313, 'Ancient orientation unveiled: II. Etruria and Rome; III. The left as the place of honour in Roman and Christian art'; F.P.Johnson, *AJA* XXVIII (1924), 399, '*Right* and *left* in Roman art', on Roman flexibility under the empire.

20 H.Seyrig, *RA* XXIX (1929), 90, n.1 (the statue-base of *two* figures from Athens there discussed is not really germane).

21 See, provisionally, M.E.Blake, *Ancient Roman construction in Italy* (Washington, 1947), 228.

22 A.Boethius, *Roman and Greek town architecture* (Göteborg, 1948), 15: *II Int. Congr. Class. Stud. 1954* (Copenhagen, 1958), IV 92. Strabo was struck by buildings of many stories in Rome, 16.2.23 (757), and could only compare Aradus and Tyre in the east, with their restricted sites, 16.2.23 and 13 (753).

23 R.MacMullen, *Roman social relations* (New Haven, 1974), 129.

24 E.Rosenbaum, *Cyrenaican portrait sculpture* (London, 1960), 13-28.

25 Gellius 19.9.7; Strabo noticed the existence of the Atellan

farce, 5.3.6 (233); Caecilius of Caleacte compared Demosthenes
and Cicero; for Virgilian influence on Greek literature see V.
Reichmann, *Römische Literatur in griechischer Übersetzung*,
Phil. supp. 34, 3 (Leipzig, 1943), 9 (also for Horatian influence) and the works cited in J.Diggle, *Euripides: Phaethon*
(Cambridge, 1970), 199, n.3; for Ovidian influence on Lucian,
J.Diggle, 202; for Latin influence on the fourth-century Tri-
phiodorus (Virgil) see A.Cameron, *Claudian* (Oxford, 1970), 20,
n.5; on the fifth-century Nonnus (Ovid and Claudian), Cameron,
11 and 20-1, esp. 20, n.7; Diggle, 180-200; on Christodorus
(Virgil), Cameron, 20, n.4. The remark of H.D.Jocelyn, *Antich-
thon* I (1967), 61, that Latin poetry does not influence Greek
poetry before the thirteenth century is curious.

L.Cestius Pius, of Smyrna, and Arellius Fuscus, perhaps
from Asia, who worked on Latin literature are perhaps shown by
their names to be of Italian origin.

26 *Milet* III, nos. 133 and 124.

27 Fr. 261 Edelstein-Kidd; the characterization in my view ad-
mirably fits Cn. Pompeius.

28 Cic. *pro Mur.* 62; Nepos, *Att.* 17.3; also Strabo 1.1.22 (13);
2, 3 and 4 (15-17). Note also the similar judgement of Diod.
34-5.33.8 (perhaps from Posidonius), G.Busolt, *Jahrb. für cl.
Philologie* (1890), 331; *FGH* 87 F 112.8; F.Münzer, *RE* IV 1505,
cites the *elogia* of the Scipiones as parallel material, implicitly rejected by F.Jacoby ad loc.; Diod. 37.8.2 for the
duty to honour men who were *propaideumenoi*. For Cato's image
as a philosopher compare Plut. *Cato Min.* 6; *Brut.* 34 with 12.

29 Dion. Hal. 15.5 (4-5). It is not surprising that Dionysius
was pathetically anxious to show that the Romans were really
Greeks.

30 For derogatory remarks in private letters see *ad Att.* 4.7.1,
7.18.3, 13.35.1; *ad fam.* 7.18.1, 13.78.1, 16.4.2; for the
notion of the decline of Greece since classical times see *ad
QF.* 1.1.16 and 27-8; *pro Flacc.* 16 and 61-2; Tac. *Hist.* 3.47;
Juvenal 3.66-80; Pliny, *Ep.* 10.40.2; A.N.Sherwin-White (1967),
62-86.

31 Cic. *de prov. cons.* 10; compare Livy 36.17.5, in the speech
attributed to M'. Acilius before the battle of Thermopylae,
'Syrian and Asiatic Greeks, the most worthless among the races
of mankind and ones born to slavery', presumably reflecting
attitudes of the first century B.C. Cic. *pro Flacc.* 9-12.

32 Cic. *pro Flacc.* 14-16; the practice documented by W.Vischer,
RhM XXVIII (1873), 380; cf. 17 for Phrygians and Mysians in
Roman assemblies.

33 Cicero was of course prepared to admit certain isolated cases
where the Romans could learn from the Greeks in the field of
public law, see *de leg.* 3.46 on the absence of any real system
of *nomophylakia* at Rome; when Cicero discussed the institution

of the tribunate, *de re pub*. 2.57-8, he admitted that it perhaps lacked a *ratio* and remarked in its defence that a similar
institution was necessary even at Sparta and on Crete; he also
admitted that if the problem of debt had been dealt with as it
had been by Solon and as it was later at Rome, the tribunate
would not have been necessary.

34 Cic. *de orat*. 1.197; W.A.J.Watson is in my view right to argue
that there was no serious Greek influence on Roman law, *Law-
making in the later Roman republic* (Oxford, 1974), ch. 16. M.A.
Trouard, *Cicero's attitude towards the Greeks* (Chicago, 1942),
33-42, further documents the belief of Cicero in the superiority of Rome in law and government, religion, military discipline, 52-9, in language (Cicero was here untypical).

35 Cic. *ad QF*. 1.1.27-8, closely paralleled in *pro Arch*. 12-14.

36 Cic. II *Verr*. 4.147 (Cicero in Syracuse - Cicero later represents the great orators of the preceding generation to his
own, M.Antonius and L.Licinius Crassus, as affecting ignor-
ance of things Greek); 4.4; see also 2.87; 4.29, 30, 33, 39,
94, 124, 134 (knowledge of Greek art); H.Jucker, *Vom Verhält-
nis der Römer* (Frankfurt-am-Main, 1950), ch.IV, further documents ambiguous Roman attitudes to Greek art. At *Parad. Stoic*.
13 and 37-8 works of art are attacked basically as manifestations of luxury.

37 Cic. *Brut*. 207 (L.Aelius); *de leg*. 1.13, 2.59; *de amic*. 1
(*ius civile*); *ad fam*. 13.1.2 (Phaedrus).

38 Cic. *Brut* 306; compare *Tusc. disp*. 2.26. I regard the reference to Molo in Rome in 87 as a doublet.

39 Cic. *Brut*. 309; note *ad fam*. 13.16.4 for Apollonius, as freedman of P.Crassus, being trained by Diodotus in Cicero's house;
9.4 for a general reference to Diodotus.

40 Cic. *de offic*. 1.1; *Ep*. fr. 1; Suet. *Rhet*. 2 for the advice to
Cicero not to be a pupil of the teacher of rhetoric in Latin,
L.Plotius Gallus (perhaps from L.Licinius Crassus).

41 *RE* Apollonius 85.

42 Cic. *Brut*. 315, with the reading of *L*; *de fin*. 1.16 for Phaedrus
and Zeno; see J.C.Davies, *CQ* n.s. XVIII (1968), 303, for the
rhetorical techniques which Cicero may have learnt from Molo.

43 Suet. *DJ* 4; Plut. *Caes*. 3 (incomplete and chronologically in-
accurate). Molo also taught a T.Manlius Torquatus, Cic. *Brut*.
245, and M.Favonius, *ad Att*. 2.1.9.

44 Cic. *ad fam*. 16.21.3 and 5; *ad Att*. 14.16.3, 18.4, 15.16, 27.3;
de offic. 1.1; Plut. *Cic*. 24 (son - teachers Leonides and
Herodes); Cic. *ad QF*. 3.3.4 (nephew). Note that Sallust assumed
Sulla to be equally well educated in Greek and Latin, *BJ* 95.3.

45   Dio 51.15.6 with Bowersock (1965), 60-1.

46   Val. Max. 2.2.3, see Cic. *de fin.* 5.89; Roman magistrates,
     whether Cicero or Verres, of course continued to use interpre-
     ters for official purposes.

47   *Utra voles lingua*, *Orator* 235; *in utriusque orationis facul-
     tate*, *de offic.* 1.1; see also *utraque lingua* in Hor. *Sat.*
     1.10.23; *utriusque linguae* in *Odes* 3.8.5; *hekateros* in the
     edict of Paullus Fabius Maximus, Sherk 65, line 30 = U.Laffi,
     SCO XVI (1967), p.20, line 30; later examples in Pliny, *NH*
     12.11; Quint. *proem.* 1; 1.1.14; Stat. *Silvae* 5.3.90; Martial
     10.76.6; Pliny, *Ep.* 3.1.7, 7.25.4; Gellius 17.5.3; Suet. *Gram.*
     1; *Aug.* 89; *Claud.* 42; Plut. *Luc.* 1; Philostratus, *VS* 2.10.5;
     Dio 69.3.1; *ILS* 7761 (A.D. 229); Ammianus 15.13.1; D. 45.1.1.6;
     note the existence in Italy of the late republic and early
     empire of *omnium linguarum histriones*, Suet. *DJ* 39.1; *Aug.* 43.1;
     the actors of Tac. *Ann.* 14.15.1 are *pantomimi*, see E.Koester-
     mann ad loc.

48   The main sources are Strabo 13.1.54 (608); Plut. *Sulla* 26.

49   T.P.Wiseman, *Greece and Rome* n.s. XXI (1974), 162-4, see also
     Cic. *Brut.* 174; *de leg.* 1.53; compare Antonius' marriage of
     Athena, perhaps in imitation of Antiochus IV, who *se simulabat
     Hierapoli Dianam ducere uxorem* (Licinianus XXVIII, p.5, lines
     213 Flemisch = 9 Bonn).

50   H.W.Parke and D.E.W.Wormell, *The Delphic oracle* (Oxford, 1956),
     nos.593 (cf. Dion. Hal. 1.49.3), 438-41, 596.

51   Crawford (1974), no.419/2.

52   L.Licinius Crassus owned two *scyphi* by Mentor (Pliny, *NH* 33.147),
     Varro owned a bronze statue by him (154) and admired his work
     (Nonius 99, 16 M = 141 L), compare Diodorus of Lilybaeum owning
     pocula by him (Cic. II *Verr.* 4.38); *mentoreum opus* epitomized
     silver ware for Propertius, 1.14.2, 4.9.13, also for Juvenal
     and Martial, G.Lippold, *RE* XV 966-7.
        For perfumes see J.Colin, 'Luxe oriental et parfums mas-
     culins dans la Rome Alexandrine (d'après Cicéron et Lucrèce)',
     RBPh XXXIII (1955), 5.

53   Sherk 22, lines 2-3; for his praetorship see also Cic. *pro Corn.*
     cited by Asconius 74C with comment of Asconius; for his use of
     adsentio, not *adsentior*, in senatorial debates see Varro in
     Gellius 2.25.9; Quint. 1.5.13.

54   H.Peter, cccliii-cccliv.

55   Asconius 13C; cf. 69C. There is nothing to be made of the his-
     torian L.Aelius Tubero, legate of Q.Cicero in 61 (Cic. *ad QF.*
     1.1.10), to be distinguished from Q.Aelius Tubero, probably of
     the triumviral period, whose fragments are in H.Peter, 308-12;
     or of L.Scribonius Libo, whose *Annalis* (*Liber*) is used by Cicero
     in working out the names of the ten legates who settled Greece

in 146 (*ad Att*. 13.30.3, 32.3, perhaps also 44.3; see E.Badian, *Hommages Renard*, Coll. Lat. CI, 54-65).

56 For a critique of his oratorical style see *Brut*. 238; the absence of mention of his history is without significance, compare 95 on C.Sempronius Tuditanus and 110-16 on P.Rutilius Rufus. Macer was condemned before Cicero as praetor *de repetundis* in 66.

57 Compare *Brut*. 228 for a discussion of Sisenna as an orator (also 259) and a more favourable estimate of his historical style. I am not persuaded that Sisenna treated Sulla in his history in a way analogous to that in which Cleitarchus is supposed to have eulogized Alexander, against H.Peter, cccxlii-cccxliii.

58 Sent to Atticus early in 60 (*ad Att*. 1.19.10, 20.6).

59 Cic. *ad Att*. 2.1.1, published in due course, Nepos, *Att*. 18.6.

60 Cic. *ad Att*. 2.1.1 (Posidonius), 1.20.6 (others); an earlier attempt to get Archias to celebrate Cicero's consulship in verse came to nothing, *pro Arch*. 28; *ad Att*. 1.16.15.

61 See, recently, J.M.André, 'Cicéron et Lucrèce', *Mélanges Boyancé* (Rome, 1974), 21. Contrast the interest displayed at Rome in the *didascalia* of the Athenian theatre, L.Moretti, *Ath*. n.s. XXXVIII (1960), 263-81.

62 See H.Dahlmann, *RE*, Supp. VI 1174.

63 Cic. II *Verr*. 4.4 (for the term *idiotes* compare Strabo 1.2.8 (19)); compare Cicero's admiration of the way in which Greek literature was appreciated everywhere, *pro Arch*. 23.

64 M.A.Trouard (n.34), 45-51, documents the defence that Rome would in due course have reached the same level as the Greeks, but had had other things to do with her time; also the defence that Rome put such things as geometry and philosophy to practical purposes; J.Vogt, *Ciceros Glaube an Rom* (Stuttgart, 1935), 24, documents the defence that Greek culture helped to bring out Roman virtues; A.E.Wardman, *Rome's debt to Greece* (London, 1976), 150-1, documents the Roman emphasis on their sages as a defence against the lack of philosophers.

65 Cic. *pro Mur*. 58-66; Cicero admits the flattery, *de fin*. 4.74.

66 For the Roman concern with appearances see *pro Mur*. 62; and compare Lucian, *de mercede conductis* 25 for the insincerity of Roman interest in Greek culture. H.D.Jocelyn (1977), 323, concludes that Greek philosophy had little real influence in Rome.

67 See, for instance, L.Moretti, *RFIC* XCIII (1965), 283-7, for the Epicurean Philonides interceding for Laodicea with the Seleucid authorities after the murder of Cn. Octavius.

68   See the characterization of A.E.Douglas commenting on Cic.
     Brut. 239; further ritual compliments appear at *pro Sest.* 107;
     pro Balb. 15.
         W.S.Anderson (1963) likewise also argues that Pompeius
     was a patron of the arts in the interests of prestige; I am
     unable to follow his argument that Pompeius with his *philoi*
     played a decisive role in the emergence of the *consilium prin-
     cipis*; this emerged from traditional Roman institutions.

69   Plut. *Pomp.* 78; App. *BC* 2.85.358 (lines of Sophocles); Plut.
     Pomp. 79; Zonaras 10.9 (speech).

70   W.S.Anderson (1963), 34.

71   Note that he advocated proscription in 49, Cic. *ad Att.* 9.11.3.

72   Anderson (1963), 28.

73   Note the detailed emulation of Alexander involved and compare
     the later gifts perhaps of Lucullus and certainly of Ap.
     Claudius Pulcher and Caesar and the intended gift of Cicero.

74   Plut. *Luc.* 1; compare *Luc.* 4 and *Sull.* 6; as an orator Lucullus
     is described simply as *acutus* by Cicero, *Brut.* 222, compare
     Plut. *Luc.* 33, a good and thoughtful speaker, and the more ex-
     tended eulogy in *Luc.* 1.

75   Plut. *Luc.* 1; Lucullus claimed that the *barbara et soloeca* in
     the work were inserted deliberately, Cic. *ad Att.* 1.19.10,
     clearly not acquainted with it; I see no reason to suppose that
     the Greek piece on the Marsic War known to Plutarch is by Lucullus.
         For the type of competition involved compare Sisenna's
     challenge to Hortensius to memorize the proceedings of an auc-
     tion, Sen. *Contr.* 1, pref. 19; Quint. 11.2.24; also Cic. *Brutus*
     301.

76   Strabo 12.3.11 (546); Plut. *Luc.* 42.1-4.

77   Cic. *pro Arch.* 21; *ad Att.* 1.16.15; see *Acad. pr.* 2.4 for cele-
     brations in Greek and Latin of the deeds of Lucullus.

78   *Acad. pr.* 2.4.11 and 61, compare Plut. *Luc.* 42.1-4; *Luc.* 28
     (treatise).

79   Cic. *ad Att.* 6.1.25, with commentary of D.R.Shackleton Bailey;
     Herodes is presumably also the teacher of M. Cicero junior in
     44 (n.44), perhaps also the general of *IG* II 488 (so F.Münzer,
     RE VIII 920) = *IG* II-III^2 1051.

80   App. *BC* 2.88.368; Athens was the symbol of Greek civilization.

81   App. *BC* 4.65-7.278-83 (Rhodes); Bowersock (1965), 33, n.1
     (Alexandria).
         A city could also profit from its religious aura, note
     the case of Hieracome and Perperna, P.Servilius Isauricus and
     others, Tac. *Ann.* 3.62, Aphrodisias and Sulla, Delos in 67,

Eleusis and the two sides in 48 (App. *BC* 2.70.293; compare the
initiation of Sulla).

82 Strabo 13.1.66 (614); Posidonius, fr. 253 Edelstein-Kidd.

83 My view of Posidonius is thus radically different from that of
P.Treves, in *La filosofia greca e il diritto romano* (Acc. Naz.
dei Lincei, Quad. 221), 27, speculating that Posidonius was
led by his own rootlessness to formulate the notion of the
cosmopolis.

Chapter 10. The beneficial ideology

1 B.Keil, *Aelii Aristeidis Smyrnaei quae supersunt omnia* II
(Berlin, 1898), XXX; J.J.Reiske, *Opuscula medica ex monumentis
Arabum et Ebraeorum* (Halle, 1776), 5.

2 B.Forte, *Rome and the Romans as the Greeks saw them* (Rome, 1972),
395-415, provides a broader range of evidence than Palm (1959),
60-2, but is entirely lacking in sophistication or penetration.
Boulanger (1923), 341-91, is still valuable.

3 Oliver (1953) assembles a mass of comparative material; see
also below, n.57.

4 Boulanger (1923), 381; B.P.Reardon, *Courants littéraires grecs*
(Paris, 1971), 127-42. Still less can be derived from an emphasis on Aristeides' sincerity as asserted by H.Bengtson, 'Das
Imperium Romanum im griechischer Sicht', *Gymnasium* LXXI (1964),
160-6.

5 An approach indicated by Bleicken (1966). I have been unable
to see W.Gernentz, *Laudes Romae* (Diss., Rostock, 1918).

6 The Roman tradition is given by F.Christ (1938) and by L.R.Lind,
'Concept, action and character: the reasons for Rome's greatness', *TAPhA* CIII (1972), 235-84; cf. also E.M.Sanford, 'Contrasting views of the Roman empire', *AJP* LVIII (1937),436-56.

7 E.g. *Anth. Pal.* 16.40 (Crinagoras); Dion. Hal. *Ant.* 2.9.2-3;
Plut. 314C; Dio 1.20, 3.83-5; App. *BC* Pf. 1-11; Arist. 27.24-6,
21.5-7, 35.5-11.

8 A. von Stylow, *Libertas und Liberalitas* (Munich, 1972); contrast
A.H.M.Jones (1974), 62-4, 81.

9 C.P.Jones (1971), 32-4.

10 J. von Arnim, *Leben und Werke des Dio von Prusa* (Berlin, 1898);
A.N.Sherwin-White, *The letters of Pliny* (Oxford, 1966), 675-9.

11 Philostratus, *VS* 214 (Loeb); Arist. 50.63; C.A.Behr, *Aelius
Aristeides and the Sacred Tales* (Amsterdam, 1968), 3; L.Robert,
Etudes Anatoliennes (Paris, 1937), 207-22, produced strong

evidence for property near Hadrianoutherae, but this need not disprove Philostratus' reference to Hadriani.

12 Gal. 6.755, 14.17, 6.552, 10.561. Arabic sources (Rosenthal (1975), 35) said his grandfather was a surveyor and his great-grandfather head of the carpenters' guild. He himself may have participated in politics, 6.412, possibly in the *boule* of Pergamum: his opinions were markedly Platonic and oligarchic (cf. 10.10–11, 5.303).

13 B.Baldwin, *Studies in Lucian* (Toronto, 1973), 12–14; on peasants, Gal. 17B.49.

14 Gal. *Comm. VI in Epid. II*: *CMG* V 10.1, p.402; G.Strohmaier, 'Übersehenes zur Biographie Galens', *Philologus* CXX (1976), 117–22.

15 Bowersock (1969), 114–16.

16 Bowersock (1969), 43–88, esp. 45–7.

17 H.G.Pflaum, 'Lucien de Samosate, archistator praefecti Augusti', *MEFR* LXXI (1959), 281–4; for Plutarch, Syncellus 659; Suda s.v. Plutarchos, with C.P.Jones (1971), 34 and V.Nutton, *CQ* n.s. XXI (1971), 271.

18 Bleicken (1966), 267–9; F.Christ (1938), 103–10; A.D.Nock, *JTS* n.s. V (1954), 250: note esp., among primary sources, *Anth. Pal.* 16.61 (Crinagoras); Strabo 288; Epict. 3.13.9, 4.5.17; Plut. 317A–C, 408B; Arist. 23.54; *IGR* III 721, III 1376; *SIG* 797–8; *OGIS* 458; *AGIBM* 894; *IPriene* 105.35–6.

19 Arist. 26.76–84, 35.35–6. The attempt of C.P.Jones, 'Aelius Aristeides, Εἰς βασιλέα, *JRS* LXII (1972), 134–52, to prove the authenticity of this speech is not convincing.

20 Arist. 26.11–13, 100; cf. Irenaeus 4.46.2–3, and on the same *topos*, Menander 230 (cited throughout in the pagination of Walz).

21 Palm (1959), 114–16: cf. Athenagoras, *Leg.* 1.

22 Tertullian, *De anima* 30; a similar, if ironic, comment on African prosperity may be deduced from *Anth. Pal.* 7.626.

23 Plut. 814F; Dio 31.111; Bleicken (1966), 240–63.

24 Hence the part played by concord in the speeches of Dio and Aristeides and even in Galen, 19.46; note also Lucian, *Dem.* 64; Philostr. *VA* 1.15; Plut. 824D; M.Aurelius, quoted by Arist. 23.73; Menander 250; *IG* XII 5.906; *EG* 877b; C.P.Jones (1971), 114–15.

25 Oliver (1953), 891–2; Bleicken (1966), 243, n.40.

26 Arist. 20.15. The same words are also applied to the sack of Eleusis, 22.1.

27 Arist. 27.32, 23.11; Gal. 14.217 (cf. Rosenthal (1975), 35). The opinion of a Jewish rabbi that Gen. 1.31 'Behold it was very good' applied to the Roman empire is characterized by Schürer-Vermes-Millar (1973), 381, n.126, as a minority view among the Jews.

28 Plut. 814D. The theory of *origo* as determining a man's obligations develops from the mid-second century: see D.Nörr, 'Origo', *Tijdschr. v. Rechtsgeschiedenis* XXXI (1963), 525-600.

29 Oliver (1953), 958; note also the use of the words in *GVI* 1975.

30 F.Christ (1938), 113-14; Statius, *Silv.* 5.3.185.

31 *Anth. Pal.* 6.236, 9.285 (Philip); cf. Philo, *Leg.* 552, 556; App. pref. 8.

32 Oliver (1953), 958-80, although his choice of examples is largely irrelevant; J.Triantophyllopoulos, 'Griechisch-römische Nomokrasie vor der Constitutio Antoniniana', *Akten VI Kongr. Epigr.* (Munich, 1973), 169-91.

33 L.Mitteis, *Reichsrecht und Volksrecht* (Leipzig, 1891), remains fundamental; Sherwin-White (1973), 312, 392; Talamanca (1971); Wieling (1974); H.Wolff, *Die Constitutio Antoniniana und Papyrus Gissensis 40.1* (Diss., Cologne, 1976), 80-7, 114.

34 Bardesanes, *Liber legum, Patr. Syr.* 1.2, 598, 602; Greg. Thaumaturgos, *Paneg. ad Origenem* 1.7, *Patr. Graec.* 10.1052, rightly rejected by Wieling (1974), 372; *contra*, V.Arangio-Ruiz, 'L'application du droit romain en Egypte après la Constitution Antoninienne', *Bull. Inst. Eg.* XXIX (1946-7), 94-6.

35 Menander 227, cf. L.Robert, 'Les femmes théores à Ephèse', *CRAI* 1974, 176-81; on Menander's date and the problem of authenticity, see Talamanca (1971), 475-7; H.Maehler, 'Menander Rhetor and Alexander Claudius in a papyrus letter', *GRBS* XV (1974), 305-11.

36 Wieling (1974), 373, criticizes Talamanca (1971), 456, for applying *politeuometha* (M. 202) to both public and private law, but the context and Menander's other references show that Wieling's insistence on public law alone would have been rejected by Menander; cf. Talamanca (1971), 554.

37 Talamanca (1971), 482-3, 502, 557; Wieling (1974), 372-3, but his arguments are of variable worth.

38 CJ. 8.52.1; J.A.C.Thomas, 'Custom and Roman law', *Tijdschr. v. Rechtsgesch.* XXXI (1963), 43-52; E.Levy, *Gesammelte Schriften* I (Cologne, Graz, 1963), 291-3.

39 CJ. 6.23.9; contrast CJ 6.32.2 (Valerian and Gallienus), which apparently allowed it. Presumably the *privilegium speciale* was

available to (some) *civitates liberae*.

40 CJ. 10.32.36 (383): a mother's *origo* or *domicilium* was no
    longer to be taken into account in determining the *origo* of
    a son.

41 L.Mitteis, *Reichsrecht und Volksrecht* (Leipzig, 1891), 161-4;
    J.A.C.Thomas, *Tijdschr. v. Rechtsgesch.* XXXI (1963), 43.

42 Arist. 26.100. For a fuller exposition of the argument of
    this paragraph see 'Two notes on immunities', *JRS* LXI (1971),
    57-60.

43 Sherwin-White (1973), 428-9.

44 Repeated by Arist. at 24.31; cf. Artemidorus 1.13; Apollonius
    of Tyana, *Ep.* 44; Musonius 9 (p.42, Hense).

45 F.Christ (1938), 81-3; used by Arist. 23.62 and Menander 202.

46 G.Strohmaier, 'Der Arzt in der römischen Gesellschaft: Neues
    aus der arabischen Galenüberlieferung?' *Acta Conventus XI
    Eirene* (Warsaw, 1968), 69-70; Gal. 14.62.

47 Arist. 26.100; Eusebius, *Dem. Ev.* 7.2.22; *Laud. Const.* 16.7.

48 A.H.M.Jones (1974), 102.

49 F.Millar, 'Emperors at work', *JRS* LVII (1967), 9-19.

50 Plut. 814C; in general, see C.P.Jones (1971), 110-21.

51 F.Christ (1938), 92-7.

52 Agathias, *Hist.* 2.17; cf. also G.W.Bowersock, *Augustus and the
    Greek world* (Oxford, 1965), 157.

53 Arist. 19; cf. Arist. 20; Philostr. *VS* 214-16.

54 W.H.Buckler, 'T. Statilius Crito, Traiani Aug. medicus', *JOÄI*
    XXX (1936-7), Beibl. 5-8.

55 Arist. 32.15; Gal., 14.217-18, reports that the emperors pro-
    vided drugs for friends and subjects in need.

56 Dio 48.8; Philostr. *VA* 5.32; Plut. *Cato Maior* 23.3; Philo, *Leg.*
    147. Dio, 2.79, implicitly compares his position as adviser
    to Trajan with that of Aristotle to Alexander.

57 Arist. 26.74-85; Menander 230; P.A.Brunt (1974); A.Michel, 'De
    Socrate à Maxime de Tyr: les problèmes sociaux de l'armée dans
    l'idéologie romaine', *REL* XLVII (1969), 237-51.

58 Gal. 10.632-3, possibly augmented from another (Galenic?) source
    in the biography of Galen by al-Mubaššir (Rosenthal (1975), 35);
    Roman buildings in general are also mentioned in a Jewish source,

Babylon Talmud, *Shabbat* 56b. I have also excluded the arithmetical poem of Metrodorus on the road distances between Gades and Rome (*Anth. Pal.* 14.121) and such epigrams as that of Philip on the new mole at Puteoli (*Anth. Pal.* 9.108).

59 Discussed in detail by P.M.Duval, 'Construction d'une voie romaine d'après les textes antiques', *BSAF* 1959, 176-86; cf. also F.Lämmli, *Homo faber* (Basle, 1968), 71.

60 Above, n.18.

61 Epigraphic references include: *ILS* 9469; *AE* 1926, 77; *NdS* 1888, 621; *CIL* X 6849; *ILS* 291, 5866; see also R.Paribeni, *Optimus Princeps* (Messina, 1927), 120-49; G.Radke, *RE*, Supp. XIII (1973), 1513-15, 1641-2; T.Pekary, *Untersuchungen zu den römischen Reichstrassen* (Bonn, 1968), 8-10.

62 Cf. L.Friedländer, *Sittengeschichte Roms*, ed. 10 (Leipzig, 1922), 318-20, for Roman roads reputedly surviving in use until the sixteenth century.

63 Not that the literary evidence is much better: the test of a good emperor in the Sibylline Oracles 12 and 13 is the crude one of peace or war, and consequent gifts to cities; see Sherwin-White (1973), 430-2.

64 L.Robert, 'Epigrammes relatives à des gouverneurs', *Hellenica* IV (Paris, 1948), 35-114.

65 Especially the honorary decrees for magistrates, foreign judges, doctors and athletes; only when the magnates of the east themselves become Roman officials are such magistracies regularly considered worthy of fulsome commemoration, e.g. *IPerg. Ascl.* 21; *IGR* III 173, 174; *ILS* 9471; *SEG* 17.584; *Hellenica* 11-12, 463-4; Nock (1972), 732-3.

66 E.g. *EG* 858-60; *GVI* 1107; Nock (1972), 727-30.

67 *GVI* 1156, 1099 (= *EG* 434), 818, 1112; cf. also *GVI* 1068 (Athens), 1983 (Syria); *TAM* 3.127 (Solyma and Termessus).

68 Cf. *EG* 903-8, 911-14, 919; epigrams and commemorative inscriptions continue to be erected to local magistrates but, as Robert noted, *Hellenica* 4 (1948), 109, they became far rarer.

69 Firmicus Maternus 4.4.4, 3.5.21; cf. R.MacMullen, 'Social history in astrology', *AncSoc.* II (1971), 113.

70 Menander 233, deriving in part from Arist. 26.31-3, but attributing greater power and independence to the governor.

71 Although Menander, like Philostratus in his *Lives of the Sophists*, in no way implies a break with the cultural and civic traditions of the past; indeed he expects them to stretch well into the future.

72 E.Levy, 'Von römischen Precarium zur germanischen Landleihe', *ZSS* LXVI (1948), 17-25.

73 P.Brown, 'The rise and function of the holy man in late antiquity', *JRS* LXI (1971), 80-101, esp. 85-7.

74 As in the famous case of Polemo, Philostratus, *VS* 112-14, with Bowersock (1969), 48-9, and T.D.Barnes, 'In Attali gratiam', *Historia* XVIII (1969), 383-4. For Aristeides himself, see Bowersock (1969), 30-42, and my note, *JRS* LXI (1971), 52-4.

75 This situation, which can be posited of Greece, Asia Minor and possibly Syria, did not obtain in Egypt, according to A.K.Bowman, 'Some aspects of the reform of Diocletian in Egypt', *Akten XIII Intern. Papyrologenkongr.* (Munich, 1974), 43-51, where there was an attempt made to foist more administrative responsibility onto the *curiales*, probably as a result of problems and difficulties elsewhere in the empire. This may also represent a reversion to the norm and a reaction against the earlier domination of the central government and administration in that province.

Chapter 11. Rome's African empire under the Principate

1 I wish to thank C.R.Whittaker, B.D.Shaw and R.P.Saller for critical comment on an earlier draft of this paper. I am particularly grateful to C.R.Whittaker for sharing ideas as well as bibliographical references.

2 I am concerned only with the more obvious material benefits, economic, social and political. I do not, for example, discuss the possible advantage for those at the top of the social pyramid of being culturally allied with the imperial power.

3 Only one side of the argument is presented by A.Demans, 'Matériaux et réflexions pour servir à une étude du développement et du sous-développement dans les provinces de l'empire romain', in H.Temporini, ed., *Aufstieg und Niedergang der römischen Welt*, II 3 (Berlin, 1975), 3-97.

4 C.Lepelley, 'Declin ou stabilité de l'agriculture africaine au Bas-Empire? A propos d'une Loi de l'empereur Honorius', *AntAfr* I (1976), 135ff.

5 Pliny's assertion that the senators owned half of Proconsularis (as it then was) need not be believed. For possible estates of Augustus, see *CIL* VIII 12314 (Bisica); *ILT* 213 (Sidi Habich); cf. Pliny, *NH* 18.94-5. Note the *vicus Augusti* near Vaga. Augustus may have inherited a marble quarry at Simitthus from Agrippa. See I.Shatzman, *Senatorial wealth and politics* (Brussels, 1976), 366, citing *CIL* VIII 14580-2 (*officina Agrippae*)and the use of the marble in Augustan public buildings in Rome. A (Numidian) 'royal quarry' (*officina*

regia) is also attested, see *CIL* VIII 14578-9, 14583; this probably became imperial property under the empire.

6   See D.J.Crawford (1976); Millar (1977), 133ff.; T.Kotula, 'Rozwój Terytorialny i Organizacja Latyfundiów w Rzymskiej Afryce w Okresie Wczesnego Cesarstwa', *Eos* XLVI (1952-3), 113ff.

7   Agennius Urbicus in C.Thulin, ed., *Corpus Agrimensorum Romanorum* I (1913), 45. On the source of this passage Professor O.A.W.Dilke kindly gave me this opinion: 'Agennius Urbicus is late, but at least fifty per cent of his text seems to be taken almost verbatim from an early empire writer, thought by Lachmann to be Frontinus. Whether Frontinus or not, I think he and Thulin are right in thinking so, and it may well be of Frontinus' period.' The relevant passage comes from the early writer. The evidence for private *saltus* in the late republic and early empire is summarized in Haywood (1938), 28ff., 83ff.

8   P.Leveau, 'Paysanneries antiques du pays Beni-Menacer: à propos des "ruines romaines" de la région de Cherchel (Algérie)', *BCTH* VIII (1972), 3ff., at 19.

9   Cf. Amm. Marc. 29.5.13 (a *fundus Petrensis*, built up *in modum urbis*); John Matthews, 'Mauretania in Ammianus and the Notitia', in *Aspects of the Notitia Dignitatum*, ed. R.Goodburn and P. Bartholomew, BAR Supplem. Series XV (1976), 157ff.

10 *ILAlg*. II 616; cf. 615. One of the men was C.Arrius Antoninus, cf. the advocate and consul of c. A.D. 170, *PIR*[2] A 1088. This inscription is to be set alongside another from Cirtan territory discussed in N.Charbonnel and S.Demougin, 'Un marché en Numidie au IIIe siècle après J.-C.', *RHDFE* LIV (1976), 559ff.

11 Imperial property is indicated at *CIL* VIII 18813, Aquae Thibilitanae (Hammam Meskoutine), 9 km from Thibilis, and not far from the provincial border with Africa Proconsularis. On Cirta and its territory, see *ILAlg*. II p.40; U.Laffi, *Adtributio e contributio* (Pisa, 1966), 135ff.

12 App. *BC* 4.54; cf. L.Teutsch, *Das Städtewesen in Nordafrika in der Zeit von C.Gracchus bis zum Tode des Kaisers Augustus* (Berlin, 1962), 65ff. (Sittius); Vitruv. 8.3.24ff. (Julius): *cuius erant totius oppidi agrorum possessiones*.

13 I use 'African' in this and later sections to designate African-born individuals, whatever their ultimate family origins.

14 The first consular was a Pactumeius, one of two brothers adlected *inter praetorios* by Vespasian, consul in the 70s. See *ILAlg*. II 642-4 (Cirta). Other early consulars: P.Pactumeius Clemens, *suff.* 138, *ILAlg*. II 645; Q.Lollius Urbicus, *suff.* c. 135, *ILAlg*. II 3446, 3563, 3605, etc.; M.Cornelius Fronto, *suff.* 143; etc. In general, Fronto, *ad amicos* 2.10: *Alii quoque plurimi sunt in senatu Cirtenses clarissimi viri*.

15 The phrase giving the location of the property is corrupt (*et unum fundum invenit etiam*), but cf. Stat. *Silv.* 4.5.54-5 (Veii); *CIL* XI 3816 (near Veii).

16 Tac. *Ann.* 12.23; Dio 52.42.6-7, 50.25.6; Suet. *Cl.* 23.2.

17 A clear case is Herodes Atticus, consul (143), sophist and grand seigneur of Attica, *PIR*[2] C 802. Athens also attracted the historian Arrian, consul (129), and in his adopted city archon (145-6) and prytanis (166-7, 169-70), *PIR*[2] F 219. Their contemporary at Ephesos, P.Vedius Antoninus Phaedrus Sabinianus, was first of his family to attain senatorial rank but seems to have made little use of it. He is conspicuous as magistrate, envoy and benefactor of Ephesos. See e.g. *IBrit.Mus.* III 491 (= *Syll*[3] 850); 492.

18 For African *viri clarissimi* at home in the late empire, see e.g. *CIL* VIII 1633; 24069.

19 See n.14 above.

20 This is a theme of E.J.Champlin, 'An historical study of Fronto of Cirta', D.Phil. thesis, Oxford, 1976, ch.1.

21 *ad M.Caes.* 1.10.5 (ed. van den Hout, pp.22-3; A.D. 143, the year of his consulship). Cf. Stat. *Silv.* 4.5.45-6: *non sermo Poenus, non habitus tibi / externa non mens; Italus, Italus.*

21 *ILAlg.* II 638. This man is probably the learned Iulius Celsinus, dubbed 'The Numidian' by his friend A.Gellius, who helped Fronto in a duel with a self-confident *grammaticus.* See A.Gell. 19.7.2, 10.1 and 11.

23 S.Gsell, C.A.Joly, *Khamissa, Mdaourouch, Announa.* III *Announa.* (Alger, 1918), 81ff.; see *PIR*[2] A 754,757.

24 For a famous example, see *MEFR* 75 (1963), 398: C.Septimius Severus, procos. of Africa in 173-4, and his legate L.Septimius Severus, at Leptis Magna. For equestrians in employment in Africa, see Jarrett (1972), e.g. nos.7,9,14,17,23,58,59, etc.

25 This inscription was brought to my attention in this connexion by Miss Joyce Reynolds.

26 The clearest cases concern army officers. See Jarrett (1972), e.g. nos.5,8,15,37,41,42, etc. For possible examples of ex-procurators at home, see nos.47,82,89,92,100,126. Cf. Duncan-Jones (1967), 168-9.

27 See the lists compiled by Duncan-Jones (1967) and Pflaum (1968).

28 Equestrians of Cirta and environs: *ILAlg.* II 10,11,29,35,36,479 = *ILS* 6858, 481,500,528,529,560,569,617,648,649,685-6,689,690, 696,697,705,794(3),796,798(1+),799, 3610-11; *CIL* VIII 5534,18912 = *ILS* 6856. Equestrian officials from Cirta and environs: *ILAlg.* II 570; 665 = *ILS* 1437; 671 = *ILS* 5549; *CIL* VIII 5532; 18909 = *ILS* 9017; 18892; *BAC* 1917, p.336.

29 For African society as reflected by Apuleius see the admirable
    thesis of E.Matthews, 'The social background of the Apologia
    and Florida of Apuleius', B.Phil. thesis, Oxford, 1968; also
    H.Pavis d'Escurac, 'Pour une étude sociale de l'Apologie
    d'Apulée', *AntAfr* VIII (1974), 89ff.

30 The wealth of the curial class is discussed by Duncan-Jones
    (1963).

31 Some scholars have assumed that small-scale landownership in
    North Africa was essentially linked with the imperial policy
    of assigning land to discharged soldiers. See H. d'Escurac
    Doisy, 'Notes sur le phénomène associatif dans le monde paysan',
    AntAfr I (1967), 59ff., following P.Romanelli, 'Brevi note
    sulla distribuzione della piccola e grande proprietà agricola
    nell'Africa Romana', *Atti del primo congresso nazionale di
    studi romani* (Rome, 1929), 340ff. This seems unlikely. 200-300
    soldiers were demobilized each year in normal circumstances
    (some of whom may not have settled on the land); their life-
    expectancy after discharge would have been low; and land was
    also assigned to tribesmen (I discuss this below). It remains
    likely that veterans had better title to their land than tribes-
    men, and that they had a better chance of maintaining their pos-
    ition because of the tax-free status of their land.

32 See R.P.Duncan-Jones, 'Some configurations of landholding in
    the Roman empire', in M.I.Finley (ed.), *Studies in Roman Prop-
    erty* (Cambridge, 1976), 18ff.

33 Jones (1964), 636.

34 Brunt (1971), 589ff.; cf. Gascou (1972), 24ff.

35 Romanelli (1959), 207.

36 Cf. *CIL* VIII 885 = 12387: *pagus Mercurialis veteranorum Mede-
    litanorum*; 20834 = *ILS* 6885 (Rapidum).

37 For the details see Gascou (1972). Many of Augustus' colonies
    also had a strategic purpose.

38 H. d'Escurac-Doisy, op.cit. n.31; Gascou (1972) (Verecunda and
    Lambaesis).

39 Jones (1964), 652-3, citing *IRT* 880 (A.D. 244-6); P.Trousset,
    *Recherches sur le limes Tripolitanus du Chott El-Djerid à la
    frontière tunico-libyenne* (Paris, 1974). Earlier work by
    Goodchild (and Ward-Perkins) may be conveniently consulted in
    Joyce Reynolds, ed., *Libyan studies: select papers of the late
    R.G.Goodchild* (London, 1976), chs.2-4.

40 *CIL* VIII 22786 a,f,k = *ILS* 9375 (A.D. 29-30). For refs. see
    most recently Bénabou (1976), 433, 438.

41 A.Berthier, 'Nicibes et Suburbures: nomades ou sédentaires?',
    BAA III (1968), 293ff.

42 For this view, see J.Lancel, 'Suburbures et Nicibes: une in-
    scription de Tigisis', *Libyca* III (1955), 289ff.

43 J.Despois, *Le Hodna (Algérie)* (Paris, 1953), III.

44 The inscription was published by L.Leschi, 'Une assignation de
    terres en Afrique sous Septime Sévère', *Etudes d'épigraphie et
    d'histoire africaines* (Paris, 1957), 75ff. Bénabou (1976),
    172, following Leschi, thinks the recipients were *coloni par-
    tiarii*, but does not see that they were tribesmen.

45 The economic significance of the nomads, and particularly their
    role as seasonal labourers, were first brought home to me by my
    colleague C.R.Whittaker in a paper delivered to a colloquium in
    Cambridge in September 1975. These matters are fully discussed
    in his forthcoming paper 'Land and labour in North Africa'.

46 For the tariff list from Zarai (*CIL* VIII 4508), see conveniently
    Haywood (1938), 80ff.

47 T.Précheur-Canonge, *La vie rurale en Afrique romaine d'après les
    mosaiques*, n.d., planche 1, photo 1. I owe this reference to
    Elaine Matthews.

48 The military confrontation with the nomads is the subject of
    Rachet (1970), see esp. ch.2. For regular soldiers guarding es-
    tates, see *CIL* VIII 14603 = *ILS* 2305 (late J/Cl., *saltus Philo-
    musianus*).

49 See e.g. *ILAlg.* I 1927, with R.Syme, 'Tacfarinas, the Musulamii
    and Thubursicu', in P.R.Coleman-Norton, ed., *Studies in Roman
    economy and society in honor of A.C.Johnson* (Princeton, 1951),
    113ff.; *CIL* VIII 22729 (Gigthis); Gascou (1972), 134ff. (Turris
    Tamelleni).

50 The laws are best known from the imperial *saltus* inscriptions.
    See conveniently Haywood (1938), 89ff. For a full discussion,
    C.Courtois *et al.*, *Tablettes Albertini* (Paris, 1952).

51 The phrase is from A.Piganiol, 'La politique agraire d'Hadrien',
    Les Empereurs romains d'Espagne (Paris, 1965), at 135. See also
    Bénabou (1976), 181. Both writers refer to Rostovtzeff, who was
    evidently the source of their views. See Rostovtzeff (1957),
    367ff., 405ff.

52 See W.L.Westermann, 'Hadrian's decree on renting state domains
    in Egypt', *JEA* XI (1925), 165ff. There is a hint of a possible
    parallel to the African legislation in an unpublished inscrip-
    tion from Delphi involving civic land. See *BCH* 1944-5, 75
    (A.D. 125).

53 L.Leschi, 'La vigne et le vin dans l'Afrique ancienne', in
    Etudes d'épigraphie et d'histoire africaines (Paris, 1957),
    80ff.

54 J.Peyras, 'Le Fundus Aufidianus: étude d'un grand domaine romain

de la région de Mateur (Tunisie du Nord)', *AntAfr* IX (1975), 181ff. The points I have discussed here were raised in an earlier article: see Garnsey (1976).

55 *ILAfr.* 568. For A.Gabinius Quir. Datus pater see also *CIL* VIII 26467-9; *ILAfr.* 515; *ILTun.* 1511. I follow J.Carcopino, 'Fermier général ou sociétés publicaines?', *REA* XXIV (1922) 13ff., who stands by the reading of the stone (*conductoris*), rejecting the emendation (*conductori*) which turns Gabinius into a grand *conductor*.

56 See Jones (1964), 417-19, 788-9.

57 See Brunt (1976).

58 If (*exempli gratia*) the *curiales* were 25,000 out of 8 million Africans (see Duncan-Jones (1963), 170), they made up 0.3 per cent of the population.

59 J.Kolendo, 'Sur le colonat en Afrique préromaine', *Neue Beiträge zur Geschichte der alten Welt*, II (Berlin, 1965), 45ff.; Kolendo (1976), 23ff. Cf. H.Kreissig, 'Bemerkungen zur Produktionsweise in Nordafrika (vorrömische Zeit), *Afrika und Rom in der Antike*, ed. H.-J.Diesner, *et al.* (Halle, 1968), 135-42. The thesis of continuity between Roman and pre-Roman periods, advanced tentatively in the text, is argued fully by C.R. Whittaker in his forthcoming paper 'Land and labour in North Africa'.

60 Gsell (1928), I 302 n.2, 465, II 299ff., IV 47. The main texts, not all referring specifically to agricultural slaves, are Diod. 14.77, 20.69.2; Just. 21.4.6; Polyb. 15.18.1; App. *Lib.* 9,15, 24,59; Livy 21.45.7, 29.29.2; Sall. *Bell. Iug.* 44.5.

61 The evidence of the mosaics is inconclusive. Joyce Reynolds writes from Tripoli that it was not the intention of the Zliten mosaicists depicting agricultural workers to show Negroid types or black faces.

62 The evidence is presented in full by Gsell (1932), 397ff. I am not convinced by the thesis of E.M.Schtajerman, *Die Krise der Sklavenhalterordnung im Westen des römischen Reiches*, tr. W. Seyfarth (Berlin 1964), 185-204.

63 Gsell (1932), 407 n.1, suggests implausibly that they were 'des serfs tenanciers'.

64 Cf. D. 20.1.32: '*Praediorum pars sine colonis fuit, eaque actori suo colenda ... tradidit adsignatis et servis culturae necessariis.*'

65 Gsell (1932), 401-2.

66 This is implied by the frequent references in inscriptions to free *coloni*, especially on imperial estates. The *saltus* inscriptions refer once to *servi domini*, but their functions are not specified (*CIL* VIII 25902, IV ℓ.39).

67 M.Hombert, C.Préaux, *Recherches sur le recensement dans l'Egypte romain* (Leiden, 1952), 170.

68 On taxation under the Principate see Jones (1974). I have also derived considerable benefit from P.A.Brunt, 'Direct taxation under the Roman Principate', London University Special Lectures, Jan. 1972, unpublished.

69 The Roman army in Britain numbered perhaps 40-50,000 men, see S.S.Frere, *Britannia* (London, 1967), 157ff. Africa, in contrast, was garrisoned by c. 12-13,000, see Ch.-Picard (1959), 7; cf. Rachet (1970), 61.

70 Pol. 11.25.9-26.1; cf. Livy 28.25.9-10 (*exactores*, who could only have been soldiers). In any case tribute was commonly exacted as a *stipendium*, a levy of cash for the payment of soldiers, or of kind for their supplies. See now J.S.Richardson 'The Spanish mines and the development of provincial taxation', *JRS* LVI (1976), 139ff., esp. 147ff.

71 See Bénabou (1976), 448ff.

72 See R.Cagnat, 'L'annone d'Afrique', *Mém. acad. inscr. belles-lettres* XL (1916); G.Ch.-Picard, 'Néron et le blé d'Afrique', *Cah. Tun.* XIV (1956), 163ff.; G.Rickman, *Roman granaries and store buildings* (Cambridge, 1971), 307ff. at 309. H.Pavis d'Escurac, *Le préfecture de l'annone service administratif impériale d'Auguste à Constantin*, Bibl. des éc. franc. Ath. et Rome, CCXXVI (1976).

73 The tithe brought in 3 mill. *modii*, Verres was ordered to buy 3 mill. more at 3 HS per *modius*, and a further 800,000 *modii* at 3½ HS per *modius*.

74 F.Zevi, A.Tchernia, 'Amphores de Byzacène au bas empire, *AntAfr* III (1969), 173ff.; A.Carandini, 'Produzione agricola e produzione ceramica nell' Africa di età imperiale', *St. Misc.* XV (1970), 95ff.; A.Carandini, C.Panella, 'Ostia III', *St. Misc.* XXI (1973), 327ff.; 560ff.

75 For a good recent discussion, see Ramsay MacMullen, *Roman government's response to crisis A.D. 235-337* (New Haven, 1976), ch.6.

76 Hyginus (ed. Thulin, *Corpus Agrimensorum Romanorum* 1 (1913), 168-9) writes of fifths and sevenths, and Dio 38.26 of a tithe (in Bithynia). Insofar as *publicani* were present in Africa at least in the early decades of the empire, and insofar as the tax-farming system was more oppressive than the main alternatives, Africa was at a disadvantage in comparison with Spain and Gaul, which did not have *publicani*.

77 Recently, P.A.Brunt (1974), 90ff., at 105; cf. 108.

78 Brunt (1974), 99, n.46, utilizes *ILS* 9195 (= *CIL* XI 7554). But see the revised reading in *AE* 1952, 34.

79 H.M.D.Parker, *The Roman legions* (2nd ed., Cambridge, 1958), 176.

80 J.Lesquier, *L'armée romaine d'Egypte d'Auguste à Dioclétien*
    (Cairo, 1918), 206; G.Forni, *Il Reclutamento delle Legioni da
    Augusto a Diocletiano* (Milan, 1953), 219-20.

81 J.F.Gilliam, 'The veterans and the "praefectus castrorum"', *AJP*
    LXXVII (1956), 359ff.; J.C.Mann, 'The raising of new legions
    during the Principate', *Hermes* XCI (1963), 483ff.

82 Africans serving in elite corps fall into a different category.
    See *CIL* VI 2663 (praetorians); 3884 iii 21, v 4 (Sev.); 2384
    ii 5 (Sev.) (urban cohort; there was also an urban cohort in
    Carthage. See *CIL* VIII 2890, 8395; *AE* 1916, 80, etc.).

83 Cf. Brunt (1974), 105: 'Auxiliary units were normally posted to
    regions other than those where they had been raised.'

84 An early example from Spain is Livy 24.49.7 (212 B.C.). The
    best-known of several cases from a later period is the *turma
    Salluitana* that served Pompeius Strabo (*ILS* 8888) and was
    constituted from several different tribes. The force of 3,000
    Gallic *equites* collected by Caesar in 49 for civil war use
    (*Bell. Civ.* 1.39.2) was formed in a similar way. This point
    is discussed by D.Thomas in an unpublished paper on the army
    and the administration of native peoples.

85 Mauri: see R.Cagnat, *L'armée romaine d'Afrique* (Paris, 1913),
    262; *RE* IV 315-16. Musulamii: *AE* 1939, 126 (Dom.); *CIL* XVI 35
    (Syria, A.D. 88). Numidae: *AE* 1939, 126; *CIL* XVI 35. Gaetuli:
    CIL V 5267 = *ILS* 2721; *CIL* V 7895; 7007; *RE* I 1243; IV 286-7.

86 Rachet (1970), 161; Bénabou (1976), 124.

87 Spanish auxiliaries used by Scipiones: Livy 25.33.6. Furnished
    under agreements: Badian (1958), 117ff.; App. *Iber.* 44 (179
    B.C.); 52 (151 B.C.); etc. In Africa an important role in re-
    cruitment was played by the *praefecti gentium*, as was recog-
    nized long ago by Cagnat (op.cit. n.85), 263ff., cf. *CIL* XI
    7554 (= *ILS* 9195), with *AE* 1952, 34 [pra]ef(ecto) gentis
    Numidar(um), dilictat(ori) [tir]onum ex Numidia lecto[r(um)].
    Other references in Brunt (1974), 106-7.

88 R.Cagnat (op.cit. n.85), 287ff.

89 J.Gascou, 'Inscriptions de Tébessa', *MEFR* LXXXI (1969), 537ff.;
    M.Leglay, *Les Gaulois en Afrique* (Bruxelles, 1962), at 9.

90 Th.Mommsen, *Ges. Schr.* VI 29; G.Forni (op.cit. n.80), 126-8 (in
    general); 212 cf. 204ff.; (Africa). For auxiliaries (not in
    Africa), K.Kraft, *Zur Rekrutierung von Alen und Cohorten an
    Rhein und Donau* (Bern, 1951), 50ff.

91 See Brunt (1974), 109ff.

92 For refs. see P.Garnsey, *Social status and legal privilege in*

the *Roman empire* (Oxford, 1970), 245ff.

93 See the major contributions of Broughton (1929); L.Teutsch (op.
    cit. n.12); and Gascou (1972). For a recent discussion with
    refs. see Bénabou (1976), 394-425.

94 *Publicani* may still have collected the African *stipendium* in
    the early decades of the Principate (see *ILS* 901), but they
    probably worked through the city authorities (cf. Cic. *ad Att.*
    6.2.5). In any case, the cities had replaced tax-farmers al-
    together as tribute-collectors by the second half of the second
    century at the latest (see Apul. *Apol.* 101; D. 50.1.17.1, 50.4.
    3.10-11, etc.). Taxes were at no stage collected by an army of
    centrally-controlled imperial officials. For cities and army
    recruitment, see the brief discussion in Brunt (1974), 114-15,
    and next note.

95 C.Thulin, ed., *Corpus Agrimensorum Romanorum* 1 (1913), 45.

96 The *pagus* which could conscript an influential patron was in
    the best position to defend its interests. The *patroni* of the
    pagus (and *civitas*) of Thugga have recently been studied, al-
    though not in this connexion, by Cl.Poinssot, 'M. Licinius
    Rufus: patronus pagi et civitatis Thuggensis', *BCTH* V (1969),
    215ff.

97 See the fundamental study, drawing especially on Italian evi-
    dence, of Martin Frederiksen, 'Changes in the patterns of
    settlement', *Hellenismus in Mittelitalien, Koll. in Göttingen,
    Juni 1974, Abhandl. der Akad. der Wiss. in Gött.*, Phil.-Hist.
    Kl., Dr. Folge, XCVII (1976), 341ff.

98 See *CIL* VIII 8210 = *ILS* 6864 (2nd half, 3rd c.): *soluta con-
    tributione a Cirtensibus*. The reference is to Milev, one of
    the three subsidiary colonies of the Confederation. There is
    no reason to suppose that any of the numerous minor centres
    within Cirtan territory were upgraded before the fourth cen-
    tury, if at all.

99 The public benefactions of patrons to their client cities are
    better known and easier to document than the services they
    must have exchanged with individual members of the local aris-
    tocracy. It is not hard to imagine, for example, that indi-
    vidual decurions looked after the economic interests of their
    superiors based in Rome.

100 According to Pflaum (1970), 109-10, the Romans were displaying
    sensitivity, on the one hand to their Punic subjects who wanted
    to preserve their own constitutions, and on the other to Roman
    veteran colonists in the area. Gascou (1972), 226ff. correctly
    recognizes that a policy of municipalization was detrimental to
    the interests of Carthage (and notes that the award of the *ius
    Italicum* was compensatory), which he considers was threatening
    to become a 'state within a state'. In my view Severus was
    more alive to the advantages for the fiscus and the army of a
    multiplication of administrative units than to any political

threat from cities with vast territories.

101 Garnsey (1974).

102 Similarly, we should I believe accept Dio's comment on the
     famous Edict of Caracalla: 'nominally he was honouring them,
     but his real purpose was to increase his revenues' (77.9.5).

103 On nomenclature, see Bénabou (1976), 591ff., with full refer-
     ences.

104 E.g. for the period before Caesar, see Romanelli (1959), 109;
     Brunt (1971), 219.

105 See also *ILAlg*. I 2195: a man of Madauros who *domumque tenuem
     ad equestrem promovit gradum*.

106 See *CIL* VIII 4243 + 18502; 4196-7 (Verecunda); *ILAlg*. I 2070;
     2130; 2201 (Madauros); *CIL* VIII 4594 + 18649 (Diana); cf. 4594:
     the same person, but not designated *vet.* in the latter inscrip-
     tion. Sons and descendants of veterans, especially plentiful
     in the veteran colonies, usually give no indication of their
     origins.

107 See e.g. *CIL* VIII 7080 (Cirta; ex-centurion married to a
     flaminica IIII col. Cirtensium); cf. 7958 (Cirta); 12370; *AE*
     1912, 179 (Thuburbo Maius).

108 On Gigthis see Gascou (1972), 137ff.; M.G.Jarrett, 'Decurions
     and priests', *AJP* XCII (1971), 513ff., at 533; cf. 538.

109 See R.Syme (op.cit. n.49), 125.

110 J.Gascou, 'Inscriptions de Tébessa', *MEFR* LXXXI (1969), 556ff.

111 J.Gascou, 'Le *cognomen Gaetulus*, *Gaetulicus* en Afrique romaine',
     MEFR LXXXII (1970), 723ff.

112 See H.-G.Pflaum, 'Remarques sur l'onomastique de Cirta', *Limes
     Studien* XIV (Basel, 1959), 100ff.

113 For Sittius, see above n.12.

114 See Sherwin-White (1973), 241ff.; 341ff.

115 Evidence (covering the period A.D. 140-280) and bibliography in
     Bénabou (1976), 460. For a full discussion, see E.Frézouls,
     'Les Baquates et la province romaine de Tingitane', *BAM* II
     (1957), 65ff.

116 W.Seston, M.Euzennat, 'Un dossier de la chancellerie romaine:
     la Tabula Banasitana. Etude de diplomatique', *CRAI* 1971, 468ff.

117 G.Ch.-Picard, 'Deux sénateurs romains inconnus', *Karthago* IV
     (1953), 121ff. at 127, citing H.-G.Pflaum, *Les Procurateurs
     équestres sous le Haut-Empire romain* (Paris, 1950), 184-5. But

Pflaum's lists (which now need correction and updating) produce
a figure of 12.5% for the period Hadrian to the end of Commodus,
and for the third century one of 27.5% (see pp.192ff.).

118 G.Ch.-Picard (op.cit. n.117), 127, citing and correcting G.
     Barbieri, *L'albo senatorio da Settimo Severo a Carino, 193-285*
     (Rome, 1952), 441. Cf. Mason Hammond, 'The composition of the
     senate A.D. 68-235', *JRS* XLVII (1957), 74ff., at 80: 14%, reign
     of Septimius Severus. For the third century I have seen con-
     jectures of 12.5% and 14%: see, respectively, Millar (1967),
     178, and C.R.Whittaker, *Herodian* (ed. Loeb), II p.187. The most
     optimistic assessment is that of A.R.Birley, *Septimius Severus*
     (London, 1971), 336ff., who conjectures that 19% of the 'most
     prominent' men under Severus were 'more or less certainly Afri-
     can', and in the case of an additional 14% 'a strong probability'
     points to Africa as their place of origin. The figures would
     be higher if the 11% whom he regards as of undiscoverable *origo*
     were eliminated. Clearly the whole subject requires systematic
     investigation. There is no reliable list of African senators.
     That of A.Pelletier, 'Les sénateurs d'Afrique proconsulaire',
     Latomus XXIII (1964), 511ff., is inaccurate and incomplete even
     for Africa Proconsularis.

119 Rachet (1970); Bénabou (1976), livre 1.

120 I pass over for reasons of space the matter of the survival of
     Punic or Libyo-Punic political institutions. See T.Kotula, *Les
     curies municipales en Afrique romaine* (Warsaw, 1968); 'Remarques
     sur les traditions puniques dans la constitution des villes de
     l'Afrique romaine', *Africana Bull.* XVII (1972), 9ff.; W.Seston,
     'Des "portes" de Thugga à la constitution de Carthage', *Rev.
     Hist.* CCXXXVII (1967), 277ff.; Cl.Poinssot, 'Sufes maior et
     princeps civitatis Thuggae', *Mélanges Piganiol* (Paris, 1966),
     1267ff.; B.D.Shaw, 'The undecemprimi in Roman Africa', *MusAfr*
     II (1973), 3ff. Nor do I discuss the survival of local cul-
     tures in Africa, especially in the countryside. See F.Millar
     (1968). Brunt (1976), 170ff. has an excursus on vernacular
     languages in the empire as a whole.

121 This theme is developed by A.N.Sherwin-White, *Racial prejudice
     in Imperial Rome* (Cambridge, 1967).

122 *ut homines dispersi ac rudes eoque in bello faciles quieti et
     otio per voluptates adsuescerent.*

123 Cf. Brunt (1976), 162.

124 P.Monceaux, *Les Africains. Etudes sur la littérature latine
     d'Afrique* (Paris, 1894); M.D.Brock, *Studies in Fronto and his
     age* (Cambridge, 1911), 161ff.; M.Leglay, 'La vie intellectuelle
     d'une cité africaine des confins de l'Aurès', *Hommages à L.
     Herrmann*, Collection Latomus XLIV (1960), 485ff.; W.Thieling,
     Der Hellenismus in Kleinafrika (Leipzig, 1911); T.Kotula,
     'Utraque lingua eruditi: une page rélative à l'histoire de
     l'éducation dans l'Afrique romaine', *Hommages à M.Renard*, Coll.
     Latomus CII (1969), 386ff.; H.Pavis d'Escurac, 'Pour une étude

sociale de l'Apologie d'Apulée', *AntAfr* VIII (1974), 89ff., at 96ff.

125   M.Leglay, *Saturne Africaine: Histoire* (Paris, 1966); Bénabou (1976), 261ff.

126   Leglay (op.cit. n.125), 61ff.; 314ff., citing Tertullian, *Apol.* 9.2-3, among other texts, plus archaeological evidence.

127   Tertullian, *Apol.* 25.12ff.; Min.Felix, *Octavius* 25. Later critics of traditional justifications for Roman imperialism also happen to be African. See Lactantius, *Inst. Div.* 5.16ff.; Augustine, *de civ. dei* 19.21. The fact that Tertullian is inconsistent in the opinions he expresses on state and empire does not affect the present argument. See R.Klein, *Tertullian und das römisches Reich* (Heidelberg, 1968).

128   On this subject, Professor G.W.Clarke has written to me: 'My strong impression is that they conveniently exploit a western (general) tradition about the nature of the gods, and that a special provincial bias is probably a chance perception given the nature of the surviving evidence.'

129   On this question see the summary by R.Markus, 'Christianity and dissent in Roman North Africa: changing perspectives in recent work', in D.Baker, ed., *Schism, heresy and religious protest* (Cambridge, 1972), 21-36.

Chapter 12   Jewish attitudes to the Roman empire

The following abbreviations are used in this article:
B = Babylonian Talmud, J = Palestinian (Jerusalem) Talmud.

1   I Macc. 8.23-30 (Josephus, *Ant.* 12.414-19); 12.1-4 (Jos. *Ant.* 13.163); 14.25; Jos. *Ant.* 13.559-66.

2   Ps. Sol. 8.9-22; cf. 2.3, 13-15. In 17.5-8, 22 it is the Hasmonean rulers who are blamed.

3   Ps. Sol. 17.23-6; cf. Orac. Sib. 3.46-53.

4   Orac. Sib. 3.356ff., etc. On the background to this work and its dating see V.Nikiprowetzky, *La troisième Sibylle* (Paris, 1970).

5   *Ant.* 17.299-314. Cf. *Ant.* 14.41, a similar argument before Pompey in 63 B.C.

6   Philo, *Leg.* 157, 317; cf. Jos. *BJ* 2.197. The expense was probably borne by the emperor, notwithstanding Jos. *C.Ap.* 2.77. A similar sacrifice instituted by the Persians (Ezra 6.10) was still being performed during the Hasmonean War (I Macc. 7.33). The Roman sacrifice, however, was discontinued in the summer of 66 (Jos. *BJ* 2.409); Josephus calls this act *tou pros Romaious polemou katabole*.

7   Hananiah the *segan* of the Priests, Mishnah Aboth 3.2, B Abodah
    Zarah 4[a]. The date is probably the last years of the temple.
    The parallel text in Aboth de Rabbi Nathan B 31 (end) inserts
    what may be a fragment of such a prayer: 'may it reign over us
    for all time'. Cf. Philo, *In Flaccum* 49; 1 Timothy 2.2.

8   A possible exception is *Megillath Ta'anith, 'The Scroll of
    Fasts'* (ed. H.Lichtenstein, *HUCA* VIII-IX (1931/2), 257-351), a
    document celebrating nationalist victories. It was never re-
    ceived into the canon of rabbinic literature.

9   Mark 12.17. Cf. I.Abrahams, '"Give unto Caesar"', in *Studies
    in Pharisaism and the Gospels*, First Series (Cambridge, 1917),
    62-5.

10 Mishnah Aboth 3.5. *Hakkanah* may mean 'the zealot'. Cf.
    Hananiah the *segan* of the Priests, Aboth de Rabbi Nathan A 20.

11 See above, n.6.

12 See Song of Songs Zuta 2.10; cf. Allon (1961), 74-5.

13 See T.Rajak, *CQ* XXIII (1973), 351-2.

14 Aboth de Rabbi Nathan A 4, B 6. See J.Neusner, *The development
    of a legend* (Leiden, 1970), 113ff.

15 On the relationship between the various versions see J.Neusner,
    op.cit. 228-34.

16 Taught by Yohanan bar Nappaha, B Gittin 56[b], Lamentations Rabba
    1.5.31.

17 See the collection of (mainly Babylonian amoraic) sayings, B
    Shabbath 119[b]-120[a]. Cf. Tosefta Menahoth 13.22; J Yoma 38[c]; B
    Yoma 9[b]; Pesahim 118[b].

18 I Baruch 1.15-17. See the account of reactions to the crisis
    of A.D. 70 in M.Simon, *Verus Israel* (Paris, 1948), 19-28.

19 I Baruch 1.11-12 (NEB). For Nebuchadnezzar, Belshazzar, Baby-
    lon, read Vespasian, Titus, Rome. The writers of this period
    commonly applied the names of the Babylonian captivity to their
    recent conquerors. For the prayer see above, n.7.

20 See E.M.Smallwood, 'Palestine c. A.D. 115-18', *Historia* XI
    (1962), 500-10.

21 For the literature, ancient and modern, see Schürer-Vermes-
    Millar (1973), 529 (and p.533 for the rabbinic evidence).

22 The various theories are set out in V.Tcherikover *et al.*,
    Corpus Papyrorum Judaicarum I (Cambridge, Mass., 1957), 90,
    n.84.

23 Trajan died at Selinus in Cilicia.

24 See Schürer-Vermes-Millar (1973), 543. 'Star' is an allusion
    to Numbers 24.17.

25 B Sanhedrin 98^{a-b}. For the sentiment cf. Judah I, B Yoma 10^a.

26 Haninah ben Abbahu, J Ta'anith 64^a. The reading *Romi* for *Dumah*
    is ascribed to a text of Rabbi Meir. Similarly in Pesikta de
    Rab Kahana 68^a, Isaiah 34.7 is read as 'Romans shall come down
    with them'. Eleazar ben Pedat in the late third century is the
    author of several such interpretations, e.g. Genesis Rabba 10.7
    (cf. Leviticus Rabba 22.4; Ecclesiastes Rabba 5.8.5; B Berakhoth
    62^b; J Shabbath 8^c); 61.7 (cf. Exodus Rabba 9.13; Pesikta
    Rabbati 17.8).

27 Yohanan, Genesis Rabba 76.6, Leviticus Rabba 13.5, B Abodah
    Zarah 2^b (= Shebuoth 6^b). Other examples: Genesis Rabba 44.17;
    Exodus Rabba 51.7; Leviticus Rabba 13; Song of Songs Rabba
    6.10.1; Midrash Psalms 18.11.

28 E.g. Pesikta Rabbati 14.15, 17.8; Midrash Psalms 15.1.

29 E.g. Genesis Rabba 63.9 (quoted above), 70.8; Leviticus Rabba
    13.5.

30 Leviticus Rabba 29.2 (= Pesikta de Rab Kahana 151^b). This
    elaboration derives from a homily of the second-century rabbi
    Meir, cf. ibid. and Midrash Psalms 78.6. Other homilies of
    Samuel bar Nahman on the same theme: Genesis Rabba 73.7
    (= 75.5); Deuteronomy Rabba 1.20 (cf. Abbahu, Genesis Rabba
    78.14).

31 Midrash Psalms 10.6, 17.12. Cf. Esther Rabba 3.5, where Esau
    is the father of the twins.

32 Levi, J 'Abodah Zarah 39^c; cf. B Shabbath 56^b; Sanhedrin 21^b;
    Song of Songs Rabba 1.6.4.

33 B Megillah 6^a. The authority is a Babylonian, Ulla, but the
    legend is likely to have a Palestinian origin.

34 Exodus Rabba 1.31, B Sanhedrin 98^a. Cf. Vermes (1975), 223-4.

35 Rabbinic references to Roman institutions are collected in S.
    Krauss, *Paras veromi battalmud ubammidrashim* (Tel-Aviv, 1948);
    cf. S.Lieberman, 'Roman legal institutions in early Rabbinics
    and in the Acta Martyrum', *JQR* XXXV (1944), 1-55.

36 Genesis Rabba 63.6, Midrash Psalms 14.3.

37 E.g. Genesis Rabba 63.13.

38 Hiyya bar Abba, Genesis Rabba 63.10; cf. B Gittin 57^b. Yohanan
    rebuts this charge, B Shabbath 149^b. See also Orac.Sib. 5.387.

39 Pesikta Rabbati 12.4-5; Genesis Rabba 63.8 (Abba bar Kahana),
    75.1.

40   Simeon ben Lakish, Genesis Rabba 2.4 = Pesikta Rabbati 33.6.

41   Levi, Ecclesiastes Rabba 1.7.9.   Cf. Hama bar Haninah, Genesis
     Rabba 66.7; Abba bar Kahana, Leviticus Rabba 15.9; Yohanan, B
     Pesahim 118[b].   See S.Lieberman, *JQR* XXXVI (1945), 344-70.

42   Ecclesiastes Rabba 1.7.9; Esther Rabba 1.17; cf. B Pesahim 119[a].

43   Simon, Genesis Rabba 65.1, Leviticus Rabba 13.5, Midrash Psalms
     80.6.   Cf. Isaac, Genesis Rabba 63.8.

44   Judah ben Simon, Genesis Rabba 49.9.   Cf. Yose, Exodus Rabba
     18.5.

45   Genesis Rabba 37.2, 63.10.   See S.Lieberman, *JQR* XXXV (1944),
     24-5.

46   This subject is discussed more fully by Glatzer (1962, 1975).

47   See above, p.268.

48   Above, p.271.

49   Deuteronomy Rabba 1.20; cf. Genesis Rabba 78.14 (Abbahu).   For
     the messianic use of this verse see above, n.24.

50   See W.Bacher, *Die Agada der palästinensischen Amoräer* (Strass-
     burg, 1892-9), I 252ff. on Yohanan's attitude to Rome.

51   Genesis Rabba 63.6, 76.6; Leviticus Rabba 13.5; B Pesahim 118[b];
     'Abodah Zarah 2[b] (= Shebuoth 6[b]).

52   B Baba Metzi'a 84[a]: he was apparently a *leistes*.

53   E.g. B Sanhedrin 98[b]; Genesis Rabba 63.6; Leviticus Rabba 13.5.

54   B Yoma 9[b]; cf. Song of Songs Rabba 8.9.3.

55   Song of Songs Rabba 2.7.1.   See Allon (1961), 77; Baer (1961),
     114; Glatzer (1975), 15.

56   Tanhuma (ed. Buber), *Debarim* suppl. 3.

57   Genesis Rabba 63.6, 10; cf. 63.14, 64.2.

58   Genesis Rabba 75.1; Leviticus Rabba 7.6.

59   Though not entirely.   Messianic risings recur spasmodically in
     the Byzantine empire.   See A.Sharf, *Byzantine Jewry* (London,
     1971), esp. Appendix I, a tenth-century apocalyptic 'Vision of
     Daniel'.

BIBLIOGRAPHY

Note. The purpose of this bibliography is to provide a list of the works cited in the text and notes which are concerned either wholly or in the main with imperialism in the ancient world. The only exceptions to this rule are the few general works which it would be too cumbersome to keep on repeating in the notes. All other studies are fully documented in the notes wherever they are relevant.

Journal titles have been abbreviated according to the initials used by *Année philologique* or in a fashion which is self-explanatory. Other abbreviations refer to ancient authors or to standard collections of inscriptions, legal texts, etc., which it is hoped will be familiar to most readers.

The bibliography for B.J.Kemp, 'Imperialism and empire in New Kingdom Egypt'—is located on pp. 368ff.

Accame,S. (1941). *La lega ateniese del sec. IV A.C.* Rome

Allon,G. (1961). 'The attitudes of the Pharisees to the Roman government and the house of Herod', *Scripta Hierosolymitana* VII 53-78

Amit,M. (1965). *Athens and the sea.* Brussels

Anderson,W.S. (1963). *Pompey, his friends, and the literature of the first century B.C.* Berkeley

Andrewes,A. (1971). 'Two notes on Lysander', *Phoenix* XXV 206-26

Astin,A.E. (1967). *Scipio Aemilianus.* Oxford

Badian,E. (1958). *Foreign clientelae.* Oxford

Badian,E. (1964). *Studies in Greek and Roman history.* Oxford

Badian,E. (1966). 'Alexander the Great and the Greeks of Asia', *Ancient society and institutions. Studies...Victor Ehrenberg,* 37-69. Oxford

Badian,E. (1968). *Roman imperialism in the late republic.* 2nd ed. Oxford

Baer,Y. (1961). 'Israel, the Christian church, and the Roman empire from the time of Septimus Severus to the Edict of Toleration of A.D. 313', *Scripta Hierosolymitana* VII 79-149

Barreca,F. (1968). 'Quand Carthage dominait Sardaigne', *Archéologia* XX 74-80

Barreca,F. (1971). 'Sardegna', in *L'espansione fenicia nel Mediterraneo* = *Studi Semitici* XXXVIII 7-27

Barreca,F. (1974). *La Sardegna fenicia e punica.* Sassari

Bénabou,M. (1976). *La résistance africaine à la romanisation.* Paris

Bengtson,H. (1944). *Die Strategie in der hellenistischen Zeit* II. Munich

Bengtson,H. (1962). *Die Staatsverträge des Altertums* II. Munich

Blackman,D. (1969). 'The Athenian navy and allied naval contributions in the pentecontaetia', *GRBS* X 179-216

Bleicken,J. (1966). *Der Preis des Aelius Aristides auf das römische Weltreich.* Nachr. der Akad. der Wiss. zu Göttingen, Philol.-Hist. Kl. 1966,7. Göttingen

Boulanger,A. (1923). *Aelius Aristide et la sophistique dans la province d'Asie au IIe siècle de notre ère.* Paris

Bowersock,G.W. (1965). *Augustus and the Greek world.* Oxford

Bowersock,G.W. (1969). *Greek sophists in the Roman empire.* Oxford

Briscoe,J. (1972). 'Flamininus and Roman politics, 200-189 B.C.', *Latomus* XXXI 22-53

Broughton,T.R.S. (1929). *The Romanization of Africa Proconsularis.* Baltimore

Brunt,P.A. (1961). 'Charges of provincial maladministration under the early Principate', *Historia* X 189-227

Brunt,P.A. (1963). Review of H.D.Meyer (1961). *JRS* LIII 170-6

Brunt,P.A. (1965). 'Reflections on British and Roman Imperialism', *Comp. Stud. Soc. Hist.* VII 267-88

Brunt,P.A. (1971). *Italian manpower 225 B.C. - A.D. 14.* Oxford

Brunt,P.A. (1974). 'Conscription and volunteering in the Roman imperial army', *Scripta Classica Israelica* I 90-115

Brunt,P.A. (1976). 'The Romanization of the local ruling classes in the Roman empire', *VIe Congrès international d'études classiques, Sep. 1974, Madrid*, 161-73

Capelle,W. (1932). 'Griechische Ethnik und römischer Imperialismus', *Klio* XXV 86-113

Cawkwell,G.L. (1956). 'A note on the Heracles coinage alliance of
   394 B.C.', *NC* ser.6, XVI 69-75

Cawkwell,G.L. (1963). 'Eubulus', *JHS* LXXXIII 47-67

Cawkwell,G.L. (1973). 'The foundation of the second Athenian confederacy', *CQ* XXIII 47-60

Charles-Picard,G. (1959). *La civilisation de l'Afrique romaine.*
   Paris

Christ,F. (1938). *Die römische Weltherrschaft in der antiken
   Dichtung.* Tübingen

Christ,K. (1974). 'Caesar und Ariovist', *Chiron* IV 251-92

Cimma,M.R. (1976). *Reges socii et amici populi Romani.* Milan

Collins,J.H. (1972). 'Caesar as political propagandist', in H.
   Temporini (ed.), *Aufstieg und Niedergang der römischen Welt*
   I.1, 922-66. Berlin

Colloque de Dijon (1974). *L'idéologie de l'impérialisme romain,*
   Colloque de Dijon les 18 et 19 Oct. 1972, Publications de
   l'Université de Dijon XLVI. Paris

Crawford,D.J. (1976). 'Imperial estates', in M.I.Finley, ed.,
   Studies in Roman property, 35-70, 173-180. Cambridge

Crawford,M.H. (1974). *Roman republican coinage.* Cambridge

Dahlheim,W. (1968). *Struktur und Entwicklung des römischen Völker-
   rechts.* Munich

Deininger,J. (1971). *Der politische Widerstand gegen Rom in
   Griechenland.* Berlin

Derow,P.S. (1973). 'Kleemporos', *Phoenix* XXVII 118-34

Drexler,H. (1959). 'Iustum bellum', *RhM* CII 99-140

Duncan-Jones,R.P. (1963). 'Wealth and munificence in Roman Africa',
   PBSR XXXI 159-77

Duncan-Jones,R.P. (1967). 'Equestrian rank in the cities of the
   African provinces', *PBSR* XXXV 147-88

Earl,D.C. (1961). *The political thought of Sallust.* Cambridge

Erxleben,E. (1969-71). 'Das Munzgesetz des delisch-attischen
   Seebundes', *APF* XIX 91-139, XX 66-132, XXI 145-62

Erxleben,E. (1975). 'Die Kleruchien auf Euböa und Lesbos und die
   Methoden der attischen Herrschaft im 5. Jh.', *Klio* LVII 83-100

Feyel,M. (1942). *Polybe et l'histoire de Béotie au IIIe siècle avant notre ère*. Paris

Finley,M.I. (1965). 'Classical Greece', in *Trade and politics in the ancient world* (2nd Intl. Conference of Econ. Hist., Aix-en-Provence 1962), 11-35. Paris and The Hague

Finley,M.I. (1968). *Ancient Sicily*. London

Finley,M.I. (1973a). *The ancient economy*. London

Finley,M.I. (1973b). *Democracy ancient and modern*. London

Finley,M.I. (1976). 'Colonies - an attempt at a typology', *Transac. Roy. Hist. Soc.* 5th ser., XXVI 167-88

Flacelière,R. (1937). *Les Aitoliens à Delphes: contribution à l'histoire de la Grèce centrale au IIIe siècle av. J.-C.* Paris

Flach,D. (1976). 'Der sogennante römische Imperialismus. Sein Verständnis im Wandel der neuzeitlichen Erfahrungswelt', *HZ* CCXXII 1-42

Frank,T. (1933-40). *An economic survey of ancient Rome*, 5 vols. Baltimore

Garbini,G. (1966). 'I fenici in occidente', *Stud. Etr.* XXXIV 111-47

Garnsey,P. (1974). 'Aspects of the decline of the urban aristocracy in the Empire', in H.Temporini, ed., *Aufstieg und Niedergang der römischen Welt* II.1, 229-52. Berlin

Garnsey,P. (1976). 'Peasants in ancient Roman society', *J. of Peasant Studies* III 221-35

Gascou,J. (1972). *La politique municipale de l'empire romain en Afrique proconsulaire de Trajan à Septime-Sévère*. Paris

Gauthier,P. (1966). 'Les clérouques de Lesbos et la colonisation athénienne au Ve siècle', *REG* LXXIX 64-88

Gauthier,P. (1973). 'A propos des clérouques athéniennes du Ve siècle', in M.I.Finley, ed., *Problèmes de la terre en Grèce ancienne*, 163-86. Paris and The Hague

Gelzer,M. (1963). 'Die Anfange des römischen Weltreichs', *Kleine Schriften* II 3-19

Glatzer,N.N. (1962). 'The attitude toward Rome in third-century Judaism', in *Politische Ordnung und menschliche Existenz. Festgabe für Eric Vogelin*, 243-57. Munich

Glatzer,N.N. (1975). 'The attitude to Rome in the Amoraic period', *Proceedings of the Sixth World Congress of Jewish Studies* II 9-19

Goar,R.J. (1972). *Cicero and the state religion.* Amsterdam

Graham,A.J. (1964). *Colony and mother city in ancient Greece.*
Manchester

Gschnitzer,F. (1958). *Abhängige Orte im griechischen Altertum,*
98-112. Munich

Gsell,S. (1928). *Histoire ancienne de l'Afrique du Nord.* 3rd ed.
Paris

Gsell,S. (1932). 'Esclaves ruraux dans l'Afrique romaine',
Mélanges G.Glotz I 397-415. Paris

Hampl,Fr. (1957). 'Stoische Staatsethik und frühes Rom', *HZ* CLXXXIV,
reprinted in Klein (1966)

Hampl,Fr. (1959). 'Römische Politik in republikanischer Zeit und
das Problem des Sittenverfalls', *HZ* CLXXXVIII, reprinted in
Klein (1966)

Harris,W.V. (1971a). 'On war and greed in the second century B.C.',
AHR LXXVI 1371-84

Harris,W.V. (1971b). *Rome in Etruria and Umbria.* Oxford

Hasebroek,J. (1926). *Die imperialistische Gedanke im Altertum.*
Stuttgart

Hasebroek,J. (1928). *Staat und Handel im alten Griechenland.*
Tübingen (English translation: London, 1933)

Haywood,R.M. (1938). *Roman Africa* = T.Frank, ed., *An economic survey of ancient Rome* IV. Baltimore

Heinen,H. (1973). *Untersuchungen zur hellenistischen Geschichte
des 3. Jahrhunderts v. Chr.* (*Historia,* Einzelschriften 20).
Wiesbaden

Heuss,A. (1949). 'Der erste punische Krieg und das Problem der röm.
Imperialismus', *HZ* CLXIX 457-513

Hoffmann,W. (1960). 'Die römische Politik des 2. Jahrhunderts und
das Ende Karthagos', *Historia* IX 309-44, reprinted in Klein
(1966)

Hoffmann,W. (1972). 'Karthagos Kampf um die Vorherrschaft im Mittel-
meer', in H.Temporini, ed., *Aufstieg und Niedergang der römischen
Welt* I.1, 341-63. Berlin

Holleaux,M. (1920). *Rome, la Grèce et les monarchies hellénistiques
au IIIe siècle avant J.-C. (273-205).* Paris

Humphries,S.C. (1969). 'History, economics and anthropology: the
work of Karl Polanyi', *History and Theory* VIII 165-212

Jarrett,M.G. (1972). 'An album of the equestrians from North Africa in the emperor's service', *Epigraphische Studien* IX 146-232

Jocelyn,H.D. (1977). 'The ruling class of the Roman republic and Greek philosophers', *Bull. Rylands Libr.* LIX 323-66

Jones,A.H.M. (1940). *The Greek city from Alexander to Justinian.* Oxford

Jones,A.H.M. (1957). *Athenian democracy.* Oxford

Jones,A.H.M. (1964) *The later Roman empire 284-602*, 3 vols. Oxford

Jones,A.H.M. (1974). *The Roman economy.* Oxford

Jones,C.P. (1971). *Plutarch and Rome.* Oxford

Klein,R., ed. (1966). *Das Staatsdenken der Römer.* Darmstadt

Kolendo,J. (1976). *Le colonat en Afrique sous le Haut-Empire.* Annales littéraires de l'Université de Besançon CLXXVII. Paris

Larson,J.A.O. (1955). *Representative government in Greek and Roman history*, ch.3. Berkeley and Los Angeles

Latte,K. (1960). *Römische Religionsgeschichte.* Munich

Lepore,E. (1972/3). 'Otto anni di studi storici sulla Sicilia antica e concluzioni de Congresso', *Kokalos* XVIII/XIX 120-45

Levi,M.A. (1973). 'Le cause della guerra romana contro gli Illiri', *PP* XXVII 317-25

Liebmann-Frankfort,T. (1969). *La frontière orientale dans la politique extérieure de la République romaine.* Brussels

Lotze,D. (1970). 'Selbstbewusstsein und Machtpolitik', *Klio* LII 255-75

Magie,D. (1950). *Roman rule in Asia Minor to the end of the third century after Christ.* Princeton

Marshall,F.H. (1905). *The second Athenian confederacy.* Cambridge

Mattingly,H.B. (1966). 'Periclean imperialism', *Ancient society and institutions. Studies...Victor Ehrenberg*, 193-223. Oxford

Meiggs,R. (1972). *The Athenian empire.* Oxford

Merante,V. (1970). 'Sui rapporti greco-punici nel Mediterraneo occidentale nel VI secolo A.C.', *Kokalos* XVI 98-113

Merante,V. (1972/3). 'La Sicilia e Cartagine dal V secolo alla conquista romana', *Kokalos* XVIII/XIX 77-103

Meyer,H.D. (1960). 'Abfall und Bestrafung von Bündnern im delisch-attischen Seebund', *HZ* CXCI 497-509

Meyer,H.D. (1961). *Die Aussenpolitik des Augustus und die augusteische Dichtung*. Cologne

Millar,F. (1967). *The Roman empire and its neighbours*. London

Millar,F. (1968). 'Local cultures in the Roman empire: Libyan, Punic and Latin in Roman Africa', *JRS* LVIII 126-34

Millar,F. (1977). *The emperor in the Roman world (31 B.C. - A.D. 337)*. London

Moscati,S. (1966). 'La penetrazione fenicia e punica in Sardegna', *MAL* ser.8, XII 215-50

Mossé,C. (1962). *La fin de la démocratie athénienne*. Paris

Nesselhauf,H. (1933). *Untersuchungen zur Geschichte der delisch-attischen Symmachie*. *Klio*, Beiheft 30. Leipzig

Niemeyer,H.G. and Schubart,H. (1971). 'Toscanos et Trayamar', in *L'espansione fenicia nel Mediterraneo* = *Studi Semitici* XXXVIII 150-60

Nock,A.D. (1972). *Essays in religion and the ancient world*. Oxford

Oliver,J.H. (1953). *The ruling power: a study of the Roman empire in the second century after Christ through the Roman oration of Aelius Aristides*. Trans. Amer. Phil. Soc., n.s. XLIII, part 4. Philadelphia

Oppermann,H., ed. (1967). *Römische Wertbegriffe*. Darmstadt

Palm,J. (1959). *Rom, Römertum und Imperium in der griechischen Literatur der Kaiserzeit*. Lund

Parke,H.W. (1930). 'The development of the second Spartan empire', *JHS* L 37-79

Perlman,S. (1968). 'Athenian imperial expansion in the fourth century', *CPh* LXIII 257-67

Perlman,S. (1976). 'Panhellenism, the polis and imperialism', *Historia* XXV 1-30

Pflaum,H.G. (1968). 'Les juges des cinq décuries originaires d'Afrique romaine', *AntAfr* II 153-98

Pflaum,H.G. (1970). 'La romanis.ition de l'ancien territoire de la Carthage punique', *AntAfr* IV 75-117

Polanyi,K. (1957). *Trade and market in the early empires*. Glencoe

Rachet,M. (1970). *Rome et les Berbères: un problème militaire d'Auguste à Dioclétien*. Brussels

Roloff,H. (1938). *Maiores bei Cicero*. Göttingen

Romanelli,P. (1959). *Storia delle Provincie Romane dell'Africa*. Rome

de Romilly,J. (1954). 'Les modérés athéniens vers le milieu du IVe siècle', *REG* LXVI 327-54

Romstedt,M. (1914). *Die wirtschaftliche Organisation des athenischen Reiches*. Diss. Leipzig

Rosenthal,F. (1975). *The classical heritage in Islam*. London

Rostovtzeff,M. (1957). *Social and economic history of the Roman empire*. 2nd ed. Oxford

Ryder,T.T.B. (1965). *Koine Eirene*. Oxford

Schäfer,A. (1887). *Demosthenes und seine Zeit* I. 2nd ed. Leipzig

Schürer,E., Vermes,G. and Millar,F. (1973). *The history of the Jewish people in the age of Jesus Christ (175 B.C. - A.D. 135)* I. Edinburgh

Schuller,W. (1974). *Die Herrschaft der Athener im ersten attischen Seebund*. Berlin and New York

Schweigert,E. (1940). 'The Athenian cleruchy on Samos', *AJPh* LXI 194-8

Seager,R. (1967). 'Thrasybulus, Conon and Athenian imperialism, 396-386 B.C.', *JHS* LXXXVII 95-115

Sealey,R. (1957). '*IG* II^2 1609 and the transformation of the second Athenian sea-league', *Phoenix* XI 95-111

Sherk,R.K. (1969). *Roman documents from the Greek East*. Baltimore

Sherwin-White,A.N. (1957). 'Caesar as an imperialist', *G&R* IV 36-45

Sherwin-White,A.N. (1967). *Racial prejudice in imperial Rome*. Cambridge

Sherwin-White,A.N. (1973). *The Roman citizenship*. 2nd ed. Oxford

Simpson,R.H. (1959). 'Antigonus the one-eyed and the Greeks', *Historia* VIII 385-409

de Ste Croix,G.E.M. (1972). *The origins of the Peloponnesian War.* London

Strasburger,H. (1965). 'Posidonius on problems of the Roman empire', *JRS* LV 40-53

Swain,J.W. (1940). 'The theory of the four monarchies: opposition history under the Roman empire', *CPh* XXXV 1-21

Talamanca,M. (1971). 'Su alcuni passi di Menandro di Laodicea relativi agli effetti della Constitutio Antoniniana', *Studi in onore di Edoardo Volterra* V 433-560. Milan

Timpe,D. (1965). 'Caesars gallische Krieg und das Problem des römischen Imperialismus', *Historia* XIV 189-214

Timpe,D. (1972). 'Rechtsformen der römischen Aussenpolitik bei Caesar', *Chiron* II 277-95

Toynbee,A.J. (1965). *Hannibal's legacy.* Oxford

Vermes,G. (1975). 'Ancient Rome in post-biblical Jewish literature', in *Post-biblical Jewish studies*, 215-24. Leiden

Veyne,P. (1975). 'Y a-t-il eu un imperialisme romain?', *MEFR* LXXXVII 793-855

Vogt,J. (1960). *Orbis.* Freiburg im Breisgau

Walbank,F.W. (1933). *Aratos of Sicyon.* Cambridge

Walbank,F.W. (1940). *Philip V of Macedon.* Cambridge

Walbank,F.W. (1963). 'Polybius and Rome's eastern policy', *JRS* LIII 1-13

Walbank,F.W. (1964). 'Polybius and the Roman state', *GRBS* V 239-60

Walbank,F.W. (1965). 'Political morality and the friends of Scipio', *JRS* LV 1-16

Walser,G. (1954). 'Die Ursachen des ersten römisch-illyrischen Krieges', *Historia* II 308-18

Warmington,B. (1964). *Carthage.* Harmondsworth

Wehrli,C. (1969). *Antigone et Démétrios.* Geneva

Weippert,O. (1972). *Alexander-Imitatio und römische Politik in republikanischer Zeit.* Diss. Würzburg

Welles,C.B. (1934). *Royal correspondence of the Hellenistic age.*
New Haven

Wells,C.M. (1972). *The German policy of Augustus.* Oxford

Westermann,W.L. (1955). *The slave systems of Greek and Roman antiquity.* Philadelphia

Whittaker,C.R. (1974). 'The western Phoenicians: colonisation and assimilation', *PCPhS* CC 58-79

Wieling,H.J. (1974). 'Ein neuentdeckte Inschrift Gordians III und ihre Bedeutung für den Verständnis der Constitutio Antoniniana', *ZSS* XCI 364-74

Will,E. (1966). *Histoire politique du monde hellénistique* I. Nancy

Woodhead,A.G. (1957). '*IG* II^2 43 and Jason of Pherae', *AJA* LXI 367-73

Woodhead,A.G. (1962). 'Chabrias, Timotheus and the Aegean allies, 375-373 B.C.', *Phoenix* XVI 258-66

Ziegler,K.H. (1964). *Die Beziehungen zwischen Rom und den Parthenreich.* Wiesbaden

Select Bibliography for Chapter 2

Adams,W.Y. (1964). 'Post-Pharaonic Nubia in the light of archaeology. I', *JEA* L 102-20

Adams,W.Y. (1977). *Nubia: corridor to Africa.* London

Arkell,A.J. (1961). *A history of the Sudan,* 2nd ed. London

Breasted,J.H. (1906-7). *Ancient records of Egypt.* Chicago

Bull,L. (1955). 'Ancient Egypt', in R.C.Dentan, ed., *The idea of history in the ancient Near East,* 1-34. New Haven

Edel,E. (1966). *Die Ortsnamenlisten aus dem Totentempel Amenophis III.* Bonn

Edel,E. (1974). 'Zwei Originalbriefe der Königsmutter Tūja in Keilschrift', *SAK* I 105-46

Edel,E. (1976). *Ägyptische Ärzte und ägyptische Medizin am hethitischen Königshof.* Opladen

Edwards,I.E.S., Gadd,C.J., Hammond,N.G.L. and Sollberger,E. (1973). *The Cambridge Ancient History,* 3rd ed. Vol.II, part 1. Cambridge. Chapters VIII-XI and those cited in the next reference cover both the history of Egypt in the New Kingdom and what is known of the political, social and archaeological aspects of Palestine and Syria in the same period.

Edwards,I.E.S., Gadd,C.J., Hammond,N.G.L. and Sollberger,E. (1975). *The Cambridge Ancient History*, 3rd ed. Vol.II, part 2. Cambridge. Chapters XIX-XXI, XXIII, XXVI, XXVIII

Emery,W.B. (1965). *Egypt in Nubia*. London

Fairman,H.W. (1958). 'The kingship rituals of Egypt', in S.H.Hooke, ed., *Myth, ritual, and kingship*, 74-104. Oxford

Frankfort,H. (1948). *Kingship and the gods*. Chicago

Gardiner,A.H. (1920). 'The ancient military road between Egypt and Palestine', *JEA* VI 99-116

Gardiner,A.H. (1960). *The Kadesh inscriptions of Ramesses II*. Oxford

Giveon,R. (1971). *Les bédouins Shosou des documents égyptiens*. Leiden

Grapow,H. (1947). *Studien zu den Annalen Thutmosis des Dritten und zu ihnen verwandten historischen Berichten des Neuen Reiches*. Berlin

Greenberg,M. (1955). *The Hab/piru*. New Haven

Griffith,F.Ll. (1927). 'The Abydos decree of Seti I at Nauri', *JEA* XIII 193-208

Habachi,L. (1957). 'The graffiti and work of the viceroys of Kush in the region of Aswan', *Kush* V 13-36

Habachi,L. (1969). 'The administration of Nubia during the New Kingdom, with special reference to discoveries made during the last few years', in *Actes du symposium international sur la Nubie organisé par l'Institut d'Egypte...1965* = Mémoires de l'Institut d'Egypte, LIX, 65-78. Cairo

Helck,W. (1939). *Der Einfluss der Militärführer in der 18. ägyptischen Dynastie*. Leipzig

Helck,W. (1960). 'Die ägyptische Verwaltung in den syrischen Besitzungen', *Mitteilungen der Deutschen Orient-Gesellschaft* XCII 1-13

Helck,W. (1964). 'Die Ägypter und die Fremden', *Saeculum* XV 103-14

Helck,W. (1968). 'Die Bedrohung Palästinas durch einwandernde Gruppen am Ende der 18. und am Anfang der 19. Dynastie', *VT* XVIII 472-80

Helck,W. (1971). *Die Beziehungen Ägyptens zu Vorderasien im 3. und 2. Jahrtausend v. Chr.*, 2nd ed. Wiesbaden. The most detailed treatment of textual sources for Egypt's involvement in the ancient Near East, but with almost no reference to archaeology.

Hofmann,I. (1967). *Die Kulturen des Niltals von Assuan bis Sennar vom Mesolithicum bis zum Ende der christlichen Epoche.* Hamburg

Hornung,E. (1957). 'Zur geschichtlichen Rolle des Königs in der 18. Dynastie', *MDAIK* XV 120-33

Hornung,E. (1966). *Geschichte als Fest. Zwei Vorträge zum Geschichtsbild der frühen Menschheit.* Darmstadt

James,F.W. (1966). *The Iron Age at Beth Shan.* Philadelphia

Jirku,A. (1937). *Die ägyptischen Listen palästinensischer und syrischer Ortsnamen.* Leipzig

Kemp,B.J. (1972). 'Fortified towns in Nubia', in P.J.Ucko, R. Tringham and G.W.Dimbleby, eds., *Man, settlement and urbanism*, 651-6. London

Kestemont,G. (1974). *Diplomatique et droit international en Asie occidentale (1600-1200 av. J.C.).* Louvain

Kitchen,K.A. (1962). *Suppiluliuma and the Amarna Pharaohs; a study in relative chronology.* Liverpool

Kitchen,K.A. (1969). 'Interrelations of Egypt and Syria', in M. Liverani, ed., *La Siria nel Tardo Bronzo* = Orientis Antiqui Collectio, IX, 77-95. Rome

Knudtzon,J.A. (1915). *Die El-Amarna-Tafeln.* Leipzig

Liverani,M. (1971). 'Le lettere del Faraone a Rib-Adda', *Oriens Antiquus* X 253-68

Liverani,M. (1972). 'Elementi "irrazionali" nel commercio amarniano', *Oriens Antiquus* XI 297-317

Lorton,D. (1974). *The juridical terminology of international relations in Egyptian texts through Dyn. XVIII.* Baltimore and London. The absence of basic distinctions in the terminology for Nubia and western Asia suggests that the terminology might not be as precise as the book supposes.

Mazar,B., ed. (1970). *The world history of the Jewish people*, first series, vol.II, 'Patriarchs'. London. Chapters VII and X and those cited in the next reference cover the New Kingdom involvement in Palestine and the social and archaeological background, including the role of the ḫabiru.

Mazar,B., ed. (1971). *The world history of the Jewish people*, first series, vol.III, 'Judges'. London. Chapters I-IV.

Merrillees, R.S. (1968). *The Cypriote Bronze Age pottery found in Egypt*. Lund

Mohammad,M.Abdul-Kader (1959). 'The administration of Syro-Palestine during the New Kingdom', *ASAE* LVI 105-37

Munn-Rankin,J.M. (1956). 'Diplomacy in western Asia in the early second millennium B.C.', *Iraq* XVIII 68-110. Not concerned with Egypt, but a useful background study to ancient Near Eastern practices.

Oppenheim,A.L. (1967). *Letters from Mesopotamia*. Chicago. A selection from the el-Amarna letters is provided on pp.119-34.

Priese,K.-H. (1974). ''*rm* und ';*m*, das Land Irame; ein Beitrag zur Topographie des Sudan im Altertum', *Altorientalische Forschungen* I 7-41

Pritchard,J.B., ed. (1950), 2nd ed. (1955). *Ancient Near Eastern texts relating to the Old Testament*. Princeton

Pritchard,J.B. (1954). *The ancient Near East in pictures, relating to the Old Testament*. Princeton

Rainey,A.F. (1971). 'A front line report from Amurru', *Ugarit-Forschungen* III 131-49

Röllig,W. (1974). 'Politische Hieraten im Alten Orient', *Saeculum* XXV 11-23

Rowe,A. (1930). *The topography and history of Beth-shan*. Philadelphia

Rowe,A. (1940). *The four Canaanite temples of Beth-Shan*. Philadelphia

Sauneron,S. (1968). 'Les désillusions de la guerre asiatique (Pap. Deir el-Médiné 35)', *Kêmi* XVIII 17-27

Säve-Söderbergh,T. (1941). *Ägypten und Nubien; ein Beitrag zur Geschichte altägyptischer Aussenpolitik*. Lund

Säve-Söderbergh,T. (1960). 'The paintings in the tomb of Djehuty-hetep at Debeira', *Kush* VIII 25-44

Säve-Söderbergh,T. (1963). 'The tomb of the Prince of Teh-khet, Amenemhet', *Kush* XI 159-74

Säve-Söderbergh,T. (1967-8). 'The Egyptianization and depopulation of Lower Nubia', *Kush* XV 237-42

Säve-Söderbergh,T. (1969). 'Die Akkulturation der nubischen C-Gruppe im Neuen Reich', *XVII. Deutscher Orientalistentag...1968* =

Zeitschrift der Deutschen Morgenländischen Gesellschaft,
Supplementa I 12-20. Wiesbaden

Schulman,A.R. (1962). 'The *N'rn* at the Battle of Kadesh', *JARCE* I
47-53

Schulman,A.R. (1964a). 'Some observations on the military background
of the Amarna period', *JARCE* III 51-69

Schulman,A.R. (1964b). *Military rank, title and organization in
the Egyptian New Kingdom.* Berlin

Several,M.W. (1972). 'Reconsidering the Egyptian empire in Palestine during the Amarna Period', *PEQ* CIV 123-33

Simons,J. (1937). *Handbook for the study of Egyptian topographical
lists relating to western Asia.* Leiden

Simpson,W.K. (1963). *Heka-nefer, and the dynastic material from
Toshka and Arminna.* Philadelphia

Smith,H.S. (1976). *The fortress of Buhen; the inscriptions* (Excavations at Buhen, II). London

Smith,W.S. (1965). *Interconnections in the ancient Near East; a
study of the relationships between the arts of Egypt, the
Aegean, and western Asia.* New Haven and London

Spalinger,A. (1974). 'Some notes on the Battle of Megiddo and reflections on Egyptian military writing', *MDAIK* XXX 221-29

Stadelmann,R. (1967). *Syrisch-Palästinensische Gottheiten in
Ägypten.* Leiden

Théodoridès,A. (1975). 'Les relations de l'Egypte pharaonique avec
ses voisins', *Revue Internationale des Droits de l'Antiquité*
XXII 87-140

Trigger,B.G. (1965). *History and settlement in Lower Nubia.* New
Haven

Trigger,B.G. (1976). *Nubia under the Pharaohs.* London

Vandersleyen,C. (1971). *Les guerres d'Amosis, fondateur de la XVIIIe
dynastie.* Brussels

te Velde,H. (1967). *Seth, god of confusion; a study of his role in
Egyptian mythology and religion.* Leiden

Vercoutter,J. (1959). 'The gold of Kush', *Kush* VII 120-53

Ward,W.A. (1972). 'The Shasu "bedouin"; notes on a recent publication', *JESHO* XV 35-60

Yadin,Y. (1963). *The art of warfare in Biblical lands, in the light of archaeological discovery.* Jerusalem

Ziskind,J.R. (1968). *Aspects of international law in the ancient Near East.* University Microfilms, see *Dissertation Abstracts International* A, XXVIII, no.10 (Apr. 1968) 4975-6A, order no. 68-8631

and Roman army 243; and Roman taxation 190,241; senatorial land
tenure in 227; slave cultivators in 236,237
Iulius *see* Julius

Jacob (i.e. the Jews under Rome) 269-80 *passim*
Jerusalem 258-60,262,278
Jews, the
  in New Kingdom Egypt 55
  in Persian empire 173
  in Roman empire: Roman-Jewish alliances 256-7; Roman conquest of
    258-60; complex attitude to Rome 258-81; revolts 241,262-9;
    zealotry 261-5,279; messianism 261-81 *passim*
Judaea 242,260-1
Julius Caesar
  in Britain 182; in Gaul 162-3,164,172,178-83; and Germans 179-81,
    182; in North Africa 224,243,250; and clemency 183-4; and citizen-
    ship 185; and expansionism 170,179; and Greek culture 199,200,206;
    imperialism of 178-83; and the just war 176,180,183; on justice
    188,189; quality of public opinions 159,161; rivalry with Pompey
    163,179,202,206
justice and law, quality of
  in New Kingdom Egypt 17-18
  Roman 173-4,183-91,211-15,275

Kadesh 18,44; battle of 15,16
Karnak 11,18,37
Kerma 21,22,26,29
king cult in Egypt 8-15,30,32,38,53
King's Peace 129,133
koinos: usage of term 212
Kumidi 47,49
Kush 21-2,29,30

Lambaesis 231,232,242,243
land use and ownership in provinces
  Athenian empire 115-17,122,123
  Carthage 60,74-6,88-9
  New Kingdom Egypt 30-4